D1738584

CROSSING THE DIVIDE

THE ADST-DACOR DIPLOMATS AND DIPLOMACY SERIES

For more than 220 years an extraordinary group of men and women have represented the United States abroad under all kinds of circumstances. What they did and how and why they did it are not well known by their compatriots. In 1995 the Association for Diplomatic Studies and Training (ADST) and Diplomatic and Consular Officers, Retired (DACOR) created a book series to increase public knowledge and appreciation of the efforts of U.S. diplomats around the world in the service of their country. The series seeks to demystify diplomacy by telling the story of those who have conducted our foreign relations, as they saw it and lived it.

John Holdridge was intimately involved in the historic events surrounding the establishment of relations between the United States and the People's Republic of China. Responsible for East Asia on the National Security Council staff in 1969–1973, he helped President Richard Nixon and his national security advisor, Henry Kissinger, prepare for their first visits to China and accompanied them there. He was present in Shanghai when the historic framework agreement was completed and announced on 28 February 1972. Relations between the two countries have been guided ever since by these events and by the subsequent agreements on January 1979 and August 1982. Ambassador Holdridge's personal account of the background and negotiations for these agreements thus sheds light on the challenges that continue to confront the important United States-China relationship.

STEPHEN LOW, President, ADST
ROBERT H. MILLER, President, DACOR

CROSSING THE DIVIDE

An Insider's Account of Normalization of U.S.–China Relations

John H. Holdridge

**An ADST-DACOR Diplomats
and Diplomacy Book**

ROWMAN & LITTLEFIELD PUBLISHERS, INC.
Lanham • Boulder • New York • Oxford

ROWMAN & LITTLEFIELD PUBLISHERS, INC.

Published in the United States of America
by Rowman & Littlefield Publishers, Inc.
4720 Boston Way, Lanham, Maryland 20706

12 Hid's Copse Road
Cummor Hill, Oxford OX2 9JJ, England

British Cataloging in Publication Information Available

Library of Congress Cataloging-in-Publication Data
Holdridge, John H.
    Crossing the divide : an insider's account of the normalization of U.S.–China
relations / John H. Holdridge.
        p. cm.—(ADST-DACOR diplomats and diplomacy series)
        Includes bibliographical references and index.
        ISBN 0-8476-8504-7 (cloth : alk. paper).—ISBN 0-8476-8505-5 (paper : alk.
paper)
        1. United States—Foreign relations—China.   2. China—Foreign
relations—United States.   3. United States—Foreign relations—
1945–1989.   I. Title.   II. Series.
E183.8.C6H65   1997
327.73051'09'045—dc21   96–52875
                                                                        CIP

ISBN 0-8476-8504-7 (cloth : alk. paper)
ISBN 0-8476-8505-5 (paper : alk. paper)

Printed in the United States of America

♾ ™ The paper used in this publication meets the minimum requirements of
American National Standard for Information Sciences—Permanence of Paper for
Printed Library Materials, ANSI Z39.48—1984.

Contents

Photographs follow page 160

Foreword

Those of us who have spent a good part of our lives in our nation's capital are too often aware that the reporting of current events is best captured by the term "revisionism." Self-serving machinations by incumbent political parties combined with the less than discriminating reporting of the Washington press seldom provide the public an accurate description of current events. It remains the burden of serious scholars, historians, and national security professionals to set the record straight. John Holdridge meets the criteria of both professional and scholar, and his description of the relations between the United States and the People's Republic of China from 1945 to the present is must reading for every American interested in the accurate reporting of the evolution of America's post–World War II relationship with China.

Not only our common educational background (we are both graduates of West Point) but our service together on the National Security Council staff in the early 1970s and also during my time as secretary of state when I chose John Holdridge to be assistant secretary for East Asian and Pacific affairs have shaped our individual assessments. These common experiences and others unique to Holdridge's extensive background in Asia have molded converging attitudes between us on the subject of U.S.-China affairs.

Looking ahead to the turn of the century, perhaps the greatest international challenge facing the United States is the management of our relations with China. In a world no longer dominated by the politics of the Cold War, many have begun to question the policy of cooperation with China, which has been that of every administration since the 1970s. Some are even urging a policy of containment, which is the precursor to animosity and confrontation. Recognizing that the "Middle Kingdom" is fundamentally different than the World War II regimes in Germany, Italy, or Japan, had we chosen not to deal with each of these with patience and cordiality but rather pursued an aggressive if not arrogant insistence on their immediate adoption of American standards of political pluralism, human rights, or even fair trade, the world today might be a different place. Indeed, it would be difficult to visualize the emergence of the economically viable democratic models Germany, Italy, and Japan represent today.

The People's Republic of China is not a defeated enemy. It is, however, an inevitable international superpower. China's relationship with the United States may well be the pivotal determinant of international peace and stability as well as continued Pacific economic success. Perhaps the greatest danger to this relationship is the tendency of contemporary political leaders to overlook the commitments made by every American president since the early 1970s and the reasons for which they were made. This is the gist of John Holdridge's historical contribution, which should be carefully read by the political authorities who are today shaping our relations with China.

ALEXANDER M. HAIG, JR.
November 1996

Preface

China and its relations with the United States have been very much on my mind since my twelfth year, 1937, when I had the opportunity to visit several Chinese cities and to live for over two months in Beijing, then known to Westerners as Peking and to the Chinese government as Peiping. At that point in history the "anti-Japanese Resistance War," as the Chinese called it, was about to break out, and tensions in Beijing were palpable. From where my family resided in the former College of Chinese Studies in the northeast quadrant of Beijing known as the Tartar City, I witnessed Japanese troops marching through the Chaoyang gate of the city wall for maneuvers outside, and I frequently encountered Chinese irregular troops drilling in the city armed only with traditional two-handed swords. The Japanese ship on which we had voyaged from Osaka to Tianjin (Tientsin) had been crowded with Japanese troops, lending more weight to a sense of impending conflict.

Impressed by the political and martial electricity in the air, I read every English language newspaper and photojournal about China that I could get my hands on and asked questions of everybody. Chiang Kai-shek's "New Life Movement" was seemingly catching on in northern China, leading to a new sense of nationalism, especially among students. I saw patriotic slogans papered everywhere, and I heard Chinese Boy Scouts and troops loudly sing patriotic songs as they marched throughout Peking. The Chinese Communists were far away, and the people's patriotism was buoyed by the Chinese Nationalist defeat of troops from "Manchukuo" (the area of Northeast China seized by Japan in 1931–1932), backed and trained by Japan, who had attempted and failed to seize territory in the Chinese provinces of Suiyuan and Jehol.

How I managed to travel to China relates to an old song called "The Monkeys Have No Tails in Zamboango" sung by U.S. Army troops in the Philippines during that now-dead period of American colonialism. One of the verses went:

> Oh, we'll all go up to China in the springtime
> We'll all go up to China in the springtime
> We'll all go up to China on a great big ocean linah
> Oh, we'll all go up to China in the springtime.

That's exactly what my family did. My father, a U.S. Army officer stationed in the Philippines, had saved enough money to finance an extended trip that began in February 1937 and took us to Hong Kong, Canton, Shanghai, Kobe, Kyoto, Tokyo, Osaka, Tianjin, and finally, Peking, which we reached around the first of March. In those days it was possible for officers and their families to visit China and then pick up a U.S. Army transport ship at Qinhuangdao near Tianjin for the long journey back to the United States, since the army still maintained its 15th Infantry Regiment in Tianjin. My family didn't leave Beijing for my father's next posting in the United States until well into May 1937, or less than two months before the 7 July Marco Polo Bridge (*"Lugouqiao"*) incident that initiated what the Chinese called the Anti-Japanese Resistance War, which merged with World War II after Pearl Harbor.

Despite the hordes of beggars on Hatamen Street (now *Ruijin Lu*), China's vitality and cultural richness overwhelmed my consciousness; I was awestruck by the glories of the Temple of Heaven, the Forbidden City, and the Summer Palace. The sights and sounds of China in that era have remained part of me since I was twelve; I made up my mind then that if the chance ever came to return to China, I would take it.

After a year at Dartmouth College, I entered the U.S. Military Academy at West Point. As a cadet at West Point from 1942 to 1945, I still thought of returning to China. In 1937 I had met in Peking Major (later Major General) Frank Roberts, U.S. Army, West Point class of 1920. Major Roberts was a Chinese language student in China as well as an assistant military attaché there. He was aboard the U.S.S. *Panay* in the Yangtze River when the ship was attacked and sunk by the Japanese in 1937 after the *Lugouqiao* incident. Roberts was one of those who had managed to make his way ashore, and for his performance under fire he was awarded the Navy Cross—an unusual honor for an army officer. I hoped that I could follow in Major Roberts's footsteps, at least in being able to study Chinese after graduation from West Point.

This chance finally opened up for me in 1948, but only after I had left the military following a period of duty in South Korea and had joined the

U.S. Foreign Service. While I was still studying Foreign Service basics at the Foreign Service Institute, Philip Sprouse, then the office director of the Office of Chinese Affairs, called me in and asked if I wanted to study the Chinese language and area under State Department auspices. The plan was for me to take an intensive language course at the Foreign Service Institute, then go to Cornell University for a year, and finally finish my studies at the State Department's Chinese language school in Beijing. I accepted immediately.

I couldn't have been more fortunate in beginning my study of Chinese language and area at Cornell, in a class of five that included two other Foreign Service officers: Art Rosen and Steve Comiskey. Our instructors were outstanding. The director of Cornell's East Asia Studies Program, Knight Biggerstaff, had served in China during World War II at the American embassy in Chungking and had a hands-on knowledge of both China and the Chinese language. He taught Chinese history from the practical standpoint, giving his students a feel for the long sweep of Chinese history and culture, from the earliest beginnings up to the modern period. Our professor of Chinese language and literature, Harold Shadick, had been an English teacher at Yenching University in Beijing before World War II, but he had also used his time there to acquire a profound knowledge of Chinese literature, both in the original classic *wen yan* style and in translation. We had two Chinese language instructors: Charles Hockett, a linguistic scientist with an analytical knowledge of Chinese; and a Chinese native speaker, Lydia Wu, who taught both written and spoken Chinese (Mandarin, albeit with a very slight Shanghai accent).

One of the features of our Chinese studies at Cornell was a Far Eastern studies seminar that covered the interrelationships of Asian cultures, in which various professors from the East Asian Studies Department participated. It was there that I met my wife, Martha, who sat across the seminar table from me. Altogether, my own experiences and those of my colleagues at Cornell were extremely rewarding.

Because of political and military events on the China mainland in 1949, it became impossible now to proceed to Peking for advanced language training and area studies. This was a disappointment in more ways than one, since I had promised Martha during our courtship that I would take her to China. In lieu of sending us to Beijing, the State Department sent its new Chinese language officers to Harvard. At Harvard, we were joined by an additional Foreign Service officer, Paul Frillman, who had been both a Lutheran missionary in Changsha, Hunan Province (where he acquired a thick Hunan dialect that would have been intelligible to Mao Zedong), and the chaplain of the famous "Flying Tigers." Harvard's emphasis was more on the Chinese classics than on the contemporary scene, but we did have the opportunity to sit at the feet of the late John K. Fairbank during his discussions with two graduate students, K. C. Chao and Benjamin Schwartz, who were working, respectively, on *A Documentary History of Chinese Communism*, and *Chinese Communism and the Rise of Mao*. (I consider Ben Schwartz's book a seminal work and strongly believe that its conclusions remain valid today.)

Others who taught us at Harvard were Professors Edwin Reischauer, John Hightower, Francis X. Cleves, and Yang Lien-sheng, all of whom broadened our foundations in Chinese studies. Thus fortified, we all went from there to our first Foreign Service assignments in the latter half of 1950. By that time, the United States had already broken off diplomatic contacts with the People's Republic of China (PRC) and pulled out its diplomats.

By beginning my Foreign Service career in the China field when I did, I found myself either on the fringes of, or directly involved in, the tortuous process of trying to keep up with the events on China's mainland, attempting to discern the directions of Chinese policy, and helping make recommendations affecting the future course of U.S.-China relations. The process was tortuous because, while the People's Republic of China was— and is—a vast country vital to American interests, it was tightly closed to American diplomats. As part of the process of reporting on China, I spent a total of seven years, during two tours, in Hong Kong, which was as close as Americans could get to China, but which gave us some feel for what was happening across the border. For some years I also helped to defend the international position of the "Republic of China on Taiwan." (Maintaining nondiplomatic relations with Taiwan remains an important element in U.S. policy.)

By 1968, however, events in China, such as the developing confrontation between Moscow and Beijing, plus the obvious need for the United States to be able to open contacts with a country having the world's largest population and a constantly growing strategic and diplomatic importance, led me to join some colleagues in concluding that our Taiwan-centered policy was at a dead end. I, among others, became convinced that the best interests of the United States lay in opening up a constructive dialogue with China in which both countries could overcome mutual suspicions, establish some sort of peaceful coexistence, and maintain "normal" diplomatic relations. This book is the story of how the United States and China worked to "normalize" (the Chinese term is "*zheng chang hua*") our diplomatic relations between 1968 and 1979, and how that relationship has developed up to the present.

My part in normalizing diplomatic relations with China required more than a few job shifts and household moves. After my second tour in Hong Kong, I returned to Washington for assignments between 1966 and 1969 as deputy director and then director of the Office of Research for East Asia and the Pacific in the Bureau of Intelligence and Research at the Department of State. In July 1969 I was transferred to the National Security Council under Dr. Henry A. Kissinger as his senior staff member for East Asia and the Pacific, where I spent the next four years. In 1973 Martha and I went to China (I did finally make good my promise to her!), where I was one of two deputy chiefs of mission (DCM) of the U.S. Liaison Office in Beijing. The other was Alfred Lesesne Jenkins, who represented the Department of State, while I in effect represented the National Security Council; thanks to both our efforts, the unusual two-DCM arrangement worked well.

After serving in Beijing I was named ambassador to Singapore and then assigned as national intelligence officer for East Asia and the Pacific on the National Intelligence Council. In 1981, I was appointed assistant secretary of state for East Asia and the Pacific, and from 1983 until 1986 I was ambassador to Indonesia, after which I retired from the Foreign Service.

My basic purpose in writing this book is to present events in history, in many of which I myself participated, that were critical to the normalization process of bringing China and the United States closer together. I hope that American historians, businessmen, students, and members of the public in general will find these events and my analyses of them both interesting and valuable. Many episodes have not been brought to light elsewhere, and my intention in citing them is to fill some important gaps in history. A key aspect has been to outline the differences between the United States and China that have affected our relationship, both in the past and in the current period. Besides the Taiwan issue (see below), these differences include Chinese sales of advanced arms and nuclear technology to what might be best described as "rogue states," China's monitoring of its manufacturers' piracy of U.S. intellectual property, access to the Chinese market by U.S. business interests, and Chinese resentment of American moralizing over human rights, lack of democracy, and other perceived shortcomings of the Chinese system.

I also hope that in the United States, government officials, members of Congress, business people, and the American voters will reflect on my account of the long-drawn-out normalization process when addressing current difficulties in U.S.-China relations. Above all, I would want my American readers to understand the central issue of U.S. relations with

Taiwan, and how it was necessary for both the United States and China to find ways to put this issue aside to proceed with normalization. It was fortunate from the standpoint of regional and world peace that such ways were found, and they worked very well until a new generation of U.S. leaders came along who either forgot or never understood the difficulties of normalization. These lessons provide significant clues as to how issues between our two countries can be resolved, or at least managed more effectively. On neither side do we need another quarter-century of confrontation in the U.S.-China relationship, a relationship that is valuable to each of us in the cause of regional and world stability, as well as in our respective domestic economies and politics.

In transcribing Chinese personal or place names, I have grappled with the problem that two different sets of romanization are used in transcribing Chinese: the modified Wade-Giles system originally used by the Kuomintang authorities on the China mainland and still used on Taiwan, and the *pinyin* system used in the People's Republic of China on the mainland today. Whenever I have referred to pre-1949 events or to personages connected with the former group, I have used the modified Wade-Giles nomenclature; whenever I have referred to events or personages connected with what is now the PRC, I have used the *pinyin* system.

As this book's subject is the normalization of United States relations with the People's Republic of China, and as that normalization necessarily required this country to recognize the PRC as "China" and the government on Taiwan as "Taiwan" or as the "Nationalists," when I refer to "China" or "the Chinese" in the post-1949 period it is to the People's Republic of China and its citizens.

I wish to give my heartfelt thanks to those who have reviewed my manuscript and made suggestions based on their own recollections: former ambassador U. Alexis Johnson, who filled in some blanks concerning the early period of U.S.-China ambassadorial-level talks; former assistant secretary of state William P. Bundy, who added many details of the period before I went to the National Security Council in July 1969; former ambassador Marshall Green, who as assistant secretary of state was one of the key players in the earliest days of the normalization process; former ambassador Arthur Hummel, whose contributions to the talks with the Chinese on arms sales to Taiwan were a critical factor in their success; and FSo William Rope, who as office director of the State Department's Office of Mainland China Affairs in many cases "held the pencil" while these talks were going on. Particular thanks go to Gerald S. Stryker, formerly of the United States Information Agency, and Arthur Rosen, who for many years was president of the U.S. National Committee on U.S.-

China Relations, who painstakingly went over the full text word by word and made many excellent suggestions. I add my deepest appreciation to my daughter, Patricia Johnson, who undertook the formidable task of editing this work, and to my wife Martha, who was always a part of my "team" in China and elsewhere, and who has supplied constant encouragement and logistical support.

I want to extend my deep appreciation to the law firm of Popham, Haik, Schnobrich & Kaufman, Ltd., which, because of its interest in world events and China in particular, gave generous support to the Association for Diplomatic Studies and Training (ADST) to help publish this book in the ADST-DACOR Diplomats and Diplomacy Series. I am also grateful to the China Industrial Information Institute (C3i), which similarly supported the association's work on the book. The institute's assistance to the Chinese in drafting laws and providing training for occupational safety and health demonstrates to me the value of the continuing process both sides began in the early 1970s of normalizing relations between our two countries. Also, my deep appreciation goes to Dr. Wang Chi, cochairman of the United States–China Policy Foundation, which was established to address the political and economic issues between the two countries with a view towards increasing each nation's understanding of the other, hence helping to improve their basic relationship. The foundation's assistance was, and is, of great value in helping me to present my thoughts on this relationship to the public. And, of course, I cannot fail to mention the invaluable contributions of ADST, which led me by the hand through the intricacies of bringing my book to print and working with the publisher to this end.

Bethesda, Maryland
December 1996

Chapter 1

Root Causes of United States–China Differences

In the years immediately following World War II, a great rift developed between the United States and what most Americans used to call "Communist China" or "Red China" but that became the People's Republic of China (PRC) on 1 October 1949. This rift was so profound that three decades passed before it was bridged through normalizing U.S.–China relations, that is, opening diplomatic ties and maintaining a relatively conventional diplomatic give-and-take. Before proceeding with the story of normalization, or *zheng chang hua*, some background is essential to appreciate why the process of normalizing U.S.–PRC relations required so much time.

Above all, problems between the United States and the People's Republic of China in the immediate postwar period can be attributed to the immense ideological void that lay between our two countries. On one side stood the United States, the world's most powerful capitalist state, which beginning in 1948 found itself engaged in a "cold war" with the Soviet Union, and which was a long-time supporter of the Chinese Nationalist (Kuomintang or KMT) government. On the other side stood the People's Republic of China, a country led by founding members of the Chinese Communist Party (CCP), which proclaimed it "leaned to one side"[1]— that of the Soviet Union—and that in 1949 won a long revolutionary struggle against the KMT government.

Between these two ideological poles lay a chasm that few American or Chinese leaders cared to bridge. Clearly, both sides experienced misunderstandings, suspicions, and mistakes of judgment due to the personalities and ideological convictions of the policy-makers in the two countries. The differences between the two countries' cultural and philosophical

1

traditions also played a significant part (see chapter 15). In addition, the United States and China were sharply divided on many specific issues, concerning Korea, Taiwan, and Vietnam, for example. Divisions developed long before it was clear that the Communist leaders would rule China.

Early Grievances

Numerous specific episodes in the immediate post–World War II period of U.S. relations with Chinese Communist leaders help to explain the ensuing rift between the United States and China.[2] The complaints of the United States included the expulsion of American missionaries and businessmen from areas held by the Chinese Communists and the difficulties American diplomats encountered in trying to get the Chinese Communists to negotiate with the Nationalists, whom the American public strongly supported, and to whom the U.S. government had given $2 billion in military and economic aid during the Chinese civil war. A case in point is the failure of the "Marshall Mission," a group of U.S. diplomatic and military officials under General of the Army George C. Marshall, who had been sent to China in 1946 to try and bring the Nationalists and Communists together in a joint post–World War II government.

American grievances were intensified during the final days of the Chinese revolution. Chinese Communists accorded harsh treatment to the U.S. diplomats whom the State Department deliberately left in the path of advancing Chinese Communist forces to learn if it might be possible for the United States to establish relations with the victorious regime. First to feel the bite of China's ill will was the U.S. Consulate General in Shenyang, known then to Americans as Mukden, where the Communists seized Consul General Angus Ward and imprisoned him for thirty days in solitary confinement. When the advancing armies reached Beijing, Communist leaders told Consul General O. Edmund Clubb that he and his staff were not to be treated as diplomats but as private citizens, and they apparently went out of their way to make life difficult for the Americans.[3] Ambassador John Leighton Stuart in Nanjing ran into a similar situation, made all the more poignant for him because many of the senior Chinese leaders, including Huang Hua (later Chinese foreign minister), had been students of his when he was president of Yenching (now part of Beijing) University.

What finally forced the United States to remove its official presence from China was a decision by the Chinese to take over the former U.S. Marine barracks in Beijing, which, following the withdrawal of the Marines, had been occupied by the U.S. Consulate General staff and used as their office building. The Chinese order "requisitioning" the building was given to Consul General O. E. Clubb on 6 January 1950; on 10 January the U.S. government, after repeated consultation with the Consulate General, directed Mr. Clubb to inform the Chinese that if they proceeded to carry out this order, the United States was prepared to withdraw all its official personnel from China. The Chinese nevertheless proceeded, and on 14 January 1950, the State Department issued a press release in Washington announcing its intention to withdraw all official personnel from China.[4] After this edict was carried out, no U.S. official returned to China on a permanent basis until May 1973, and full diplomatic relations were not established until 1979.

From the point of view of the Chinese Communists, mutual problems with the United States were primarily related to their power struggle with the KMT following the Japanese surrender in 1945. Chinese Communist leaders perceived a pro-KMT bias on the part of wartime U.S. Ambassador to China Patrick Hurley and believed that his efforts to help reconcile differences between them and the KMT were but an attempt to buy time for the KMT.[5] Communist suspicions of U.S. as well as KMT intentions during the Marshall Mission discussions in 1946 contributed greatly to the mission's failure to mediate the formation of a coalition government. In addition, the Chinese Communists chafed at U.S. limitations on military assistance to them during the war against Japan, when the United States actually maintained a military presence known as the "Dixie Mission," under Colonel David Barrett, in the Communist headquarters at Yan'an. Furthermore, they bitterly resented the U.S. assistance to the Kuomintang, specifically its transporting of KMT troops after the war into Manchuria where major Communist-Kuomintang battles were to take place. As the Communist armies consolidated power and eventually swept victoriously south from Manchuria, they were in no mood to negotiate with the U.S. diplomatic and consular missions that were left behind to test their intentions toward the United States. And because by that time they were committed to "lean to (the) one side" of the Soviet Union, Chinese leaders appeared to have few regrets concerning the final withdrawal of the U.S. diplomatic missions in early 1950.

The issue of detention of citizens illustrates on a small scale the uncooperative and suspicious tenor of early relations between the United States and Communist China. While other problems were developing in the late 1940s, Chinese students in the United States who had acquired knowledge of sensitive technologies were not permitted to return to China (although most were returned by 1950). For its part, the PRC detained American missionaries and businessmen who had remained in China after the PRC was established, plus the pilots and crew of military aircraft downed during alleged intrusions of Chinese territory. Some of the latter were shot down over China during the Korean War, a period during which U.S.-China relations became cemented in acrimony.

The Korean War

China's entry into the Korean War contributed significantly to the estrangement between the United States and China. According to press reports, the Korean War cost the United States 54,246 men killed in action, not counting many thousands of wounded and the 8,177 missing in action still not accounted for.[6] China likewise lost hundreds of thousands. Up to that point, it might have been possible to negotiate terms for mutual diplomatic recognition; however, the Korean conflict helped set that timetable back two decades.

China's participation in the Korean War may be attributed in considerable part to a climate of opinion dominant in the Communist world at the time that existing Communist regimes should everywhere promote revolution. The chief proponent of this philosophy, Joseph Stalin, sought to push forward the frontiers of communism as far as he could wherever and whenever opportunities opened. One such opportunity was in Korea, which had been divided into two zones since the end of the Japanese War in 1945: the Soviet Union occupied the northern section, and the United States occupied the southern section. A Joint U.S.-Soviet Military Control Commission was supposed to meet regularly to establish the parameters of a unified Korea, but the U.S. delegates on the commission soon found that the Soviets were unwilling to discuss unification in any realistic way.

As a young lieutenant in the U.S. Army, I was stationed in Korea from 1945 to 1947, and I was aware of the frustrations our delegation encountered. Major General Archibald Arnold, the father of a West Point classmate of mine, was the chief of the U.S. delegation, and from him and his son, Arch Jr., I heard enough to convince me of the Soviets' obstructionism. The Soviets gave no sign of willingness to give up their hold on the zone they occupied and instead busied themselves in setting up a government under Kim Il Sung. Kim was a dedicated Communist for many years and had been trained partly in those areas of China held by the Chinese Communists. In addition, the Soviets early on had applied themselves to the task of organizing, training, and equipping a North Korean army. Before my departure from Korea in November 1947, I learned in a briefing from the G-3 of the 7th Infantry Division to which I had been assigned that by then the North Korean forces numbered some 250,000 men and possessed both artillery and tanks.

In contrast to the strength of the North Korean army supported by the Soviets, South Korea in 1947 had what was still called the "Korean Constabulary," which was trained only as a paramilitary force and equipped mainly with weapons captured from the Japanese. Attached to my engineer battalion was a constabulary company that had the sole duty of helping to guard the U.S. heavy equipment we were using around the city of Seoul. The Korean Constabulary was no match in numbers, training, or equipment for the army of North Korea. The United States eventually realized the discrepancy in power between the two Koreas and began to train and equip a South Korean army, but this move was much too late—the North Koreans enjoyed an advantage of several years.

The main instance of U.S. short-sightedness about Korea was diplomatic, not military. On 12 January 1950, Secretary of State Dean Acheson spoke before the National Press Club in Washington, D.C. and there defined the U.S. "defensive perimeter" in East Asia, namely, specific places that the United States would be prepared to defend. Significantly, the perimeter he described did not include South Korea: "The defensive perimeter runs along the Aleutians to Japan and then goes to the Ryukyus. . . . [and] to the Philippine Islands. . . . So far as the military security of other areas in the Pacific is concerned, it must be clear that no person can guarantee it against military attack. . . . Should such an attack occur . . . the initial reliance must be upon the people attacked to resist it."[7]

A week earlier, President Harry Truman had also given a press conference in which he made it plain that the United States would not intervene in the "Chinese civil war" by helping to defend "Formosa" (Taiwan) or by providing the "forces there" with military assistance.[8] Combined, these two statements sent a clear public message that the United States's strategic interests in Asia were very narrowly defined. To explain this limited definition of interests, one can only speculate that our policy makers did not wish to engage the United States in a land war on the continent of Asia. However the omission of Korea from the American "defensive perimeter" occurred, it provided the opportunity for Stalin and the North Koreans under Kim Il Sung to try to unify Korea on their own terms by force of arms.[9] The attack on South Korea came on 25 June 1950. Compelled by President Truman's decision to react militarily, the United States found itself, regardless of prior intentions, fighting a land war in Asia.

In October 1950, when the counterattack by the United Nations forces under Supreme Commander General Douglas MacArthur neared the Yalu River that divides Korea from China (some units actually reached the river), "Chinese People's Volunteers" came into the fighting in great numbers. China's entry was presumably driven by at least three motives: to rescue a "fraternal socialist state" from destruction; to assist Stalin in his plan to extend communism's frontiers; and to safeguard China's own borders. The PRC had been established only a year earlier, and its leaders likely were highly sensitive to what could have been a significant external threat to its control.

Whatever the reasons for China's entry into the Korean War, the United States had ample warning. In early October 1950, State Department personnel at the U.S. Consulate General in Hong Kong briefed me on my way to my first State Department posting in Bangkok, Thailand. They knew that the entire Chinese Communist Fourth Field Army under the command of Marshal Lin Biao was moving by rail from South China northwards towards the Korean border. General MacArthur's intelligence chief, Major General Charles Willoughby, apparently chose to disregard such intelligence in his briefings to MacArthur. This intelligence was backed up by specific warnings from Zhou Enlai, passed to the United States through Indian Ambassador to China Pannikar, that if the United States crossed the former line of demarcation between North and South, the Demilitarized Zone (DMZ), China would enter the conflict. In retrospect, U.S. intelligence and the warnings given through Ambassador Pannikar should have been given greater weight.

In any event, the three years of bitter fighting in Korea left a legacy of hostility in U.S.-China relations. In 1953, when the long, drawn-out armistice talks at Panmunjom on the de facto border between North and South finally ended the fighting in Korea, representatives from the "Chinese People's Volunteers" sat with representatives from North Korea across the table from American and South Korean representatives. This was the first high-level contact between U.S. and Chinese officials since World War II, but it was not one that helped to bridge the gap between us.

Besides the actual fighting and the loss of lives on both sides, an additional factor related to the Korean War must have strained U.S.-PRC relations: the U.S. insistence during the truce talks that there be no forced repatriation of POWs. This resulted in some 14,000 Chinese POWs refusing to return to China and going instead to Taiwan once the fighting had stopped. The Chinese retaliated by talking a handful of American POWs into refusing repatriation to the United States in favor of going to China. (Almost all of these Americans eventually returned to the United States, some with Chinese wives and with children. While assigned to the U.S. Consulate General in Hong Kong in the early 1960s, I assisted some of them in their return to the United States.)

As a consequence of China's combat role in Korea, the U.S. government imposed a complete embargo on trade with the PRC, and it banned travel by Americans to "those areas of China under Communist control." The government also barred traditional Chinese goods such as handicrafts, foodstuffs, and medicines from entering the United States unless accompanied by a "certificate of origin" showing that the country of manufacture was not the PRC. These regulations were in effect for years, and a whole generation of U.S. diplomats labored to enforce them. Although the Chinese resented these regulations, their economic effects on the PRC were slight. Other U.S. actions consequent to China's role in Korea affected China more deeply; these actions concerned the Chinese Nationalist government on Taiwan.

The Status of Taiwan

Foremost among the many subsequent issues dividing the United States and the People's Republic of China was that of Taiwan, the island bastion to which the Kuomintang (KMT) government retreated in 1949 after the China mainland fell to the Chinese Communists. The United States had maintained only a token diplomatic presence on Taiwan while it was sounding out the possibilities of establishing a modus vivendi with the PRC. Also, as noted above, President Truman initially eschewed any military involvement with the defense of Taiwan, though he did order what later became known as the "Taiwan Strait Patrol," an occasional passage by a destroyer through the Taiwan Strait intended to keep an eye on what was happening on both sides of the strait.[10] China's entry into the Korean War became the catalyst not only for an expansion of U.S.-KMT diplomatic ties but also for a growing U.S. security interest in Taiwan. This security interest included an order from President Truman to the U.S. 7th Fleet to "neutralize" the Taiwan Strait and a resumption of military aid to the KMT forces on Taiwan. The U.S. diplomatic commitment to Taiwan included recognizing the KMT-led "Republic of China" (ROC) as the sole representative of China, maintaining an embassy in the ROC capital of Taipei, and supporting it in international bodies such as the United Nations. As of this time, KMT policy called for "recovery of the mainland."

In support of its security interest in Taiwan, the United States concluded a mutual defense treaty with the ROC in December 1954, which called on both sides to consult together on steps to be taken in the event of an external threat against the island of Taiwan or the ROC-held Pescadores islands in Taiwan Strait.[11] The U.S. Senate ratified this treaty on 9 February 1955. It was immediately denounced by the Chinese as an attempt to "legalize" the so-called "U.S. occupation of Taiwan." The PRC subsequently flexed its muscles in the Taiwan Strait by seizing Yijiang Island, located 210 miles north of Taiwan, and by initiating an aerial bombardment of the ROC-held Dachen Islands, located somewhat to the northwest of Taiwan and closer to Taiwan than to the China mainland. The bombardment presaged an amphibious assault on these islands. The United States, fearing a military debacle if the islands were defended by the ROC, prevailed upon Chiang Kai-shek to permit the U.S. Navy to evacuate ROC forces from the Dachens back to Taiwan.

This episode surely had a bearing on the drafting of the "Formosa Resolution" in the U.S. Congress. This was passed in July 1955 after President Eisenhower called on Congress to extend U.S. security coverage of Taiwan to include the "Offshore Islands" of Quemoy and Matsu adjacent to the China mainland province of Fujian should the United States judge that safeguarding these territories was necessary to "assure the defense of Formosa [Taiwan] and the Pescadores."[12]

The identification of the United States with Taiwan was intensified during the McCarthy period in the early 1950s. Supported by many American conservatives, Senator Joseph McCarthy carried on a vendetta against the State Department for allegedly being riddled with "card-carrying Communists," many of whom he accused of playing a prominent role in "losing China to the Communists." Among those McCarthy accused were well-respected career diplomats John P. Davies, John Carter Vincent, and John S. Service, all of whom had served in China before and during World War II, who had reported favorably on Chinese Communist actions (particularly those related to organizing mass support against Japanese forces and to agrarian reform) and on the corruption rampant in the Kuomintang. In this same period, Dr. Walter Judd, a former medical missionary to China and by then a member of Congress, organized an American grass-roots organization called the "Committee of One Million," which unalterably opposed contacts between Americans and Chinese Communists and threw its moral backing to the ROC on Taiwan. (The ROC supported the Committee of One Million financially.) On this group's board of directors were a number of distinguished Americans, including General Albert S. Wedemeyer, who had succeeded General Joseph Stilwell as commander of U.S. and ROC forces in China during

World War II, and Democratic Senator Paul Douglas. As a result of these kinds of activities, anticommunist, anti-PRC sentiment solidified throughout the United States.

As a measure of the official U.S. attitude toward the PRC-ROC equation at the time, then-Assistant Secretary of State Walter S. Robertson had a habit in conferences with visiting diplomats of beginning remarks on China by stating that the Chinese Communists had "killed 20 million people" in establishing their government. While working on the "China Desk" (or CA) at the State Department in 1958, I often sat in on Robertson's conversations with visiting diplomats, and I heard him use this line many times.

Anticommunist sentiments were also expressed by Secretary of State John Foster Dulles, who besides being an expert in international law was an elder of the Presbyterian church, saw communism as an evil force, and hence was a staunch anticommunist. In speaking to the Foreign Service Association at the time of his appointment by President Eisenhower in 1953, he stunned the assembled Foreign Service officers, including me, with the remark "some of you are loyal." I well remember the shock that Dulles's words generated among these dedicated Foreign Service officers. At any rate, official as well as popular American sentiment against communism was such in the 1950s that the country's unity with the ROC was continually reinforced.

Tensions over Taiwan between the United States and the PRC at times grew to the point where the two nations came close to military confrontation and tested the U.S.-ROC Mutual Defense Treaty. One crisis, mentioned above, was the PRC bombardment of the Dachen Islands in the Taiwan Strait. Another crisis occurred in August and September 1958, when the PRC conducted a campaign of intensive artillery bombardment of the offshore islands of Quemoy and Matsu, which the United States had specifically included in the "Formosa Resolution." The United States assured the resupply of the Quemoy garrison by using its warships to escort ROC naval vessels to Quemoy's three-mile limits while its carrier-borne aircraft kept a careful watch overhead. (Matsu was considerably farther away from the Chinese mainland than Quemoy and did not require the same degree of U.S. involvement.) During this resupply effort, several clashes occurred over the Taiwan Strait between PRC aircraft and U.S.-supplied ROC aircraft, in which PRC-flown MIG-15s and MIG-17s were shot down by U.S.-built F-100s.

To the People's Republic of China, U.S. support of Taiwan represented interference in China's internal affairs and prevented the consummation of the Communist revolution and the full unification of the nation. To this day, reunification of Taiwan with the mainland remains the most persistent issue of concern to the PRC in its relations with the United States. As long as the United States retains "unofficial" relations with Taiwan as well as a security responsibility through arms sales to Taiwan as provided for in the "Taiwan Relations Act" of 1979, the PRC cannot be free to proceed with reunification on its own terms. The PRC is also limited in its use of military force against Taiwan under the terms of three joint communiqués reached with the United States, which are discussed below.

The Vietnam War

A decade after the Korean War, the United States again found itself involved in a war on the Asian mainland, this time in Vietnam. Once U.S. military units became directly committed in Vietnam in the mid-1960s, Chinese antiaircraft, engineer, and logistical units entered Vietnam and assisted the North Vietnamese in keeping lines of communication open in the face of U.S. air attacks. Although neither China nor North Vietnam ever admitted the presence of these troops, worries persisted in the United States about becoming involved in a land war in Asia, as in Korea, with the PRC a major opponent. These worries influenced the United States to hold back in its air attacks on the North Vietnamese port of Haiphong and on rail and road communications between Hanoi/Haiphong and China, along which vital Soviet military assistance flowed to North Vietnam. It was not until the latter stages of the Vietnam War—specifically, after Hanoi's so-called "Easter Offensive" of March 1972 and the American "Christmas bombings" of December 1972—that the United States lifted these restrictions.

One bizarre feature of this era in U.S.-PRC relations was a constantly growing number of PRC "serious warnings" to the United States for intrusions into PRC territory, stemming for the most part from U.S. overflights of the PRC-claimed Paracel Islands, which lie in a nearly direct line between the northern part of South Vietnam and locations in the Philippines where the United States had bases. The PRC also charged that territorial violations were being made elsewhere along its borders by U.S. warships and reconnaissance aircraft, particularly in the Taiwan Strait where for many years the Navy maintained the Taiwan Strait patrol (see above). The implication of these warnings was that the PRC, at some later and unspecified date, would demand redress for such violations of its territory, but it never did. Nearly five hundred of these "warnings" were issued by the PRC before the Nixon administration brought them to a halt in November 1969.

Throughout the Vietnam War, the PRC spoke of having a "lips and teeth" relationship with Vietnam, even though the Soviet Union was the preponderant foreign influence in Vietnam. However, as Soviet-PRC relations began to deteriorate, China increasingly resented the Soviet influence in Vietnam, and Chinese relations with Vietnam deteriorated as a result. At one stage in the hostilities, the Chinese manifested their displeasure by interfering with Soviet arms shipments moving by rail across China to North Vietnam.

There were some direct confrontations involving the United States and China in the Vietnam War. Certainly U.S. bombings inflicted casualties among PRC troops,[13] and presumably some U.S. aircraft were shot down by PRC antiaircraft fire. In at least two instances, U.S. aircraft that had intruded into China were shot down and the pilots killed. Such confrontations were few; nevertheless, the period was hardly conducive to normalization of U.S.-PRC relations.

Tibet

An issue in U.S.-China relations that muddied the waters and further complicated the process of normalization was the American public's reaction to events in Tibet, which the Chinese had occupied in 1950. Their suppression of the uprising of Khamba tribesmen in March 1959 led in May of that year to the flight to India of Tibet's spiritual and temporal leader, the Dalai Lama. In the United States sympathy for the Dalai Lama poured forth; he was asked by private American groups to visit the United States and speak about the troubles of Tibet, which he did. Although the U.S. government in no way sponsored the Dalai Lama's visit, it interposed no objection to the visit. The Dalai Lama's highly—and favorably—publicized visit to the United States undoubtedly stirred up strong resentment within the Chinese government, where it smacked of foreign interference in China's internal affairs. Nevertheless, despite the American public's sympathy toward the Dalai Lama and Tibet, at no time did U.S. government policy support the Dalai Lama as the leader of an independent country, even though the Central Intelligence Agency (CIA) supported Khamba forces staging raids from Nepal into Tibet.

The U.S. position toward Tibet was, and is to this day, to regard it as "autonomous under Chinese suzerainty." Originally this position was based upon Taiwan's policy toward Tibet, which was accepted in

Washington so as not to offend this ally. It has remained in effect since normalization of relations with the PRC in order to avoid further complications in an already complicated relationship. The Dalai Lama has continued to make frequent visits to the United States, despite Chinese sensitivities, and the American public has sustained its interest in the human rights situation in Tibet.

Sino-Soviet Ideological Issues

Of the many issues affecting the state of U.S.-China relations, perhaps none besides Taiwan has been more significant than the ideological dispute between China and the Soviet Union. Despite the PRC's pro-Soviet "lean to one side" policy in the immediate post–World War II period, ideological harmony between China and the Soviet Union began to dissipate in the latter half of the 1950s, replaced by increasingly bitter relations and finally by open hostility. A recurrent point of contention between the two Communist giants was what China dubbed Soviet "revisionism," as evidenced in part by the Soviet Union's moderation of its hostile posture towards the United States, the "leader of the imperialist camp." Since China took the ideological high road of staunchly opposing "United States-led" capitalism and "imperialism" at any cost, and the Soviet Union moderated its anti-United States stance, deteriorating Sino-Soviet relations necessarily hindered U.S.-China rapprochement in the 1960s. Paradoxically, increasing Sino-Soviet hostility later contributed to the normalization of U.S.-China relations in the 1970s.

Complex ideological differences arose between the Chinese Communist Party (CCP) and the Communist Party of the Soviet Union (CPSU) as early as the mid-1930s. At that time the mainstream leadership of the CCP was dominated by a faction of Moscow-educated "returned students" who espoused the Soviet view that organization of the urban proletariat was the key to the victory of the Communist revolution and the development of socialism.

This faction was opposed by another headed by Mao Zedong, who maintained that the revolution in each country had to reflect its own unique characteristics, and that in the absence of a strong urban proletariat in China (peasants comprised 85 percent of China's population), the revolution had no alternative but to take the countryside as its base and go on from there. Mao's thesis was that the countryside and its peasants should be organized to surround the cities to bring about the ultimate seizure of power, and that building socialism afterwards had to focus first on the countryside. It was Mao's "different approach to socialism" that prevailed in China; still, the CCP and the CPSU maintained very close relations until the late 1950s.

A watershed in Sino-Soviet relations was Khrushchev's February 1956 speech to the twentieth Congress of the CPSU, in which he denounced Stalin and advocated a less restrictive atmosphere in the Soviet Union. The CCP, no doubt with some misgivings, stood by the Soviets during the unrest in Eastern Europe that followed Khrushchev's speech; PRC Premier Zhou Enlai even toured Eastern Europe in the latter part of 1956, following this unrest, to proclaim, in effect, that the socialist camp had to have a leader, and that leader was the Soviet Union. Nevertheless, ideological disagreements following a meeting of Communist parties in Moscow in November 1957 marked the beginning of indirect CCP attacks on the CPSU by means of blasts against Yugoslav "modern revisionism," clearly intended as warnings to the Soviets not to stray from the revolutionary path (as defined by the CCP).

When ideological points of dispute coincided with China's practical, nationalistic concerns regarding Soviet economic and military support of China, the bitterness of the Chinese anti-Soviet polemic escalated dramatically. According to information received by the State Department, Khrushchev in a visit to Beijing in July 1958 attached conditions unacceptable to the Chinese for Soviet support of the PRC's campaign against the offshore islands in the Taiwan Strait, including the establishment of Soviet naval communications centers in China and operational control of the PRC Navy.[14] By some Soviet accounts, Chairman Mao indicated to Soviet leaders that same year that in a nuclear war China would be prepared to sacrifice half of its 600 million inhabitants on the assumption that the 300 million people left would allow China—and the revolution—to survive.[15] Perhaps as a consequence of Mao's stance, in 1959 Khrushchev repudiated a 1957 USSR-PRC "Agreement on New Technology for National Defense" that was to aid China in developing nuclear weapons and the missiles needed for their delivery.

With publication of an article entitled "Long Live Leninism" in the CCP publications *Red Flag* and *People's Daily* on 6 April 1960 (ostensibly commemorating the ninetieth anniversary of Lenin's birth),[16] the CCP directly targeted the Soviets in a pointed attack on their ideological purity and zeal. The article portrayed the Soviets as archetypal "modern revisionists" who had betrayed the goals of the October Revolution by insisting that the victory of socialism throughout the world could be attained without the use of force. The article maintained further that in the light of the presumed superior military power the Soviet Union possessed relative to the United States and its allies, the Soviets should not fear war when assisting the world revolutionary movement, though it result in a major conflict. Perhaps the most significant—certainly the most disquieting—feature of the article was that it publicly discounted the effects of a nuclear war by asserting that if one actually occurred, "on the ruins of the old civilizations the victorious peoples will build an even more beautiful future for themselves." (The heavy play given to this article in China's domestic and international press releases suggests that Mao Zedong probably wrote "Long Live Leninism," or at least edited it to final form.)

The CCP continued a virulent ideological polemic against the CPSU from 1960 well into the 1970s and even the 1980s. Two themes recurred: the validity of "different roads to socialism" and the CPSU's alleged abandonment of fundamental Marxist-Leninist teachings. Mao Zedong in his role as the apostle of revolutionary philosophy in China strongly opposed first Khrushchev's, and later, Brezhnev's, willingness to accept a period of "peaceful coexistence" with the United States as a way-stop on the road to the eventual victory of socialism. Khrushchev in particular was attacked for arguing that this victory could be attained peacefully through demonstrating the superiority of the "socialist system" in economic as well as political terms. As the polemic broadened, the United States more and more found itself caught in the middle as the hapless initiator of Chinese wrath against the Soviets, which led in turn to a stifling of U.S.-PRC contacts.

According to Mao and the CCP, socialism could only be attained as a result of violent revolution and bloodshed, and the least that the Soviets could do was to "keep the line drawn between the enemy and ourselves"—this enemy, of course, being the United States. The CCP further maintained that "the revolution must be carried through to the end, both at home and abroad," and that it was the "proletarian international duty" of the socialist countries to support "wars of national liberation" wherever these occurred.

The Soviet Union reacted to the CCP's attacks on its policies and its revolutionary "adventurism"—especially in light of Mao's apparent willingness to engage in nuclear war—by abruptly terminating its economic support of the PRC. In July 1960, three months after the publication of "Long Live Leninism," Premier Khrushchev withdrew all Soviet economic assistance to China, including technicians and blueprints for factories being constructed with Soviet assistance. Soviet economic aid, which had begun in 1954 following a Khrushchev-Bulganin visit to Beijing, was funding what the PRC called the "hard core" of its modern industrial development, encompassing over 140 large factories and other major projects, such as a bridge across the Yangtze. Its loss was a staggering blow. Chinese editorials around this time noted with some bitterness that the USSR was also demanding repayment for all the arms it had provided China during the Korean War. Underscoring the economic hardship to China, the Soviet pullout occurred just as Mao Zedong's utopian "Great Leap Forward" was collapsing, and near-famine conditions had developed in many parts of China. Khrushchev's actions must have been seen by the PRC as a terrible betrayal.

For the next four years China took every opportunity to criticize the Soviet Union; the Soviet Union in turn pointedly avoided supporting its one-time socialist ally, as when it sided rhetorically with India instead of China in the Sino-Indian border dispute of 1962. Still, it was not until 1964 that China publicly broke with the Soviet Union, on the occasion of a conference called by Moscow of "World Workers' and Communist Parties" in December of that year. Zhou Enlai and his entourage joined the other main Communist apostate, Albania, in resisting Moscow's efforts to impose the CPSU's leadership on the world Communist movement. When the majority of the conference voted to expel Albania from their community, China accompanied Albania in walking out of the conference, never to return to the Soviet fold.

China's confidence in the ultimate victory of its own revolutionary cause was buoyed in 1964 by its first successful nuclear test. An article written by PRC Defense Minister Lin Biao ("Long Live the Victory of People's War") in September 1965 gives an insight into Beijing's basic world view in that period.[17] As described by Lin, the "victory of socialism" appeared imminently attainable through a process modeled on the successful CCP revolution: revolutionary forces in the "countryside" of the world, that is, the developing countries, would surround the "cities" of the world, that is, the developed countries headed by the United States, and then seize power.

It should be noted that Lin Biao in his article ruled out the direct intervention of a "socialist" state such as China in a "people's war." The task of achieving victory in each country was to be left "primarily" to its revolutionary masses. The socialist countries should, of course, provide appropriate material support, in keeping with Mao Zedong's dictum on the international proletariat duty of socialist states to support wars of national liberation. According to Stanley Karnow, this section of Lin Biao's article was really "an announcement that China had no plans to intercede militarily in Vietnam."[18] In these terms, China was on the offensive ideologically and strategically, but remained on the defensive tactically. Still, when Lin Biao's article is placed alongside "Long Live Leninism," it can be seen that China patently advocated a higher risk of war between the East (the "socialist camp") and the West (the United States and its allies). From the CCP's point of view, the militarily superior USSR could and should have taken on this risk, even if the less well-armed China remained in the background (as was the case with PRC aid to Hanoi).

The year 1966 brought the "Great Proletarian Cultural Revolution" to China, when Mao Zedong's determination to "carry the revolution through to the end, both at home and abroad," reached enormous dimensions. Although the primary targets of the Cultural Revolution were CCP leaders who had "departed" from Mao Zedong's revolutionary ideals, during frequent mass rallies in Tian An Men Square (the large area just outside the entry to the Forbidden City, known as the "Gate of Heavenly Peace," or Tien An Men, three words in Chinese) and in a stream of editorials in CCP journals, the Soviet Union and the United States were both routinely and fervently denounced, the former for "revisionism," the latter for leading the "imperialist camp."

In effect, in its acrimonious polemic against both the Soviet Union and the United States, China claimed for itself the role of defender of the faith, "pure" Marxist-Leninist communism. What the CCP's stance on Marxist-Leninist doctrine meant for U.S.-China relations was that the United States continued to be the PRC/CCP whipping boy for all ills of the world, the main threat to world peace, and an ideological opponent second only to the revisionist USSR. The corollary was that the United States constantly saw China in an opponent's role. The onset of the Cultural Revolution made CCP antipathy toward the United States worse, even as party-to-party relations between the PRC and the USSR deteriorated.

China's Support for "People's Wars"

A point that needs to be underscored is that Beijing's dogma on "support for wars of national liberation," with its related backing of "people's wars," cast a shadow over U.S.-China relations for many years in a political-military as well as ideological sense. China helped the Communist Party of Burma oppose the Burmese government; it played some role, along with the Soviet Union, in aiding the New People's Army in the Philippines; it gave at least moral support to the Communist Party of Indonesia; and it was actively engaged in instigating and assisting the Communist Party of Thailand to conduct a guerrilla insurgency against the Thai government. Since the United States had mutual defense treaties with both Thailand and the Philippines, Chinese involvement in the internal affairs of these countries remained a contentious issue.

In Thailand's case, Chinese help included not only arms, equipment, and training, but also sponsorship of a radio broadcast from Yunnan Province, known as the "Voice of the People of Thailand," designed to stir up mass resistance to the legitimate Thai government. China supported Thai guerrillas (many were actually Sino-Thai) in the Thai resistance movement in remote mountain areas such as northeast Thailand, the main theater of operations. With U.S. contributions of arms and equipment under the so-called "Nixon Doctrine," the Thai army was able to contain the insurgency, particularly as many of the guerrillas lost heart and returned to their urban home environments.

There are allegations that the Chinese had a major share of the responsibility for the abortive effort by the Indonesian Communist Party to seize governmental power in 1965, culminating in a failed coup d'état on 30 September 1965, in which President Sukarno was implicated, and in which seven senior Indonesian military officers were murdered by Indonesian Communists. It seems likely that the Chinese had some advance knowledge that a coup attempt was in the making, since the head of the Communist Party of Indonesia, Aidit, called on Mao Zedong in Beijing in July 1965. Moreover, China had given considerable political backing to Sukarno in his efforts in build "Nasakom" (a merger of nationalism, socialism, and communism) in Indonesia, and in his decision to walk out of the United Nations. While Sukarno was in power in Indonesia, relations between China and Indonesia were close. However, it is doubtful that China had any more advance notice of the date of the coup in Jakarta than did the United States. Reports from Beijing on 1 October 1965, the day after the coup, which was also the Chinese National Day, indicate that during the national day parade, the senior Chinese leadership withdrew from the Tian An Men reviewing position for some time, suggesting that the top leaders were surprised by news of the Indonesian coup and needed to discuss its implications on the spot.

But the failed coup did not, as some writers have claimed, mark the end of China's identification with "wars of national liberation." What brought a significant change in Chinese policy on this score was the end of the Vietnam War and China's consequent hope to improve its relationships with the Southeast Asian nations, particularly those of ASEAN (the Association of Southeast Asian Nations). Mao Zedong's death in September 1976 may have speeded a policy reassessment. At any rate, a change in China's policy was stated publicly in 1978, when Deng Xiaoping made a visit to Burma. There he made a speech declaring that China would not let Communist party-to-party relations interfere with friendly state-to-state relations, implying that Chinese support for "wars of national liberation" had come to an end as a declared feature of national policy. Previously, China had maintained that state-to-state relations should not preclude good relations between the CCP and other Communist parties, no matter what the role being played by those parties. One can only speculate that Deng Xiaoping was attempting to scrap the ideological legacy of Mao Zedong in favor of a much more practical policy. Sometime in this period the "Voice of the People of Thailand" fell silent.

U.S.-China Contacts amid the Freeze

Despite the sour relationship that prevailed for so many years between the United States and the People's Republic of China, contacts between the two did take place, and for a time on a fairly regular basis. These contacts initially included the 1951–1953 Panmunjom talks that ultimately brought an end to the Korean conflict. Next were the talks that began in April 1954 intended to stop the fighting between the Vietminh and the French in Indochina, where PRC Premier Zhou Enlai represented China and Secretary of State John Foster Dulles represented the United States as allies of the principals. It was during the opening of these talks in Geneva that the episode occurred of John Foster Dulles's refusing to shake Zhou Enlai's hand—an event the Chinese apparently neither forgot nor forgave, for Huang Hua mentioned it to me when Dr. Henry Kissinger made his secret visit to China in 1971 (see chapter 3).[19] Despite Dulles's attitude, Chinese present at Geneva hinted to one of their U.S. counterparts that with the attainment of a truce in Korea, it might be possible for the two countries to enter a "new stage" in their relations.[20] Subsequent to the opening of the Geneva talks, consular representatives of the United States and China met sporadically in Geneva to address the question of citizens of each country detained in the other.

A broader range of contacts was opened in 1955 when Zhou Enlai, following the April 1955 Bandung Conference of Nonaligned Countries, proposed in a press conference that the United States and China undertake high-level talks to reduce tensions, including those arising from the Taiwan issue. After some soul-searching, Secretary Dulles took up Zhou's offer and suggested that the consular-level contacts in Geneva be raised to the ambassadorial level.[21] The first in a series of ambassadorial talks began in Geneva on 1 August 1955. The U.S. representative was U. Alexis

Johnson, then ambassador to Czechoslovakia; the PRC representative was Wang Bingnan, the PRC ambassador in Warsaw.

Considerable haggling over the agenda for these talks ensued during August and early September, with the United States pressing for discussions on the release of its citizens held in China before proceeding to other matters, and the PRC seeking a review of a broad range of differences between the two countries, including Taiwan and the withdrawal of U.S. forces from the Taiwan Strait area. Eventually, on 10 September 1955, an "Agreed Announcement" was adopted for an agenda that covered (1) "appropriate" measures that would be taken by each side so that citizens of the other could "expeditiously exercise their right to return"; and (2) "other practical matters at issue." This last was a catchall that could be used for discussion of whatever questions each side considered germane. The Taiwan question obviously fell into this final category, although the PRC also wanted to address elimination of the U.S. trade embargo and other matters.

The initial stages of the ambassadorial-level talks saw some results on the first agenda item. The United States had already permitted Chinese students and teachers in the United States who wanted to return home to leave; China for its part allowed forty-one of the Americans detained there, both military and civilians, to depart. Despite the Agreed Announcement, however, many of those convicted by the PRC of having violated Chinese laws remained in PRC hands pending the expiration of their sentences, and the United States's suspicions of PRC bad faith were therefore inevitable.

On item two of the agenda, the talks in their initial period focused on a draft submitted by the United States of a joint communiqué under which both sides would agree to renounce the use of force to achieve national objectives. Given Taiwan's importance to both sides, the Taiwan issue figured early on as a major element in the discussions. Ambassador Johnson was instructed by Secretary Dulles to attempt to gain Chinese acceptance of a renunciation of the use of force in general terms, but without suggesting that China abandon its position on Taiwan or the right to defend itself. This would permit a kind of live-and-let-live situation in which the Taiwan issue could remain dormant while other issues were addressed. Ambassador Wang rejected this approach, arguing that China had no intention of using force either in advancing international objectives or against the United States. He went on to say that Taiwan was a strictly internal matter for China and that the U.S. "occupation" of Taiwan was preventing its "liberation" by the Chinese people.

On 8 October, Johnson made a detailed, formal statement to Wang concerning U.S. policy towards Taiwan to the effect that neither side would be renouncing its views, its right to pursue its policies peacefully, or its right to defend itself. All the United States wanted, he said, was that the Chinese join it in renouncing the use of force, both generally and in the Taiwan area. The two ambassadors then agreed that the two sides should submit written texts and attempt to reconcile the respective versions.

The Chinese draft, submitted by Wang on 27 October 1955, first cited the obligations of United Nations member states to settle international disputes peacefully, then went on in more specific terms to say that "the PRC and the United States agreed that they should settle disputes between their two countries without resorting to the threat or use of force." In addition, though, Wang also called for a meeting of foreign ministers to address the question of "relaxing and eliminating the tension in the Taiwan area."[22] Wang's ploy, if successful, would have been tantamount to separating the Taiwan issue from the ambassadorial-level talks and from the list of issues that could be settled peacefully. Moreover, a bilateral Dulles-Zhou Enlai meeting (as opposed to the multilateral Geneva talks in 1954) would be a step in the direction of recognition of China by the United States. Wang's proposal was rejected by the United States. With this rejection the talks stagnated. Both sides held to their positions, and the United States in addition insisted that the PRC release all American prisoners as a prerequisite to progress on any other issue.[23]

During this series of exchanges, the hand of John Foster Dulles was apparent. When Wang's draft language was received in Washington, Dulles personally inserted the words "including the dispute in the Taiwan Strait" immediately following Wang's formulation on settling disputes between the two countries peacefully.[24] (Here Dulles's training as an international lawyer, characteristically seeking specificity, came into play.) Wang refused to accept Dulles's written reformulation of his draft.

Another issue at the talks was that of mutual travel of journalists, which arose in August 1956 when Zhou Enlai shrewdly struck a chord with the American press by removing a Chinese ban on travel of U.S. journalists to China and by issuing invitations to fifteen American news organizations to send representatives to China for a one-month tour. Dulles refused to lift the U.S. ban on citizens' travel to China. When the State Department subsequently received a great amount of press criticism, Dulles one year later relaxed the ban to permit twenty-four news organizations to send representatives to China for a six-month trial period, which could be extended provided these journalists could report freely; however, no reciprocity was offered to Chinese journalists, who, as Ambassador Johnson explained, would have to meet U.S. visa requirements on a case-by-case basis. Again, Ambassador Wang rejected this arrangement.[25]

Despite this impasse, the ambassadorial-level talks continued more or less regularly (biweekly and then monthly) until December 1957, when Johnson announced to Wang his forthcoming departure to assume an appointment as United States ambassador to Thailand. Johnson also informed Wang that his replacement at the talks would be Johnson's deputy, Edwin W. Martin, who was given the personal diplomatic rank of minister for the talks but did not then hold the title of ambassador. Wang immediately protested this move as an attempt to downgrade the level of the talks, and the PRC subsequently refused to set the date for the next meeting.[26]

Eventually, in July 1958, the United States appointed a new representative of suitable rank to replace Alexis Johnson: Jacob D. Beam, who was ambassador in Warsaw. By this time the PRC was preparing for its campaign against Quemoy and Matsu, and it did not initially respond to the appointment of Ambassador Beam. The near-confrontational situation that then developed in the Taiwan Strait between the United States and the PRC, however, evidently caused some cooler heads in Beijing to prevail; on 6 September 1958, Zhou Enlai broadcast a statement that, while accusing the ROC of attempting to use the offshore islands as bases from which to attack the China mainland, also proposed a resumption of the ambassadorial-level talks "for the defense of peace."

The United States promptly agreed. The outcome, after several meetings between Jacob Beam and Wang Bingnan in Warsaw, was that although the United States made it clear that it was not about to allow the offshore islands to fall into the hands of the PRC, it would "respond to a Communist cease-fire by persuading the Nationalists to forego the use of Quemoy and Matsu as bases for attacks against the mainland."[27] In short, while the bulk of American public opinion at that time firmly supported the territorial integrity of Taiwan, most Americans would almost certainly have opposed the use of the offshore islands as military bases for the recovery of the China mainland or American military intervention to defend those bases if used to attack the mainland.

The position of the United States was formalized in a joint U.S.-ROC communiqué signed in Taipei, Taiwan, at a meeting between Secretary of State Dulles and ROC President Chiang Kai-shek on 23 October 1958. Obviously, the critical nature of the issue in U.S.-Taiwan relations was such as to require a personal visit by Secretary Dulles to resolve it. Dulles's mission was twofold: to grant "face" to President Chiang and to hold the ROC back from provocative actions against the China mainland. In the joint communiqué, the United States for its part acknowledged that "under the present circumstances the defense of Quemoy, together with the Matsus, is closely related to the defense of Taiwan and Penghu [the Pescadores]"; the ROC then asserted, under considerable persuasion from the United States, that "the principal means of successfully achieving its mission ['the restoration of freedom to its people on the mainland'] is by the implementation of Dr. Sun Yat-sen's Three People's Principles and not the use of force."[28]

The so-called Taiwan Strait crisis had already abated at the time of Dulles's visit to Taipei, although for years the PRC carried on an alternate-day bombardment of Quemoy and Matsu just to show that its military power could not be discounted (and that China had not suffered a psychological setback by backing away from a confrontation with the United States). To justify their bombardment, the Chinese leaders used the formula, "fight-fight, stop-stop; half-fight, half-stop"—a line that even they found hard to explain to the Chinese people. Propaganda shells fired by both Taiwan and the PRC made up much of the artillery exchanges in the Taiwan Strait.

The Warsaw ambassadorial-level talks between the two countries limped along for another twelve years, but with little progress until their entire relationship began to change. Nevertheless, despite the seeming lack of movement in the talks in the post-1958 period, former assistant secretary of state William P. Bundy asserts that they did serve the very important purpose of assuring the Chinese that the United States bore no hostility toward China and in addition did not seek the destruction of the Communist regime in Hanoi.[29] According to Secretary Bundy, these points were repeatedly hammered home as late as February 1968 and certainly would have had a bearing on China's shift in policy towards the United States.

The history of U.S.-China relations in the period between the end of World War II and the end of the 1960s is a contradictory one. On the one hand, the period witnessed a continuing confrontation between China and the United States: early diplomatic frictions, the Korean War, U.S. support for Taiwan and the near-conflict in the Taiwan Strait, the Vietnam War, Tibet, the impact of the Sino-Soviet polemic on China's attitude toward the United States, and Chinese support for "people's wars" and "wars of national liberation." On the other hand, there were groping efforts on the part of both countries to open a dialogue and at least begin to address the larger issues between them, as exemplified by the ambassadorial-level talks in Geneva and Warsaw. But it is no exaggeration to say that the confrontational elements in this relationship outweighed the more positive ones, so much so that normalization of diplomatic relations was impossible.

Chapter 2

The United States and China Turn towards Normalization

1968: A Soviet-Influenced Thaw

The year 1968 saw the beginning of a warming in U.S.-China relations after years of chill. Ironically, the catalytic agent that started the thaw was introduced by Moscow rather than Beijing or Washington. The impetus for China to reassess its relations with the United States was almost certainly the Soviet Union's suppression of the incipient trend toward democracy in Czechoslovakia: the "Prague Spring." On 20–21 August 1968, Soviet paratroopers and tanks, as well as troops from the "fraternal socialist states," invaded Prague under what became known later as the Brezhnev Doctrine. A *Pravda* article of 26 September 1968 provided the ideological underpinnings for the Soviet actions: "Every Communist party is responsible not only to its people, but also to all socialist countries and the world Communist movement. . . . Communists in the fraternal countries could not allow themselves to remain inactive in the name of an abstract principle of sovereignty while watching one of their number fall into the process of antisocialist degeneration."[1]

The implications of this ideology for the "fraternal socialist states" was obvious. If any of them deviated from the communist ideological "norm" and went down the slippery path of "antisocialist degeneration," it then became the duty of the remaining members of the socialist camp to set the errant member back on the right course, even to the extent of using force, and quite in disregard of the concept of national sovereignty. Inevitably, the leader of the socialist camp was the Communist Party of the Soviet Union (CPSU). As the "vanguard party," that is, the first Communist party to undergo the process of revolution and attain victory as a

23

result, it considered itself the repository of ideological wisdom for the rest of the fraternal socialist states and therefore entitled to take action against Communist brothers to ensure their fidelity to socialist principles. The difference between the Soviet response to the Prague Spring and to the 1956 Hungarian uprising was that the Soviets chose to bring in other fraternal states to discipline the Czech leader Dubcek, rather than act alone, as they had following the previous uprisings in Poland, East Germany, and Hungary.

There can be little doubt that the Chinese, privy to the debates raging within the international Communist movement during this period, got the message very quickly. After all, if the Czechs had displayed "anti-socialist degeneration" by attempting to implement democratic reforms, the PRC by virtue of its long and increasingly bitter ideological debate with the USSR had challenged the USSR much more rigorously on the vital issues of what roads lead to socialism—that is, on what means were proper to bring about the seizure of power both within a country experiencing revolution and in an international context. In both arenas, certainly, once Khrushchev had seized power after Stalin's death, the key question between China and the USSR was whether or not the "victory of socialism" could be attained without bloodshed. There was no disagreement on the need for blood to be shed internally in overthrowing the old ruling classes, but internationally Khrushchev argued—especially after his 1959 visit to the United States—that victory could be attained just by demonstrating the "superiority of the socialist system" over capitalism, especially U.S. capitalism. Pending attainment of this victory, the two systems could coexist more or less peacefully, although with no cessation of ideological warfare.

Mao Zedong, on the other hand, persisted in maintaining that no victory could be possible without bloodshed. Moreover, Mao Zedong held that the victory of socialism in each country had to be based on the particular conditions of that country, rather than blindly following Soviet insistence on relying upon the urban proletariat to lead the revolutionary struggle. In Mao's view, China, as an overwhelmingly rural country with but a minuscule urban proletariat, had no option but to base the revolution on the rural proletariat, that is, the peasantry. In short, Mao supported the concept of "different roads to socialism," which was sheer heresy to the Soviet Union. Hence, if both the Czechs and the Chinese were sinners from the Soviet point of view, the Chinese sins had to be far more serious, because the Chinese ideological stand was a direct challenge to Soviet leadership of the world Communist movement.

Subsequent to the Soviet-led invasion of Prague, heated discussions surely must have been conducted within the confines of CCP headquarters in Beijing's Zhongnanhai area in the Forbidden City, where the top leaders lived and worked, about what to do in the face of Soviet willingness to use force against a fraternal socialist state in order to drag it back onto the "correct" path. It can be hypothesized that the Chinese decided to concentrate first and foremost on reducing the external threat against them posed by the Soviet Union and to relegate their differences with the United States to a secondary place. The Soviet Union shared a common frontier with China of several thousand kilometers, while the United States, despite its involvement in Vietnam and its large military presence in Southeast Asia, did not appear anxious to challenge China militarily or to establish a permanent military presence in Southeast Asia. On the contrary, the impact on American public opinion of North Vietnam's 1968 Tet offensive added up to a possible U.S. desire to get out of the region entirely. The scattered U.S. border incursions and overflights of China connected with the Vietnam War could be viewed in a much less alarming light than that cast by the Soviet invasion of Prague. Furthermore, in the long-lived if intermittent and inconclusive ambassadorial-level talks in Geneva and Warsaw, the United States had repeatedly assured the PRC of its peaceful intentions (see chapter 1).

In any event, on 17 September 1968, less than a month after the Soviets and "fraternal" forces entered Prague, the U.S. Department of State sent a letter to the Chinese via the PRC embassy in Warsaw proposing a resumption of the virtually moribund ambassadorial-level talks. To the amazement of the U.S. side, not only was the Chinese response affirmative, it was given in the startlingly brief time of two days.[2] There was a rather condescending tone to the Chinese reply: "If you really want to proceed with these talks, we might as well go ahead with them." The reply went on, however, to make a point that certainly caught the attention of the China watchers in the Department of State, to the effect that "it had always been the policy of the People's Republic of China to maintain friendly relations with all states, regardless of social system, on the basis of the Five Principles of Peaceful Coexistence." Peaceful coexistence, even with the United States, on the basis of the Five Principles? Astonishing! Not since Zhou Enlai had proposed the ambassadorial-level talks in 1955 (see chapter 1) was there such a positive move from China.

Abortive Attempts to Renew the Ambassadorial Talks

Nothing less than a significant shift in policy toward the United States could have been at the heart of China's willingness to revive the Warsaw ambassadorial-level talks under the conditions of "coexistence" that the Chinese themselves suggested. For literally years, they had been firing cannons filled with rhetoric at the Soviets for their even daring to suggest that peaceful coexistence could be possible with the United States. This whole issue was, as indicated in chapter 1, one of the most crucial elements in China's anti-Soviet polemic. And yet, in the span of just a few days, the PRC's stance on this cornerstone of its doctrine appeared to shift a full 180 degrees.

It would have been unrealistic to assume that the PRC expected its revised approach to relations with the United States to relieve it from the threat of a Soviet military move, but presumably there were those in Beijing who argued that a start had to be made. For one thing, the military weakness of the People's Liberation Army (PLA) must have been of great concern to China's leadership, even though Soviet forces in the Mongolian People's Republic and along the Chinese border at this time were at considerably lower levels than in ensuing years. By mid-1968 Mao Zedong's Cultural Revolution had brought chaos, or near-chaos, to many parts of China, and a significant proportion of the PLA had been diverted from military duties to restoring some semblance of order in the country, even to the point where PLA commanders became responsible for managing factories and enterprises. This, combined with the Soviet-led invasion of Czechoslovakia, must have made China's leaders feel that their border with the Soviet Union was particularly vulnerable to invasion by the powerful Soviet military forces. Chinese military concern over a possible Soviet attack was manifested in Mao's call for people throughout the country to "dig tunnels and store grain."

Although Beijing's statement of its new "coexistence" policy towards the United States looked to American China watchers like a radical policy departure, it can be argued from the Chinese point of view that this was not in fact a shift in policy or ideology. Since the days of the Communist revolution it had been a general principle of the CCP, laid down by Mao Zedong, to fight one enemy at a time and to carry out a "dual policy" of unity and struggle towards its adversaries. Thus, the CCP might unite with an adversary in order to resist a common enemy, even if the adversary were to be "struggled" against later on.[3]

By November 1968 the United States and China had reached an agreement for their ambassadors to meet in Warsaw in February 1969. Unfortunately, the effort of both sides to restore contacts through the medium of the Warsaw talks started to fall apart before the talks even began. The responsibility lay entirely on the Chinese side, where criticisms from some top leaders over the merits of reopening a dialogue with the United

States surfaced almost as soon as the Chinese sent their reply to the United States. These criticisms were apparent in a series of editorials in CCP mouthpieces such as *Red Flag* and *People's Daily*, which flagellated the already deposed CCP Senior Vice Chairman Liu Shaoqi for having advocated "peaceful coexistence," along with the many other transgressions attributed to him during the "Great Proletarian Cultural Revolution" that was still proceeding in China at a high pitch.

Editorials of this stripe continued through 1968, indicating that disagreements persisted within the CCP concerning the new policy departure toward the United States. In retrospect, one cannot but wonder whether the principal dissidents weren't those who later emerged as the "Gang of Four," who, following the death of Zhou Enlai in January 1976, attempted to take the reins of power from a Mao Zedong in failing health. These individuals were Mao's wife Jiang Qing; Zhang Chunqiao, "leading member" of the CCP Shanghai Municipal Revolutionary Committee; Yao Wenyuan, minister of the state council (and Politburo member) in charge of culture; and Wang Hongwen, assumed to be a protégé of Jiang Qing from Shanghai. These four consistently used the theme of "ideological purity" as a weapon against people such as Zhou Enlai who favored a less ideological, more pragmatic policy. At this time, Minister of Defense Lin Biao, designated as Mao Zedong's successor, also appeared to be on the side of the ideologues (though later he, too, was denounced after he perished in an abortive coup against Mao). All of these individuals had identified themselves with Mao Zedong in his effort, through the Cultural Revolution, to purge the CCP and the country at large of anyone who opposed Mao's utopian goal of "carrying the revolution through to the end." Against such politically motivated zealots, it was remarkable that China ever responded favorably to the U.S. proposal to resume the Warsaw talks.

My own involvement with U.S. efforts to open a relationship with the PRC began at just this time. As director of the Office of Research and Analysis for East Asia and the Pacific in the State Department's Bureau of Intelligence and Research (INR/REA), I was responsible for providing daily briefings to Assistant Secretary of State for Far Eastern Affairs William P. Bundy on significant intelligence items affecting his area of responsibility. Accordingly, I helped to keep him up to date on the apparent controversy going on within the CCP over the merits of responding favorably to the U.S. overtures. I was by no means the only one involved in the briefing process, however; certainly the then-director of the Office of Chinese and Mongolian Affairs in the State Department's Bureau of East Asian and Pacific Affairs (EAP), Paul Kreisberg, was following the same data available to me (mostly translations from the PRC press), and he came to the same conclusions concerning the internal CCP controversy.

What brought an untimely end to the whole U.S. endeavor to create an opening to the PRC was the January 1969 defection to the United States of the PRC chargé d'affaires in The Hague, who quietly dropped out of a second-story window of the PRC embassy and made his way to the U.S. embassy, where he was granted asylum. The opponents in Beijing of improved Sino-American relations must have been waiting for just such an opportunity, for shortly thereafter a PRC announcement from Beijing canceled the scheduled Warsaw talks because the United States refused to return the diplomat who had defected.

By this time, however, the veil had been torn away from whatever modicum of normalcy remained in Sino-Soviet relations. Zhou Enlai had used the occasion of a visit to China by an Albanian military delegation in September 1968 to reveal that over the years the Soviets had violated Chinese borders more than 2,000 times. (Violations included overflights, incursions of personnel, or intrusions of Soviet shipping on the Amur and Ussuri Rivers into waters claimed by China.[4]) China also charged that hundreds of thousands of square miles of Chinese territory had been taken away from China as a result of unequal treaties dating back to the times of the czars. In a move very uncharacteristic of the security-conscious Chinese, they took the Albanian military delegation to the Chinese missile-launching site at Shuangchengzi, as if to reassure the Albanians, China's only "socialist" allies during this era, that the PRC did, in fact, possess nuclear resources capable of reaching the Soviet Union (USSR), and that the PRC was not defenseless. The same point was directed, of course, to the USSR and the world at large.

Although Beijing's cancellation of the scheduled February 1969 Warsaw talks seemed to stop China's moves towards rapprochement with the United States, China's military problems with the USSR actually grew more acute. On 8 March 1969, Chinese and Soviet troops engaged in a series of clashes over possession of the small island of Zhenbao, or Damansky, in the Ussuri River, in which the Chinese first drove Soviet border guards off the island and a week later were themselves driven off by an enormous Soviet artillery barrage. The rival claims to the island derived from conflicting interpretations of where the riverine boundary lay between the two countries: along the center of navigation, which would have placed Zhenbao on the Chinese side, or in the middle of the main channel, which would have placed it on the Soviet side. But the March 1969 military exchanges certainly could be traced back to the decade-long ideological dispute between the PRC and the USSR, as exacerbated by

Khrushchev's withdrawal of Soviet aid to China, the Brezhnev Doctrine, and the record of Soviet transgressions of China's borders. What had begun as an ideological dispute had also turned into a nationalistic confrontation.

In April 1969 the CCP held its Ninth Party Congress, and for the two weeks the congress was in session China's anti-Soviet invective fell off sharply, as if behind the scenes the PRC was making a last effort to ease tensions with the Soviet Union. Nothing actually came of any such effort, if indeed it had actually occurred. The PRC had also made an overt effort to remove the tensions from Sino-Soviet relations when USSR Premier Kosygin made a refueling stop at Beijing airport in September 1969 while returning to Moscow from Ho Chi Minh's funeral in Hanoi (Ho had died on 3 September). Zhou Enlai used the occasion to discuss the issues that had developed between the two Communist powers. Zhou told Kissinger (in my hearing) that Kosygin had agreed on a number of points suggested by the Chinese, including to hold a discussion of the riverine boundary between the two countries, to draw back troops from both sides twenty kilometers behind their common frontiers to reduce the chances of border clashes, and to discuss the actual location of the Sino-Soviet borders.[5] Zhou added, however, that everything Kosygin had promised in Beijing was repudiated by the Soviets once he had returned to Moscow, thus leaving the Chinese even more embittered.

For years thereafter, Sino-Soviet relations were marked by a heavy Soviet military buildup along the Chinese border, with a very sharp increase of Soviet forces in 1969–70, something of a matching Chinese military response within the PRC's capacity to do so, and continued military and political tensions. It was at about this time that the underground shelters called for by Mao Zedong were actually built in many cities in China. Underground Beijing was reputed to be honeycombed with tunnels and shelters (one of which I toured in 1973).

The accession to power in Washington of the new Nixon team in 1968 brought with it a president and members of his staff and administration (including senior personnel in the Department of State) who would work hard and long, and with considerable success, to bring an end to the extended break in U.S.-China relations. China's worries over the potential for a military confrontation with the Soviet Union provided a backdrop for the positive Chinese response to U.S. efforts at rapprochement after Nixon's election. Despite the historic success of the Nixon administration's push for an improvement in relations between the two countries, the first real initiatives, such as the September 1968 letter from the United States to China, had already originated with the State Department.

1969: Normalization Further Pursued
by the Nixon Administration

Although American public opinion in the 1940s, 1950s, and early 1960s was prepared to continue upholding the concept that Taiwan represented "China," popular support for the U.S. policies of isolating the PRC and embargoing trade with it began to erode in the mid 1960s. Pressures for opening up cultural and commercial contacts with the PRC continued to grow, and as indicated above, a degree of U.S. government responsiveness was evident in the efforts of the State Department to reopen the Warsaw talks in 1968–69.

An important voice in this process was that of Richard Nixon, who in an article in the October 1967 *Foreign Affairs* argued strongly that it was in our long-term national interest, although not while the Vietnam War was still an issue, to open up relations with the PRC, a country with a massive population (at that time, 600 million people) and with important global strategic, political, and economic influences.[6] Later, as president, Richard Nixon often asserted in emphatic terms to visiting dignitaries that given China's size, population, and strategic potential, "It's far better to talk to the Chinese than to fight them." (As a member of the National Security Council staff taking notes on these Nixon conversations, I frequently heard President Nixon state this position.)

Almost immediately after his January 1969 inauguration, President Nixon asked for a U.S. government policy study to determine whether a change in U.S. policy toward the PRC might be desirable, and if so, what steps might be taken to implement such a change. The process used to make this study was newly established by the president's assistant for national security affairs, Henry A. Kissinger. Kissinger was an ideal choice for this position. He was often a difficult taskmaster, but of the many American officials I have known, he was head and shoulders above all but a few in getting to the heart of an issue, that is, defining and acting on what national interest was involved and in cutting away lesser, or fringe, matters.

Kissinger's study format was a system of "NSSMs" (National Security Study Memoranda) and "NSDMs" (National Security Decision Memoranda), in which the terms of reference of each study were laid out by the National Security Council (NSC) and overseen by a senior interdepartmental group (SIG), which was chaired by a representative of the Department of State. The China study, NSSM 14, was but one of a whole series of such policy studies undertaken with respect to critical foreign policy questions and relationships; however, my belief is that the basic inspiration behind the China NSSM came from Richard Nixon himself.

The China study SIG was chaired by Winthrop G. Brown. Ambassador Brown was senior deputy assistant secretary of state in the Bureau of East Asian and Pacific Affairs, then headed by Marshall Green, previously ambassador to Indonesia, who had been appointed assistant secretary shortly after the Nixon administration took office. I participated in the NSSM 14 study in two capacities: first, as office director of INR/REA, and then as senior staff member for East Asian and Pacific affairs on Kissinger's staff, a position I assumed in early July 1969.

NSSM 14 was completed in July 1969. It recommended several unilateral steps the United States should take to begin improving U.S.-PRC relations: elimination of the "certificate of origin" requirement on importation of Chinese traditional goods into the United States, and relaxation of the Korean War–era embargo on U.S. exports to China to permit the export of nonstrategic goods. These recommendations were approved by the SIG, accepted by the administration, and put into effect between July and December. Another unilateral move that the Nixon administration made toward the PRC was the November 1969 cessation of the Taiwan Strait patrol, the periodic cruise by a U.S. destroyer through the Taiwan Strait occasionally near, but outside, the PRC's territorial limits (see chapter 1).

It was against the background of the U.S. initiatives to open a relationship with the People's Republic of China that later in July 1969 President Nixon embarked on a round-the-world tour that took him to the mid-Pacific splashdown of the first moon-landing mission and then to Guam, the Philippines, Indonesia, Thailand, South Vietnam, Pakistan, Romania, and France. While on Guam, he enunciated the so-called "Nixon Doctrine," which had as its basic point the position that the United States should not be more concerned with the threat of internal subversion in a friendly country than was that country itself, and that while the United States would supply military equipment to allies to deal with an internal threat, it would not contribute manpower. With affected countries, the United States would, however, continue to provide an umbrella—a nuclear umbrella if necessary—against external threats. The adoption of this new policy by the Nixon administration must have been watched with interest by the PRC, possibly as another indication that the United States had no hostile intent toward China.

An additional major step in the efforts of the United States to create an opening toward China occurred during President Nixon's round-the-world trip. On Air Force One, flying between Indonesia and Thailand,

Kissinger asked me in my capacity as senior staff member for East Asian and Pacific affairs to draft a message proposing to the Chinese that the United States and the People's Republic of China get together to discuss an improvement in relations. The line of my resulting draft was that, while many difficulties had arisen between the two countries over the last two decades, we should look to the future rather than to the past and should meet to resolve our differences. Kissinger gave a typical grunt and then took my draft back to the president's compartment on the aircraft, which was the last I saw of it. This was my first experience with Kissinger's characteristic work style: he gave assignments but did not provide feedback, and frequently gave the same assignment to several of his staff members, none of whom knew what the others were doing. Presumably a message along the lines of my draft was indeed sent to the PRC, either through the Pakistanis from Lahore, the next stop, or the Romanians from Bucharest.

This was the earliest attempt to find at least a semidirect communication link to Beijing. Both Pakistan and Romania maintained particularly close relations with the PRC, although Romania, being a "socialist" state allied with the USSR, presented security problems. Paris was also considered as a possible communication channel, and while some contacts were later instituted there between the Chinese embassy and U.S. Military Attaché General Vernon Walters, the Pakistan track ultimately became the preferred one.

Preparation of the message to be sent to Beijing while airborne in Air Force One was indicative of the way the entire issue of U.S.-China relations was to be handled during President Nixon's term of office: control was to rest firmly in the hands of the president and Kissinger, and the State Department was to be kept out of all major substantive decisions, its role limited to backstopping the White House on lesser matters once the main decisions had been reached. Kissinger's grasp of policy implications made a perfect complement to President Nixon's determination to run U.S. foreign policy from the White House. President Nixon made his attitude toward the State Department very plain in late 1969 during a meeting he held in the White House Cabinet Room with Kissinger and all the NSC senior staff. The occasion was the publication of President Nixon's first foreign policy report to Congress, prepared entirely by the NSC, with no input or clearances from the State Department. After telling us that the White House, rather than State, would handle all sensitive foreign policy issues, not only those affecting China, President Nixon went on to say in a revealing way, "If the State Department has had a new idea in the last twenty-five years, it is not known to me."

President Nixon's negative attitude toward the State Department was at least partially derived from the rather shabby treatment he received at the hands of some of our overseas diplomatic missions while he traveled abroad as a private citizen after serving as Eisenhower's vice president. Marshall Green speculates also that the Nixon antipathy toward the State Department stemmed from the Republican "massive retaliation" doctrine towards the Soviet Union, which was generated when Nixon was vice president but was not heartily endorsed by State. Still, some U.S. diplomats treated Nixon quite well, including Marshall Green, who was ambassador to Indonesia when Nixon visited Jakarta and sat up with him until all hours of the night to discuss world issues. Green recalls having advocated an improvement in our relations with China, and this was in April 1967, some six months before Nixon's crucial *Foreign Affairs* article appeared. In 1969 President Nixon appointed Green assistant secretary of state for East Asia and the Pacific, perhaps as an outgrowth of their 1967 meeting. Nixon and Kissinger both manifested confidence in U. Alexis Johnson, who was deputy under secretary for political affairs in the State Department during much of the Nixon administration. Nixon's negative attitude toward the State Department prevailed, however, which made my life as a Foreign Service officer detailed to the National Security Council more than a little complicated.

To the message sent to Beijing in July 1969 there was no immediate PRC response. Evidently impatient over Beijing's silence, Kissinger met in early October with U.S. Ambassador to Poland Walter J. Stoessel Jr. while he was in Washington and directed him to find a suitable diplomatic occasion to make contact with the senior PRC representative in Warsaw (at the time, this was the chargé d'affaires, Lei Yang, Ambassador Wang Bingnan being away on leave, or perhaps being subjected to criticism during the PRC's Cultural Revolution) and again propose a resumption of the Warsaw talks. I was present on this occasion. According to Marvin and Bernard Kalb, Ambassador Stoessel disobeyed his instructions, or at the minimum dragged his feet, until further messages from Kissinger ordered him to comply or else.[7]

It is highly unlikely that Stoessel, a senior career diplomat, would disobey orders from the White House, which, even if originated by Kissinger, bore the imprimatur of the president. Nor did Kissinger voice any particular criticisms of Stoessel later on. The more likely scenario is that while Kissinger and Nixon were thirsty for quick results, Stoessel felt he had to wait for an appropriate time and place to make his approach.

In any event, Stoessel took the opportunity presented by (of all things!) a Yugoslavian fashion show on 3 December to which the Warsaw diplomatic corps had been invited to catch up with PRC Chargé Lei Yang as he was leaving with his interpreter and duly propose a resumption of the Warsaw talks. Lei Yang, although visibly surprised at this contact, referred the matter to his government. Beijing's answer was a high-profile visit on 11 December by Lei Yang to the American embassy, in which Lei arrived in his massive and unmistakable *"Hung Qi"* ("Red Flag") limousine flying the PRC's national five-star red flag, to convey the PRC's acceptance; a few days later Ambassador Stoessel paid a return visit to the PRC embassy in his Cadillac, which flew the American flag. The foreign press in Warsaw was quick to take note of this ostentatious exchange of visits and to infer that something was up between the two countries.

Something was indeed up. On 8 January 1970, it was announced in both Beijing and Washington that the Warsaw talks would resume on 20 January 1970. In Washington, the U.S. spokesman took care to refer to China as the "People's Republic of China," according it a new, higher status in U.S. policy terms than ever before, for the U.S. government had always before referred to the PRC as "Red China" or "Communist China." There is no doubt that the tensions along the Sino-Soviet border had a bearing on Beijing's response. The Soviet Union had proceeded with the large-scale buildup of military forces along the Chinese border that it began in the summer of 1969, following the Zhenbao Island incident; by September the size, strength, and composition of the Soviet forces had reached levels that suggested the possibility of a Soviet attack on China, particularly against the PRC's nuclear production installations.

In this regard, Kissinger had met with Allen Whiting of the University of Michigan and with me at San Clemente in late August 1969 to discuss the possibilities of a Soviet attack. Whiting (author of a book entitled *China Crosses the Yalu*, a study of the PRC's entry into the Korean War) was predisposed to put forward scenarios in which force would enter into Communist calculations for the purpose of achieving political objectives. To be sure, Whiting had the example of the entry of Soviet tanks into Prague to bolster his case that the USSR *would* move. However, it seemed to me implausible that the Soviets would really take the plunge, since the Chinese could be relied upon to resist strongly, and any clash would consequently be of epic proportions far exceeding anything the Soviets had encountered in Budapest or in Prague.

One element in this equation was that the PRC had tested its first nuclear weapon in October 1964 and had developed a thermonuclear weapon in 1966. Popular mythology of the time suggested that if the Soviets were to move against China, they would strike first at the PRC's nuclear capabilities, that is, at the gaseous diffusion plant near Lanzhou. But thanks to Soviet assistance prior to 1962, the PRC already possessed a medium-range ballistic missile (MRBM) delivery capability, which, even if rudimentary, was nevertheless able to hold significant areas of the USSR hostage, since launch sites were masterfully dispersed and camouflaged.

Following this discussion on the likelihood of a Soviet attack on China, Kissinger charged a few members of the U.S. policy-making community to study what response, if any, the United States might make in the face of a Soviet attack on the PRC. This effort was conducted in the "tank" of the Joint Chiefs of Staff in the Pentagon, where I represented the NSC. All that we were able to come up with in practical terms was that the United States would direct a strong political campaign against the Soviets in the United Nations and in other public forums; still, a contingency plan for such action did result.

With the threat of a Soviet invasion of China as a backdrop, the joint U.S.-PRC announcements in early 1970 of a resumption of the Warsaw talks set the stage, or so it seemed at the time, for the United States and the PRC to get together to address our respective differences and to see what could be done to improve relations.

1970: New Channels in U.S. Normalization Overtures

Tangible efforts by the two countries to address their differences began to take form in 1970. Following up the exchanges between Walter Stoessel and Lei Yang, ambassadorial-level meetings were held on 20 January and 20 February. Instead of directing Stoessel to air the usual litany of complaints against the PRC, the State Department instructed him for the first of these meetings to introduce a dramatic new element into the talks: the suggestion that emissaries be exchanged. Nixon and Kissinger had intended that State Department efforts to open communications with the PRC include some departure of this nature, but the department on its own initiative suggested that high-level emissaries be sent by each side to the other's capital to discuss not only differences, but also what might be done to improve relations. In addition, the department instructed Stoessel to express the "hope" that the United States could reduce troop strength in the Taiwan areas as tensions in the region abated.

The State Department's initiative was in fact a logical follow-up of its letter to the Chinese in September 1968. These instructions were quickly cleared by the White House and the NSC.[8] Under the guidance of Assistant Secretary of State Green, the two State Department officers most immediately involved in these early normalization efforts were Deputy

Assistant Secretary of State Winthrop Brown and Paul Kreisberg, office director of what was then known as "Asian Communist Areas"—both in EAP.

Nor were the Chinese hesitant about new departures. At the 20 January meeting, after Stoessel had made his proposal, there was a pause on the Chinese side while Stoessel's words sunk in, and then Lei Yang responded with the expected statement that he would inform his government of what had been said. However, he added the following, undoubtedly based on prior instructions from Beijing:

> We are willing to consider and discuss whatever ideas and suggestions the U.S. Government might put forward in accordance with the five principles of peaceful coexistence, therefore really helping to reduce tensions between China and the U.S. and fundamentally improve relations between China and the U.S. These talks may either continue to be conducted at the ambassadorial level or may be conducted at a higher level or through other channels acceptable to both sides.[9]

Just as the talks began to progress, the negotiation process began to be complicated by the different approaches of the White House and the State Department to "reducing tensions between China and the U.S." When the department's draft instructions for the 20 February meeting arrived at the NSC for clearance, no further mention had been made of the exchange of high-level emissaries, an omission that surely would have caused very negative reactions in Beijing and that certainly caused such reactions in the White House. In *White House Years*, Kissinger discusses various reasons why the State Department seemingly got cold feet, which he suggests revolved about the presumed adverse effects that a positive Chinese response could have on U.S. relations with a wide range of allies (including Taiwan), neutrals, and the Soviet Union.[10] Marshall Green has explained to me that from the State Department's perspective, there was no objection per se to the concept of an exchange of high-level envoys, but rather a fear that the United States might be giving up too much, with consequent ill effects on U.S. relations with friendly East Asian countries, without receiving a reasonable quid pro quo.[11] Paul Kreisberg, who helped to draft this particular set of instructions in the State Department, observed also that there was concern that a high-level exchange of officials might complicate U.S. relations with the Soviet Union.[12]

In any event, the White House prodded the department into reintroducing the emissary proposal, along with other statements of a conciliatory nature vis-à-vis the PRC, which separated it from the Soviet Union as an adversary in U.S. policy considerations and certainly demonstrated the United States's continued interest in following along the course set in the 20 January meeting. Moreover, in the 20 February meeting, Ambassador Stoessel told Lei Yang, "It is my government's intention [no longer a 'hope'] to reduce those military facilities which we have in the Taiwan area as tensions in the area diminish."[13] This positive approach was reflected in Lei Yang's response at the 20 February meeting, in which he accepted the U.S. proposal to send an emissary to Beijing for high-level talks.

The U.S.-China policy-making process then became more complicated for both countries. No date for the next ambassadorial meeting had been set during the 20 February meeting, and immediately after its results were reported to Washington, a great debate began between the White House and the State Department over the merits of actually accepting the Chinese offer to receive a U.S. emissary and when to hold the next meeting. The United States was on the hook: to retreat would blow the whole approach to the PRC sky-high, and yet as State perceived the issue, the Chinese were likely to exploit the U.S. position to gain power and influence in East Asia at our expense, particularly with respect to North Vietnam, Japan, the Soviet Union, and Taiwan, not to mention creating a firestorm in Congress. Accordingly, the department wanted to slow the momentum of the emissary proposal by discussing the modalities under which the emissary would be received. Given the long history of U.S.-PRC tensions and conflicts, especially the accepted policy in the United States of regarding Taiwan as the sole representative of "China," this position was understandable. What State did not have, and what might have helped considerably to clear the air, was background knowledge of the White House efforts to open communications with the PRC, including its backchannel messages sent via sources friendly to both countries.

The Impact of Cambodia

Meanwhile, events outside the immediate sphere of the ambassadorial-level talks began to affect basic U.S.-PRC relations and create more difficulties. On 18 March, General Lon Nol, commander of the Cambodian armed forces, staged a coup d'état in Cambodia that unseated Cambodian chief of state Prince Sihanouk, away on a foreign tour at the time. The reason for this coup was the North Vietnamese and Viet Cong violation of Cambodian sovereignty, with Sihanouk's tacit consent, by using areas of Cambodia along the border with South Vietnam as bases from which to attack U.S. and South Vietnamese forces in adjacent areas of South

Vietnam. There must also have been personality clashes between Sihanouk and Lon Nol, who, regardless of any faults he may have had, appeared to be a strong nationalist and resentful of the North Vietnamese presence in Cambodia that Sihanouk tolerated. Lon Nol soon proclaimed an anti-Communist policy and promised that the Vietnamese and Viet Cong Communists would be driven out of their Cambodian bases. He also closed the port of Sihanoukville through which military supplies had been reaching the Communist forces, in substantial part from China, and appealed to the United States for aid.

Sihanouk, who was in Moscow when the coup occurred, flew on to Beijing, where he received a warm welcome. He was permitted to set up a government in exile in Beijing, which the Chinese promptly recognized. Over a period of years Sihanouk had made a special point of cultivating the Chinese, probably in hopes that they would help to balance off the pressures exerted on him by North Vietnam. The Chinese propensity to stand by "old friends" made it improbable that they would turn him away, even had they wanted to.

What drew the United States into this equation was the Vietnamese Communists' reaction to the Cambodian coup. After waiting a few days to see what might transpire in the wake of the coup, Vietnamese Communist and Viet Cong troops east of the Mekong River began to attack Cambodian army units between Phnom Penh and the South Vietnamese border to assure uninterrupted use of the "sanctuary" this territory provided for carrying out operations against South Vietnam.

By 18 April, the ill-led and ill-equipped Cambodians had fallen back to the Bassac River, only five kilometers from Phnom Penh. A complete Cambodian military collapse appeared possible, with all of Cambodia, not just the traditional "sanctuary" areas, falling into the Communists' hands for use to back up their campaign against the U.S. and South Vietnamese forces. This could have undermined the entire U.S. "Vietnamization" effort of withdrawing U.S. troops from South Vietnam as South Vietnamese troops became trained and equipped to take over. I had the task of drafting a memorandum from Kissinger to President Nixon for a full meeting of the NSC, outlining the possible adverse consequences for the United States of a Communist victory in Cambodia. At the NSC meeting, which took place on 22 April, participants considered such consequences and decided to initiate a series of graduated steps to prevent such a victory. This decision led in turn to a U.S. and South Vietnamese cross-border operation against the Communist sanctuaries, which began on 1 May and lasted until the final withdrawal of all U.S. troops on 30 June.

Regardless of the pros or cons of the U.S. operation into Cambodia, it had the side effect of stopping the ambassadorial-level talks between China and the United States in Warsaw dead in their tracks. After considerable wrangling, an agreement had been reached between the White House and the State Department to hold the next session on 30 April or any date thereafter convenient for the Chinese. (Among other items of discussion regarding the timing of the next meeting was the scheduled 22 April visit to the United States of Chiang Ching-kuo, then vice premier of the ROC.) When the 30 April date was put forward to the Chinese by our embassy at Warsaw, they in turn suggested 20 May, and the United States accepted. However, after the U.S. cross-border operation into Cambodia, the Beijing press became increasingly critical, indeed vitriolic, about the operation. Then, on 18 May, the New China News Agency (NCNA) carried a statement that due to the U.S. "invasion" of Cambodia it would be inappropriate to continue the talks. The NCNA release, which was also printed in a special box in all the leading Chinese newspapers, was signed simply, Mao Zedong. [14] The talks then ceased.

In any event, Kissinger had by then come to the conclusion that the Warsaw channel was too "constrained." [15] He must also have calculated that careful, secret preparations were required if a United States-China meeting was to take place and succeed.

The Paris Channel

Despite the cold water thrown on U.S. contacts with China by China's highest authority and the implication that contacts between the United States and China had been definitively broken off, Kissinger had already been attempting to activate another channel of communications with the Chinese using the U.S. military attaché in Paris, Major General (later Lieutenant General) Vernon A. Walters, and General Walters's Chinese opposite number, Chinese military attaché Fang Wen. Even before the break-off of the Warsaw talks, during a visit to the United States, General Walters had been given a letter by Kissinger to deliver through this channel to the Chinese ambassador in Paris, Huang Zhen, saying that President Nixon was prepared to send a high-level representative to Paris to hold secret talks with the Chinese if the latter thought that such a means of communication would be helpful. General Walters was to add verbally that this high-level U.S. representative would be Kissinger. [16]

On 27 April, 1970, General Walters attempted to deliver this message to the Chinese military attaché by approaching him at a Polish embassy reception to declare that he had a letter to deliver to the Chinese government from the president. He succeeded only in getting the latter to stutter, "I'll tell them, I'll tell them, I'll tell them," before dashing off into the night.[17]

General Walters was to help the White House to communicate privately with the Chinese government on subsequent occasions, delivering messages and arranging meetings in Paris between Kissinger and Huang Zhen. The accounts of Walters and Kissinger vary somewhat, but it is clear that the general played a vital role in keeping open the confidential communication channels between Washington and Beijing as Kissinger pursued expansion of U.S.-China ties in 1970 and 1971.[18] (Where Walters seems to have been particularly active was in setting up the arrangements for Kissinger's second, public, visit to China in October 1971, when he flew to China in an Air Force plane, not secretly by the backdoor flight the Pakistanis had provided for his first visit in July 1971. Since everything connected with the China opening was on a "need to know" basis, I did not inquire into the communications channels.)

Renewal of Contacts

As Dr. Kissinger relates the sequence of events,[19] sometime around July 1970 the Chinese apparently had reconciled their inner policy conflicts, following a period of noticeable belligerence toward the United States. China and the United States both made conciliatory gestures in the following period. On 10 July Beijing announced the release of Catholic Bishop James Walsh, who had been sentenced in 1958 to twenty years imprisonment as a spy, and also announced that Hugh Redmond, another American detainee in Shanghai, had committed suicide. The U.S. government, for its part, permitted the export to China of heavy-duty trucks made by Italy, which, in accordance with Chinese stipulations, were fitted with General Motors diesel engines. (The Italians ended up taking Chinese frozen pork as payment for the trucks.)

Despite the State Department's fears of the possible adverse consequences of loosening up U.S. policy towards China, as far back as 1963, Marshall Green, as consul general in Hong Kong, had sent the department a series of cables recommending reductions in restrictions on travel and trade and improvements in our official references to China. (I was chief of the consulate general's political section at the time.) These had been well received by then-Assistant Secretary of State Roger Hillsman but ran into bureaucratic obstacles in other government agencies that prevented their adoption. Senior State Department officials were prepared to take steps such as these to promote an enhanced dialogue with China, if not a precipitous reconciliation. Adoption by the United States of such steps as the 1969 changes in U.S. trade and travel policy as well as the export to China of the GM truck engines were evidence of our good faith in resuming a dialogue with the PRC.

Bishop Walsh's release by the PRC appeared to have less generous motives: during his imprisonment he had developed incurable cancer, and he was carried across the border into Hong Kong on a stretcher; the good bishop did not survive his release for too many months. Nor was China's release of the news of Hugh Redmond's suicide much of a positive gesture. At any rate this seeming change of heart on Beijing's part towards the United States should be attributed to the palpable increase in the Soviet threat along China's borders mentioned above. It may also be that the Chinese took positive note of the changes in trade and travel policy towards the PRC. Still, there was no Chinese reply to U.S. overtures of May–October 1970.

On 1 October there was a symbol of a change in attitude on China's side that Kissinger thought State Department officials too unsubtle to notice: the appearance on top of the Tian An Men, or Gate of Heavenly Peace, in Beijing of the American writer Edgar Snow and his wife standing next to Chairman Mao Zedong to review China's 1 October National Day parade. Perhaps this signal, if it was one —Edgar Snow thought that it was and regarded it as an expression of Mao's devoting his personal attention to U.S.-China relations—had been intended to indicate a change in the Chinese stance toward the United States. However, many Americans looked upon Edgar Snow, author of the book *Red Star Over China*, as a pro–Chinese Communist fellow traveler and his appearance next to Mao as simply an illustration of the slogan then much in vogue in China that "we have friends all over the world." The 1970 National Day parade in Beijing was noticeably short on distinguished foreign visitors, thanks to the Sino-Soviet diatribe and the international revulsion against the excesses of the Cultural Revolution; China, we assumed, wanted to display all the friends that it could find. Edgar Snow's subsequent reports of his conversations with Mao at Tian An Men and in the chairman's study, however, later threw a much different light upon this public juxtaposition of the Snows with Chairman Mao and surely would have created some response by the United States had Edgar Snow made any attempt to get in touch with us.

Instead, President Nixon made a definite but much less subtle effort to send a signal to China in an October issue of *Time* magazine, in which he declared that he viewed China as a world power, if not today, then in twenty years, and he hoped to visit China before he died; if he could not make the trip, he hoped his children could.

What eventually appears to have broken the communications logjam between the United States and China was the intercession of third parties in Washington and in their home capitals to act as postmen between Washington and Beijing after an October 1970 event that brought significant numbers of chiefs of state or heads of government to the United States. This was the observance in New York of the twenty-fifth anniversary of the founding of the United Nations. President Nixon personally honored the occasion by inviting these senior statesmen from around the world to Washington for a dinner at the White House. This dinner turned out to be a remarkable affair, in which leaders from both East and West, hostile and nonhostile nations, came together in a common social event rarely seen in the history of the world. Each leading personage was accompanied by an American aide for the reception in the ballroom that preceded the dinner, and I found myself in the remarkable position of introducing Vice President Chen Cheng of the Republic of China on Taiwan, for whom I served as aide, to Nicolae Ceauçescu, president of Romania.

While the statesmen were in Washington for the occasion, Nixon had private meetings with many of them. In Kissinger's account of the UN anniversary, he recalls that President Nixon made a point of telling President Yahya Khan of Pakistan, during their 25 October meeting in the Oval Office, of the U.S. interest in improving relations with China, knowing that Yahya Khan was planning a visit to Beijing in November. Nixon described a U.S.-China rapprochement as essential, declared that the United States would never join a condominium against China, and offered to send a high-level secret emissary to Beijing: Ambassador Robert D. Murphy, former governor Thomas E. Dewey, or Henry Kissinger. Nixon followed this same line with Ceauçescu in their Oval Office meeting, but in addition stressed his desire for good relations with both China and the Soviet Union. Later that same evening, at the dinner, Nixon used Ceauçescu's presence to offer a toast that stressed the many common interests of the United States and Romania and pointed out the good relations Romania had with the United States, the Soviet Union, and the "People's Republic of China," the first use of China's official name by an American president. (The reaction of ROC Vice President Chen Cheng is unfortunately not recorded.) Just so that Ceauçescu would not miss the point, Kissinger reiterated it in a conversation at Blair House on 27 October.[20]

Some weeks later, Pakistan president Yahya Khan returned from his visit to Beijing, which had lasted from 10 to 15 November. Pakistan ambassador Hilaly informed the White House that Yahya Khan had brought back a "message" from Zhou Enlai for President Nixon stating that, speaking on behalf of not only himself but also Chairman Mao and Vice Chairman Lin Biao, China had always wanted to settle the Taiwan issue peacefully with the United States and to this end was willing to receive a special envoy from the United States in Beijing. In this message, Zhou acknowledged that China had received numerous communications from the United States, but this was the first, to quote Kissinger, that had come "from a Head, through a Head, to a Head. The United States knows that Pakistan is a great friend of China and therefore we attach importance to the message."[21] In short, China was willing to accept a high-level U.S. emissary in Beijing, if solely to discuss the Taiwan question.

After discussions between Dr. Kissinger and President Nixon, a reply was duly sent, which, while expressing an interest in addressing the Taiwan issue and in fact a willingness to reduce U.S. troops on Taiwan as tensions in the region subsided, also stated that the meetings should not be limited only to the Taiwan question but might address other steps designed to remove tensions and improve relations. In the meantime, by December 1970, a secure channel of communication was set up in Paris, via General Walters, to Chinese ambassador Huang Zhen. Walters established this link himself, under White House instructions, by "crashing the gate" of Huang Zhen's residence in the Paris suburb of Neuilly.[22]

In this fashion the year 1970 ended, with more than a little backstage activity, but nothing on the front stage on which to base a concrete shift in basic policy. Nevertheless, a means (presumably secure) for Beijing and Washington to talk to one another had been opened, the two sides had reached agreement on the visit of a senior U.S. representative to Beijing, and they had begun to work out an agenda to include not only Taiwan, but other issues as well.

Chapter 3

Secret Flight To Beijing, 1971

Once the means of communicating with Beijing had been established, the material task of improving U.S.-PRC relations could begin. In early spring of 1971 Dr. Kissinger summoned me to his office and told me to begin preparing "the books" for a visit by him to Beijing later in the year. According to his memoir, *White House Years*, the interim following Yahya Khan's favorable message from the Chinese had been used to establish additional indirect contacts with them to ascertain China's degree of seriousness about pursuing talks.[1] Of this I personally knew little except that Pakistan, by way of back-channel communications with Ambassador Joseph S. Farland in Islamabad, rather than the secret Paris link, appeared to be turning into the preferred channel.

By "preparing the books," Kissinger meant creating a detailed set of briefing papers in loose-leaf binders. These were to include a scope paper describing what the situation in China was believed to be at that time and what we hoped Kissinger's visit would accomplish, his opening statement, and a series of position papers touching on every conceivable issue that might come up in his talks in Beijing. The position papers followed a set form: first came a description of the particular issue being addressed, for example, tensions on the Korean Peninsula, where both the United States and the Chinese had interests; next was a brief outline of the anticipated Chinese position; and finally a section entitled, "your response." Books of this sort were assembled for any of Kissinger's significant meetings, and his staff were well accustomed to providing what he desired.

Among the papers for the China visit, those dealing with the Soviet Union and Vietnam, both areas in which Dr. Kissinger had been deeply involved personally, were to be prepared by him; China and all other East Asian issues were left to me, as senior staff member for Asian and Pacific affairs. In my position papers on other East Asian issues, I drew heavily on the body of knowledge I had acquired in my service in East and Southeast Asia—pre-1950 Korea, Hong Kong, Thailand, and Singapore, and also visits to the Philippines, Japan, post-1953 Korea, Taiwan, Vietnam, and Indonesia.

The Soviet papers were written by Kissinger, possibly with the help of Winston Lord, his personal aide-de-camp, and by Commander (later Admiral) Jonathan Howe, USN, who dealt with strategic matters. Also involved in preparing the Vietnam papers was William "Dick" Smyser, who worked solely on Vietnam within the National Security Council staff and was very close to Kissinger in this regard.

All preparations were to be extremely closely held and accomplished entirely within the NSC. No word was to reach the ears of anyone outside our inner circle, particularly in the State Department, which Kissinger regarded as particularly leak-prone.

While all our efforts to be well prepared for Kissinger's visit to Beijing were helpful, one aspect of this process was particularly critical: Since Chinese propaganda against the United States alleged that in various ways we in the United States were trying to interfere in PRC-Taiwan relations or block Taiwan's reunification with the China mainland, I included in Kissinger's opening statement the phrase, "the United States is not seeking two Chinas, an independent Taiwan, nor a one-China, one-Taiwan solution." It was essential to make these points about Taiwan at the very outset, in order to allay any Chinese suspicions about U.S. intentions in seeking rapprochement with China. Differences over Taiwan had been at the heart of the Sino-U.S. dispute for twenty years and had twice almost brought the two countries into a shooting war. The sole declared reason that Zhou Enlai had agreed to talks was to discuss the Taiwan question, even though pressing strategic considerations growing out of the Sino-Soviet dispute would surely be involved as well.

It was important, figuratively speaking, to get the United States out of the Taiwan Strait and allow the parties most directly concerned to work out their future relationship without continued U.S. involvement. The wording of Kissinger's opening statement aimed to tackle the Taiwan issue head-on in such a way as to make it possible to discuss the other problems affecting U.S.-China relations. I must confess that I did not have any particular solution in mind as to how the concerned parties might resolve the status of Taiwan, but I believed strongly that the Chinese on both sides of the Taiwan Strait would sooner or later find a way to overcome their ideological prejudices and reach a realistic accord.

Work on "the books" proceeded relatively smoothly and fairly rapidly in view of the possible time constraint, for we did not know when Kissinger's trip would actually take place. It was helpful that during this time the Chinese invective against the Soviet Union was continuing at a high pitch, while that directed against the United States, though still present, had dropped to a much lower level. This indicated that China continued to believe the Soviets constituted a direct military threat to China, while the United States, despite the Vietnam War, did not.

The confidence of the drafters was greatly improved about this time by the publication in the 20 April 1971 issue of *Life* magazine of an account of Edgar Snow's meeting with Mao Zedong on 10 December 1970. As Snow reported, Chairman Mao had mentioned that he would be happy to talk to Nixon, either as president or as a tourist. Mao's attitude was based on the fact that "the U.S. was getting out of Vietnam." This was China's first public endorsement of a possible easing of the tensions with the United States, and by China's highest political source at that. Snow's article gave us great encouragement by suggesting that we were on the right track and that an improvement in U.S.-China relations was possible. At this point China, and Mao personally, seemed to be discounting previous ideological difficulties with the United States. The president added to the atmosphere of forward movement by saying that he, too, along with his wife and daughters, would like to visit China.

We NSC staffers were already familiar with what Snow had written about a meeting he had been granted with Mao in January 1965, when Mao had referred to his "meeting God" fairly soon and had gone on to speak about China's "revolutionary successors" taking one of two possible roads: one leading towards continuing the revolution, and the other doing "bad things" and negating it. "Future generations would decide these things for themselves," he said, "and in accordance with conditions we could not foresee. . . . The youth of today and those who came after them would assess the work of the revolution in accordance with values of their own."[2] In these words can be seen Mao's reason for implementing the Cultural Revolution, namely steeling the younger generation in revolutionary struggle so they might uphold the values of Mao's generation.

Snow went on to say that Mao's voice then dropped away, then he half-closed his eyes and added, "A thousand years from now all of us, even Marx, Engels, and Lenin, would probably appear rather ridiculous."[3] Through these words it would seem that even the chairman was far less than sure that the "new Chinese man" he had hoped to create—and would try once again to mold through the coming Cultural Revolution—would actually come into existence. The efforts of Mao and his would-be successors to fortify China's youth with revolutionary values would prove to be a recurring stumbling block in the process of U.S.-China rapprochement.

China Steals a March through "Ping-Pong Diplomacy"

While the NSC drafters were hard at work preparing for Dr. Kissinger's visit to Beijing, a Chinese table tennis, or Ping-Pong, team temporarily stole the normalization impetus from U.S. policy-makers. China sent its Ping-Pong team to Japan in April to take part in an international tournament at Nagoya in which an American team also participated. Evidently with Zhou's encouragement, the members of the two teams met without difficulty in a friendly atmosphere, and out of these meetings came an "official" invitation for the U.S. team to visit China.

There can be little doubt that the invitation came from Zhou Enlai personally, albeit with appropriate clearances from others in the Chinese hierarchy. It was an inspired and theatrical piece of diplomacy that had all the attributes of Zhou Enlai's sophistication, wisdom, and sense of tactical and strategic planning. Zhou must have foreseen the dramatic nature and consequences in world politics of a visit to China by a senior U.S. representative such as Kissinger, which was almost certain to take place later that year, and rather than allow the United States to claim the credit for a diplomatic breakthrough, he took steps to see that China, not the United States, would be regarded as the initiator of improved relations.

The Ping-Pong team's visit to China was approved by the State Department and the White House. That visit, together with a reciprocal visit by the Chinese team to the United States, completely eclipsed in the world press the less spectacular moves the United States had been making toward improving U.S.-China relations, such as further removing restrictions on travel and nonstrategic trade. When Zhou, in a reception for the U.S. team at the Great Hall of the People 14 April 1971, spoke of the visit opening a new chapter in the history of the Chinese and American people, the international press went wild.

The team deserved the considerable acclaim it received. Graham Steenhoven, president of the U.S. Table Tennis Association and a very modest-appearing man, came to the White House to describe his experiences and those of his team. Steenhoven seemed a little abashed by all the publicity and by the interjection of a sport such as Ping-Pong into international diplomacy. However, that the U.S. team had been thoroughly trounced by the Chinese meant nothing in terms of the political goodwill he and his team had engendered. We in the NSC were frankly a little put out by being upstaged by Zhou Enlai, Steenhoven, and the American Ping-Pong team, but could not but give Zhou the greatest credit for his perspicacity in jumping ahead of us in the matter of improving U.S.-China contacts.

Meanwhile, within the NSC the drafting of the books continued, and by mid-June we were fairly well finished. About this time, President Nixon took a few days' vacation in his "Florida White House" on Key Biscayne, and Kissinger was asked to stop by for a few days for a little rest of his own and to show the president what the drafters had accomplished. Accordingly, accompanied by Winston Lord, Jonathan Howe, and me, plus several secretaries, Kissinger took a night flight in a U.S. Air Force Learjet to Homestead Air Force Base south of Miami, flew by helicopter to the president's personal landing pad, then drove to our respective lodgings.

The presidential helipad was as close as staff members got to Nixon on this visit. The good doctor stayed at a villa adjacent to the president's; we others spent the time reviewing for the umpteenth time what we had written, swimming in the Florida-style, fully screened-in swimming pool at our own quarters, occasionally meeting with Kissinger to make some alteration in our texts that had occurred to him, and reading and rereading Edgar Snow's *Life* magazine account of his session with Chairman Mao. It was at this time that I began to appreciate Edgar Snow's personal contributions to improved U.S.-China relations, accepting that while Snow certainly had a bias in favor of Beijing, his purpose was the same as ours, that is, to bring China and the United States together. In a way, Snow's encouraging account became our road map for the future.

An episode at Key Biscayne had the potential to derail the White House's secret endeavors to improve U.S.-China relations. One afternoon the president and Kissinger went for a cruise in Biscayne Bay as a guest of Nixon's close friend Bebe Rebozo. During the cruise, Kissinger bore the precious books along with him to show to the president. Upon the return from this excursion the books were inadvertently left aboard Rebozo's boat. With hearts beating at much more than normal speed, we summoned a car from the Florida White House motor pool and sped to the dock where the boat was kept; to our enormous relief we found the books were still there, and as far as anyone could tell, untampered with. No leaks occurred, then or later.

Against this backdrop, the wires were kept humming between Beijing and Washington with complementary messages that made a meeting of representatives from the two countries all the more likely. Ambassador Farland in Islamabad was the link for the "backchannel" messages. Those from the Chinese continued to focus on discussion of the Taiwan issue. From the standpoint of the United States, discussion of Taiwan was acceptable but with the addition of "other related issues." The Chinese did not raise objections to this last phrase, and the date of a meeting in Beijing between Kissinger and Premier Zhou Enlai came ever closer, these two having been chosen as our countries' respective representatives.

In the meantime, another issue arose to complicate U.S.-China relations: the question of UN representation for China, then held by Taiwan, but increasingly under pressure from both domestic and world opinion to be opened to Beijing, either as a replacement for Taiwan (advocated by the Communist bloc and its supporters) or together with Taiwan in some formula that would find a place for both. Kissinger's preoccupation, as he has written in *White House Years*, was to keep the State Department from saying anything publicly that might in some way interfere with the growing prospects for a meeting between himself and Premier Zhou Enlai.

The State Department was entirely unaware of what had been transpiring between Beijing and the White House, and it had actually set up a special office headed by a colleague of mine, Harvey Feldman, to pursue the matter of keeping Taiwan in the United Nations and keeping China as far away from membership as possible. Some solutions being considered involved granting China the Security Council seat and Taiwan the General Assembly position; another solution was a complicated formula involving a trade-off between calling Taiwan's retention an "important question" requiring a two-thirds rather than a simple majority, which might help Taiwan hold onto its UN seat.

Fortunately, the Chinese never raised the UN question with us and proceeded as if they fully understood that the arbiters of the U.S.-China contact were the White House and China, and not the State Department. Eventually, the date for the Zhou Enlai–Henry Kissinger meeting was set for 9 July 1971 in Beijing. This was not the best time for China, since North Korea's Kim Il Sung was scheduled to be there at the same time; Chinese forbearance in acceding to U.S. wishes was very evident in the way that the date was chosen. Having made the decision to accept a meeting, the Chinese seemingly went out of their way to assure its success.

Into the Wild Blue Yonder

Kissinger was extraordinarily sensitive about security for the Beijing trip, so the whole venture was cloaked in utmost secrecy. Some people maintain that we should have at least clued in the Japanese, but such are the pressures of Japanese politics that Eisaku Sato, the prime minister at the time, would almost certainly have found himself in deep trouble later if he had not said something at least to members of his own party. Any public disclosure of the mission, Dr. Kissinger frequently remarked, would have resulted in our negotiating not with the Chinese, but with the *New York Times* and the *Washington Post* over the nature and content of U.S.-China policy.

For security purposes the visit to Beijing was to be sandwiched into a tour of Vietnam, Thailand, India, and of course Pakistan, with the excuse that Kissinger needed to visit the Asian subcontinent. The route was Andrews Air Force Base (AFB) in Washington, D.C.; Travis AFB in California; Elmendorff AFB in Anchorage, Alaska; Yokota AFB outside Tokyo, Japan; Than San Nhut AFB in Saigon; Don Muang airport in Bangkok; the Pakistani AFB in Rawalpindi (Islamabad was still under construction as Pakistan's new capital); a fuel stop in Tehran; Le Bourget Airport in Paris for talks between Kissinger and North Vietnamese representative Le Duc Tho on ending the Vietnam War; across the Atlantic to a refueling stop at Loring AFB in Maine; and finally, El Toro Marine Corps Air Base near San Clemente in California, where the president was staying.

The addition of other foreign stops required quite a bit of extra work for the NSC staff, since position papers were required for meetings with the top leaders in each country, including President Thieu in Saigon, Prime Minister Thanom in Bangkok, Prime Minister Indira Gandhi in India, and President Yahya Khan in Pakistan. Dr. Kissinger also had papers for his meetings with the Iranian foreign minister in Tehran and for his session with Le Duc Tho in Paris.

Finally, 1 July came, the day we began our historic voyage. We drove out to Andrews Air Force Base in a cortege, or as the White House preferred to put it, a "motorcade," consisting of Winston Lord, Richard Smyser, two secretaries from the NSC, Diane Matthews, Florence Gwyer, and me, as well as an unexpected addition from the office of the Pentagon's liaison officer on the NSC, a U.S. Navy chief yeoman who was a competent secretary and about whom I will say more later. Harold Saunders, an NSC colleague who covered South Asia and the Middle East, joined our party to lend verisimilitude to our stops in India and Pakistan. At Andrews we waited for what seemed an interminable time in the VIP room for Kissinger to join us; when he finally arrived, accompanied by two Secret Service agents (Jack Ready and Gary McCleod) and his special assistant, David Halperin, we boarded our aircraft and, at long last, took off into the unknown.

A government aircraft had to be used as far as Pakistan and then beyond (but certainly not into China!) to assure secure communications, but for various reasons the only one available at the time was a converted tanker, a KC-135, normally used by the commanding general of the Air Force's Tactical Air Command. The one advantage our aircraft possessed was that it had a full encrypted-communications capability. Kissinger occupied a large cabin in the rear of the aircraft, complete with its own "head," but for the rest of us, the aircraft was tortuously cramped. We found ourselves disposed in rows of two facing each other across narrow desks on either side of a central aisle, with so little space that our knees constantly bumped. (When every so often Dr. Kissinger would emerge from his quarters and stride along the narrow aisle, frequently wearing a dressing gown, to examine the messages that had been received, the scene was reminiscent of a Roman galley, with the captain directing imperiously from the stern and the rowers laboring uncomfortably in banks of two along the hull!) Chairs could not be tilted back without hitting those in the row behind, and there was barely enough room on the desks between our seats for a typewriter, much less all the "books" we had compiled for the trip. These were packed in large, black leather briefcases that took up considerable space.

Our stops at Saigon and Bangkok were standard—formal meetings with Kissinger's official counterparts, with little to be said other than that the United States would continue to support these two allies. In Saigon, there was a session with President Thieu and Vice President Nguyen Cao Ky at the presidential palace, with assurances that they could rely on the United States to maintain financial and military backing for its South Vietnamese ally. At Bangkok, we met with Prime Minister Thanom, plus his close associates Air Chief Marshal Dawee and Foreign Minister Thanat Khoman. To them we conveyed much the same message as the one we had passed along in Saigon. We also received a briefing on the situation along the Thai-Laos border and on the state of the insurgency in northeast Thailand.

In India, our visit was less routine. Our ambassador, former senator Kenneth Keating from New York, had arranged a dinner, the guest list of which included Prime Minister Indira Gandhi, Foreign Minister Swaran Singh, and other senior Indian officials. All appeared somewhat baffled at this visitation by Dr. Kissinger and his party, especially since U.S.-Indian relations were not particularly good at that moment thanks to the Bangladesh situation, and the Indians knew that the next stop would be Pakistan, a country with which India's relations were far from cordial, given the overt Indian support for the mujahadeen rebels against Pakistan in what was then East Bengal. There were immense suspicions in the minds of the Indians as to what we might be up to—suspicions focused, fortunately, on what our intentions might be in Pakistan rather than on any other possible issues. The dinner conversation was cordial but strained. Kissinger has noted in his own book that at each stop he touched upon the desirability of the United States improving relations with China, using the "Ping-Pong diplomacy" theme to make his point, but not otherwise stressing the relationship with China.[4]

And finally, Pakistan. Here we were met with suitable protocol and a warm welcome at the Rawalpindi airport and conveyed to quarters set up for us in a Rawalpindi hotel. Only the support staff remained there; those of us going on the mission to Beijing were moved to the presidential guest house maintained by the Pakistan government and used by President Yahya Khan for visitors of high estate. Keeping up the veneer of protocol, Ambassador Farland had arranged a luncheon for us at the newly completed embassy residence in Islamabad.

The public itinerary called for Kissinger to remain in Pakistan for forty-eight hours, the same amount of time spent in India so as to balance off the two rivals, but the actual plan was for Kissinger, upon his arrival, to start complaining about a stomach upset, which would provide an excuse for President Yahya Khan to offer his rest house in Murree, a hill station not too far from Islamabad, as a place to recover. A motorcade would actually be sent there with Kissinger presumably aboard, with enough of his staff to lend substance to the illusion. David Halperin, his staff assistant, was one of those assigned to make the trip. In the meantime, the trip to Beijing would take place aboard a Pakistan International Airlines Boeing 707 that had been specially arranged for us.

The evening of our arrival in Pakistan, 8 July, President Yahya Khan gave an elaborate dinner for Kissinger and his party, attended by an array of senior Pakistani officials headed by Foreign Minister Sultan Khan. In addition to Yahya Khan's spreading the word that Kissinger would be going off to Murree in the morning to "recover" from his stomach ailment, he took Sultan Khan, Kissinger, and me aside to inform us that to assure our welcome in Beijing, the Chinese had sent a small delegation to fly with us. This was the first we had heard of Chinese passengers being aboard the PIA aircraft, but we assured Yahya Khan that the gesture was welcome and appreciated.

Then we returned to the guest house for some last-minute packing and for what little sleep we could muster. Wake-up time was set for 3:30 A.M. When that moment came, we gathered up our luggage and loaded ourselves into nondescript private cars so as not call attention to our movement, in the remote event anyone would be awake and watching at that hour. I have a distinct memory of Kissinger hunched over in the back of a red Volkswagen Beetle with a hat pulled down over his head and wearing dark glasses. Sultan Khan, whose memory may be better than mine, insists that Kissinger was in a blue Datsun that he, Sultan Khan, personally drove. After twenty-five years, it's hard to recall every detail. At any rate, our several cars sped through the darkened, silent streets of Rawalpindi to the airport and over to the military side. There a PIA Boeing 707 was waiting for us, with a ramp up against its open forward door and its jet engines ticking over ready for a fast getaway. We piled out of our cars and up the ramp, and our baggage was whisked into the cabin.

At the top of the ramp, sure enough, we were greeted by several distinguished Chinese personages: Zhang Wenjin, who had a long history of close association with Chinese Premier Zhou Enlai dating back to the Marshall Mission days (and whose father had been a Chinese manager of the Chase Bank in Tianjin in the 1930s), and Wang Hairong, Mao Zedong's mother's grandniece.[5] Also there were Tang Longbin, an official of the Chinese Foreign Ministry's Protocol Department, and Tang Wensheng, known more familiarly to us as Nancy Tang, who had been born in New York City and who was to serve as interpreter. For those who had been forewarned, this meeting was no surprise, but for the two Secret Service agents, being met by these individuals from China was a complete shock, as was the news of our destination.

Once we had boarded, the aircraft promptly headed out onto the runway and began its takeoff, while we sorted ourselves out and prepared for the journey. The Pakistanis had divided the aircraft into three sections: a forward, first-class section where the working-level passengers sat; the usual tourist section in the back where spare Pakistani flight crews and attendants took their places; and a special mid-cabin section complete with double bed where Kissinger was ensconced in solitary splendor. His accommodation resembled a VIP howdah on an elephant's back—surely something the Pakistanis had arranged in deference to memories of the Mogul Dynasty!

Perhaps unconsciously, the Americans all seated themselves on the right-hand side of the aisle in the front cabin, while the Chinese sat on the left. In addition to our distinguished emissaries, several Chinese pilots also sat in this section, ready to take over the navigation duties once the aircraft had passed into Chinese airspace.

Soon after takeoff we were treated to one of the most spectacular sights in the world. The PIA aircraft kept climbing and in about a half-hour was at an altitude of some 25,000–30,000 feet. About this time, the sun was rising, and we could look down into the deep defiles of the Hindu Kush. Even more spectacular, the pink light of early morning illumined first the tips of Daughalgiri and later K-2, which protruded from the snow-covered Hindu Kush range like a shark's tooth, far overshadowing the other peaks. Looking at the twisted land below and the gigantic mountains above, one wondered how any human being could possibly make his way through this terrain, much less climb the two peaks we had just passed. But dedicated mountaineers had conquered both.

Breakfast was served, and shortly afterwards two small events took place that illustrated our common humanity. First, after breakfast had been cleared away, a Pakistani steward passed a tray filled with small boxes of cigarettes to each passenger; none of the Americans smoked, but a Chinese pilot-navigator sitting immediately across the aisle from me looked surreptitiously to the left and right to see if he was observed, dove into the cigarettes with both hands, and in an instant had somehow disposed of a large number of the small boxes around his person. This seemed a hopeful sign that he was human, and that China was still China.

The next episode came shortly thereafter, when Kissinger asked me if I had any extra shirts. In the excitement of packing and leaving the guest house at Rawalpindi, he said, he had forgotten to pack the shirts he had brought along specifically for the China trip, and he now found himself with no spares. I was happy to give him three new ones packed by my wife—fortunately short-sleeved so arm length didn't matter, although Kissinger complained about the collars. (On my return home, close inspection of a fourth shirt's label revealed that the shirts had been made in Taiwan.) In his own reminiscences, Kissinger attributes his shirt shortage to David Halperin's forgetting to pack them; at any rate, the episode showed that Kissinger, too, was human.

Talks in Beijing

On we flew to Beijing, crossing in Chinese airspace over some most desolate country. This was the Takla Makan, the great desert across which silk caravans used to work their way, and which now appears to be a major source of underground oil. Upon finally reaching Beijing, for secrecy's sake we did not land at the usual Beijing airport but at a military airport south of the city adjacent to a factory where I later heard that China builds its guided missiles. We landed about mid-morning on 9 July, and as we taxied toward the small group of welcomers awaiting us, Zhang Wenjin explained that we were being met by Ye Jianying, a marshal when the People's Liberation Army still maintained distinctions in rank (but who never objected when he was addressed as *Yuan Shuai*, or marshal), newly appointed ambassador to Canada (later foreign minister) Huang Hua, and Director of Protocol Han Xu (later ambassador to the United States). With them as interpreter was Ji Chaozhu, a Foreign Ministry official trained at Tufts and Harvard before he returned to China in 1951. (Ji later became deputy undersecretary general of the United Nations.)

In typical Chinese fashion, we were welcomed, sorted out according to rank, and placed in limousines in the proper protocol order. Kissinger was in the lead vehicle, a *"Hong Qi,"* ("Red Flag") of the same type Lei Yang had used in December 1969 to call on Walt Stoessel in Warsaw—a Cadillac-sized but purely Chinese-designed and Chinese-built vehicle reserved exclusively for VIPs. With him was, of course, Ye Jianying accompanied by Ji Chaozhu. Interpreter Nancy Tang and I followed in another *Hong Qi.* My escort was Huang Hua, a Yenching graduate who spoke fluent English but chose to speak in Chinese and use an interpreter. The others in our party rode in the ubiquitous *Shanghai*-model "limousines" (loosely copied after an older-model Mercedes-Benz) used by lesser officials. All the car windows were curtained, so it was virtually impossible to see either in or out except for surreptitious peeks around the edges of the curtains.

No sooner had the motorcade begun to move than Huang Hua broached with me a matter that evidently weighed heavily in the minds of many of the Chinese: U.S. Secretary of State Dulles had refused to shake Premier Zhou Enlai's hand, Huang Hua said, when attending the Geneva Conference on Indochina in 1954. I was rather taken aback by Huang's having raised this seventeen-year-old episode out of the blue. I could only conclude that the Chinese were apprehensive over the possibility that Kissinger might follow Dulles's example when he met with Premier Zhou for our talks, which we had already learned were to begin later that day after we had enjoyed lunch. I hastened to assure Huang Hua that we hadn't come all this distance by such a circuitous route with such a high degree of secrecy just to repeat the errors of previous administrations, and that Zhou Enlai should have no apprehensions about a handshake. We were looking to the future, not the past.

The motorcade took us from the airport to the Diao Yu Tai, the Chinese government's most elaborate guest house, located in the western suburbs of Beijing. When I peeked at Beijing through the car curtain, it appeared to be almost a ghost city. The few pedestrians moved slowly, their faces impassive, as if they were suffering some form of combat fatigue as a result of the Cultural Revolution, which was then winding down. Virtually no vehicles were on Chang An Jie, the broad avenue that skirts the southern edge of the Forbidden City and the Tian An Men, or Gate of Heavenly Peace. The quietness in this huge city was eerie, an enormous change from the bustle and noise of the "Peking" I had known in 1937. (This was even more true at night, when there were no dogs barking, people shouting, or vendors calling out their special cries for the wares they were selling as they had in earlier times; nighttime in Beijing was deathly silent.)

Once at the Diao Yu Tai, or "Fishing Pavilion," where high court officials of past dynasties had fished ceremonially on certain days of the year, we drove through a gate where we were confronted by a large concrete screen exhorting "*Wei Ren Min Fu Wu*," or "Serve the People," in characters painted in red in the style of Mao Zedong's distinctive calligraphy. We also took note of the presence of People's Liberation Army guards at the gate, leading us to believe that our leaving the area would not be welcomed. Once inside, we settled down into our respective rooms in one of the numerous villas that had been built in that area without, however, doing damage to the small lakes and surrounding willow trees that dotted and beautified the area. I, of course, had already informed Dr. Kissinger of Huang Hua's remarks about the Dulles-Zhou Enlai episode in Geneva in 1954. We then had lunch hosted by Ye Jianying, and awaited Zhou's arrival.

Premier Zhou arrived at approximately 3:30 that afternoon, striding into our villa alone from his "*Hong Qi*" to find Kissinger awaiting him with outstretched hand. Zhou and Kissinger then shook hands. The hall area where the two met burst into a glare of lights created by the flash bulbs and high-intensity lamps carried by about thirty or so reporters and others who were gathered on the steps leading to the second floor and scattered around the hall itself. This handshake, duly recorded for posterity, certainly helped to assuage Chinese feelings wounded by John Foster Dulles's snub to Zhou Enlai at Geneva.

We then went into a small conference room at the back of the villa, with the U.S. representatives seated on one side of a green-baize-covered conference table with soda water bottles and glasses at each place—a typical Chinese/Eastern European touch—and with Zhou Enlai, Ye Jianying, Huang Hua, and Zhang Wenjin seated on the other side. Ji Chaozhu and Nancy Tang sat behind the other Chinese leaders and officially interpreted for both our sides. (My Chinese was adequate for daily communications, but not up to interpreter standards, although I was able to verify the accuracy of the interpreters' translations of Kissinger's remarks.)

Zhou indicated that it was a Chinese custom always to let the distinguished guests speak first. Kissinger began with rather lengthy opening pleasantries, and then, as I waited impatiently, he finally did address matters of substance with the crucial words regarding Taiwan: the United States did not seek two Chinas, a one-China, one-Taiwan solution, nor an independent Taiwan. Zhou's response was instantaneous and positive.

"Good," Zhou said, "these talks may now proceed." In other words, it seemed, if Kissinger hadn't started by addressing the Taiwan issue, which was at the top of the Chinese agenda, any further discussions might well have been stopped dead or at least stalled. As it was, the talks proceeded on to cover a broad range of global topics, with both Zhou and Kissinger clearly enjoying the exchange. The Taiwan issue did not figure in this discourse, since from the Chinese standpoint, it had already been appropriately addressed in Kissinger's opening statement. As he noted in *White House Years*, "Taiwan was mentioned only briefly during the first session,"[6] but as just outlined, it was mentioned in such a way as to diminish, if not entirely eliminate, for the time being its role as an item of contention in U.S.-China relations.

On our side of the table, Kissinger sat in the middle, with me on his right and Dick Smyser and Winston Lord on his left. Our two Secret Service agents sat in a back row behind us. Our small party was quite outnumbered by the Chinese, who in addition to the top people had several rapporteurs recording what had been said in Chinese characters, presumably to assure that no word or nuance was missed. Lord, Smyser, and I were also scribbling away on our side, aided by the time used by the Chinese interpreters, which gave us enough leeway—just!—to record what had been said. Zhou did not use a "book" such as ours but merely had a penciled list of topics to cover, and Kissinger, not to be outdone, put away his own book; nevertheless, I am sure that he had studied and restudied the contents frequently enough to be thoroughly at home with them. The atmosphere was serious, but not tense. We continued in this way for several hours, until Zhou decided it was time for us to break for dinner. Afterwards we resumed the talks, not breaking up until nearly midnight. We reviewed many aspects of the world scene but also focused upon the heart of the discussions: that what was at stake was the wording of a jointly agreed announcement on a visit to China by President Nixon, an announcement that would not focus upon Taiwan as the central issue—a focus the Chinese desired (and we desired to avoid).

Before the discussions had actually begun, I had taken Huang Hua aside and asked whether, despite the shortness of our time in Beijing, it would be possible for Kissinger on his first visit to China to see something of Beijing's ancient glories—the Temple of Heaven, perhaps, or the Forbidden City, or even the more distant Summer Palace, all of which I remembered from my time in Beijing in 1937. Huang thought that something might be arranged for the morning of the following day. Accordingly, that day, 10 July, began with a visit to the Forbidden City, which the Chinese had thoughtfully closed entirely to the general public so as to maintain secrecy. Escorted by Huang Hua, we went first to a small palace complex on the western side of the Forbidden City, or *Gu Gong*, as it is known to the Chinese, and inspected a dazzling display of "Historical Artifacts Excavated During the Cultural Revolution"—an effort, perhaps, to assure visitors that the Cultural Revolution, despite many credible reports to the contrary, had not resulted in the destruction of China's cultural legacy at the hands of the Red Guards, but had actually enhanced it. Among these treasures were two jade funerary body suits worn by a noble of the Han Dynasty and his wife on the theory that jade would act as a preservative of their mortal remains. This was the first time that these remarkable items had been shown to non-Chinese.

Following our tour of this exhibit, we drove to the Forbidden City's imposing Meridian Gate, or *Wu Men*, which we walked through, and then we viewed the three "Peace" halls located behind the first immense courtyard. We concluded with a visit to the private quarters of the Empress Ci Xi, which Huang Hua admitted to me had been considerably torn up by Red Guards during the Cultural Revolution, but which had been completely restored. The Americans in our party were thoroughly impressed by the Forbidden City and found this brief introduction to China a major event on our schedule. But under Huang Hua's prodding, we had to move on to a "duck luncheon," which had been promised to us by Premier Zhou Enlai, in the Great Hall of the People. Again our concern was to maintain secrecy, and our motorcade proceeded not to one of the main entrances to the Great Hall, but to a small entrance under one of the sets of broad steps to the building. Here we were crowded into a small elevator not much larger than an American telephone booth and lifted to a floor containing the Fujian Room, where we were both to dine and continue our discussions. Zhou Enlai met us there.

The trip to the Forbidden City in July, hardly Beijing's coolest month, plus excitement and tension, caused one of our number to faint dead away shortly after we sat down to lunch. The efficient Chinese promptly whisked him away to a clinic located somewhere in the Great Hall where he could recover, while the rest of us continued our meal. After the duck luncheon, which had featured the traditional Peking duck as well as numerous other items from the duck served in various ways, Zhou insisted that we should accompany him to the kitchen to see how Peking duck was actually prepared. Once again we crowded (in several shifts) into the tiny elevator and went into the kitchen, which was one or two floors above. Here we found a spotlessly clean but empty room—empty with the exception of one small PLA soldier, clad in a white smock but wearing the standard green PLA cap with the red star, scrubbing the kitchen floor.

The stunned look on his face when he saw a band of foreigners in his kitchen guided by none other than the Chinese premier was alone well worth the trip. But Zhou also showed us the ovens where the ducks were roasted and described the use of fruitwood, apple or cherry, to impart a special flavor to the duck. This whole episode shows the great hospitality, graciousness, and effort to put us at ease displayed by Premier Zhou Enlai, surely one of contemporary China's greatest leaders. His courtesy was shared by Huang Hua, the epitome of a professional diplomat, and by Ye Jianying, the bluff and hearty veteran soldier.

The afternoon's discussions, following up those on the previous day, became hot and heavy. Among other issues, the Chinese raised the questions of alleged U.S. rearming of Japan, calling it a threat to China, to which Kissinger replied that the rearmament was in response to the Soviet Union's powerful military buildup in the region, that it did not threaten China, and that the U.S. military presence acted as a stabilizing influence on Japan and a brake against a resumption of Japanese militarism. Moreover, the U.S. nuclear umbrella over Japan, a country that in any event was strongly antinuclear due to memories of Hiroshima and Nagasaki, served to deter Japan from developing its own nuclear capability. The U.S. and Chinese problems with the Soviet Union were mentioned, but not stressed. Another issue was the Korean Peninsula, where again Kissinger pointed out that the U.S. military presence did not threaten the region but rather helped to stabilize the military balance. He took the position that it was in the interests of neither China nor the United States to see tensions increase on the Korean Peninsula. The subject of Vietnam was largely side-stepped, except to reiterate each country's support for its respective Vietnamese side. Kissinger also described his secret talks with North Vietnam's representative to the Paris talks, Le Duc Tho.[7]

The major issue that emerged then and later that evening, though, was the wording and timing of the joint announcement that would be released simultaneously in the United States and Beijing saying that President Nixon would visit China the following year. Agreement on a Nixon visit was almost certain; the terms of the announcement had yet to be determined. The problem here was that the United States wished to avoid mentioning Taiwan in this context, while the Chinese insisted on a reference to Taiwan. After a hard day of talks, our party returned to the Diao Yu Tai for dinner, while Zhou went his separate way, saying that he would return to our villa after dinner, perhaps around 9:30 or 10:00 P.M., to continue the talks.

Then came a period of anxious waiting. Nine-thirty came with no Zhou; 10:00 and 11:00 passed still with no sign of the absent premier.

Kissinger became nervous and asked me to take a walk with him in the garden of the Diao Yu Tai, where we would not expect to be bugged, to discuss what might be holding things up. My surmise at the time was that the issues we had raised during our afternoon conversations with the Chinese were still being debated hotly at the topmost echelons of the Chinese Communist Party, and recalling from previous analysis of Chinese propaganda statements how exchanges of congratulations between the People's Liberation Army (PLA) and the Soviet Red Army on their respective Army Days had been noticeably more cordial than party-to-party communications, it also seemed likely that on practical grounds there might still be pressures among the weapons-deficient Chinese military for closer relations with the Soviet Union. Thus, it was possible the PLA might be one of the problems. Chairman Mao Zedong himself would almost certainly have a strong voice in any deliberation going on.

In retrospect, it would seem that the main dissent emerged from the group later described as the "Gang of Four" (mentioned in chapter 2): Jiang Qing, Wang Hongwen (who at one time was thought to be Mao's designated heir), Zhang Chunqiao, and Yao Wenyuan—four ideologues probably motivated not so much by ideology as by a desire for sheer power. Taking an orthodox anti-American line might have strengthened their hands in any ensuing power struggle for the succession to Chairman Mao, who was already in failing health.

Just when we were ready to give up, around 11:15 P.M., Zhou appeared and resumed his talks with Dr. Kissinger. After about an hour, though, he excused himself and designated Huang Hua to work out with us the text of an announcement on the Nixon visit. We waited another interminable period for Huang Hua to appear, and when he finally did so, long past midnight, the version of the announcement that he presented was found unacceptable by Kissinger because it would have made the United States the party that had sought the visit and because Taiwan figured prominently in it. Thanks to the Chinese, the differences were finally reconciled early the following day.[8] The gist of the announcement was that President Nixon had accepted a Chinese invitation to visit China early in 1972. The Chinese leaned over backwards to be accommodating to the U.S. requirements; they seemed as anxious for a resolution as we were.

The time for the announcement was settled upon as 15 July in the United States, when President Nixon was to make a speech before the Los Angeles World Affairs Council beginning at 9:30 P.M. Los Angeles time. Given the fifteen-hour time difference between China and the U.S. West coast, this would have been at 12:30 P.M. Beijing time the next day, which was satisfactory to the Chinese. It was further agreed that in the future the contact point between China and the United States would be Paris, via Chinese Ambassador Huang Zhen and U.S. Military Attaché General Walters.

It seemed that the concessions over the language of the announcement of the Nixon visit were all on the Chinese side, most notably their agreeing to drop any reference to Taiwan. Our speculation was that the Chinese concern over the military threat from the Soviet Union was sufficient to outweigh other considerations in their deliberations over the wording of the announcement. It was evident that they greatly wanted the Nixon visit to take place.

Zhou Enlai joined us the next day to host a lavish celebratory luncheon at our Diao Yu Tai villa, but excused himself shortly afterwards. During the luncheon, however, he turned the talk to the Bangladesh fighting, noting that China had continued to support Pakistan and probably would be the last country to recognize an independent Bangladesh. Chinese propaganda had been extremely critical not only of India, but also of the Soviet Union for its support of the Indian position. As Zhou departed and was being seen off at the door by Dr. Kissinger and myself, I heard him remark to Kissinger that China had received a note from the Soviet Union about Bangladesh and that "we [the Chinese] would have to think about this." It was during this same luncheon that Kissinger stunned Nancy Tang and her Chinese colleagues by telling Ms. Tang that she could become president of the United States, while he could never achieve such a distinction: she was a "native-born" American, and he was not. (Her father had been editor of a Chinese Communist newspaper in New York.)

At this point, our main concern was getting back to Pakistan in time to resume our schedule, which had been released to the press and had to be followed to avoid suspicions about our real itinerary. The luncheon broke up, and we hastened back to our rooms, packed, boarded our limousines, and returned to the airport. As Kissinger has recounted, in his conversation with Marshal Ye Jianying en route to the airport, the two touched upon Ye's history as a young man deciding to join the Communist Party and upon his experiences as a cavalry platoon leader on the Northern Expedition of 1927–1928. The way the conversation was recounted to me at the time differed somewhat from what Kissinger wrote later[9]: Ye remarked that fifty years earlier, when the Communist Party had been established, he and other early members never envisaged the necessity (the Party had been established on 1 July 1921) of still remaining in the senior positions of leadership. They had anticipated that younger generations would come along to assume command. But this had not happened. "Here we are," Ye continued, "and here *you* are!"

In short, Ye appeared to be wondering why the Communist Party, after all these years, had failed to produce a generation of revolutionary successors willing to fight the kind of battles fought by Chairman Mao and his contemporaries, making it necessary for an already elderly group of leaders such as himself to stay on indefinitely. Even more, events had forced the Communist Party to reconcile its differences with a country, the United States, which hitherto had been regarded as one of China's worst enemies. The seeds of future internal ideological and political troubles clearly were already present and growing, judging from the delays in China's coming to terms on the announcement of the Nixon visit. Ahead lay many challenges to the Chinese leadership decisions that had brought Kissinger to China; those challenges were to render more difficult the establishment of future normal relations between the world's most populous country and the world's most powerful country.

Nevertheless, China had gained considerably, as had the United States, from beginning this new relationship between our two countries, both of which were involved in difficult—and dangerous—relations with the Soviet Union. Moreover, the basis had been laid for a new look by China at the outside world—one that helped to bring it more intimately into the global political and economic mainstream in a positive position to influence international affairs. For the United States, nearly a quarter of a century of official hostility had been struck down, and normal contacts between the American and Chinese peoples could be envisaged. The two and one-half days Kissinger and his party had spent in Beijing were truly historic.

A significant aspect of this opening contact was that it had occurred while the Vietnam War was still raging, with China and the United States supporting opposing sides. It takes no great stretch of imagination to perceive that China had placed improvement of relations with the United States at a higher priority than placating North Vietnam, although it could be assumed that China was confident that the "people's war" would lead to an eventual victory by Hanoi regardless of Kissinger's visit. However, China's subsequent handling of its ties with Vietnam suggests that it really wasn't anxious to see the North Vietnamese prevail if this meant an intrusion of Soviet interests into areas close to China.

Back to the United States via Paris

At the airport we bade a hasty farewell to our Chinese hosts on the apron of the runway where we had landed and then took off aboard the aircraft that had brought us to Beijing. The PIA aircrew had prepared a lavish luncheon for us, which for protocol reasons we were obliged to sample, leaving us near the bursting point. We arrived back at Rawalpindi late in the afternoon and rushed with our baggage to the USAF aircraft, already prepared for takeoff. There was barely enough time for farewell amenities with the ever-helpful Pakistanis before we were airborne.

Then began the ordeal of writing up a summary account of the meetings for Kissinger to send to the president and following up the summary with a detailed, word-for-word reconstruction of what each participant, Chinese and American, had said. After the two and one-half days in Beijing, our party was approaching exhaustion, but it fell to my lot and that of Winston Lord to do the work. Fortunately, the secretaries had enjoyed their stay in Pakistan and were quite fresh. What Lord and I did was first to go over our more or less verbatim notes together and reach an agreed version, and then dictate to one of the secretaries aboard the aircraft. One of these was the U.S. Navy chief yeoman mentioned earlier, Charles Radford, who managed to make extra copies of what came his way to report to the Joint Chiefs of Staff, and who even went through the "burn bags" of discarded materials waiting to be destroyed for extra information. To the credit of the Joint Chiefs, there were no public leaks from that direction, but there was considerable consternation in our midst when we learned months later that Chairman of the Joint Chiefs of Staff Admiral Thomas Moorer had about as complete a fill-in on the Kissinger China visit as we did, and in fact had been clued in almost from the start.

Our next stop was a fairly brief one at Tehran, where Kissinger and the Iranian foreign minister met in the airport VIP lounge while the rest of us wandered around. The airport looked like a U.S. Air Force base, crowded with rows of F-4s and C-130s. Following that stop we went on to Paris, which we reached long after dark. Kissinger stayed at the ambassador's residence, while the rest of us were put up at the Hotel Crillon, conveniently located next door to the U.S. embassy. Our stay in Paris involved one small subterfuge: Kissinger wanted to meet with North Vietnamese representative Le Duc Tho but definitely did not want the press to know about this session. To resolve the quandary, it was officially given out that he would spend the afternoon with me reviewing the various aspects of the trip (omitting any reference to China, of course), and I duly turned up at the front door of the ambassador's residence to force my way in through a crowd of press people. Once I was inside, Kissinger escaped the building through the back door and went on to his meeting with Le Duc Tho, while I spent the entire afternoon dictating from my notes the highlights of our stops in Saigon, Bangkok, New Delhi, and Islamabad/Rawalpindi to one of our secretaries, Diane Matthews.

That same evening our journey resumed (though not before Kissinger had put in a public appearance at a well-known French restaurant with an attractive American female correspondent, Meg Olmer), and we jumped across the Atlantic to Loring AFB in Maine for refueling. From there we continued on to El Toro Marine Corps Air Station, from whence, in the early hours of the morning, we helicoptered to the president's private helipad at San Clemente, where he was present to meet us. And a bedraggled crew we were! Bone-tired, grimy from the long trip, and with our clothes considerably wrinkled, we hardly looked like the same people who had departed from Andrews AFB only about a week before. Fortunately, nothing was required of the working staff that day except to recover somewhat.

The following two days were fully occupied, though, since a careful script had to be worked out to inform our close friends and allies about the trip, timed just in advance of the president's World Affairs Council meeting in Los Angeles to minimize the chances of a leak to the press. To help inform our friends and allies, Dr. Kissinger brought Secretary of State Rogers and Under Secretary of State U. Alexis Johnson in from Washington with the especially delicate tasks of helping to pass the word to ambassadors of key countries about the trip and the president's upcoming announcement, so that at least a modicum of advance warning would be given. Because there had been an announcement from the San Clemente Western White House that the president was going to make a "major foreign policy statement" in his World Affairs Council speech, the general public had some advance warning as well.

The task of officially informing the ambassadors of our allies was to be accomplished by long-distance telephone. Of the East Asian ambassadors to be contacted, Alexis Johnson drew the Japanese ambassador and the Taiwan (Republic of China) ambassador, and I drew many of the rest. I remember in particular the reaction of the South Korean ambassador, who after a long moment of silence had the grace to say that he hoped that the new relationship with China would work out well for the cause of peace, and he supposed that in any event it was bound to happen some day. In the communications with the various ambassadors, we were careful to point out that our relations with their respective countries would remain unchanged. In the case of Taiwan, though, President Nixon later sent Ronald Reagan, then governor of California, on a special mission to placate Chiang Kai-shek, who was shaken.

President Nixon's brief announcement of Dr. Kissinger's trip, of the Nixon administration's concern to improve relations with China in the cause of peace, and of his own planned trip to China, stunned the world.

The reaction from most Americans as well as most of our allies was positive, even euphoric, with the notable and predictable exceptions of Japan and Taiwan and their supporters.

American television later showed clips of Japanese Prime Minister Sato watching the televised report of the Nixon speech. The intensity of his reaction was striking, more so because it lacked the traditional Japanese inscrutability; Sato was visibly grim and shaken by this particular development. As noted, we have been criticized for not giving at least Prime Minister Sato a few more hours warning, but it was our firm belief that he would have been under irresistible political compulsion to use this information for Japanese domestic political purposes had it been made available to him earlier. Sato quite clearly had wanted to make the breakthrough to China in advance of the United States and felt politically exposed when he was bypassed, especially since we had pressured the Japanese against any such move themselves. Japan ultimately established normal diplomatic relations with China in October 1972, or over seven months before the United States established an official presence in Beijing.

President Nixon's announcement was the culmination of months—even years—of effort by not only the NSC and Dr. Kissinger but earlier ongoing efforts of the State Department as well. Through the changes of history as well as the work of forward-looking individuals, normalization of relations with China was an idea whose time had come. Yet Kissinger and other thoughtful foreign policy-makers in both China and the United States were fully aware that the joint announcement was in fact only a beginning of much more hard work that would be necessary to make the seeds of past efforts bear fruit in the future.

Chapter 4

Preparations for the Nixon China Trip

Having accomplished a dramatic breakthrough in U.S.-China relations, the next tasks of Dr. Kissinger and his team were the preparations for President Nixon's visit to China. This inevitably required addressing a host of details, such as the timing of the visit, who should be in the official party, what was to be included in the joint communiqué covering the visit, what places the president should visit other than Beijing itself, and what topics he should discuss with the Chinese. On this last issue, in addition to matters of grand political-military strategy, there were more mundane matters, such as the questions of Chinese assets that had been frozen by the United States and of properties formerly owned by Americans that had been seized by the Chinese. All of these issues and more would need to be considered.

20 October Trip to China

The multiplicity of details to be addressed would have inundated the NSC staff, and accordingly, Kissinger agreed to bring the State Department into the planning. He also agreed to have a State Department representative accompany his party on his next visit to China, scheduled for 20 October 1971, in agreement with the Chinese. The representative was Alfred Lesesne Jenkins, who was office director of the Office of Mainland China and Mongolian Affairs, or CM as it was known in the department. Considerable liaison was also required with Marshall Green, the assistant secretary of state for East Asia and the Pacific, Jenkins's immediate superior.

Al Jenkins and his people were soon put to work preparing their own "books" for the second Kissinger visit, much as the NSC had prepared for the first, except that the books they were to prepare would concern the practical, bilateral issues affecting U.S.-China relations; the NSC staff would prepare the books on the more politically sensitive issues, particularly those dealing with the Soviet Union and Vietnam. There were, in fact, to be two sets of books.

For my own part, not too long after returning from the July China visit, I was asked to try my hand at drafting a first cut of the joint communiqué to be issued at the conclusion of the Nixon visit. Not knowing where to start, I modeled my first attempt on some of the other joint communiqués that had been issued following visits by senior foreign dignitaries to Beijing for meetings with Chairman Mao, working into the text such purely bilateral U.S.-China issues as seemed appropriate. I began this effort about 1 September, after spending the ensuing time on other matters involving our relations with the other countries of East Asia and the Pacific. It came as no great surprise to me later that the final version of what became known as the "Shanghai Communiqué" bore little resemblance to my initial version. But as all veterans of the federal bureaucracy know, just having a piece of paper on hand from which to work is a great help in reaching a final version.

The preparations proceeded against a background of two complications: the State Department's continued efforts to keep "Red China" out of the UN, or at least to maintain a position in the UN for Taiwan; and, of more mysterious domestic political import for China, the alleged coup attempt against Mao Zedong by Lin Biao, who had been designated Mao's successor by the Ninth Party Congress in April 1969.

Lin Biao's attempted coup was said by the Chinese press to involve an attempt by Lin and a group of supporters to blow up a train on which Mao was riding, and according to what little news reached the outside world, it was exposed by Lin's own daughter. The crisis period had evidently been in the first week of September 1971; the first news filtered out to the rest of the world only in early October of that year, after the 1 October National Day parade in Beijing was canceled. The coup's exposure and consequent failure ended with the flight of Lin Biao and a planeload of supporters toward the Mongolian People's Republic, over which the aircraft purportedly ran out of fuel and then crashed and burned, killing all aboard. To this day, the whole episode remains shrouded in mystery, with the Chinese claiming that all bodies were so badly burned that identification was impossible.

The White House and the State Department hardly knew what to make of such a startling development, and we wondered if our plans to visit China on 20 October would be affected by the incident. As it turned out, the trip proceeded as planned, although not without signs that Beijing was in a state of tension. The only immediate effect was that the Chinese indicated that they would like us to defer public announcement of the next Kissinger visit until 5 October.

With the ice broken between Beijing and Washington, preparations for the October trip proceeded fairly rapidly, and by mid-October we were all, NSC and State alike, ready to proceed. Our complement on this trip, in addition to Al Jenkins, also included several members of the so-called advance party, whose job it was to scout out "photo opportunities" and to lay out a preliminary schedule for President and Mrs. Nixon to follow. The route was more direct than the one taken on Kissinger's secret trip to Beijing: first to Hawaii via Travis AFB for several days in which, theoretically, to polish up our papers; thence to Guam; and from there direct to Shanghai and then Beijing.

The stop on the big island of Hawaii was utterly delightful, Kissinger having drawn upon his relationship with the Rockefeller family to put the staff members in the Mauna Kea Beach Hotel, where, to be absolutely candid, we did absolutely nothing for two days but enjoy the climate and scenery. Kissinger himself stayed at the headquarters of the Rockefeller Ranch, located a considerable distance from the beach—much to his annoyance. The rest stop was very helpful, though, in relaxing tensions before the China visit.

The night before we took off for Guam, Kissinger gave a reception for the members of the staff, aircrew, and local dignitaries, and I took this opportunity to present him with a little memento prepared by Martha: a handy, dandy practice kit for using chopsticks, since his unfamiliarity with these implements had cost him some embarrassment the previous July. The kit consisted of three types of chopsticks—wood, ivory, and silver—plus an assortment of different items to be picked up by the chopsticks: mothballs, marbles, and wood chips. At an appropriate point in the reception I called the guests together and explained the nature of the practice kit, much to Kissinger's discomfiture, and I then presented it to him. I can't recall any other occasion in my tenure with him during which he was absolutely speechless.

At Shanghai we were met by protocol representatives of the Shanghai municipal government plus several mid-level representatives from the Foreign Ministry in Beijing, including Ni Yaoli and Xu Shangwei, who remained connected with the U.S.-China negotiations. (The main welcome had been saved for our arrival in the capital city.) While the aircraft was being refueled, we were driven to a Western-style guest house not far from Shanghai's Hongqiao Airport. There, a lunch was waiting for us, hosted by Zhang Chunqiao, who as one of the principal members of the yet-to-be-named "Gang of Four," was presumably already deeply involved in the ideological dispute going on at the topmost levels of the Chinese Communist Party over both doctrine and the succession to Mao Zedong. To us, the luncheon was remarkable for two things: first, the principal dish was a Shanghai special delicacy called "dragon, tiger, phoenix," which turned out to be snake, some species of cat, and chicken; second, the guest house was opulent, of timbered Tudor style complete with coat of arms over the fireplace and fine overstuffed Western furniture. Our hosts told us that this had formerly been the residence of a Western businessman; the house and furnishings certainly gave us a glimpse of the sumptuous lifestyle of the prewar wealthy foreign business community in Shanghai.

On the next leg of our trip two Chinese navigators took over. This was a formality only, since our aircraft (in this case, Air Force One, the president's own aircraft) was equipped with two inertial navigation (IS) systems capable of giving accurate fixes on latitude and longitude at any time and in any part of the world. The regular navigator later described to me the "interesting" reactions of the two Chinese navigators when they saw the inertial systems. It appeared that they had looked around the cockpit, which was far more sophisticated than anything they were familiar with, had noted the IS instruments, had immediately grasped the significance of the devices, and then had ignored them completely, as if the IS systems did not exist. They had navigated the aircraft between Shanghai and Beijing strictly by eyeball, with one navigator sitting behind the other to peer over the latter's shoulder and to make hand motions for "left" or "right."

Reception in Beijing

Our welcoming party in Beijing was much the same group who had welcomed us in July, with Ye Jianying as its leader, but with Foreign Minister Ji Pengfei also a member of the party. We were ensconced in the same guest house in the Diao Yu Tai as before; however, one rude surprise awaited us in each room—a special bulletin from the New China News Agency in English reprinting a *People's Daily* editorial calling on the "peoples of the world" to overthrow the American "imperialists and their running dogs." Kissinger had no intention of accepting this act of discourtesy and had me collect all of the offending items and turn them over to one of the Chinese protocol officers assigned to us, on the grounds that they must have been left by a previous party. There was no further mention of this article, which we took to be a calculated effort to see how we would react to such a pointed slap (as opposed to the signs all over Beijing that conveyed variations of the same theme but that were taken by us to be a more or less normal part of the background). Again, the opponents of a U.S.-China détente in the Chinese hierarchy evidently wanted to have their voices heard. Actually, Zhou Enlai later mentioned obliquely to Kissinger that the United States shouldn't pay too much attention to what the Chinese called "firing empty cannons of rhetoric," or "*kai kong pao.*"

Our October visit differed from the previous one in one major respect: it was publicized. Our arrival was mentioned in the *People's Daily* the following morning. On page one there was a box briefly noting that Dr. Henry Kissinger, the national security adviser to U.S. President Nixon, had arrived in Beijing for talks with Chinese officials and had been met at the airport by Ye Jianying; the principal members of both the arriving and welcoming parties were also listed by name.

This modest publicity was a far cry from the secrecy of our previous entry into Beijing and was especially significant considering the enormous readership of the *People's Daily*. This news must have come to the average Chinese, steeped in anti-U.S. propaganda, as a lightning bolt. The mention of Ye Jianying was particularly important, since not only was he one of the most senior members of the Chinese Communist Party, he was also the top-ranking officer of the People's Liberation Army; accordingly, mention that he had greeted Kissinger would have conveyed to the Chinese people that the PLA leadership backed the U.S.-China meeting. Given the wonderment that Chinese reading this brief *People's Daily* article must have felt at the news, it was clear that by publishing even a few details of the Kissinger visit, the top Chinese leadership wanted to let the people know that something new was in the wind regarding U.S.-China relations.

Other examples showed the Chinese leadership's desire to publicize this visit. As Kissinger notes in *White House Years*, the *People's Daily* published photographs of Premier Zhou Enlai together with Kissinger and the rest of our group,[1] but even more striking were the circumstances of a "cultural event" arranged for us in the Great Hall of the People on the evening following our arrival in Beijing. Our host was, of all people, Mao Zedong's wife, Jiang Qing. Jiang Qing was famous for having become the arbiter of Chinese (communist) culture and the sponsor of many revolutionary-style dramas and operas. We went from the Diao Yu Tai after dinner and were astonished when we entered the theater to find it packed with an audience of approximately five hundred people, apparently senior cadres (officials) and their wives. Ye Jianying and Huang Hua were also present, along with other senior Chinese officials.

For this special event Jiang Qing wore a three-quarter length black bombazine dress just short enough to reveal that she was wearing black high-button shoes. (Both of these items went out of style in the West in the 1890s, but they were considerably more fashionable than the drab, shapeless pants and jacket usually worn by both men and women in China.) The audience literally gasped when Jiang Qing and Dr. Kissinger walked down the aisle together and took their places in a center row. They created quite an "odd-couple" impression—two of the most unlikely partners that the world could produce at that particular moment—but it was obvious that our Chinese hosts, once again, wanted to make a political statement.

The program that evening also contained surprises. The main event was to be one of Jiang Qing's "revolutionary" operas (that is, a combination of a contemporary political theme sung in the *kun qu* style of the traditional Beijing opera) entitled "Ode to the Dragon River," a story of poor peasants building a dike against flooding despite the machinations of a Kuomintang agent. The program opened, however, with the public appearance—evidently the first in years—of the Beijing Philharmonic Ensemble, which under the baton of its conductor, Li Delun, proceeded to play Beethoven's Sixth, or "Pastoral," Symphony. The playing of Western music caused a stir in the audience, which surely was only accustomed to hearing the "revolutionary" music that saturated the television and radio broadcasts to the complete exclusion of all other music. I regarded the addition of Beethoven's Sixth to the program as having major political implications for the future (described later), since it could only have been sanctioned, if not suggested, by Jiang Qing, who had almost single-handedly purged Chinese literature and art of anything that could not be construed as "revolutionary." And she evidently liked Beethoven, at least the lilting melodies of his Pastoral Symphony!

There was an intermission between the two presentations, in which the members of our party tried, with some difficulty, to make small talk with Jiang Qing and her party in a reception room adjacent to the theater. Once the cultural event was over, around 11:30 P.M. on a very dark night, we proceeded immediately to the Diao Yu Tai by way of Chang An Jie, Beijing's main street, and found ourselves back in the real world of post-Lin Biao Beijing. The streets were absolutely empty except for our motorcade, but under the street lamp hanging at every road intersection, standing in the dim cone of light it cast, was stationed a PLA soldier armed with an AK-47. The dark city, the armed soldiers, and the absence of pedestrians and traffic all created an eerie impression. We were unable to judge whether the armed guards were there for our protection or for general public order and discipline connected with the aftermath of the Lin Biao episode.

The cultural evening did not end our public exposure. The following day we traveled by car to the Great Wall and the Ming Tombs, both famous tourist sites forty to sixty kilometers from Beijing, and we again found an unusual level of security precautions along our route: at every junction of a side road with the main Ming Tombs–Great Wall road stood a white-jacketed policeman. At the wall itself there were many Chinese visitors who silently absorbed our presence.

The morning of the following day we visited the Summer Palace (I He Yuan), about an hour's drive from Beijing, with Ye Jianying as our host and tour guide. It was a gloriously clear fall day, although a cold wind was blowing. The Summer Palace is one of the main recreational spots for the Chinese citizens of Beijing and, because days off from work do not necessarily coincide with weekends, the area was crowded with ordinary Chinese enjoying their holiday and obviously taking a good look at our party and its high-level escort. There was much staring and comment, since the *People's Daily* article had given the people a pretty good idea of who we were, and Ye Jianying was of course well known.

When we reached the vicinity of the so-called Marble Boat, built with one of the Qing Empress Ci Xi's numerous diversions from Chinese navy funds, our hosts suggested that we stop and have tea on the Summer Palace lake. They offered us three choices: first, to go out on the lake in roofed but open-sided barges, two of which were waiting for us; or to take a motor boat with a closed cabin; or if we didn't like either of these options, to go onto the Marble Boat itself, which was fully protected from the wind. It was clear, though, that the Chinese preferred the first option, the barges, which provided the greatest visibility. We then dutifully boarded the barges under the watching eyes of at least three hundred spectators, Kissinger arm-in-arm with Ye Jianying. Once settled, Kissinger looked back at the crowd and waved. The response was immediate and startling—the onlookers broke out with a sudden burst of handclapping, which seemed spontaneous. Certainly there was no sign of any orchestration.

My conclusion about this scene, then and now, was that the average Chinese was basically discontented with the pattern of life as it was then, that the unprecedented arrival of a group of high-level "American imperialists" together with a senior Chinese figure such as Ye Jianying suggested that some kind of change in this pattern was afoot, and while the nature of the change was of course unknown, any change had to be for the better. Hence the applause.

Two small episodes are worth noting about our exposures to the public, because they offer insights into Chinese society at the time. In the first, during the car ride to the Great Wall, in which Al Jenkins and I rode with Zhang Wenjin, I noticed a few miles north of Beijing a sign pointing eastward, labeled in Chinese "To the May 7 Cadre School for Literature and the Arts." This was undoubtedly where people from these walks of life were receiving political "reeducation." I remarked on this sign to Zhang Wenjin and asked him if it might be possible at some future point for the classical Beijing opera to be revived. "Oh, yes," he said, "We are practicing it now, but the time has not yet arrived to bring it back." Then, in a thoughtful mood, he went on to say, "We need to do a great deal more in our country to improve the living conditions of our people and especially to bring the economic standards of the countryside up to those in the cities." Since Zhang Wenjin was personally very close to Zhou Enlai, his remarks appeared to indicate that serious consideration was being given at high Chinese levels, certainly under Zhou Enlai's direction, to effect changes in China's economic and political system that would make the lot of the common man more agreeable. Had Zhou Enlai not died in 1976, China might have become a very different place, with reforms occurring months or even years earlier than they actually did.

The second episode was of a more personal nature. Our host during our visit to the Summer Palace, Ye Jianying, was already in his late seventies and not in the best of health. The walk around the Summer Palace was quite extensive and involved a considerable climb up to the central tower overlooking the lake; throughout the walk our young female guide (part of the Summer Palace staff) grasped Marshal Ye by the arm and assisted him, taking particular care on the stairway leading to the central tower. Her solicitude was touching and displayed a human side of Chinese Communism that I had not expected to see. The elderly Ye seemed very grateful for her help. Chinese respect for old age had demonstrably not been destroyed. Once at the summit, we were again applauded by the Chinese already there to enjoy the view and take refreshments.

Substantively, the discussions on the joint communiqué were difficult indeed, with the Chinese expressing dissatisfaction with the rather anodyne style of communiqué that I had prepared based on what the Chinese had used with other distinguished visitors. They insisted instead on something that referred to the real differences between our two countries, particularly to Taiwan, but also—probably for the record—to Vietnam, although it was already evident that Vietnam rated a lower priority with our hosts than did relations with the United States. Long discussions took place, mostly at night. Despite the intensity of the negotiations, both sides bargained in good faith, were clear and consistent in their positions, and still were flexible enough to make adjustments. Much progress was made in the space of a few short days and nights.

As we prepared to leave China for home, the basis for a successful Nixon visit had been laid, although some blank spaces needed to be filled in the joint communiqué (in fact, much haggling remained to be done during the actual presidential visit). Regarding Taiwan, Dr. Kissinger had devised phraseology, which he admits he borrowed from State Department language dating back to the ambassadorial-level talks of the 1950s, to the effect that, "The United States acknowledges that all Chinese on either side of the Taiwan Strait(s) maintain there is but one China. The United States Government does not challenge that position."[2] The dates had also been set for the Nixon visit the following year, 21 to 28 February 1972. One of the significant agreements was that neither side sought hegemony in the Asia-Pacific region and would oppose efforts by other countries to do so. "American hegemonists" had been a favorite epithet of the Chinese for the United States, and accepting this language at our suggestion was significant in showing the change in Chinese outlook. With the United States removed from the list of offenders on this score, in reality only the Soviet Union remained.

The sole issue to mar the visit was that as our aircraft was actually taxiing for the takeoff, a coded message arrived informing us that U.S. ploys to maintain Taiwan's seat in the United Nations had failed, and that China had just been voted in as a member of both the General Assembly and the Security Council, replacing the "Republic of China" on Taiwan. Our effort to make the vote on Chinese membership an "important question" requiring a two-thirds majority had failed. The Chinese had, of course, already been aware of the vote, but had not taken the opportunity to crow over it to us.

The news about the UN vote was hardly surprising. It would have been only a question of time before China was voted into the UN to replace Taiwan, given China's gradual reemergence into world politics, especially with its boost in diplomatic stature after President Nixon's announcement of the United States's interest in improving relations with China in the cause of world peace. The problem was a domestic one for the United States, since Taiwan's friends rallied together to release a storm of protest, and the president was obliged to send a personal representative, the then-governor of California, Ronald Reagan, to assure Chiang Kai-shek that the United States would continue to support his regime. Kissinger personally had already extended this assurance to Taiwan (Republic of China) Ambassador James Shen at a dinner given by Ambassador Shen shortly after our return from the July visit. The atmosphere during that dinner was very strained, but at the same time, Shen was simply bursting with curiosity about our reactions to conditions on the China mainland. He deserves great credit for having preserved his dignity and integrity under very difficult circumstances.

The Chinese wasted no time in appointing an ambassador to the UN, Huang Hua, who had been serving as ambassador to Canada. Toward the end of 1971 I joined with Kissinger and Winston Lord at a dinner for Ambassador Huang in New York City hosted by Vice President Nelson Rockefeller at the Century Club, an exclusive Manhattan gathering place for writers and scholars rarely seen by Foreign Service officers. We flew up to La Guardia aboard an Air Force Learjet, and on the way into Manhattan, Kissinger nervously kept asking Lord, who organized the session, if he had made the appropriate arrangements for the wine at the dinner, to which Lord invariably gave the same reply—"yes." On arrival at the Century Club, we saw that each place was set with at least five separate wine glasses. Winston had outdone himself.

The dinner was fascinating in that Vice President Rockefeller had obviously not been put into the loop on all the background information connected with the opening to China. He was almost mesmerized at hearing from Kissinger and Huang Hua, whom Kissinger and we NSC staffers now looked upon as an old friend, the amount of sensitive information that we had made available to the Chinese in the course of the two Kissinger visits. He also seemed surprised to hear the state of the arrangements for the visit to China by President Nixon. Lord and I barely had a chance to eat, since as note-takers it was our job to record all the details of the dinner conversation as close to word-for-word as we could manage.

One final official visit to China was necessary before the presidential visit actually took place. This was made by General Alexander Haig, then Kissinger's deputy. He made his trip in January 1972 to finalize communications and other logistical arrangements and presumably pick up any loose threads of substance left over from the Kissinger visits. In his book *Caveat*, General Haig writes that the Chinese treated his visit like a dress rehearsal for the Nixon visit, and they tried—once again—in their exchanges with him to employ language, presumably on Taiwan, that would have been highly offensive to the United States. Haig steadfastly resisted this ploy, which was then dropped. The Chinese made clear to Haig, though, the rather low priority that China attached to its relationship with Vietnam. Haig maintains that Zhou Enlai indicated to him in their conversations, albeit indirectly, that the United States should not lose in Vietnam, and based on previous observations cited earlier, there is no reason to doubt Haig's accuracy.[3] Events of March 1972 would amply bear out this low Chinese appraisal of their relations with Vietnam (see chapter 6).

Final Preparations for the Nixon Visit to China

The beginning of 1972 brought an enormous outburst of energy concerning China in both the National Security Council and the State Department. "The books," of course, had to be prepared for President and Mrs. Nixon's visit to China, but in a different format from anything the NSC had done before, since it had to be assumed that President Nixon was unfamiliar with many or most of the issues that would be discussed with the Chinese, with the exception of U.S. relations with Vietnam and with the Soviet Union. Indeed, the main book prepared for the president was more of a tutorial, with analyses as accurate as we could provide of the major personalities he was likely to meet, along with outlines of the major policy issues confronting the two sides. In addition, we included recapitulations of the Kissinger-Zhou Enlai talks of July and October 1971, plus excerpts of articles on China by leading sinologists and perceptive recent visitors to China.[4]

The State Department was preparing its own set of books for Secretary of State William Rogers, and, it hoped, for the president as well. Secretary Rogers was to accompany the president on his trip to China; assisting Rogers would be Marshall Green, assistant secretary for East Asia and the Pacific; Al Jenkins, who had been on Kissinger's October 1971 trip to China; Charles Freeman, a Foreign Service officer fluent in Chinese, who was to go as interpreter for both the president and the secretary; and a sizable State Department entourage. There were to be two separate levels of meetings in Beijing, one level between President Nixon and Premier Zhou Enlai in which the global and critical foreign policy questions would be addressed, and the other level between Secretary Rogers and Foreign Minister Ji Pengfei to address bilateral questions.

The State Department books covered U.S.-China bilateral issues such as the question of American citizens still remaining in China (as of early 1972 a few remained, some voluntarily and some involuntarily), and the question of Chinese assets frozen by the United States from the time China had entered the Korean War; on the Chinese side there was the matter of substantial amounts of American property in China that the Chinese had seized following their defeat of the Kuomintang. Issues such as these, while secondary to the major policy issues in U.S.-China relations, still required settlement as part of the normalization process. They were assigned entirely to the State Department.

In addition to addressing the bilaterals, the State Department also was responsible for some of the major elements of foreign policy that the NSC included in its books, but though the papers were duly sent to the NSC and forwarded to Dr. Kissinger, whether or not they were passed on to the president is a question only Kissinger can answer. In fact, several weeks later in Beijing, I was asked to bring the president's "book" to him from his suite in the guest house, and the only item I found there was a familiar black-bound volume that we in the NSC had prepared. As already indicated, both the president and Kissinger saw to it that foreign policy, at least in its most critical aspects, was run by the White House, not the State Department. As for the bilaterals, Kissinger and the president were happy to leave these matters for Secretary Rogers to discuss with the Chinese.

At the same time that both we in the NSC and the staff of the Office of China Mainland Affairs in the State Department were working on the books for the president's trip, we were being deluged with advice, some good, mostly bad, volunteered by people outside the U.S. government, suggesting to the president what he should do or say while in China. All of this had to be screened and appropriate "thank you" letters drafted, with the able assistance of Richard Solomon, a respected China scholar (later assistant secretary of state for East Asia and the Pacific, ambassador to the Philippines, and president of the United States Institute of Peace), and John S. Froebe, a career Foreign Service officer well known for his hard work and attention to detail, who had learned Chinese and served at a number of East Asian posts.

Among all the outside advice we received I particularly valued one item: a neat looseleaf binder presented to me personally by a California businessman named Harned Hoose, who was the nephew of Dean Pettis, the pre–World War II head of the College of Chinese Studies in Beijing (then Peking). Hoose had spent a good part of his childhood until high school living with Dean Pettis, and he spoke fluent colloquial Chinese. He was able to contribute useful insights into traditional Chinese cultural traits and practices, which he carefully had catalogued and tabbed in his binder for our use.[5]

Among the duties of the NSC East Asia/Pacific office staff was assisting in the selection of the gifts President and Mrs. Nixon would present to their various Chinese hosts during their visit to Beijing. These had to be carefully chosen to match the rank of the recipient. On each of Kissinger's trips the Chinese had given everyone in his party mementos (such as cloisonné vases), carefully graded in size and value according to the recipient's rank, and it was firmly resolved in the White House that our side could do no less. While we anticipated that President Nixon would certainly meet Chairman Mao Zedong and also hold extensive discussions with Premier Zhou Enlai, we had no idea whom Mrs. Nixon would meet—Jiang Qing? Madame Zhou? Both? We had to be prepared with the appropriate number and gradations of gifts.

The practical question that occupied the attention of my NSC people, as well as the White House staff and protocol office at State, was what particular American items would be suitable to take to China as gifts? Our own past performance had hardly matched that of the Chinese; for example, on the secret trip to Beijing in July 1971 we took a moon rock brought back by our astronauts, which was given to our hosts to be presented to Chairman Mao Zedong. This was received by the Chinese with what appeared to be a certain amount of polite disdain. (The syndrome seemed to be that if the Chinese hadn't invented it or acquired it on their own, it didn't exist, as illustrated in the case of the Chinese navigators who apparently couldn't see our inertial navigation system.) Obviously, on the presidential visit we would have to do much, much better.

The gifts finally chosen for the senior Chinese were impressive sets of ceramic birds made by Boehm, the celebrated New Jersey ceramic artist. These were unique and very lifelike copies of typical American birdlife. For the lesser officials we chose items such as silver bowls, cigarette lighters, and cuff links, all bearing the president's seal. We also took along sufficient spares to assure that nobody would be left out.

Besides the presents for Chinese officials, the president wanted to provide gifts to the Chinese people as a symbol of American friendship—something (or things) distinctly American. After much thought, two gifts were selected for the people of China: a pair of Alaskan musk oxen, a male and a female, for presentation to the Beijing zoo, and a well-developed California redwood tree for the president to plant. The tree he took was not small. A few weeks later at Travis AFB I watched its loading. Even with branches folded back against the trunk it was a distinctly difficult job to fit it through the door of one of the presidential VC-137s.

With these details—and myriad others—taken care of, all was ready for the history-making trip of President and Mrs. Nixon to the People's Republic of China.

Chapter 5

The Nixon China Trip and the Shanghai Communiqué

The day set for President and Mrs. Nixon to leave Washington for China was 17 February 1972. When that date finally came, it seemed almost anticlimactic to those of us on the NSC staff who had been working on this project for so long. On a typically cold, wet Washington February day Winston Lord, Jonathan Howe, two secretaries, Diane Matthews and Julie Pineau, and I boarded our White House limousines and proceeded to Andrews AFB, where we waited for the presidential party. Dr. Kissinger, as was customary, arrived later.

When the president and his immediate party reached Andrews aboard a helicopter from the White House lawn, there was little ceremony. A kind of enclosure similar to a sheep pen had been set up between the gate to the VIP room and Air Force One, into which a large number of reporters and TV cameramen had been crammed. The president stopped only long enough to provide what has generally become known as a "photo opportunity" and say a few optimistic words about his China trip, after which he and Mrs. Nixon walked up the ramp and waved good-bye, the door slammed shut, and the aircraft took off. According to protocol, the rest of the passengers and crew were already aboard, and in short order we proceeded to our first stop at Travis AFB for refueling.

A feature of Nixon's trip that the Chinese had not previously encountered was the very large press party that accompanied the president aboard two chartered Pan American Airways Boeing 707s. The press was ubiquitous throughout the trip, and Ron Ziegler, President Nixon's press secretary, was along to take care of the host of journalists, television personalities, and their crews. Barbara Walters, Eric Sevareid, and Walter Cronkite, among others, came along.

As was usual in presidential trips of this nature, in addition to the press flying separately, a press pool of reporters occupied the tourist-class seats in the after end of the president's Air Force One. Members of the NSC staff along with Secretary Rogers's party and lower-ranking members of the White House personal staff were forward of the press section in what normally would have been the first-class section of the plane. The more senior personnel, including Dr. Kissinger, were in a special section just ahead of us. The president's cabin was located forward of the senior staff section and behind the cockpit, crewspace, and communications equipment.

The flight proceeded from Travis AFB to Hickham AFB in Hawaii, where there was a two-day layover for physical adjustment, so that the jet-lag factor for President and Mrs. Nixon wouldn't be so great (the time difference between Beijing and Washington is thirteen hours). We of the NSC and some of the president's personal staff spent the period in Honolulu billeted at the luxurious Kahala Hilton Hotel on what the president's schedule called "staff time." We rarely saw the president and Kissinger at the Kahala. They stayed at the commanding officer's residence at Kaneohe Marine Air Base some miles further down the road. For the rest of us, our work had either already been done or lay ahead of us in China, and we simply relaxed and enjoyed the numerous amenities of the Kahala Hilton. It was something of a compliment from Kissinger that there were no last-minute demands from him for changes in any of the papers we had prepared for the president. Again, the rest-stop was helpful in easing tensions before the momentous China visit.

On 21 February a Marine helicopter settled down on the golf course adjacent to the Kahala to take us to Hickham Field, where the presidential party reassembled at the Hickham VIP building for the flight to Guam. (From Guam, after an overnight, we would fly direct to Beijing.) We boarded the aircraft in the midst of a lively Hawaiian send-off—complete with leis, hula girls, military band, and spectators from the military families—arranged by Admiral Noel Gayler, then commander in chief, U.S. Pacific Forces (CINCPAC). Shortly thereafter we were airborne.

A Cold Arrival in Beijing, and a
Meeting with Chairman Mao

If our departure from Hawaii was a happy and colorful one, our welcome in China on 22 February, while formal and correct, was as chilly as the weather. To be sure, we were met by officials of appropriate rank: Li Xiannian, who as vice premier of the State Council was as close to being head of state as China then possessed, and Premier Zhou Enlai, with his wife Deng Yingchao. Foreign Minister Ji Pengfei and other senior Chinese officials were present as well. The president duly inspected a military honor guard, with contingents from each of the three People's Liberation Army services, that was lined up adjacent to our aircraft. As the honor guard marched away they sang a military song well known to the Chinese, entitled the "Three Main Principles and the Eight Points of Attention." The sky was gray, the weather was cold, and there were no spectators. We spent little time boarding our limousines and driving toward Beijing along the main airport road, which was devoid of traffic.

All of the proceedings connected with the Nixons' arrival had been under the watchful and hyperinquisitive eye of the American press. The procession of U.S. dignitaries descending the ramp from the presidential plane, shaking hands with the Chinese welcoming delegation, and assembling to wait for the president to inspect the honor guard were all duly recorded by the prepositioned media. We weren't particularly photogenic for the occasion: because of the intense cold, all wore heavy overcoats, faces were pinched, and breath steamed. (I was wearing a tan camel's-hair overcoat, possibly of Chinese origin, which dated back to my undergraduate days at Dartmouth and which made me stand out conspicuously from the other more drably clad dignitaries.) From the "Shanghai" limousine in which Winston Lord, Jonathan Howe, and I were riding in the motorcade, we could not see what arrangements were made for the media people, but we knew they were doing their best to cover everything that happened. Their great moment would come that evening, when the president and Zhou Enlai were to make speeches at the welcoming banquet the Chinese had arranged for the Nixons in the Great Hall of the People.

The absence of spectators that we had observed on our arrival at the airport was even more pronounced as our motorcade proceeded toward the city. We were following a route made familiar in our two previous visits: past the San Li Tun diplomatic quarter (where there were some people watching from windows or balconies), a left turn by the Workers' Stadium to Chang An Jie, past the Tian An Men, and thence to the Diao Yu Tai guest house area. At every road intersection there were several members of the Public Security Forces posted, who were visibly holding back assorted pedestrians, cyclists, and vehicles in numbers that became increasingly dense as we approached the center of Beijing. From our car we could see that many necks were craning to see what they could of our motorcade, but such curiosity was visibly being discouraged by the public security personnel. The absence of spectators could be attributed to security considerations, but more likely politics was the cause. There were no diplomatic relations between our two countries, and serious problems, beginning with the Taiwan issue, remained to be resolved; accordingly, the Chinese leaders presumably decided to give low-key treatment in welcoming President Nixon, and they apparently discouraged popular participation. After all, the visit itself represented an incredible turn of events to the average Chinese.

At the Diao Yu Tai, our motorcade divided. The president and his party were housed in a large structure across the lake from where Kissinger's group had stayed before, which was used this time to accommodate the secretary of state's party. The presidential guest house, built in the form of a large "H" with suites and reception rooms on either side, a dining room in the center, and sleeping quarters on the floor above, promptly filled up with our Chinese hosts and their distinguished guests. Before lunch the president and Li Xiannian and their wives, along with the other Chinese dignitaries, talked together for some time through interpreters in the main reception room beneath the president's suite.

After lunch, Zhou Enlai told Dr. Kissinger that Chairman Mao wanted to meet President Nixon. Only the president, Dr. Kissinger, and Winston Lord attended the subsequent meeting. There was considerable confusion and milling around, and this may have contributed to my not being invited to the meeting. If I had been conspicuously present, perhaps I would have gone, too. In any case, Kissinger consistently held to a rule that drastically limited attendance on our side at senior meetings. I felt like a groom left at the altar, but knew enough about Dr. Kissinger's operating style not to get too upset. As luck would have it, I never did meet Chairman Mao.

President Nixon and Kissinger in their memoirs both cover in some detail the points that the president and Chairman Mao discussed.[1] What was most important about the meeting was that Mao officially put his seal of approval on the improvement of relations between China and the United States and in effect gave his blessing to progress on bilateral issues, even before major issues such as Taiwan were clearly decided. To illustrate Mao's approval of improving U.S.-China relations was the photograph, carried the following day in the *People's Daily*, of President Nixon and Chairman Mao having their talk in what was plainly Mao's study in the Zhongnanhai. Any doubts remaining in the minds of the Chinese people about what was happening in U.S.-PRC relations would have been dispelled by this photograph.

It is noteworthy that in the president's meeting with Mao Zedong,

Mao's words, according to Kissinger, came in bursts, as if the chairman was having physical difficulties.[2] Mao's physical problems, as manifested on this occasion, were to figure importantly in Chinese politics during the next few years in the struggle to succeed him.

The Banquet at the Great Hall of the People

Despite President Nixon's historic meeting with Chairman Mao, for the rest of the party and the TV-viewing American public, the big event of that day was to be the banquet given by Zhou Enlai for the Nixons and their staff members in the Great Hall of the People. In keeping with Chinese hospitality, the entire U.S. party was invited. As the moment for departure from the Diao Yu Tai approached, we began to assemble from different directions in the presidential guest house foyer, the State delegation from across the lake and the rest from various parts of the guest house itself, to await President and Mrs. Nixon. Our motorcade vehicles were already lined up outside. Standing in the hallway of the building were members of the Chinese protocol staff, plus interpreters Ji Chaozhu and Nancy Tang, and others who would accompany us to and from the Great Hall.

Just at this time, our own interpreter Chas Freeman expressed deep concern to me over his ability to do justice to translating what the president would say in his banquet speech. Translating for President Nixon on this occasion was a formidable task. The banquet was to be given worldwide television coverage, making it a centerpiece of the entire Nixon trip, and in typical Nixon style the president could not be expected to adhere to the text his speech-writers had drafted. His custom, in fact, was simply to look over the prepared text and go on from there with remarks he personally thought were appropriate to the occasion, using very little, if any, of what had been written for him. We knew the president was planning to use some quotes from Mao Zedong's poetry, a collection of which had been made available to him, but we didn't know in advance what poem he would quote or what the correct translation would be. This in particular was troubling Freeman, since it would be virtually impossible for anyone not thoroughly familiar with Mao's poems to be able to render the English back into the original Chinese.

Nearby where we talked stood Ji Chaozhu, whose competence as an interpreter had been amply and repeatedly demonstrated during the 1971 Kissinger trips to China. I asked Ji, who was to interpret Chinese to English for Premier Zhou, if he was familiar with Mao's poetry and might be able to take on the job of translating from English to Chinese on behalf of President Nixon. Without batting an eyelash, Ji said "Of course" to both questions. He was seemingly unfazed by the thought of translating the president's extemporaneous words for literally millions of people worldwide in what was an epochal event. Our dilemma was solved.

About this time, the Nixons arrived, so we boarded our vehicles and proceeded to the Great Hall. There we were met by Premier Zhou Enlai and escorted up several flights of stairs to a grandstand-like structure where we arranged ourselves with our Chinese hosts according to rank for a picture-taking event. In true Chinese style, the background was a painting of pine trees, which to a Chinese audience symbolizes long life and hence "welcome." Our hosts then escorted us into the banquet hall, which was, we were told, capable of seating three thousand guests, but seated perhaps one thousand on this occasion, including high-ranking Chinese and the crowd of press and TV reporters. TV cameras and crews were already in place. The president, Mrs. Nixon, and Dr. Kissinger were seated at Premier Zhou Enlai's table; the rest of us were seated at other tables, each of which had a senior Chinese leader as host. I found myself a few tables away with the commander of the Beijing Garrison, Wu Zhong (translatable as "militarily loyal") and the minister of electric power.

An amazing feature of the event was that as we entered the banquet hall, a PLA band in a far corner immediately struck up and began to play a medley of American folk songs. It was a heady experience to sit down to this banquet in the Great Hall of the People in Beijing to the strains of "The Arkansas Traveler," "Oh, Susanna," and "America the Beautiful." Music of a similar nature continued throughout the evening; from where, I wondered, had the PLA band acquired it.

Another heady experience was that the minister of electric power began to play the Chinese finger-game with me. In this game two players both throw out fingers from a fist and at the same time guess the total of their own and their opponent's fingers. The loser is obliged to *gan bei* (empty) his glass. In this case the glasses contained *mao tai*. (*Mao tai* was a favorite tipple of the Chinese Communists dating back to the Long March days when the Communists crossed Guizhou province on foot, and when the townspeople of Mao Tai had succored the nearly exhausted Red Army troops with their local, extremely potent—about 130 proof—home brew.) When I asked if this traditional Chinese drinking game was still popular, the minister explained that while this wasn't really revolutionary behavior, old customs persisted.

Zhou Enlai's welcoming speech and the president's response were delivered about midway through the banquet on a stage behind their table, which was decorated with the Chinese and American flags. Thanks to Ji Chaozhu, the speech translations, made before a rapt audience in the Great Hall of the People, went off without a hitch. The TV cameras were grinding away, not merely recording the event but helping to propel normalization forward. Zhou spoke warmly of the development of Sino-U.S. friendship, noting that the president had come such a long distance to inaugurate it; he mentioned no controversy such as Vietnam or Taiwan. The president replied in a similar manner, beginning with a quote from a poem by Mao Zedong that a journey of ten thousand *li* begins with but a single step, and that one should "seize the day, seize the hour," looking forward to the continued growth of U.S.-China ties and a better future for all.

In keeping with Chinese custom, after the speeches had been given, Premier Zhou and President Nixon went from table to table to exchange toasts in *mao tai* with each guest. Zhou was simply touching his lips to the glass and was not drinking—an example the president followed—but some of the responses were in the traditional Chinese *gan bei* ("bottom's up", or, literally, *dry* —meaning empty—*glass*) form. Aided only in part by the *mao tai*, the atmosphere in the Great Hall was electric. Surely everyone there, and every TV watcher, must have sensed that something new and great was being created in the U.S.-China relationship.

The party broke up once the last dish of the banquet had been served and eaten, as was customary. Here began what may be likened to a stampede of a herd of buffalo across America's prairies in the last century—a horde of guests all walked swiftly or even ran through the vast open spaces of the Great Hall to get to their cars parked in front of the steps of the building, the earlier returnees taking precedence over the later ones in the order their cars could leave. Those of us in the official party were thinking first of writing up our collective recollections and then getting some rest after a long, busy day, while the reporters were thinking of stories to be written and deadlines to be met. The Chinese, perhaps, simply wanted to go home. In one vignette that I witnessed, the newsman Eric Sevareid overtook Vice Foreign Minister Qiao Guanhua in search of an exclusive interview. He said to Qiao, "Oh, Mr. Foreign Minister, I'm Eric Sevareid!" assuming that Qiao knew who he was. Qiao, who probably had never heard of Sevareid and seemed confused by this approach, blinked his eyes owlishly behind his glasses and did not respond.

Crafting the Joint Communiqué

The program worked out for the Nixons was for President and Mrs. Nixon to spend the mornings sightseeing, and in the afternoons following lunch, for the president to meet in a conference room at the Great Hall of the People with Zhou Enlai and his advisers (and, separately, to take care of ongoing matters of state that needed his personal attention). In the evenings there were entertainment functions, followed by consultations on the day's progress or on the latest important revisions to the draft of the joint communiqué that would be issued at the conclusion of the president's visit. Dr. Kissinger held ongoing meetings with Vice Foreign Minister Qiao Guanhua to work out details of the communiqué's wording, which were cleared when necessary with President Nixon and, separately, with Premier Zhou and the Chinese Politburo; the separate versions and responses had then again to be reconciled with the opposite side.

On the afternoon of 22 February, substantive talks began, following President and Mrs. Nixon's visit to the Great Wall and Ming Tombs. Here, as the British say, I nearly blotted my copybook: the president and Kissinger moved out so promptly after lunch that I wasn't informed and had to dash to the Great Hall of the People on my own, arriving a few minutes late and earning a few cold glances from my superiors.

President Nixon and Premier Zhou discussed foreign policy considerations and world issues from their own countries' perspectives, focused particularly on matters of concern to both sides, such as our mutual problems in relations with the Soviet Union, the vexing question of Vietnam (where our interests diverged considerably), and our differing views on threats to peace in East Asia. There was some discussion in the Nixon-Zhou meetings of the strategic points of the joint communiqué. The main sticking points were Taiwan, of course, and the nature of future relations between our two countries. For the most part, however, the fine points of negotiating mutually acceptable wording in the joint communiqué were left to Kissinger and Vice Foreign Minister Qiao Guanhua. Premier Zhou occasionally sat in on their meetings for brief periods of time.

The significance of the communiqué's wording was that it would express the positions of two great countries' leaders, who attached their personal prestige to it, and that it would define the relationship between those two countries for years to come. In particular, it would officially end the estrangement between the United States and China that had prevailed for so many years.

While the president was meeting the premier, Secretary Rogers met with Foreign Minister Ji Pengfei and Ji's team of advisers in Rogers's Diao Yu Tai guest house conference room. Those latter "counterpart talks," for which Chas Freeman served commendably as interpreter for Secretary Rogers, primarily concerned the issues of Americans held in China and various claims versus assets, as described earlier. These questions were not resolved at this time, though.

The NSC staff did not participate in the morning sightseeing events, as we had already seen the historic places and had plenty of other things to do in connection with the talks. The NSC contingent, with the exception of Kissinger, spent the mornings drafting reports for the record on what had transpired the previous day. In the afternoons Winston Lord and I took notes at the president's meetings with Zhou Enlai; in the evenings we attended the entertainment functions arranged by the Chinese, afterwards attended follow-up discussions with Kissinger and Zhou Enlai or Qiao Guanhua concerning the wording of the communiqué, and then worked on our notes far into the night.

In the 22 February discussions and subsequently, the positions of the two sides began to emerge (although, to be sure, much groundwork had already been done on the communiqué prior to the president's trip). There could be no agreed statement on Vietnam, or for that matter on Laos and Cambodia, since China's ideologically driven positions were so far from our own position that no bridge was possible. The result was something unique in joint communiqués: Each side laid down its position clearly, for example, "the U.S. side stated . . . ," and "the Chinese side stated . . . ," and then we simply dropped the controversial items to go on to other matters where we could agree.

The next issue to be addressed was Taiwan, and here the language had to be very carefully chosen so that on the Chinese side there would be no departure from principle, and on ours it would not appear to either ally or adversary that we were deserting our old friend Taiwan. In wording the communiqué, it was helpful that both the CCP and the Kuomintang regarded Taiwan as part of China, for by accepting this point and affirming our interest in the settlement of the sovereignty question "by the Chinese themselves" we would affront neither side. Our job was to find wording that reduced the United States's involvement in Taiwan's defense to a degree that was nonprovocative to the PRC while not abandoning our relationship with Taiwan, and to find a formulation that the Chinese could accept calling for no use of force in reuniting the island with the rest of China. Finding exact language agreeable to both sides occupied a major part of our time.

Even on relatively simple matters, both sides put great care into the wording of the joint communiqué. Perhaps this helps to explain why the communiqué proved to be so significant as the basis for rapid growth in the relationship between the United States and the People's Republic of China. Although I was involved in the discussions and wording of the

other issues as well, my own particular contribution concerned the maintenance of ongoing ties between our two countries. Here I wrote what
was eventually included unchanged in the joint communiqué:

> The two sides agreed that it is desirable to broaden the understanding be-
> tween the two peoples. To this end, they discussed specific areas in such fields
> as science, technology, culture, sports and journalism, in which people-to-
> people contacts would be mutually beneficial. Each side agrees to facilitate
> the further development of such contacts and exchanges.

These few words served as the basis for a large-scale exchange program,
in which Chinese students, graduate students in particular, came to the
United States by the thousands for advanced education, and fewer but
still substantial numbers of Americans went to China. (Most of their students were in the physical sciences, and ours were in the social sciences.)
This paragraph was also the basis on which the U.S. government chose
two private American organizations, the National Committee on U.S.-
China Relations and the Committee on Scholarly Exchanges with China
[both the PRC and Taiwan] of the National Academy of Sciences, to handle exchanges of people between the two countries. Both organizations
still perform these functions, although with much less government input
than in the early period of improved U.S.-China relations.

The joint communiqué draft also included some other noncontroversial
elements, including the expansion of bilateral trade. In addition, the
phrase "normalization of relations between the two countries" occurred
for the first time. No date was set for normalization, and both the United
States and China accepted that the actual attainment of normalization
would be a difficult process, to be completed only at some unstated time
in the future. Taiwan was our old friend, and although President Nixon
could visit China and sign a joint communiqué involving Taiwan, this old
friend remained an active player on the East Asian and U.S. political
scene. The Chinese showed great restraint and understanding in accepting
our ongoing ties with Taiwan, but their attitude, particularly that of Zhou
Enlai, had already been positively influenced by the words Kissinger
spoke the preceding July to the effect that the United States did not seek
"two Chinas, a one-China, one-Taiwan solution, nor an independent Taiwan." That position was reiterated on the occasion of the president's visit.
In addition, the United States had shown both by word and deed that it
had no territorial ambitions in East Asia.

On 26 February, with the communiqué complete but for a few critical
paragraphs, the whole Nixon entourage traveled to Hangzhou to enjoy

the scenic beauties of the West Lake and to give the Nixons a glimpse of China other than Beijing. The entire party took advantage of the opportunity to ride around the highly scenic West Lake in launches. By this time the heavy mood that had prevailed among the NSC staff from our chilly arrival in Beijing had begun to lift, encouraged, no doubt, by the progress in the joint communiqué. In fact, the tour around the lake, which stopped at several small islands containing temples and summer houses, became very picniclike.

With the joint communiqué, the language on Taiwan remained an obstacle. After dinner at Hangzhou on 26 February, our two negotiating teams, headed on our side by Dr. Kissinger and on the Chinese side by Vice Foreign Minister Qiao Guanhua, found it necessary to meet again in a hotel midway between the buildings where the Chinese and U.S. delegations were quartered. (President and Mrs. Nixon were in a separate guest house.) On our side of the usual green baize table next to Dr. Kissinger were myself, Winston Lord, and Jonathan Howe. On the Chinese side next to Vice Foreign Minister Qiao were his principal adviser Zhang Wenjin and his interpreter Ji Chaozhu.

The crucial sticking points concerned the persistent questions of the possible Chinese use of force against Taiwan to "liberate" the island and the stationing of U.S. forces on Taiwan and in the Taiwan Strait area, which China regarded both as a threat and a violation of its sovereignty. On the latter element, the Chinese were willing to accept our contention that the United States had no territorial ambitions in East Asia and that the U.S. forces in areas other than Vietnam, from which we were withdrawing, acted as a stabilizing factor in the region. This point had been made as far back as Dr. Kissinger's first trip to China in July 1971. On the use of force by China against Taiwan, no U.S. president could leave this element unaddressed without causing a political furor back home.

For hours those of us at the table sat and attempted to find a formula that would solve the problem of Chinese nonuse of force, trying variations of wording, only to find that for one reason or another it wouldn't be acceptable to the other side. Qiao Guanhua was smoking heavily during this session, and observed that he had been told by his doctors to stop or cut down his use of cigarettes but that he expected to smoke many more "until I meet God."[3] Zhang Wenjin was a frequent contributor, which at one point brought a snort of annoyance from Kissinger. "Do I bore you?" Zhang asked, to which Kissinger replied, "You're never boring, Mr. Zhang, but sometimes you're a damned nuisance." Such was the atmosphere of good feeling around the table regardless of our differences, that these words, said jocularly, were taken as a jest at which everyone laughed. In fact, Zhang's excellent knowledge of English helped greatly, and he seemed to have a facility for coming up with wording that met the needs of both sides.

What finally emerged on Taiwan, long after midnight, was another statement by China of its policy that it was the sole legal government of Taiwan and that the island was Chinese territory, etcetera, following which the United States employed a formula acknowledging that "all people [sic] on either side of the Taiwan Strait maintain that there is but one China and that Taiwan is part of China." We then reiterated what we had been saying since July 1971; that the United States "did not challenge" China's rejection of "two Chinas," "one China, one Taiwan," or an "independent Taiwan." The U.S. statement went on to say, however, that the United States

reaffirms its interest in the peaceful settlement of the Taiwan question by the Chinese themselves. *With this prospect in mind* [emphasis added], it affirms the ultimate objective of the withdrawal of all U.S. forces and military installations from Taiwan. In the meantime, it will progressively reduce its forces and military installations on Taiwan as the tension in the area diminishes. (See appendix A for the full text of the communiqué.)

With these words, the United States began to take itself out of the Taiwan Strait, both figuratively and ultimately militarily, as an arbiter of Taiwan's future. At the same time, this formula made everything the United States was doing or would do militarily about Taiwan contingent on China's maintenance of a peaceful environment in the Taiwan Strait. If China were to insist on its right to use force against Taiwan and back up its words with military concentrations and/or operations, all bets would be off.

It was a great relief that the Chinese were willing to accept such a formulation. Kissinger deserves maximum credit for devising this way out of a painful dilemma, but Chinese willingness to compromise helped greatly. In these deliberations, it became evident that the Chinese badly wanted a joint communiqué that would suit the needs of both parties; they were prepared to meet us at least halfway to achieve their goal. While the Soviet Union did not have a representative sitting at our conference table, the threat to China of Soviet armed forces stationed along China's borders made the USSR an unseen player.

Meanwhile, other members of the president's party were going through a last-minute convulsion. The State Department contingent had not had the opportunity to inspect the draft communiqué until it was handed to

Secretary Rogers on the flight from Beijing to Hangzhou. Having been excluded from all the give-and-take, he and Assistant Secretary Green interposed several objections to the wording. Two elements above all caught Marshall Green's eye, and Secretary Rogers relayed them to the president through a reluctant Henry Kissinger. The first, in the section dealing with Taiwan, spoke of all "people" on either side of the Taiwan Strait regarding Taiwan as part of China (see preceding section). State objected to the word "people," maintaining that the inhabitants of Taiwan who looked upon the island as their home regardless of the point of origin in China of their ancestors, and who regarded themselves as "Taiwanese," would not necessarily agree that Taiwan was part of China. Satisfactory substitute wording was found by changing the word "people" to "Chinese," a proposal carried to Qiao Guanhua (and certainly through him to Zhou Enlai) that quickly gained Chinese acceptance.

The other point was more difficult. In the original draft of the communiqué as it was handed to Secretary Rogers, the United States reaffirmed continued support for the security obligations it maintained with Japan, South Korea (the Republic of Korea), the Philippines, the Southeast Asia Treaty Organization (SEATO), and the Australia–New Zealand–U.S. (ANZUS) treaty, but no mention was made of U.S. obligations under its security treaty with the Republic of China on Taiwan. According to Marshall Green, "This omission would certainly have been seized upon by the world press, and especially by those in the Republican party opposed to the president's trip [Green referred in particular to Vice President Agnew and Treasury Secretary John Connolly] to charge that the president had sold Taiwan down the river."[4]

According to Kissinger, when he raised the secretary's objection with the president, a near-explosion took place, for the president knew the wording was by that time already considered final by the Chinese, but he feared that returning home to the United States with a divided delegation would not bode well for broad-spectrum political acceptance of the terms of the communiqué.[5] Some kind of accommodation was necessary, though the president was loathe to ask for more concessions from the Chinese at that late date.

Dr. Kissinger did, in fact, seek out Qiao Guanhua for changes in the wording of the text, and he succeeded, with additional difficult negotiations, in obtaining an adjustment that reaffirmed in more general terms the special relationships that existed between the United States and several Asian countries with which we had bilateral military agreements, including the Republic of Korea and Japan, and that advocated a cease-fire between India and Pakistan in Kashmir. The Chinese would accept no mention of any U.S. security obligations to Taiwan; instead, the United States dropped the original sentence referring to specific U.S. security commitments in Asia.

There was a danger, albeit remote, that the omission of reference in the communiqué to the Mutual Defense Treaty with Taiwan, or the Republic of China, could turn the clock back to January 1950, when both President Truman and Dean Acheson had left South Korea and Taiwan outside the region of vital U.S. military concern, possibly contributing to the outbreak of the Korean War (see chapter 1). Since China would not budge on the point of specifically mentioning the U.S. military agreement with Taiwan in the communiqué, Kissinger addressed the State Department's concerns by deciding that in his briefing of the media he would make reference to the treaty with Taiwan. At the conclusion of his negotiations with the vice foreign minister, he informed Qiao of his intentions and of his hope that there would be no reaction from the Chinese. Qiao replied that he "would rely on [Kissinger's] tact."[6] Once again, Chinese flexibility had been displayed, although it was undoubtedly stretched thin.

Issuance of the "Shanghai Communiqué"

After our near all-night vigil at Hangzhou spent fine-tuning with the Chinese wording that we on the U.S. negotiating team believed would fully satisfy our needs, the presidential party reassembled on the morning of 27 February and went on to Shanghai, where we were met by Zhang Chunqiao, who, as mentioned earlier, was one of the so-called "Gang of Four." Despite Zhang's words of welcome, which included a banquet speech that evening to acclaim President Nixon's visit, he must have been, to use the Chinese expression "eating bitterness." But he performed his task with no apparent reservations. He had also scheduled an exhibition of Chinese acrobatics (*za ji*) for the Nixon party after the banquet that evening at a theater near the former Broadway Mansions Hotel. We all enjoyed that exhibition; the skill of the performers was simply stupendous.

As for the communiqué, with all last-minute obstacles gone, Chas Freeman and I were able to go over it word for word to assure that the Chinese matched the English, although we had confidence in the competence and integrity of the Chinese translators who had prepared the Chinese version of the document. We never did have problems with the Chinese with regard to accurate translations. (I was given to understand that the Soviets frequently played games of this sort, that is, not matching the Russian text with the English.)

The actual issuance of the joint communiqué, which was followed by a media briefing, took place on the afternoon of 28 February 1972, in a theater on the grounds of the Jinjiang Hotel (the Cathay Mansions before "liberation") where the entire U.S. party was billeted in Shanghai. Thus, the joint communiqué acquired the appellation "the Shanghai Communiqué" that has been used ever since. Both Dr. Kissinger and Marshall Green did the briefing, the latter handicapped by his noninvolvement in the communiqué's formulation. The task of reaffirming the East Asian defense commitments, including the one with Taiwan, was left to Kissinger, who faced a question "planted" with a friendly reporter, David Kraslow of the *Los Angeles Times*: "Why did not the U.S. government affirm its treaty commitment to Taiwan, as the president and you have done on numerous occasions?" Kissinger replied that this issue was an extraordinarily difficult one to discuss at that time and in that place, but went on to note words to the effect that "we stated our basic position with respect to this issue in the President's World Report [that is, his Annual Report to the Congress on Foreign Policy], in which we said that treaty would be maintained. Nothing has changed on that position." Kissinger went on to add that he hoped that this was all he would have to say on this subject. His request was respected.

On the whole, the briefing was quite a mob scene, with many questions hurled at the briefers from U.S. reporters all too anxious to find fault. The television reporter Barbara Walters tried to sneak out ahead of the others and score a "scoop" with her network, but when I caught her in the lobby of the theater nearly hidden (or disguised?) in a huge Chinese leather and wool overcoat, she did heed my polite suggestion that she return to the briefing.

As the American saying goes, "It was all over but the shouting." On the morning of 29 February, the presidential party and the press boarded our respective vehicles for the trip to Shanghai's Hongqiao Airport, but not before the president had personally thanked the entire hotel staff for their courtesy by shaking their hands. This made quite a scene before we departed the Jinjiang Hotel, since the Chinese were all lined up along the driveway in order of rank, from cooks to room attendants to bellhops. At the airport there was no formal send-off, but everyone, Chinese officials, U.S. government officials, airport personnel, Pan Am flight crews, media people, to the number of hundreds, were all mixed together with broad smiles and a vast sense of relief as President and Mrs. Nixon went up the ramp of Air Force One and waved good-bye. The trip had occurred, had been genuinely successful (even though it took the *Washington Post* and the *New York Times* several weeks to accept this), and a new era had definitely been launched in U.S.-China relations. The sense of euphoria was pervasive, and we who had been involved in the trip in our various capacities boarded our aircraft with a sense of immense accomplishment.

The president's successful visit to China and the issuance of the Shanghai Communiqué had opened up a new fruitful period for relations between the two countries. In addition, China's sense of insecurity about the Soviet Union must have been eased considerably by the Shanghai Communiqué now that the United States had become more of a friend than an adversary, and ultimate normalization of diplomatic relations had been accepted as a goal by both parties. This shift was also advantageous to the United States. The addition of China to what had been a bilateral U.S.-Soviet confrontation could only have complicated Soviet strategic calculations. Furthermore, the Shanghai Communiqué, as well as China's being seated in the UN, helped to turn China away from its preoccupation with internal problems and encourage it to become a much more positive and outward-looking contributor to the world community of nations—a U.S. objective from the very beginning of our negotiations.

One small sign of China's turning outward was that the Chinese asked the RCA Corporation, which had set up a ground station for satellite communications in Shanghai to cover the Nixon visit, to leave the station in place. RCA later became a further beneficiary of China's new attitude and a harbinger of greatly expanded U.S.-China trade in future years because of the help it had provided. The use of Boeing 707s by the Nixon party, whether in U.S. Air Force or Pan Am markings, may well have been what tilted China in Boeing's direction when China ordered ten 707s from Boeing for what was then its only airline, CAAC (Civil Aviation Administration of China). Significant gains for both China and the United States were plainly inherent in the Shanghai Communiqué.

Chapter 6

Following Up the Nixon Visit

A Briefing Tour of East and Southeast Asia

For Assistant Secretary of State Marshall Green and me, the Nixon visit to China did not conclude with the flight from Shanghai to Washington in what the presidential party certainly regarded as a triumphal return. President Nixon had wisely, as it proved, decided that U.S. friends and allies in East Asia should be briefed on his trip and on the Shanghai Communiqué. Green and I were designated to do the briefing. To fulfill this task, we flew to Tokyo on the president's backup aircraft, along with many of the White House staffers, which created a precedent in our flying directly north from Shanghai to Tokyo over South Korean airspace. (China and South Korea did not maintain diplomatic relations.) The alternative was to exit east from Shanghai, which would have required a long dog-leg in our flight pattern and several extra hours. In the atmosphere of good feeling between Chinese and Americans generated by the issuance of the Shanghai Communiqué, Zhou Enlai interposed no objection to the U.S. use of this flight pattern.

This direct flight from Shanghai to Tokyo made the contrast between the two particularly striking: In departing from China, we had left a country whose physical appearance hadn't changed very much from what I had remembered in 1937 or after the end of the Pacific War in 1947, when I was there on "R and R" from South Korea. Shanghai, except for the Soviet-designed Sino-Soviet Friendship Building, now termed the "Industrial Exhibition Hall," appeared exactly as I had remembered it from earlier years, only shabbier, and Beijing, in its back streets away from the government center and drab Soviet-style apartment blocks, still remained in large part a city of single-story mud or stone-walled structures reached by narrow, unpaved *hutungs*, or lanes. Hangzhou, while beautiful, had scarcely changed in two hundred years. In enormous contrast, when we crossed over the mainland of Japan and reached the Kanto plain, we were treated to a spectacle of a country undergoing phenomenal growth, with modern buildings of all descriptions coming into view, including factories, apartments, schools, bridges, and roads choked with every kind of motor vehicle. Looking down at all this energy, I couldn't help but think of what China might have become had it not been diverted by years of warlordism, civil war, and ideological extremism, and had it followed instead a course of development something like Japan's after the Meiji Restoration.

We deplaned at Yokota AFB outside Tokyo. From there we were to pick up a small U.S. Air Force jet and, starting with briefings in Japan, go on to South Korea, Taiwan, the Philippines, South Vietnam, Thailand, Malaysia, Singapore, Indonesia, Australia, and New Zealand. (No leg of our journey could last more than four hours, since the aircraft, while seating four people comfortably, had the disadvantage of possessing no toilet facilities.) Altogether, this areawide briefing would require nearly a month.

Marshall Green was met at Tokyo by his wife, Lisa, who would go along to look after his health and socialize with U.S. ambassadors' wives whom we would encounter on the trip. Green's staff assistant, Paul Cleveland (later ambassador to New Zealand and Malaysia), was also to accompany us. I was the only representative from the NSC, but having taken part in the Zhou Enlai-Nixon talks, I was perhaps in a better position than Green to address some particular concerns from our friends, such as whether or not their country was mentioned in the talks.

Our purpose was to reassure our friends and allies in Asia that their interests had not been sacrificed by the Nixon visit and the Shanghai Communiqué, but on the contrary, had been advanced as a result of the reduced tensions throughout the region that we foresaw due to the rapprochement between the two countries and the peaceful environment we anticipated would be maintained in the Taiwan Strait area. China, we believed, would hardly have agreed to the Shanghai Communiqué's language had it intended in the foreseeable future to resort to force in this area, above all in the Taiwan Strait. Understandably, convincing our allies was not an easy task, since China remained an ally of North Korea and North Vietnam and had troops in Laos, and since possible Chinese external aggression was one of the reasons SEATO (the Southeast Asia Treaty Organization) had been created in the first place.

In Japan, we briefed the Gaimusho's (Foreign Ministry's) foremost China expert, Hashimoto, and several of his colleagues. I have no doubt that while Hashimoto accepted our assurances of improved regional stability at face value, he was personally upset that a visit to China at the highest level had been made by the United States and not Japan. Japan was already preparing to open diplomatic relations with China, assuring that in this respect, at least, Japan would get there before the United States. The exchange of Japan's and China's ambassadors took place in October 1972 following a September visit to Beijing by the Japanese prime minister, Kakuei Tanaka.

Our next stop was Seoul. Of all the briefings we gave, the one with South Korean Foreign Minister Kim Yong Shik was the toughest. He grilled us for nearly three hours, and the series of questions he asked covered every aspect of the trip and every hypothetical situation he could envisage. His concern was understandable, thanks to Chinese identification with North Korea, which by 1972 had already amassed a record of annual military maneuvers and actual small-scale military incursions against the South that were hard to overlook (including the U.S.S. *Pueblo* incident). He was little soothed by our assurances that both the United States and China had declared during the Zhou-Nixon talks that we favored stability and not conflict on the Korean Peninsula. But we parted as friends, and no official outcry from South Korea followed against the Shanghai Communiqué. We also met in Seoul with then-president Park Chong Hee, who was well known to Marshall Green from the time of the May 1961 coup; Park simply expressed concern over the kind of reception we would have in Taiwan.

Taiwan, which was our next stop and the one that we had expected to be the most difficult, turned out to be less of an ordeal than South Korea. There we met with Premier Chiang Ching-kuo, President Chiang Kai-shek's eldest son. With Chiang Ching-kuo, the real power, we pointed to the open-ended nature of our talk of normalization with China and the continued validity of the U.S.–Republic of China Mutual Defense Treaty as it had been obliquely reiterated by Dr. Kissinger in Shanghai. We also stressed the section of the Shanghai Communiqué that made everything regarding Taiwan contingent upon the maintenance of a peaceful environment in the Taiwan Strait. Chiang's response was to me extremely interesting: he pointed to a model of a Lockheed U-2 surveillance aircraft on the mantelpiece of the old-fashioned fireplace in his office in the presidential office building (the *"Tsung T'ung Fu"*) and stated that as long as that remained, there would be no problem. I assume that what Chiang had in mind was not the U-2 per se, but the assurance of no break in the flow of military equipment that Taiwan was receiving from the United States. The U-2 model was a symbol of this military aid.

We also met with the ROC foreign minister and were hosted at lunch
by Deputy Foreign Minister Fred Chien, later Taiwan's foreign minister,
who was clearly unreconciled to the United States's improved relationship with China. In his parting words with the foreign minister, Marshall
Green urged that Taiwan not unleash major criticisms over the Shanghai
Communiqué, since this might tend to alienate its many friends in the
United States. Taiwan heeded these words.[1]

In contrast to our unexpectedly low-key response in Taiwan, our reception in the Philippines was one step short of pandemonium. Green and our
ambassador to the Philippines, Henry Byroade, were served with a sub-
poena to appear before the Philippine Senate the following day to explain
how the United States was "reneging on its two-China policy," and there
were calls for the Philippines to follow its own line and recognize China.
As I look back on this scene, I assume that what particularly bothered the
Filipinos was that they had been blind-sided by their big friend, the United
States. According to Green's account, the Philippine press was shrill in
calling for a deal with Beijing, and Hank Byroade told him that Mrs. Marcos had in fact just taken off for that destination and to meet Mao.[2] (I
believe, however, that she did not travel to Beijing and meet Mao Zedong
until after our liaison office opened in that city the following year.) Green
and Byroade received the lion's share of the flak, but my time came in a
press conference staged in the American embassy in which I, too, had to
take my share of intemperate questioning. We did succeed, nevertheless, in
lowering the high tide of criticism directed at the United States and at U.S.-
Philippine relations, following the lines used with other allies in Asia.

No particular problems occurred in our briefings in South Vietnam,
nor in Thailand, Cambodia, and Laos. Perhaps the Buddhist background
of these last three countries, as well as their close dependence on the
United States for military and economic assistance, accounted for their
relative calm. Cambodia's head of state, Lon Nol, was recovering from a
heart attack in the U.S. Army's Tripler General Hospital outside Honolulu during our visit to Cambodia, so we were met by Acting President
Sirik Matak in the presidential office. (Sirik Matak was a thoroughly ad-
mirable human being, who upon Lon Nol's return dropped back to a
lesser position as foreign minister and was patriotic enough to stay behind
when Phnom Penh fell to the Khmer Rouge in April 1975. For this act
of patriotism, he was shot by the Khmer Rouge.) Matak accepted our
explanations quite readily. At the time of our visit, the Khmer Rouge were
close enough to the airport to require us to take off quickly and climb
sharply. In Laos, where Ambassador Godley took us to see Prime Minister Souvanna Phouma, the atmosphere was friendly and receptive. Our

Thai friends, Prime Minister Thanom, Foreign Minister Thanat, and Air Chief Marshall Dawee, were more skeptical but prepared to give the Shanghai Communiqué a try.

In Malaysia, Prime Minister Hussein Onn was a polite and philosophic listener, and we had no real problems, despite the Chinese Communist-generated insurgency that had been going on for years. (As of 1972, a few "terrorists" were still holding out in the jungles of northern Malaysia with their leader, Chin Peng.) Onn looked to the future, and indeed, Malaysia under his successor was the first Southeast Asian nation to recognize Beijing. A beautiful collection of *kris*, or Malay swords, which Prime Minister Onn had assembled in the study where we met for our talks, served as a backdrop for our conversation.

Singapore, where we met with Prime Minister Lee Kuan Yew, was another story. Prime Minister Lee remarked that we had "just sprung the trap" on our friends in the region. Although cordial enough, he appeared suspicious of Beijing's ultimate intentions. History shows that Singapore long retained its suspicions about China and was the last ASEAN (Association of Southeast Asian Nations) country to recognize Beijing, even though it eventually permitted a branch of the (People's) Bank of China to function in Singapore and also set up trade offices with Beijing. Lee's particular problem was that about three-quarters of Singapore's population was of Chinese origin, and Singapore's officials suffered from pervasive fears as to where the sympathies lay within this element of the population. (Singapore-China relations are now quite close.)

In Indonesia, Secretary Green had to rise at 5:30 A.M from his bed at the embassy residence, where we stayed, to meet with Foreign Minister Adam Malik and other officials during a round of golf, played early in order to avoid the equatorial heat. (Malik was an especially good friend of Green, dating back to Green's time as ambassador to Indonesia.) Not being a golfer myself, I remained at the embassy residence and hence avoided the heavy tropical downpour that took place during their game. Green reappeared at about 8:30, looking thoroughly bedraggled and covered with wet mud from head to toe—hardly the image of a "striped-pants diplomat"! Although the Indonesians seemed to take the Shanghai Communiqué in stride, I recall stopping there some years later for a luncheon with the chief of military intelligence, who upon our arrival had a wall curtain pulled aside to show a mural of King Gajah Mada of the Majapahit Dynasty repelling a Chinese invasion in East Java during the Yuan Dynasty. Given Indonesian suspicions about Chinese complicity in the abortive 30 September 1965, coup and the heavy economic influence of Indonesia's Chinese population, such misgivings were understandable.

Indonesia was the next-to-last ASEAN country to establish, or, more accurately, restore, diplomatic relations with Beijing.

Australia and New Zealand were simply too far away for our four-hour government jet, so we traveled to both countries by commercial aircraft. Neither the Australians nor the New Zealanders posed any criticisms, and both seemed content to accept our assurances of keeping our military presence in East Asia and maintaining the balance of power. Marshall Green did his bit for U.S. diplomacy by playing golf with senior officials in both countries.

We briefed Australian Prime Minister William McMahon in Sydney, where he happened to be at the time, and also went to Canberra to talk to the leader of Australia's Country Party, the government being composed of a Liberal (read conservative) and Country alliance. The Country Party was anxious to see normalization of Australian-Chinese relations to sell China more of Australia's farm products, such as wheat. The Australians were under some domestic pressure from both parties to normalize relations with Beijing, and indeed, when the U.S. Liaison Office was set up in 1975, an Australian embassy was already doing business.

We found the New Zealanders fairly well wrapped up in domestic maneuverings between their Labor and Conservative parties. Nevertheless we met with both the prime minister, John K. ("Jim") Marshall, and Foreign Minister Sir Keith Holyoke. The impending elections seemed to preoccupy them more than our relations with China.

And finally, home. Marshall Green and I met with President Nixon on 23 March to report on the reaction of those we had briefed, and Green notes that Al Haig, Henry Kissinger's deputy, was also present. The president's concern was that when Green appeared before committees on Capitol Hill or on "Meet the Press," he not play up the Taiwan element; Green succeeded in following the president's wishes.[3]

For both of us, a long, tiring, but exhilarating episode had come to an end. I cannot in all honesty say that those with whom we discussed the president's China visit and the Shanghai Communiqué were convinced that our policy was correct, but they refrained from either panic or anti-American invective at the worst, and at the best, kept their equanimity and—especially in Australia and New Zealand—appeared willing to allow the new U.S. relationship with China time in which to show whatever forward steps had been gained towards a more peaceful East Asian region.

The Shanghai Communiqué and Vietnam's "Easter Offensive"

Scarcely had Secretary Green and I returned from our briefing tour before the Shanghai Communiqué, with its higher priority on China's relations with the United States than with its communist ally Vietnam, was put to the test. On 30 March coincidental with the celebration of Easter in Christian countries, the North Vietnamese began a major offensive against the South using regular North Vietnamese troops, attacking strategic areas running from the central highlands all the way to the Demilitarized Zone (DMZ). This offensive mustered enough strength to take Quang Tri City near the DMZ and to threaten the entire U.S.-South Vietnamese military presence in these areas, and it menaced the whole program of "Vietnamization," which may well have been one of its main purposes. The North Vietnamese surely must also have hoped to score an impressive military victory over the combined U.S. and South Vietnamese forces.

I also speculate that the Vietnamese were attempting, along with their other military and political objectives, to disrupt the budding ties between the United States and China. The significance of the Shanghai Communiqué as it affected China's priorities towards North Vietnam must not have been lost on the North Vietnamese. Their offensive was by no means a Viet Cong, or guerrilla operation, since the Viet Cong infrastructure and fighting capability had been virtually destroyed with the 1968 Tet Offensive; the so-called "Easter Offensive" of 1972 involved North Vietnamese regulars almost exclusively.

The Nixon administration, under the personal leadership of the president, reacted vigorously. Restrictions were removed on bombing areas such as rail centers in Hanoi and the Haiphong dockyards; roads and bridges between the Chinese border and the Hanoi-Haiphong area that hitherto had been off limits to aerial attack were targeted; and the port of Haiphong was mined by air, using a type of mine, the Mark Four Destructor, that could be set to explode by either magnetic or acoustic impulses and could also be set to allow the passage of a number of ships before exploding, thereby impeding countermine operations from locating and removing the destructors. Actually, no ship moved in or out of Haiphong Harbor from the date of the mining until the end of the conflict, when the United States itself removed the mines as part of the armistice agreement. (Interestingly, as early as the end of 1969 the question of mining Haiphong Harbor had been debated at length in the White House situation room among representatives of the Department of Defense, the CIA, and the NSC—I had sat in on these early discussions. Plans for mining Haiphong Harbor had been drawn up for contingency use but never employed.) The flow of supplies to the North Vietnamese forces was greatly impeded by all these measures.

As the North Vietnamese offensive began, Dr. Kissinger became very concerned about the possible adverse political effects of the greatly enhanced U.S. countermeasures on the political relationship we had just established with China, and on the U.S.-Soviet summit meetings scheduled for May. Since Vietnam was presumably an ally of both China and the Soviet Union, would the Chinese repudiate the Shanghai Communiqué? Would the Soviets call off the summit meetings, which were, among other things, expected to discuss arms reductions?

Before the die had been cast and U.S. forces carried out orders to broaden the air war against North Vietnam and mine Haiphong, on a Saturday afternoon in early April, an uncharacteristically disturbed Kissinger summoned a group of people, myself included, from the NSC and the CIA to the White House situation room to ask our opinion of what the Chinese and Soviet reactions might be. I believe that he was taken aback to discover that of all those present, only one individual, Winston Lord, interposed any objections to the stepped-up use of force.[4] (Lord has told me that his concerns related to the Soviets' possible cancellation of the U.S.-Soviet summit conference in May.)

Several of us took the position that both China and the Soviet Union contained many vested interests in keeping communications open with the United States. When my turn came to be questioned by Kissinger, I called attention to the way in which the Chinese, in the Shanghai Communiqué, had placed a higher priority on relations with the United States than with Vietnam, in all likelihood due chiefly to concern over its tense relations with the Soviet Union; China, having made such a dramatic change in its long-standing policy to establish ties with the United States, would probably confine its reactions to expressions of rhetorical support for Vietnam but would not otherwise intervene. My NSC colleague who handled Soviet affairs, Helmut Sonnenfeldt, took the position that the Soviets also had a decided interest in keeping the May talks on schedule and would interpose no major difficulties.

In his book *The Price of Power,* Seymour Hersh inexplicably blamed the near-total staff backing for the U.S. escalation in the war on the military background of four of those present, including me.[5] On this point, he was way off the mark. Those of us endorsing the administration's policy were doing so essentially on political grounds, not because we were a bloodthirsty gang of militarists bent on Hanoi's destruction. The United States's failure to respond vigorously to Hanoi's offensive would have suggested weakness, thus vitiating the balancing role that China wanted the United States to play vis-à-vis the Soviet Union. Such a failure also would have caused the Soviets to be all the tougher in reaching agreements on crucial matters such as arms control.

My own prediction proved correct. China unleashed a few cannons of empty rhetoric in the *People's Daily* and other CCP publications about being a "reliable rear area" for Vietnam, but that was it. No perceptible damage was done to the U.S.-China relationship, although I have no doubt that behind the scenes those in China who were basically opposed to the opening to the United States in the first place argued for a more tangible Chinese reaction to the situation in Vietnam. At any rate, the Chinese priorities established in the Shanghai Communiqué held: China's relations with the United States and movement on the Taiwan question outranked its possible consideration of military intervention on behalf of North Vietnam. Kissinger writes in *White House Years* that he sent Winston Lord to New York to warn China's UN representative, Huang Hua, to tell Beijing not to interfere in Vietnam,[6] but I am not at all convinced that this trip was necessary. In fact, it could have been regarded by the Chinese as a superfluous and egregious interference in their internal affairs. On the other hand, a prior nod to the Chinese as to what we were planning to do would probably have been welcome, if, as Al Haig has alleged, the Chinese virtually endorsed a U.S. victory over Hanoi.

Seemingly undeterred by the stepped-up U.S. military pressure, the North Vietnamese maintained their own increased military activities. It was in this atmosphere that Dr. Kissinger was negotiating with Le Duc Tho in Paris in the fall of 1972, and in September and October, the North Vietnamese actually made some concessions on conditions for ending the war, which were accepted by Dr. Kissinger. However, by November the North Vietnamese had backed away from many of these concessions, providing further impetus to our enhanced military response. The pattern of escalation led eventually to the so-called "Christmas bombings," in which U.S. B-52 strategic bombers were used against such targets as the Hanoi rail marshaling yards. Public criticism burst forth in the United States, where many had long been opposed to U.S. involvement in Vietnam. Critics of the "Christmas bombings" may say what they please, but by January 1973 the North Vietnamese political conditions for ending the fighting were back to where they had been in September and October 1972. The Paris accords were concluded shortly thereafter, ending the U.S. role in the Vietnam fighting, even though the war itself continued, with North Vietnamese fighting South Vietnamese supported by U.S. military advisers, for more than two years.

Two More Visits to China

The months of April and May of 1972 saw the White House preoccupied both with the North Vietnamese military offensive and with the Moscow summit; by June the situation in Vietnam had largely been stabilized and the Moscow summit had taken place, both to the satisfaction of the United States. In the meantime, though, events in Japan began to demand attention. Japanese Prime Minister Sato had been replaced by Kakuei Tanaka, known in Japan as "the computerized bulldozer" for his hard-driving but astute ways of doing business. About this time, the United States also began to be conscious of an unfavorable balance of trade with Japan, which in those days was regarded as intolerable—a full 3 billion dollars!

Consequently, it became expedient to pay more attention to Japan. At the same time, Dr. Kissinger wanted to maintain and develop the China connection and to brief the Chinese on the May U.S.-Soviet summit talks. As a result, preparations were made for a Kissinger trip to China and Japan in June 1972. Another trip to both China and Japan was later arranged for February 1973.

I had a special mission to perform in connection with the June 1972 trip: to leave for Japan ahead of the rest of the Kissinger party and inform Prime Minister Tanaka privately that the 3 billion dollar unfavorable trade balance was "unacceptable." This mission was accomplished by my going to Tanaka's private residence deep in Tokyo well after dark to pass the word. With me was an embassy interpreter and Robert Ingersoll, the U.S. ambassador to Japan, in whose embassy residence I stayed—or, more accurately, hid out—until I could meet with Tanaka. Tanaka's response was essentially a loud grunt, but it indicated that he had received the message and presumably would act on it. More discussions on this subject were to take place at a conference in the Kuilima Hotel in Oahu, Hawaii, between 30 August and 1 September and again at Nixon's San Clemente Western White House in January 1973. After my own meeting with Tanaka, I waited for Kissinger to arrive, to accompany him on to Beijing.

The most important outcome of the June 1972 talks in Beijing was that the U.S.-China relationship was being maintained in the wake of Vietnam's offensive. In keeping with past practice, Dr. Kissinger briefed Zhou Enlai on the U.S.-Soviet summit talks in Moscow. As before, the real manager of the Sino-U.S. relationship was Zhou Enlai rather than Mao Zedong; however, it was noticeable in our talks of June 1972 and February 1973 that Zhou was beginning to show signs of the illness—prostate cancer, although we didn't know it at the time—that eventually caused his death. At one point in the talks, carried on as usual on either side of a long green baize-covered table, a nurse unobtrusively came into the room and handed Zhou a pill, which he took.

It was during this period of talks that I obtained some idea of the unique influence that Wang Hairong, a relative of Mao Zedong, exercised in what might be considered a fairly normal diplomatic exchange.[7] In one of the meetings, Zhou had made some remark concerning the size of the Soviet embassy in Beijing, which included his estimate that in it the Soviets had over 100 automobiles. At this point, Wang Hairong got up, left the room for a few moments, and then returned with a piece of paper, which she handed to Zhou. Zhou read the paper, and told us that he stood corrected, the actual number of automobiles in the Soviet embassy was several more than he had stated in the first place. The point impressed us as trivial, and Zhou's courtesy to Wang Hairong rather extraordinary. But she was Mao Zedong's mother's grandniece, and her influence had to be acknowledged even by such a senior personage as Zhou Enlai.

On the bilateral side, in June 1972 Kissinger raised the matter of American detainees in China, who included two pilots shot down over Manchuria during the Korean War, and John N. Downey, a "U.S. government employee" who had also been shot down over Manchuria during the Korean War and sentenced to life imprisonment for espionage. The two pilots were released fairly promptly. Downey, an admitted CIA officer, whose sentence, remitted to twenty years, was to expire in 1973, was released early on "humanitarian grounds" to be with his ill mother. Once again, the Chinese demonstrated flexibility towards the United States.

Another bilateral issue left over from the Nixon visit, raised in the June talks and eventually settled in the February talks, was the question of U.S. claims against China for seized property, versus the question of Chinese assets that the United States had frozen following China's entry into the Korean War. Secretary Rogers and Foreign Minister Ji Pengfei had discussed the issue during the Nixon visit, but without resolution. Eventually, in February 1973, at the suggestion of the United States, the two sides simply agreed that the frozen assets would be exchanged for the seized property. For the Americans who had claims, this would amount to about 40 cents on the dollar in 1973 dollars. When this proposal was made, Zhang Wenjin, then presiding over the Chinese team, said, "Ah, you want a political solution to an economic question." We agreed that such was the case. Dr. Kissinger was not present on this occasion, and I represented the United States, assisted by Al Jenkins of the State Department. For Kissinger, the high point of the February visit was a two-hour meeting with Mao Zedong, in which the two reviewed U.S. and Chinese strategic relations with the Soviet Union.

Following the June 1972 Beijing visit, Kissinger returned to the United States via Japan, where the aircraft landed at Tokyo's Haneda Airport, for a brief meeting with Foreign Minister Masayoshi Ohira, who impressed

Kissinger mightily. This less-than-one-day effort was intended to ease criticisms from both the "Japan hands" in State and the Japanese themselves that Japan—clearly an economic and political power in East Asia—was being downgraded in U.S. policy. Our brief stop in Japan was followed by a two-day visit in February 1973, a longer time span that was more satisfactory to the Japanese because it was more respectful of Japanese dignity and importance.

Kissinger's February 1973 visit to China was by way of Paris and then Hanoi for discussions with the top Vietnamese leaders on their home ground about such matters as "healing the wounds of war" through such devices as expressing a willingness to ask Congress for $5 billion to be divided between North and South for reconstruction. This offer, I believe, was the source of (North) Vietnam's contention that the United States was prepared to pay "reparations," which was hardly the case. In any event, the North Vietnamese attack on the South in April 1975, together with failure to account for POWs and MIAs in accordance with the Paris agreement, mooted the question of reparations or payments to heal war wounds.[8] By making the longer Japan visit on the way home from China in February 1973, Kissinger was responding to continued hints from the Japanese, and even from the Chinese that U.S. policy was neglectful of Japan. The Japanese press was also heavily critical, although thanks to Kissinger's awe-inspiring political performance, he was often likened to a traditional Japanese Ninja.

The two-day February stop in Japan gave Ninja Kissinger an opportunity to pay courtesy calls on the most senior Japanese officials. One of these calls was made via a flight by U.S. helicopter to Karuizawa, over one hundred miles from Tokyo, where Prime Minister Tanaka, an avid golfer, maintained a residence on the edge of one of the major golf courses in the area. This visit was memorable only for being the third of three contacts Kissinger had with the prime minister, the first having been at the Kuilima Hotel in Oahu, Hawaii, in August 1972, in which U. Alexis Johnson had arranged with Tanaka for a U.S. aircraft carrier, the *Midway*, to be homeported at the former Japanese naval base of Yokusuka; the second contact had taken place during Tanaka's visit to San Clemente just a month earlier, in January 1973.

While in Tokyo in February, Dr. Kissinger's time was heavily taken up with protocol affairs such as a luncheon at the Okura Hotel with Keidanren, the Association of Japanese Manufacturers, where some U.S. views on U.S.-Japan trade could be aired. We also achieved something of a record by going to two formal Japanese-style dinners in one night, complete with geishas. I do remember the shock delivered to the Japanese security agents, not to mention the members of our party, when a lone Japanese in the hallway outside the Hotel Okura restaurant shouted imprecations and threw an object at Kissinger following the Keidanren luncheon; fortunately this object was a roll of toilet paper and not a bomb. Kissinger also met again with Foreign Minister Ohira, a very impressive and straightforward individual, who in due course became Japan's prime minister and one of the United States's best friends in Japan.

We had come a long way in 1972, but 1973 was the year in which we achieved truly striking progress of a practical nature, as opposed to mere politics, in bringing the United States and China closer together. It was in the February 1973 Zhou-Kissinger talks in China that the two sides reached the agreement for the United States and China to set up "liaison offices" in each other's capital. Within a few months those liaison offices were up and operating in both Washington and in Beijing.

Chapter 7

Opening the Liaison Offices

Zhou Enlai Opts for Liaison Offices
in Beijing and Washington

Unquestionably the most significant aspect of the February 1973 Kissinger trip to China was the decision to set up U.S. and Chinese "liaison offices" in Beijing and Washington, respectively. It had become evident to both sides from previous Kissinger visits that the time had come to put our relationship on a more permanent basis than that achieved by U.S. officials making periodic trips to China.

Prior to leaving for China in February 1973, Dr. Kissinger had asked me to draw up an options paper setting forth what kinds of missions might be established. We started from the fact that the lack of normal diplomatic relations made establishing formal embassies impossible. My thoughts had accordingly turned to the kinds of solutions other countries had used or might consider using under similar circumstances to maintain contacts at official, but less than diplomatic, levels: these included trade missions, "interest sections" of the type we had set up in Cuba, liaison offices that would be staffed by resident diplomats—a concept hitherto unknown in diplomatic history—and most unlikely, consulates, which would not necessarily carry the status of diplomatic missions.

Of the various options I presented to Kissinger, I believed that the trade mission approach offered the best chance of success. The Japanese had maintained such a relationship with China for years before 1972 with their "Liao-Takasaki" offices in Beijing and Tokyo, which had been established through theoretically nonofficial channels under the auspices of a "friendship" association on the Chinese side and a "private" business group on the Japanese side. I calculated that such an approach would offer the least political difficulty for the Chinese. Kissinger proposed such an exchange of trade missions to Zhou Enlai as his first option. Therefore, it was with considerable surprise—and pleasure—that I heard Zhou's much more forthcoming position on the matter.

After listening to Kissinger and considering the various alternatives, Zhou unhesitatingly picked the liaison office route. Moreover, after some reflection, Zhou not only requested "reciprocity" in the form of a Chinese liaison office in Washington to match a U.S. liaison office in Beijing, but he promptly laid out the parameters of the liaison offices we would set up: diplomatic privileges, flying our national flags, secure communications, security guards from our respective establishments, and help from the host nation in acquiring residential and office space. Further, he pressed for opening these offices as soon as possible. With a certain amount of checking on our side, we concluded that because of our own bureaucratic concerns, mid-May was about the earliest that the offices could be established; Kissinger and Zhou then agreed that we would immediately begin the process of setting them up.

To me, it was evident that Zhou was anxious to see the liaison offices in place and working as soon as the necessary arrangements could be made. I can only surmise that Zhou's acceptance of what to all intents and purposes was an exchange of diplomatic missions (even though at a level less than embassy status and in the absence of formal diplomatic relations), and his apparent eagerness to see the liaison offices established, reflected some of the internal convolutions in the Chinese political scene that were not apparent to outsiders. At the minimum, Zhou wanted the U.S. flag to be flying in Beijing in a way that carried some weight behind it. Of course, from our own standpoint, we were happy to oblige.

Setting Up Shop

Therefore, upon our return to Washington, we plunged into the arrangements for setting up our own liaison office in Beijing, and we put considerable effort into locating a place for the Chinese to establish their liaison office. We discovered that the Windsor Park Hotel in Washington was up for sale and conveyed this information to the Chinese, who found the premises ideal, being large enough both for office space and for staff housing, and they promptly bought it. (This process was reminiscent of the time when the Chinese had set up their United Nations mission in New York; through Kissinger's Rockefeller connections we were able to locate a hotel on Manhattan's West Side that suited their interests fully and that they promptly acquired, at a reduced price, thanks to the Rockefellers.) Considerable alteration of their Windsor Park premises would be required, though, and prior to the time that the Chinese could take possession, we arranged a large suite for them in the Mayflower Hotel, one of Washington's best.

The Chinese in Beijing were also very helpful to us in locating accommodations for the U.S. liaison office in China. To facilitate our settling in, the Chinese took over for our use a compound containing a residence and office building under construction, which originally had been intended for use by another foreign mission.

Concerning our arrangements for our own liaison office in Beijing, by far the most important questions were who would head the office and who would comprise the staff. To head the office we wanted a distinguished diplomat of prominent stature, who had a close relationship with the White House, and who would approximate both the age and experience of the senior Chinese leadership. The choice of chief of the U.S. liaison office came easily: Ambassador David K. E. Bruce, then 73 years of age, who among other influential assignments had served as ambassador both to the Court of St. James in London and to the Federal Republic of Germany in the post–World War II years. He had also been head of the delegation to the Paris talks between the United States and Vietnam on resolving the Vietnam War. He proved an ideal choice.

Under David Bruce there was to be a more or less conventional Foreign Service mission, the staff of which was selected by the Department of State, except that in order to maintain the White House connection, Dr. Kissinger determined that I would revert to my Foreign Service status and become a deputy to David Bruce. Not to offend the State Department, Dr. Kissinger agreed with State that there would be *two* deputy chiefs of mission (DCMs)—something unusual, to say the least, in U.S. diplomatic history—the other being appointed by the State Department. The State-appointed DCM turned out to be my old friend and colleague, Alfred Lesesne Jenkins, who, it will be recalled, had been with us on several of the Kissinger trips to China. Al Jenkins and I worked together in perfect harmony in our unique two-DCM relationship. As it happened, Al retired from the Foreign Service a little over a year after our mission opened, leaving me as sole deputy.

With the exception of David Bruce, the mission was composed entirely of career Foreign Service personnel, with a heavy emphasis on Chinese language officers in the substantive political and economic positions. Nicholas Platt (later ambassador to the Philippines and Pakistan and now president of the Asia Society) was chief of the political section, assisted by Donald Anderson (later consul general in Hong Kong) and James

Lilley (who later became ambassador to China). The economic section was headed by Herbert Horowitz (later ambassador to The Gambia), backed by William Rope (later principal deputy assistant secretary in the State Department's Political-Military Bureau and then a deputy assistant secretary in State's Policy Planning Council). The administrative officer, who also served as consular officer, was Robert Blackburn; the budget and fiscal officer was Virginia Schaeffer (later ambassador to Papua-New Guinea); and the general services officer was "Mo" Morin. Brunson McKinley was David Bruce's personal assistant. There were several communications technicians, as well as secretaries assigned to each section, all Department of State employees, plus a five-man Marine Guard detachment.

Altogether, at the time of our opening, twenty-six Americans were permanently assigned to USLO, as the U.S. liaison office became known, not counting a detachment of Navy SeaBees (Navy Construction Battalion personnel), who were in Beijing long enough to add extra security safeguards to the communications section and who, in their spare time, installed what every Marine Guard detachment apparently must have in its quarters, invariably called "the Marine House"—a wet bar. (More on this later.)

Our status was another important question. As noted above, the general outlines of the liaison office arrangement agreed upon by Premier Zhou Enlai and Dr. Kissinger in February were similar to those of a normal diplomatic mission. We discovered shortly after we opened the liaison office in Beijing that, with certain exceptions, we were indeed treated as a diplomatic mission. The exceptions were that we did not attend functions in the Great Hall of the People held in honor of visiting VIPs, nor was the chief of the U.S. liaison office invited to go along on the semiannual tour of various parts of China that the Foreign Ministry organized for chiefs of mission. Otherwise, we participated actively in the life of the diplomatic community, enjoyed diplomatic license tags on our cars, had ready access to the Foreign Ministry—sometimes more than we wanted— and maintained unrestricted contacts with fellow diplomats and members of the foreign press. We were also able to travel to parts of China open to foreigners on about the same basis as regularly accredited diplomats.

A small group of liaison office staff headed by Al Jenkins traveled to Beijing about 1 May to begin setting up temporary quarters in the Beijing Hotel. In 1973 there were only two sections of the Beijing Hotel: one that had been built sometime before 1937—I remember seeing it in Beijing when I was a youngster—and a more recent section that had been built since 1949 with Soviet assistance and distinguished by that characteristic

of all Soviet-assisted structures, namely instant antiquity. (A third, more
modern section was then under construction.) USLO's office opened in
the Soviet-assisted section pending completion of a new compound across
the street from the park of the Temple of the Sun, in the first of the several
new diplomatic quarters that the Chinese had built to house foreign diplomats.

To the credit of the Chinese, they had construction crews working
around the clock to finish our compound, which included a residence for
the USLO Chief David Bruce, and an office building, as well as storage
rooms (later partly turned into office space), behind the Bruce residence.
At first, all personnel resided in the Beijing Hotel, but as apartment space
became available elsewhere in one or another of the diplomatic sections
of Beijing, we very gradually began to spread out.

Meanwhile, the Chinese were making similar arrangements for their
liaison office in Washington, D.C. The chief of the Chinese liaison office
was to be the former Chinese ambassador to France, Huang Zhen. An
advance party under the deputy Chinese liaison office leader, Han Xu,
arrived in Washington in mid-April 1973, and I was happy to be able to
meet Han, who later became ambassador to the United States, at Dulles
Airport. The Chinese settled into the Mayflower Hotel with little trouble
and awaited completion of the alterations to the former Windsor Park
Hotel. The Chinese also acquired a separate residence for Ambassador
Huang Zhen and for Deputy Chief Han Xu, but these, too, needed re-
modeling.

Towards mid-May I departed Washington for Beijing, leaving Martha
to complete arrangements for our home and belongings; she would join
me later. Extremely cordial feelings existed between our two official delegations at this time. After my departure for Beijing, Martha invited members of the Chinese liaison office to an informal picnic on the Maryland
shore of the Potomac River to watch the annual canoe races. Several members accepted her invitation, headed by Deputy Chief Han Xu. American
guests included Arthur and Betty Lou Hummel (Arther later served as
ambassador to China) and colleague Richard Solomon. A good time was
had by all. Then, prior to Martha's departure for Beijing, the Chinese
mission gave a small Chinese retaurant party for her and the next day
stamped into her passport Liaison Office visa number one.

When I left Washington in early May, I went on to Beijing through
Hong Kong with David and Evangeline Bruce and Al and Martha Jenkins
(Al having returned from Beijing to accompany his wife). We spent a few
days in Hong Kong to be briefed by officers of the American consulate
general, up to then our advanced listening post for the People's Republic

of China, and to acquire items we might need in Beijing. Among other things, I bought two bicycles to be shipped to Beijing, which my wife and I used constantly. Finally, on 15 May we left Hong Kong and crossed into China at Shenzhen, having been seen off at the Kowloon railroad station by Consul General David Osborn and the head of the New China News Agency, the ex-officio senior Chinese representative in Hong Kong.

The route we followed became a familiar one: we took a train from Hong Kong (Kowloon) to the Chinese border, walked across the bridge over the Shenzhen River into China, went through customs and immigration procedures in a small building just over the bridge, from there moved upstairs in an adjacent building for lunch, and then went down a flight of stairs to board the train for Guangzhou (Canton). In Guangzhou we transferred from the train station to the airport, picked up our air tickets for Beijing, went up the ramp of a CAAC Trident, and flew to Beijing with a stop in Hangzhou for dinner. By late evening we were in Beijing, appropriately met by members of the Foreign Ministry, and on our way to our rooms in the Beijing Hotel.

At first, our entire mission was located in the Beijing Hotel, but in a few weeks a U.S. aircraft loaded with State Department office and household furniture arrived, courtesy both of the Chinese and of the U.S. Air Force. This permitted us to shift our chancery into the so-called "nine-story office building" (*jiu ceng ban gong lou*) in the San Li Tun area in Beijing's northeast quadrant. Each newly arrived mission (there were several during that period) was given a whole floor in one-half of the building, a section of which was used as a residence for the senior officer of the mission and the other section of which was used as an office. The Bruces moved into the residential section, and the rest of the staff commuted from our quarters in the Beijing Hotel to work at the office section of our floor. We were then really in business, although the formal opening of USLO awaited completion of the compound adjacent to the Temple of the Sun.

In due course, apartments began to open up, including one for the "Marine House" on an upper floor in the *Jian Guo Men Wai* apartment building, and life became much more normal. Even so, many of the USLO officers, staff, and their families were obliged to remain in the Beijing Hotel for weeks and even months pending availability of apartment spaces.

The formal opening of the United States Liaison Office in Beijing occurred 1 July 1973, with a full ceremony. With David Bruce standing on the front stoop of our newly finished chancery, flanked by his two deputies, and with all our Marines present in their dress blues, the American flag was officially hoisted. The Bruces moved into their freshly decorated residence, furnished and embellished by a professional designer sent out by the State Department's Foreign Buildings Office (FBO); the Jenkinses took over the Bruces' former suite in the nine-story building; and I moved into a similar suite on the floor below. Our American staff was supplemented with two, later three, Chinese interpreter-translators, and a Chinese language instructor (as well as assorted gardeners and household staff for the Bruces). All of our Chinese staff, both domestic and office employees, were necessarily requested from and then assigned to us by the Diplomatic Services Bureau of the Foreign Ministry, which also had connections with the Beijing Municipal Government.

It remained only for me to travel to Hong Kong to meet my wife, our two sons, who were to spend the summer with us, and our dog, all of whom had arrived in Hong Kong by ship, to complete our move into our new home. (Transporting our dog from Hong Kong to Beijing sorely tried all concerned, given the Chinese antipathy to dogs and this particular dog's unique, fiercely independent personality.)

USLO Open for Business in Beijing

We really knew we were open for business when we were called upon by visiting American delegations for briefings on the Chinese political and economic scene. One early delegation was from the National Committee on U.S.-China Relations, headed by its president, former ambassador Charles Yost, and including such well-known sinologues as Robert Scalapino of the University of California at Berkeley, the late Alex Eckstein of the University of Michigan (the United States's acknowledged expert in the field of Chinese economics), and China scholar A. Doak Barnett, all of whom had written extensively on U.S.-China relations. Another delegation was from the National Council on U.S.-China Trade, headed by its president, Christopher Phillips. Some of us were also present when the first multimillion dollar U.S.-Chinese business deal was signed, under which the Pullman-Kellogg Company would build in China an initial tranche of seven nitrogen-fixation plants for synthetic urea production, which was to be used as fertilizer. (The number of plants was later increased.)

Once USLO was established, our lives proceeded much as they would have in any Foreign Service overseas establishment, but with a difference: our mission was tiny, and our presence strange to the Chinese government—and its people. Also, we were obliged to contend with a bureaucracy whose traditions dated back at least as far as the Han Dynasty (206 B.C.E. to 220 C.E.), upon which was superimposed Marxist-Leninist dogma and, even more importantly, "Mao Zedong thought." Though we went about our professional duties in "normal" patterns, in fact we were feeling our way in new territory.

I always had the impression in our contacts with Chinese officials that they consistently operated in the firm belief that they held the moral high ground. First, we were up against what some American academics call "sino-centrism," or more popularly, the "Middle Kingdom complex," which for centuries has meant the conviction in Chinese minds that their civilization and culture are superior to anyone else's. In fact, the very name for China in Chinese, *Zhong Guo*, for "Middle Kingdom," assumes that China is the center of the civilized world, and that everyone else exists in varying states of barbarism, depending on how far their country is from China. All of China's troubles since the impact of the West had failed to dispel this attitude. Second, since Mao Zedong was the unquestioned leader in China when USLO opened, there was the added dimension in official minds that "the thought of Mao Zedong" had the answers to every question, and that foreigners who couldn't grasp this "truth" were hopeless. Negotiations with Chinese officials were in consequence very difficult, and we started with two strikes against us.

One situation in which I was personally engaged illustrates the problem well. It had been agreed even prior to the opening of our respective liaison offices that China's first cultural project in the United States would be an archeological exhibition drawn from the items discovered during the Cultural Revolution that Dr. Kissinger and his party had seen in Beijing in July 1971, including one of the two funerary jade body suits. This exhibition had been on tour to several European countries, and the Chinese and Europeans had reached an agreed text on the standards that would apply for care, handling, and shipping of the exhibits, which were, of course, priceless. When it came our turn to host the exhibition, however, the State Department's legal department posed a number of changes to this standard text, presumably to afford additional safeguards for the United States.

It was my job to present these changes to the Foreign Ministry, which received them coldly, to say the least. When the Chinese responded, they had made changes of their own that toughened up the procedures considerably from the Chinese standpoint. State's legal department then made additional changes, to which the Chinese responded as before, that is, by toughening up their own requirements. It soon became evident to me that if we wanted the exhibition at all, it would have to be on Chinese terms, and I so reported in a cable to State. The State Department then gave in, and the exhibition duly arrived in the United States on Chinese terms and was a smashing success. But several months had passed while all the negotiations were going on, wasting both our own time and that of the Chinese.

Another example of our exceptional and often trying operating environment came in the form of the telephone summonses we received from time to time to meet with someone in the Foreign Ministry, usually the deputy director of the *Mei Da Si* (Americas and Oceanian department) or the consular department. When we received such a summons, we invariably asked "what about?" and the answer invariably was the ominous words, "something to do with the liaison office." Occasionally David Bruce would go himself, depending on the rank of the individual who wanted to see us, but more often I was the officer who took the heat. And "heat" it usually was, since we wouldn't have been called to the Foreign Ministry unless someone there wanted to call attention to some lapse on our part, and we could expect a firm lecture concerning our shortcomings. I often took Don Anderson with me as interpreter; though I didn't need an interpreter, it was useful to have the extra thinking time that translation afforded me.

One summons, as I discovered after arriving at the Foreign Ministry, concerned the standard form all U.S. missions abroad supply to visa applicants, which sets forth eligibilities, visa categories, and the like. Our consular officer, Robert Blackburn, no Chinese speaker himself, had asked USLO's interpreter-translators to render this form into Chinese and then send it to the People's Publishing House for copies; he had not thought to inform USLO's Chinese-speaking officers (who all had their offices on USLO's second floor). My interlocutor on this mission, the deputy chief of the consular division, referred to the consular form and said that the workers in the People's Publishing House had felt insulted and had protested.

The offending section of the form was the part that defined those who were ineligible for U.S. visas, including persons of known poor moral repute, such as prostitutes, and—in a holdover from the McCarthy era—members of Communist parties. "Did I not know," I was asked, "that Chairman Mao was a member of the Chinese Communist Party, and that Premier Zhou Enlai was also a CCP member? Would persons such as these actually be barred from entering the U.S.?" Of course, I immediately apologized (while mentally rebuking Bob Blackburn for letting this one slip by us), assured the deputy director that I would inform my government, and also gave my assurances that this was a mistake that would not happen again. I returned to USLO to read the riot act to Bob, and told him never, never to let papers containing Chinese leave the building without having been checked by someone on the second floor. Unfortunately, despite my assurances, a few months after both Blackburn and I had left Beijing, a new administrative-consular officer took over, and the whole mess was repeated and had to be straightened out anew. Certainly episodes such as this did not help our reputation with the Chinese.

Another of these Foreign Ministry summonses was deemed important enough for us to have to call on Lin Ping, director of the Americas and Oceanian division of the Foreign Ministry, hence David Bruce went personally, with me along as his assistant. This was one of the few summonses we anticipated. The problem arose from a slip made by a visiting American officer from our Consulate General in Hong Kong (we had made a practice of inviting these officers from Hong Kong, which still had reporting responsibilities for China, to stay with one of us in Beijing from time to time to give them a glimpse of the real China). He had ridden a bicycle into an area plainly marked "Military Zone—Off Limits" and had been stopped by a PLA soldier. Although he had neglected to tell us about this episode immediately after it happened, on his way back to Hong Kong by train he stopped at Guangzhou and called to tell us the story. Thus, when the call from the Foreign Ministry came, we put two and two together, and when, sure enough, Lin Ping protested the violation of a military area by one of our officers, we were fully prepared. We told him that the officer had reported the matter to us, that our government had been informed, that the officer's offense was not intentional, and that he would be suitably reprimanded. This was about the only time, however, when we were able to figure out in advance what the actual subject would be of the Chinese protests or complaints.

As it turned out, the officer's phone call from Guangzhou was prompted by an unpleasant incident he underwent after getting off the train there, although we didn't know it at the time. When his train reached Guangzhou, and he was waiting in the train station with his wife to board the train to Shenzhen on the Chinese border with Hong Kong, he was directed to leave the waiting room by public security personnel and was taken to a small room where he was intensively interrogated for well over an hour about the incident in Beijing. This delay caused him to miss his train, which he protested. He also insisted that he had apologized to the PLA soldier who had stopped him and maintained that his entry into the forbidden zone was purely an accident. He had been riding his bicycle along a canal, he said, enjoying the scenery, and had missed seeing the "Off Limits" sign. When his words seemingly had failed to affect the questioning by the public security people, he said that he wanted to get in touch with his "Embassy" (meaning USLO) in Beijing. It was at this point that we in USLO learned about the episode through his telephone call. Perhaps because of the call, he was allowed to proceed, and he took a later train to Shenzhen. The Foreign Service officer's questioning by the Public Security Bureau helps to account for the summons David Bruce and I received to the Foreign Ministry. The incident also illustrates the climate of Chinese suspicion under which USLO operated, wherein our every move was scrutinized.

Chapter 8

Two Different Social Systems Coexisting Together

We quickly discovered that living in Beijing was almost like living on another planet as far as our accustomed norms of life were concerned. Although initially the Chinese were very helpful and went out of their way to be hospitable, little things kept happening to show us that our two respective social systems had a lot to learn about the business of coexisting. Since we were the outsiders in China, we did most of the accommodating. This was true both by choice, for we didn't wish to offend or to draw attention to ourselves, but also by necessity, in response to circumstances over which we had no control or to directives of the Chinese authorities. Of course, we were eager and interested observers of Chinese society, and judging by our experience, the Chinese people were as interested in us as we were in them; however, Chinese customs and political beliefs were very strong and could not be overlooked.

On Domestic Matters

One of the first places where we accommodated to the norms of our Chinese hosts was in our own homes. Diplomats overseas rely on hired household staff to attend to domestic chores and cook for the numerous official social functions that they hold in their homes. This is especially true for the senior officers assigned to most foreign missions, who more often than not have live-in domestic helpers because of their demanding official schedules. (Local staff also help diplomats bridge linguistic and cultural gaps in getting routine tasks done.) The work days of our Chinese household staff, consisting of a cook, a "waiter," and an *ai yi*, or house-

maid, were strictly confined to eight hours, and each of the three normally
worked roughly the same eight hours (so they could keep an eye on each
other); this meant that it would normally be impossible for the staff to be
present for functions that continued into the evenings.

For meals prepared by our household staff, we were given a choice of
breakfast and lunch or lunch and dinner. David Bruce chose to have
breakfast and lunch provided by the staff, with a cold supper left for his
wife Evangeline and him in the refrigerator. (Incidentally, he became very
fond of *mao tai*, sipping it in a small wine glass along with his supper.)
Martha and I chose lunch and dinner, so that we could more easily enter-
tain in the evenings. Because our cook was an elderly gentleman who had
worked for foreigners in Tianjin many years before and had a sense of
pride and obligation, he sometimes put in extra hours, particularly when
we gave dinner parties for fellow diplomats. For this extra effort, though,
he was regularly criticized by the waiter and the *ai yi* at the Saturday
afternoon *xue xi* (political study) sessions at the Diplomatic Services Bureau that all Chinese household staff members were obliged to attend.
(Incidentally, for the services of the staff, all foreign missions paid a set
rate to the Diplomatic Services Bureau, which in turn paid the staff only
a small fraction of that rate.) We had no doubt that each person at these
sessions was also required to report on our weekly activities. We had no
real sense of privacy in Beijing.

Then there was the matter of *xiu xi*, or rest, which was a sacred hour in
the day when the staff took time off, usually to sleep. David Bruce related
to me that on one occasion in his residence when he came downstairs
after lunch to return to work, he counted nine prostrate forms stretched
out on various sections of the downstairs floor—all workmen who were
there to complete the decoration of the residence (the staff had small
rooms for themselves behind the kitchen). Illustrating the importance to
the Chinese of *xiu xi*, I recall one occasion when several of us went to the
main market in Beijing, the *Dong Feng Shi Chang*, or East Wind Market
(named after Mao Zedong's dictum that the "East wind prevails over
the West wind"); we planned to have lunch at a restaurant that served
Western-style cuisine, but we were stopped outside by a large sign in Chinese informing potential customers that "we are now resting." We had to
change our plans.

The U.S. Marine Guards as an
"Organized Foreign Military Force"

The presence of the U.S. Marines guarding the liaison office (as they guard
all U.S. diplomatic missions overseas) was a constant source of problems

to us in Beijing. Before the day of the first official flag-raising, we had given considerable thought to the question of the Marines wearing their full-dress uniforms at the ceremony, given what we knew was a strong Chinese antipathy to the stationing of foreign military forces on Chinese territory. To express our misgivings, we sent a telegram to the State Department, copy to the commandant of the Marine Corps, expressing our concerns about offending our hosts and also about possible repercussions. The answer from the commandant was firm: the Marines *would* wear full dress on the occasion of USLO's formal opening, and State concurred. At the flag-raising ceremony the contrast between our spic-and-span Marines and the Chinese PLA guards at the gate—every diplomatic mission in Beijing had such guards—was striking. Our Marines were resplendent in their dress blues, complete with campaign ribbons earned in Vietnam, and they wore their uniforms with pride and exemplary military bearing. The PLA guards, in contrast, were wearing their usual pajama-like green uniforms that looked as if the wearers had indeed slept in them. While nothing untoward happened at the flag-raising ceremony, I'm sure the seeds were sown here that later brought us much difficulty. Undoubtedly some senior officers in the PLA took the presence of our Marines badly, especially when the Marines were wearing their uniforms, if only inside our compound but in sight of passers-by.

In addition to the uniform issue, the Marine bar turned out to be a big headache. Foreigners were starved for entertainment in Beijing: the streets were dark and mostly devoid of traffic by nine P.M.—only a few small food stalls and some stores along the main shopping street, Wang Fu Jing, were open later. As a result, the Marine bar—named the "Red-Ass Saloon" in honor of its builders, the SeaBees being known in the U.S. Navy as the "red-ass engineers"—became the social center and sole nightclub in after-hours Beijing. Abundantly supplied with alcoholic beverages not generally obtainable elsewhere plus music amplified through hi-fi speakers, it was *the* place to go.

Little by little the clientele of the Red-Ass Saloon grew to the point where it was jammed almost every night, but above all on weekends. Particularly avid fans of the bar were African students in Beijing, who evidently felt that the city was at the end of the earth, and who had practically no social contact with the Chinese, most notably with young Chinese women. The "Gunny" (gunnery sergeant) in charge of the Marine detachment at USLO was eventually forced to issue membership cards, which itself raised problems as to who would and who would not receive a card.

One episode illustrates the situation. An African student who had not received a membership card decided, in a drunken mood resulting most likely from *mao tai*, to tear up the Marine bar in revenge. However, he got off the elevator on the wrong floor and trashed the apartment directly below the Marine house, which belonged to an African diplomat. At this point we began to hear complaints from the Chinese authorities about lack of order because of the Marines, along with pointed hints that they should go. Only the arrival of Dr. Kissinger in November 1973 and his personal intercession with Zhou Enlai, with whom he was conducting further discussions along the lines of their previous talks, saved the Marines from expulsion.

But the Marines were put on notice that they were on probation. To try to reduce their high profile, we put a stop to their wearing of uniforms, both for regular duty and for special occasions. We even had to ask them not to engage in physical training such as jogging as a group, in response to another complaint about the appearance, as they ran in formation, of their being an "organized foreign military force." Also, we had to cancel the annual formal Marine Ball, held every November in every Marine unit to commemorate the Corps' foundation, after the Marines attempted to have a cake made for the occasion that bore the Marine Corps insignia. The manager of the little restaurant in our diplomatic apartment building whom the Marines asked to make the cake reported the request to the Diplomatic Services Bureau, which officially complained to USLO. We on USLO's second floor decided that to avoid trouble, the ball had to be scratched.

What finally drove the Marines out was a harmless circular they sent about April 1974 to all foreign embassies that might be interested in playing baseball, calling for the formation of a softball league and signed by "Slugger" so-and-so and "Killer" somebody else in the Marine detachment. This circular was immediately seized upon by the Chinese: we received a call from the Foreign Ministry to appear for a meeting with Lin Ping, chief of the Americas and Pacific Department, where he told us the Marines had to go because again they were comporting themselves as "an organized foreign military force." Their replacements were young U.S. Foreign Service security officers, who, while good, lacked the color and style of the Marines. Not for several years did U.S. Marines return as security guards for the liaison office, and later the embassy, where they now are—in uniform while inside the embassy.

Rank and the "Classless Society"

In the meantime, both the Americans at USLO and the Chinese were learning about each other's ways and customs. One of our surprises was learning about the privileges of rank in China. Our first clear example came within a month of USLO's establishment, when our first official U.S. "cultural" visit to Beijing took place in the form of a team of U.S. Olympic swimmers who stopped first in Canton and then worked their way up to Beijing via such stops as Changsha (in Hunan Province) and Shanghai, demonstrating their swimming prowess at each stop. They couldn't compete directly with Chinese swimmers, China not yet being a member of the International Olympic Committee, but stopwatches were very much in evidence in the audience during the tour. Having been lavishly entertained on the way, the team members wanted to give a banquet in Beijing to honor their hosts, the All-China Sports Federation. They asked USLO if we could handle the arrangements, and of course we agreed to help.

In exploring Beijing we had discovered in the part of the city to the southwest of Chang An Jie a restaurant called the Chengdu, which served an exceptionally tasty array of spicy Sichuan dishes. The Chengdu Restaurant, which had been a favorite of PLA Marshal Zhu De, was the former residence of Yuan Shikai, a warlord who had tried to set himself up as emperor of China after the collapse of the Qing Dynasty. As was typical of traditional wealthy Chinese homes, it was elaborate in design, complete with vermillion pillars, three courtyards, and lavishly painted ceilings. Its atmosphere and cuisine were both outstanding, and we visited it frequently. It seemed the perfect place to hold the swim team's banquet.

When we asked our senior interpreter-translator, "Harry" Liu, to contact the restaurant and make the necessary arrangements, the question arose (we soon learned it was inevitable in such cases): what standard did we want? (*"yau shenma biao zhun?"*), that is, how much were we prepared to pay per person? USLO members had become accustomed to a bill per person of about seven *yuan*, which had bought us an abundance of delicious dishes plus drinks, usually beer or *qi shui*, (carbonated orange juice), so we suggested this figure. Mr. Liu was aghast. There would be "high-level cadres" (*gao ji gan bu*) present, and seven yuan was far too little for such personages! The minimum acceptable amount was about 20 yuan per head, not including the cost of food and drink for the cadres' drivers, so the whole affair went to around 25 yuan each. Hearing this, Nick Platt said to Harry Liu, "Mr. Liu, I thought that China was a classless society!"—to which Mr. Liu drew himself up and said, "We are indeed a classless society, but we *do* have rank!"

This reference to "high-level cadres" became commonplace to us. Shortly thereafter, on my trip from Beijing to Hong Kong to meet my wife and sons, my aircraft was delayed overnight in Changsha, requiring a long bus ride from the airport to the Hunan Provincial Guest House. The next morning, when our bus seemed to be waiting interminably to return to the airport, I heard many mutterings from the assembled passengers about *"gao ji gan bu."* Not until a group of well-dressed individuals finally appeared did the bus depart. I had not seen them aboard the airplane, presumably because they had been in a special compartment. When Martha, our sons, and I boarded an IL-62 aircraft in Guangzhou to return to Beijing, I discovered that we were in a special compartment ourselves, large enough for twelve very comfortable seats only, sandwiched in between the normal first-class and tourist compartments. Our fellow passengers in this restricted area all gave the impression of being very highly placed. Several were PLA officers, judging from the extra pockets in their uniforms. Obviously, rank in China had its privileges, one of which was a special *gao ji gan bu* class on airplanes.

On another occasion, on our first sight-seeing venture outside Beijing, traveling by air in a Soviet-built AN-24 to the old revolutionary capital at Yan'an and the ancient city of Xian, Martha and I and our two sons, David and Geoffrey, discovered that the privileges of rank extended to rail travel. We had intended to fly back from Xian to Beijing, but inclement weather in Yan'an forced the pilot to return to Xian, whereupon I convinced our China Travel Service guide to arrange for the return trip by train. This placed us in the so-called "soft" car section of the train (*ruan wo che*), in which four people could travel comfortably in one compartment with upper and lower berths. A dining car was attached. When we went to the diner, which was about half full, the inevitable question of *"yau shenma biao zhun?"* was asked, and seeking to simplify matters I simply said to the waiter, "the same as all the others" (*"gen putung ren yiyang"*). To our enormous surprise, we were then served a seven-course dinner, complete with shrimp and Yangtze River yellow fish, which was superb.

The "others" were obviously doing very well for themselves, and no bill was presented, either to them or to us. The reason became clear the next morning as we approached the Beijing railroad station, when the "person in charge of the dining car" came to our compartment to ask, "To what unit (*dan wei*) should I send the charges?" He was considerably taken aback when I paid cash for the food we had consumed during the trip. We could only deduce that our fellow Chinese passengers were all high-ranking personages traveling on *dan wei* expense accounts, lavish ones by Chinese standards, though to us the meal costs were modest.

As Martha and I learned on this trip, traveling by train was by far the most pleasant way to see China. We usually had a whole compartment that normally accommodated four people for our exclusive use (I sometimes heard passengers who had been turned away as a result speak about those "damned foreigners"). With a dining car nearby and attendants to keep our ever-present thermos jug filled with hot water for brewing tea, we could watch the countryside pass by in considerable comfort.

In contrast to the *gao ji gan bu*, the average Chinese had very little in the way of amenities—on the train or in any other aspect of their lives. On the train, the average Chinese traveled by "hard car," or *ying wo che*, which consisted of wooden benches and wooden platforms overhead let down at night for beds. Dining accommodations consisted of whatever might be available at a scheduled stop, and at every station it was usual to see hordes of passengers pour from the cars to surround kiosks that sold tea or various kinds of food.

As far as we in USLO could determine, most Chinese were pushed around by the cadres, and their lives were quite cheerless. Workers were frozen to their jobs, though having a job brought with it a tiny apartment and a guaranteed minimum income. There was a saying about work in Beijing, "*zuo bu zuo, san shi liu*," which means "work or don't work, it's 36 yuan" (36 yuan was the minimum monthly wage at the time).

Across the street from the "nine-story office building" where we lived was the residential complex for the Beijing Heavy Industries Factory, which manufactured large-size power generators for use in hydraulic or steam-powered electric generating plants. The factory was at least seven miles from the residential complex, yet every morning at 6:00 A.M., long before sunrise during the winter months, the wired broadcasting system was turned on, martial music and propaganda blared out, and by 6:30 the workers were on their way to work by bicycle, which almost everyone preferred to riding the overcrowded trolley buses (that is, if they could afford a bicycle). They rode into the teeth of the relentless northwest wind loaded with dust from the Gobi Desert and with smoke from the high-sulfur-content coal used to generate power by most factories in Beijing.[1] About 7:00 P.M. they bicycled back, again in the darkness, but this time at least with the wind at their backs, to a simple meal and bed.

Despite the Spartan existence of average Chinese, they always, or almost always, treated us with innate courtesy and helpfulness. I remember well one incident that took place on our visit to Yan'an and Xian. I had taken along a large wad of Chinese currency, thinking it would be ample, but it wasn't. At every stop we were put up in special quarters judged suitable for the deputy chief of the U.S. Liaison Office, but unfortunately much more expensive than ordinary rooms. In the Yan'an guest house we must have received the equivalent of the presidential suite. The result was that by the time we had been in Xian for a day or so and made some tours outside the city, I ran out of money. I therefore went to the service desk at the hotel, the Shaanxi Provincial Guest House, and asked to cash a personal check made out on the First National Bank of Ames, Iowa. The small gentleman behind the counter who was, in the August heat, clad simply in khaki shorts and an undershirt and who couldn't have had a clue where Ames, Iowa, was, took my check and looked it over carefully. He disappeared into an inner room for a few minutes, returned with the observation that I was the first official American to visit Xian since World War II, this couldn't but be a positive step for U.S.-Chinese friendship, and he cashed my check!

I remember also a time when Martha and I were out bicycling and stopped at a shop that sold ceramic household dishes. We bought a "steamer," a large bowl with a vent in it used for steaming chicken. The shopkeeper went out of his way to wrap our purchase carefully and to tie it firmly on one of our bicycle racks to protect it against breakage.

Diplomats and Chinese Authorities on Having Fun in Beijing

For foreigners in China, social contact with Chinese citizens, whether they had official status or were simply ordinary people, was impermissible. Also, in the early 1970s, with the Cultural Revolution still going on, there were few public diversions such as movies or concerts (especially of a nonpolitical nature!) within China. This forced the steadily growing diplomatic corps in Beijing to fall back on its own resources for recreation, or more simply put, just to have fun. I have mentioned the attraction of the Marine bar, which of course closed when the Marines left Beijing in 1974. However, some months before the Marines departed, the Belgian ambassador held a dance and buffet dinner in his residence that was such a great success it inspired other missions to follow suit. Dance records were contributed by many missions, including ours, and afterwards the normally silent diplomatic residential areas often resounded to the sound of Western tunes not heard elsewhere in Beijing, unless by the few people who had short-wave radios to pick up foreign broadcasts. In each affair, a buffet dinner was served by the host's Chinese staff.

Inevitably, Chinese officialdom reacted with displeasure. It was simply not tolerable in Beijing for Chinese, at least, to be exposed to such frivolous social pleasures. Shortly after the first few dances the Diplomatic Services Bureau sent down word that Chinese staff members could remain in an embassy residence through the serving of the buffet dinner and then had to leave. Thereafter dancing had to await conclusion of the dinner, and any drinks served later were to be managed by the diplomats themselves. Nevertheless, the dances continued and were especially popular among representatives of African nations. Martha and I found ourselves very much included in the African-sponsored dances because we had made friends among this community by assisting in the birth of a son to the Togolese chargé and his wife, who were our neighbors. We frequently found ourselves among the few non-Africans present. Having been trained only in ballroom-style dancing, I found that I had to learn very quickly the kind of free rock-and-roll style favored by our hosts. (My adaptation was something akin to jogging in place to the beat!) When Martha and I left Beijing, the dances were still going on, and still there were no Chinese present to observe the spectacle of people having fun.

Another source of entertainment in Beijing, which several members of my own family joined, was a choral group established by John Boyd, chief of chancery of the British embassy, who was an enthusiastic singer. We usually met in his apartment once a week to sing classical Western pieces by Mozart or Handel. One high spot of the chorus was on Christmas eve 1974, when our group toured the entire diplomatic enclave to sing Christmas carols. Seeing their faces peering out of windows, I feel sure that many of the Chinese living in adjacent areas enjoyed hearing our music as much as the diplomatic community did.

Another high point for John Boyd's choral group was an event he organized at one of the Ming tombs, about 40 kilometers north of Beijing, where the deteriorated ancestral temple of one of the Ming emperors furnished an ideal platform and sounding board; there was no roof or front wall, and only the side and rear walls remained standing. The event took place in the evening and went on well after dark. The members of the chorus, along with numerous guests, enjoyed first a candle- and lantern-lit picnic, complete with appropriate wines, and then we sang.

The atmosphere was perfect. The candles glowing in various spots of the old temple floor gave a special quality to the performance, as did the sound resonating back from the walls. Everyone in our party enjoyed the program greatly. But to the very obvious dismay of a public security policeman from the area, so did the Chinese peasants from the nearby commune, who had flocked inside the gate of the temple compound to listen. They had mostly congregated near the gate, and from our elevated platform, I could see the public security policeman in his white hat and jacket jumping up and down outside the gate at the rear of the crowd of Chinese spectators, trying to get them to go home. He wasn't very successful, and only when our choral group's program was over did the spectators and listeners disperse.

John Boyd had received permission from appropriate authorities to hold this picnic-cum-concert at the chosen site, but I suspect that some-one must have been reprimanded for having allowed ordinary Chinese to witness foreigners having fun. I don't know if there were any official repercussions, for about this time Martha and I left Beijing, but the atmo-sphere in the city was such as to discourage residents from thinking about anything but politics. Indeed, a nationwide campaign was going on at the time, manifested by signs and slogans written on posters displayed throughout the city, to pull out the "poisonous weeds" represented by bourgeois, or Western, culture.

Picnics of a more conventional type were, in fact, one of the more pop-ular recreation forms in Beijing for the diplomatic community. Fre-quently on fair weekends when we did not have a social function to attend, Martha and I used to have our driver take us to the Ming tombs, where we would select one of the least-visited sites such as the *De Ling*, or "Virtuous Tomb" (because it was well away from the much-visited tomb of the Wan Li emperor, known as the "Underground Palace," which had been opened up in the 1950s or 1960s). There, we could quietly enjoy a picnic lunch and allow our dog, who was politically frowned upon, to have a little more freedom than we usually gave him. (Dogs had been judged by Chairman Mao to be nonproductive, and accordingly not permitted to be owned by the average Chinese, though to be sure I occa-sionally spotted a dog in a commune located away from Beijing city. We always walked our dog on a leash, and except for my usual daily jog with the dog just outside the diplomatic compound, we rarely took him be-yond the compound gate.)

Often we invited guests on our picnics, either from the diplomatic com-munity or visitors from the United States and other U.S. Foreign Service posts. We all thoroughly enjoyed the beauty and tranquility of the Ming tombs site, not to mention the chance to escape Beijing's perpetual smog. Our favorite season for Ming-tombs picnics was the fall, when the air was clearest, when skies were deep blue above the rounded dark green hills and the yellow-tiled roofs and faded red walls of the tomb complexes, and when the persimmon trees grown by the surrounding commune were burdened with clusters of orange-colored fruit.

Other places we went for picnics were the Ming tombs reservoir (where we once shared a traditional American-style barbecue with friends from USLO and the British and Canadian embassies), and also the Hunting Park at the Western Hills, about a 45-minute drive from Beijing. Here we could climb to the top of the tallest hill to enjoy the view and have lunch. If we didn't want to bring a lunch, we could dine at a restaurant located part way up the pathway to the summit. Unfortunately, the view of Beijing from the top was usually obscured by a black haze that hid all but the tallest of Beijing's buildings. We didn't visit the Hunting Park frequently, since it was too public to be able to take our dog. This was a favored spot for Beijing's youth to come on outings, and as I once observed, to engage in a little clandestine love-making.

Dining out was another of Beijing's more popular forms of recreation for foreigners, food being one of the few aspects of everyday life in China that was nonpolitical. Together with friends from USLO or other missions, my family and I often went to establishments such as the Chengdu Restaurant, the *Feng Zi Yuan* ("Phoenix Garden"), or a small establishment known accurately as the "Three Tables." Perhaps our favorite spot, though, was an establishment located near the *Hou Hai*, or "Back Lake," in Beijing's northern district not far from the Drum and Bell Towers. This was the *Kao Rou Ji*, or barbecued meat restaurant of the Ji family, which dated back to well before the 1911 Revolution in China (the brazier was said never to have cooled for over 300 years!). It was, I believe, still being run by the Ji family. The spot was particularly popular in the winter, when standing around a large brazier to cook one's own bowlful of thin-sliced meat (lamb, usually), mixed together with one's choice of savory sauces and spices, made one forget the cold wind outside. The liberal imbibing of *mao tai* or heated sweet rice wine added to the warmth.

There was, of course, the normal run of diplomatic entertainment—official dinner parties, national day receptions, and the like—but this was more a part of our diplomatic work than purely recreational. I do recall one memorable night when we were giving a dinner at our apartment in the nine-story building when an earthquake struck, and the whole building shook for nearly thirty seconds. We were fortunate on this occasion in having no damage, except perhaps to our emotions, but this quake presaged the earthquake of 1976 that forced many people in Beijing to live in the streets and that destroyed the entire city of Tangshan.

USLO also engaged in a considerable amount of in-house entertainment. For example, our daughter Pat organized a Halloween party for all USLO children and adults in our apartment on 30 October 1973. The guests came in traditional American-style Halloween costumes as witches, pirates, ghosts, and so forth. Several of our Marines came as a Mafia gang, with one of their number wearing a T-shirt from the back of which projected a dagger hilt surrounded by red coloring, looking for all the world like blood. As they stepped into the elevator from their quarters in the

Marine house, the presumed murder victim fell forward into the arms of his buddies as if in his death throes, to the great horror of the elderly woman who operated the elevator. When the elevator bell called her again to the Marines' floor and she saw Count Dracula waiting there for a ride, she shut the elevator door in his face, and he had to walk down the stairs. Similar scenes were repeated when the Marines entered the elevator in our apartment building. Neither elevator operator was amused. In all probability the two ladies reported the dagger incident to higher authority, which could have amounted to another black mark against our Marines.

All in all, life for us in Beijing was tolerable, certainly memorable, if not always a garden of delights. Our creative responses to the dearth of entertainment and to our circumscribed life in Beijing and the close camaraderie within USLO and the "Western" diplomatic community served both to heighten in our minds the differences between the Communist and democratic systems and to help us keep our perspectives healthy. Since the reforms of Deng Xiaoping, Beijing seems a much more lively place, and I have seen at least some of the changes during brief visits to China over the last decade. But even in the period 1973–1975 Beijing compared favorably to some of the other capitals in the region such as Ulan Bator (now spelled Ulan Bataar) in Mongolia and Pyongyang in North Korea. Conditions in North Korea must have been particularly hard on diplomats assigned there, for on visits to the Beijing airport to greet or say farewell to VIPs, I frequently witnessed foreign officials disembarking after a flight from Pyongyang with wide smiles on their faces, coming to enjoy the amenities of the Chinese capital. Our own favorite city for a break from the dull life of Beijing was Hong Kong.

Politics versus Entertainment

For the Chinese, public entertainment was even sparser than for visitors. Motion pictures of a highly politicized nature were available, but plays or opera required the recipient of the ticket to be in good political standing with his or her *dan wei* (unit). Black-and-white television was beginning to appear, but again, the content was heavily politicized. There were but a few neighborhood "pubs" where only beer was served. (Qingdao beer was very good, produced at the site of a prewar German brewery, possibly with the German recipe.) We once asked one of our drivers what he did on Saturdays after *xue xi* or on Sundays, which were free. He said he usually went to a beer-serving establishment and got drunk.

There was also revolutionary opera, the creations of Jiang Qing. Martha and I saw the popular reaction to this art form by attending a concert at a theater across from the Minzu Hotel, where the audience was almost entirely made up of workers, peasants, and soldiers. The first half of the program consisted of Chinese traditional music with a few Albanian folk songs thrown in, and the applause was deafening. The second half, after the intermission, consisted entirely of excerpts from revolutionary opera, including songs sung by the stars of Jiang Qing's major work, the "Red Lantern Classic." Not one decibel of applause came from the audience, which to us and most probably the singers was embarrassing but certainly indicative of the attitude of the crowd towards politics.

A number of us from USLO saw a similar instance of audience apathy when we went to see a revolutionary play called "Fighting on the Plain" (*Ping Yuan Zuo Zhan*), another of Jiang Qing's creations. This was a story about the peasant resistance against the Japanese on the North China plain, where there were no mountains to provide cover, so—in the words of the program—the peasants themselves had to serve as the mountains. The villain was a mustachioed, jack-booted Japanese officer complete with samurai sword, and the hero a young Chinese student dressed typically in a long Chinese gown. (He was a covert Communist, of course.) The denouement came with a dazzling display of Chinese acrobatics, when guerrillas drawn from among the peasants attacked the Japanese headquarters, resulting in the complete destruction of the Japanese garrison. Not even the acrobatics moved the audience, which got up and left the theater as soon as the lights went on without giving even a smattering of applause. The only sounds came from behind the closed curtain, where a high-ranking cadre was congratulating the cast, which was applauding him for his praise. The whole play was blatantly anti-Japanese; so much so that a Japanese delegation seated behind the Americans got up and left well before the play was over.

Political indoctrination was a relentless part of life in China, with new campaigns every few months. In the late 1960s and early 1970s, Chinese citizens were subjected to propaganda about the "rustproof screw," Lei Feng, a PLA soldier who died less than gloriously by running his truck into a light pole in Harbin, but whose personal effects were filled with encomiums for Chairman Mao and how important it was to subordinate self to the needs of the state. Everyone in China was supposed to emulate Lei Feng. After the Lei Feng campaign, a new one came along for "national self reliance," or "*zi li geng sheng*" in Chinese, which was pushed hard for months. An insight into the popular reaction to this campaign occurred right in front of me, when a young employee of the nine-story building asked our elevator operator, a dragon-like middle-aged woman, if she wouldn't sew back the ear-flap of his winter hat, which had torn away. Her response was, "Hmph. Why don't you exercise a little *zi li geng sheng* and fix it yourself!"

Martha's and my own most vivid memory of the application of political campaigns, coupled with a view of the harsh life endured by the ordinary people on the communes, occurred when we visited a production brigade (a subunit of a commune consisting usually of a traditional Chinese farm village) outside Luoyang. The brigade's party secretary had organized every able-bodied person in the brigade between the ages of six and seventy-five to "emulate Da Zhai," which was a commune in eastern Shanxi province where the hills characteristic of that region had been leveled to permit the use of machinery such as tractors. In this case, in a similar setting, everybody was out toiling away with hand tools to turn hillsides into flat land. (In my own opinion, terraces would have made much better sense.)

Incidentally, there were three slogans prevalent in Chinese propaganda at this time: *"nong ye xue Da Zhai"* ("farmers, study [or emulate] the Da Zhai commune" in eastern Shanxi); *"quan guo xue Jie Fang Jun"* ("everyone, emulate the People's Liberation Army"—the epitome of discipline, selflessness, hard work, and honesty); and *"gong ye xue Da Qing"* ("workers, emulate Da Ching"—a major oil field in northeast China, which thanks to the workers' efforts had been brought into production in a short period of time).

Family Life and Indoctrination of Youth in Beijing

As far as we could tell, the result of such an existence among the people was a pervasive indifference to the constant political exhortations, plus a tendency to turn inward to the family circle for comfort and pleasure. But even the ages-old institution of the family was under threat, for during our stay the hated "down to the countryside" movement was in effect, which required all but a favored few of the year's junior middle-school graduates (who were approximately fifteen or sixteen years of age) to go to the countryside, usually miles and miles away from the rest of their families, to work for an indefinite period of time and become revolutionary-minded by experiencing something of the "struggle" their forefathers had endured. These "educated youths," as they were called, despite years of political indoctrination beginning with kindergarten, neither relished their assignments nor were welcomed by the peasants in the communes to which they were assigned, since they constituted an economic burden to house and feed, and they knew little about farm work. But "politics was in command," and down they went. (Also sent down to the country- side were many thousands of adults who were judged to have political shortcomings. They were sent to the so-called "May 7 Cadre Schools" for indefinite periods to study Marxism-Leninism and Chairman Mao's writings, as well as to harden themselves through physical labor.)

Martha and I witnessed a departure of educated youth to the country- side from our apartment window one morning, when we were awakened by the sound of drums, cymbals, and songs. When we peered out, we saw large numbers of young people from the adjacent Chinese housing estate being loaded onto trucks. The atmosphere was supposed to be festive, but was in fact rather glum. I noticed that there were many posters attached to the trees of the Chinese housing estate, and later that day I made it a point to read them. Not only were there congratulations to the educated youth being sent to the countryside to work, but also congratulations to the *parents* of these young people who had "sent" their children down to the countryside, as if the parents had made the choice for themselves.

There was no doubt in Martha's and my minds that there were heavy hearts not only among the young people leaving but among those left behind. Usually those sent down were able to return only for a few days during the "Spring Festival" (at the lunar new year) to be with their fami- lies, but there were few other exceptions. The impression we had was that the time spent by the educated youth in the countryside was open-ended. For many, this was the end of school and the beginning of work and a hard new life.

Illustrating the effect on the families left behind, on one occasion Mar- tha paid a call on the wife of the British deputy chief of mission and found her household in turmoil. The *ai yi* had just received a letter from her daughter in Northeast China, where she had been sent to a state farm, announcing that she had become engaged to marry a young man on the same state farm, who was himself not from Beijing but from some place in the northeast. What this meant was that the daughter would lose her Beijing family registration, or *hu kou zheng*, in favor of her husband-to- be's Northeast China registration. She would no longer be able to visit Beijing on holidays to see her family. The *ai yi*'s misery—she was in tears—was intense. Americans in Beijing were used to looking for subtle clues to how the Chinese people felt about their lives; it was rare to see such a demonstration of emotion.

It seemed to us that fairly large numbers of young people in Beijing were spared from being "sent down," many of whom became PLA guards of diplomatic compounds or found make-work jobs in residential complexes such as ours. It's my guess that these youths had good political connections that exempted them from the treatment accorded the rest of their peer group.

We witnessed the political indoctrination to which all Chinese young people were subjected whenever we visited a school, from kindergarten on up to university level. In the kindergartens, a favorite program was almost invariably presented to us in which five- or six-year-olds appeared dressed in costumes typical of China's national minorities and sang patriotic songs, one of which was "I Greatly Love Beijing's Tian An Men." Later, in primary school, it was a common practice in the spring to send whole classes for a day to the communes just outside Beijing to help with the spring planting. From our apartment window Martha and I could hear these young people singing, evidently with some enthusiasm, the People's Liberation Army song "The Three Main Principles and the Eight Points of Attention" as they marched in military formation to the countryside.

Enthusiasm waned as students entered junior middle school and the day of being sent down approached. When we asked students what they thought of being sent down, the invariable answer was, "I will go wherever the government wants to send me." Their tone, however, suggested deep reservations. Once, at the Western Hills, we glimpsed from a hillside a young couple passionately embracing, and we felt the greatest sympathy for those young lovers. The chances were that when sent to the countryside, they would go to different destinations and never see each other again.

Other Cultural Contrasts

The political content of their curricula ruled out Chinese schools as a consideration for USLO children to attend, even if the Chinese would have consented. For various reasons the American children and their parents also ruled out the other options, the French or the British-style Pakistani school, so USLO set up a one-room school for the half-dozen or so USLO children of elementary school age. (I called it our "little Red schoolhouse.") The teachers were USLO dependents (our daughter Pat, Al Jenkins's daughter Sara, and several others), since we couldn't bring in professional teachers on diplomatic passports, which we felt was a necessary precaution in those first days of the new U.S. diplomatic presence in Beijing.

USLO's unusual American school was located in the broad hallway and porch just outside our apartment's front door. It was furnished with a State Department blackboard and typing tables and wooden chairs, cut down to size, and with painted packing crates. For materials and curriculum we relied on the Calvert correspondence system, supplemented by materials from Department of Defense schools in East Asia; by the talents of USLO officers and their dependents, who did everything from writing a Christmas play for the children to perform, to teaching them Chinese (I myself taught a miniclass on the U.S. Civil War); and by field trips to such places as tofu and noodle factories, to the Forbidden City and the Summer Palace, and to the Temple of the Sun park to play "King of the Mountain" or softball. Wherever they went, our schoolchildren were the center of attention for Chinese passers-by, who stared at the exuberant American youngsters with sometimes expressionless, sometimes curious, and only sometimes smiling faces. There were occasions when our pupils expressed frustration with their restrictive lifestyles and disdain for the Chinese political slogans and the cult of Chairman Mao. On the whole, however, they seemed to enjoy their unique school in Beijing.

In the midst of the spartan way of life of the average Chinese, we in USLO, along with other foreign diplomats, lived comfortably. We had access to the "Friendship Store," which contained a range of clothing, household goods, giftware, and foodstuffs often not available in the Chinese markets (even caviar from the region near Dalian). We also had access to the International Club near the USLO compound, open to foreigners and high-level cadres only, which offered a restaurant, tennis courts, and a swimming pool. Our housing was pleasant and fairly spacious, even lavish by local standards.

The discrepancies between our living standards and those of the Chinese surrounding us were sufficient to cause resentments among elements of the people who came into daily contact with foreigners. Most Chinese suppressed their feelings, but occasionally resentments broke out into the open. One such episode occurred in the small branch of the Friendship Store in our San Li Tun residential quarter, where an employee of the butcher shop whose job it was to haul frozen animal carcasses out of the freezer on an overhead rail to be chopped up for sale to foreigners, took the bill-hook used to pull the carcasses, went storming outside the Friendship Store, and in a rage struck down the first foreigner he encountered. This happened to be the wife of a French diplomat, who was pushing her little boy in a stroller just outside the store. Fortunately, while she suffered a jagged cut over the ear, she was not seriously injured; her attacker then rushed across the street into the Iraqi embassy compound from which he was dragged by the omnipresent PLA guards. We heard that he was later shot.

Another instance of antiforeign resentment came just before Martha's and my departure from Beijing, when a diplomat attached to one of the embassies adjacent to USLO one evening drove his wife on a shopping trip for fruit to a well-stocked fruit store on Wang Fu Jing just across from Beijing's major department store, the *Bai Huo Da Lou*. No parking was permitted on Wang Fu Jing, but the diplomat thought that by sitting in the car with the engine running while his wife dashed inside, he could escape the ban. At that point a member of the public security force, or a policeman, appeared on the scene, and in no uncertain tones told the diplomat to put his car in the parking lot of the *Bai Huo Da Lou*. The diplomat tried to argue that his wife would be out in just a moment, but the policeman was adamant. He raised his booted foot and bashed in the door of the diplomat's car. The chastened diplomat then moved his car to the parking lot.

These are but a few of many examples of the cultural contradictions that we experienced while in Beijing or when we were allowed to travel outside the capital city. (All travel had to be approved in advance by the Foreign Ministry and the Public Security Bureau; all too often our requests to travel would be answered with, *"Bu fang bien"*—"It's inconvenient"—which effectively cut us off from huge areas of China.) Other Western writers, notably the Belgian diplomat Simon Leys in his book *Chinese Shadows*,[2] have gone into far more detail about the clash of Western and Chinese cultures.

Credit at least must be given to Chinese leadership for the fact that over 1 billion Chinese people were fairly well fed, clothed, housed, and educated, even if politics dominated the scene, the niceties of life were absent, and life was fairly grim for the vast majority. I have profound doubts that many Chinese outside the *"gao ji gan bu"* level enjoyed their lot or the system itself, but this was the only life and system they had, and in classic Chinese style, they made the best of it.

One must also acknowledge the efforts made by the Chinese leadership to improve the medical care provided to the masses of people in China. In Beijing there were two major medical colleges, the former Rockefeller Hospital medical school, now known as the "Capital Hospital," and the Institute of Chinese Native Medicine, located on Beijing's ring road north of San Li Tun. The latter taught Chinese traditional medical practices such as acupuncture and moxibustion and herbal treatment, along with a goodly input of more modern techniques. Both modern and traditional techniques undoubtedly had useful functions; certainly one could expect a Chinese doctor to have training in both. As to acupuncture, I personally witnessed major operations in which acupuncture techniques were the sole anesthetic, and a visiting friend who had a relapse of a chronic back ailment was treated successfully by acupuncture at the Capital Hospital.

Outside the big cities, there were thousands of so-called "barefoot doctors" who made at least rudimentary health care available to all the people. The "barefoot doctors" were young people who had been given a six-months or so crash course in both Western and traditional medical techniques and who were able to handle the more conventional ailments without calling on physicians. Thus, despite the ever-present admonitions to "put politics in command," the needs of the people were being given due attention.

Conditions in the early 1970s certainly seemed more tolerable for those in the cities than for peasants on the communes, though now that appears to be changing. On a trip to Shanghai in 1992 our guide spoke rather bitterly about the increased income enjoyed by peasants in the "townships" (these have replaced the "communes"), as compared to the lot of workers and intellectuals in the cities. I often recall the words spoken to me in October 1971 by Zhang Wenjin about the Chinese leadership's concern to improve living standards in the countryside. (The words "living standards" were never used; "the material condition of the masses" was the catch phrase.) Manifestly, during our stay in Beijing, the seeds were already present that later grew into the reforms of Deng Xiaoping, who must have perceived the apathy and disregard for politics that pervaded Chinese society. These reforms for the most part remain in effect today, if only in economic rather than political matters, but I am convinced that economic reforms will in due course drag political reforms along in their wake.

Chapter 9

USLO and Internal Chinese Political Developments

The "Restoration of Names"

Almost from the moment that the United States Liason Office (USLO) set up shop in Beijing we became aware of a factional struggle going on within China's leadership. Our evidence was a constant propaganda theme in the *People's Daily* and other Chinese Communist publications— *Red Flag* (the Party's monthly journal), *Gong Ren Ri Bao* (*Worker's Daily*), *Guang Ming Ri Bao* (*Brightness Daily*), the paper allegedly of the intellectuals, and, in fact, every major Chinese journal. The issue was a campaign to criticize Confucius, China's great philosopher who had lived around the sixth century B.C.E., during the so-called "Spring and Autumn" period and who, while seeking but never attaining high political rank, left a profound impression on subsequent Chinese political and moral thought. The issue on which Confucius was being criticized was "restoration of names." This referred to his recommendation that experienced leaders from the feudal social order that had been overthrown in favor of unitary political states be restored to positions of responsibility so that their talents could be employed by the new rulers.

A word is necessary here about Mao Zedong's "Great Proletarian Cultural Revolution." After the failure of Mao's "Great Leap Forward," (1958 until the early 1960s) the more pragmatic members of China's leadership had in the early 1960s eased Mao into what he himself called the "second line" and had proceeded to downgrade ideology and run China more on pragmatic rather than solely ideological grounds. Nevertheless, Mao's prestige remained great. During the period 1962–66, he was able to reach out to China's younger generation, many of whose members

143

were dissatisfied with the entrenched bureaucracy and with the rewards the revolution had brought them. From among these youth Mao organized the "Red Guards" to oppose his critics.

On 18 August 1966, Chairman Mao staged a massive rally of the Red Guards in Beijing's Tian An Men square. Flanked by the deputy minister of defense and head of the armed forces, Lin Biao, Mao in an emotional address enjoined the assembled young people to "storm the Party headquarters," where his critics were to be found. With this rally as a starting point, the Red Guards were unleashed nationwide to strike at anybody and anything not considered sufficiently revolutionary. Assisting Mao to direct his "revolution within a revolution" were his wife Jiang Qing, Zhang Chunqiao from Shanghai, Wang Hongwen, and "commissar of culture" Yao Wenyuan.

For some five years, a reign of terror gripped China. The Red Guards wreaked destruction on many of China's cherished cultural legacies, and they publicly humiliated any person they suspected of being "antirevolutionary," especially among China's intellectuals. The Red Guards often removed such "antirevolutionary" intellectuals from their jobs and imprisoned them: literally thousands of Chinese men and women spent years studying politics and doing manual labor at the "May 7 Cadre Schools" set up by Mao and his supporters to "reeducate" the intellectuals.

During the Cultural Revolution, many top officials fell by the wayside, including Liu Shaoqi, long considered second only to Mao in the party hierarchy but who died in prison from pneumonia, and Marshal Chen Yi, who for many years had served loyally as mayor of Shanghai and foreign minister and who died in this period from unspecified causes. Among the major targets of the Red Guards was Liu Shaoqi's wife, Wang Guangmei, who was denounced for wearing silk dresses, furs, and strings of pearls on trips abroad.

The inevitable result of such "storming" was massive internal chaos. Among the few individuals holding China together were Premier Zhou Enlai and, in all likelihood, several PLA leaders, all of whom must have seen China's vulnerability to outside attack during the upheavals, and who must have realized the great extent to which the internal fabric of the country had been strained. Zhou Enlai did a remarkable job of staying in Mao's good graces, while at the same time keeping enough of the governmental structure together to prevent its collapse. By the fall of 1968, even Mao perceived that the Red Guards had gone too far. In a fit of anger he sent 30,000 of them from Beijing to the old revolutionary capital at Yan'an to learn more about the real revolutionary struggle of the Chinese Communist Party (CCP) and placed many key industries under the direct control of the People's Liberation Army (PLA).

It was precisely during this period that China's opening to the United States occurred, virtually removing the possibility of a U.S. attack on China and leaving only the Soviet Union as a continuing—and very potent—threat. It speaks volumes about the Chinese judgment about the overriding menace of the Soviet Union that they were willing to overlook ideological considerations and make such a drastic shift in policy vis-à-vis "U.S. imperialism," and to take steps towards establishing a relationship with the United States.

The Cultural Revolution was winding down when Dr. Kissinger's party arrived in July 1971, but the ideologues were still around, even by 1973. By that time Mao Zedong had begun to show signs of increasing infirmity, including periods of loss of lucidity.[1] What was happening as USLO opened was in effect a power struggle, with ideology as its platform, for the succession to Mao. The power struggle was between the more realistic elements, headed by Zhou Enlai, and those closely identified with Mao and his so-called "Mao Zedong thought," which took as its objective "carrying the revolution through to the end, both at home and abroad."

I have never believed that the Maoists were all that motivated by ideology, but rather used ideology primarily as a weapon against their opponents in the power struggle. Wang Hongwen had replaced Lin Biao as Mao's putative heir, Lin having died following his abortive anti-Mao coup (see chapter 4). When the anti-Confucius campaign was juxtaposed with current Chinese political developments, it became obvious to us in USLO that the target of the campaign to criticize Confucius was Zhou Enlai. To keep the country running, Zhou had protected and eventually "restored" many of the people whom Mao Zedong had targeted during the Cultural Revolution, notably Deng Xiaoping.

Deng Xiaoping had reappeared in public for the first time since 1966 on 1 May 1973, at the annual observances in Beijing of May Day, which was simultaneously being celebrated throughout the entire Communist world as Labor Day. Deng, as general secretary of the CCP, had been an early target of the Cultural Revolution, and his reappearance created a sensation (among other "crimes," he had been accused of liking to play the nonrevolutionary Western card game of bridge). In the interim, Deng reportedly had fled from Beijing to Canton, where he had been sheltered from the Red Guards by Ye Jianying.

Zhou's move to bring Deng Xiaoping back into the limelight must have stemmed from a judgment that Zhou's ideological opponents no longer had the strength to block this move in the wake of the massive damage inflicted upon China by the Cultural Revolution. China also faced a new threat from the Soviet Union. An additional factor was probably the realization that to survive, China needed leaders with Deng's pragmatism and grasp of realities. Moreover, although Mao must have approved Deng's return, Mao's illness, or whatever it was that caused his lapses from lucidity, was worsening, as his better moments were increasingly interspersed with episodes of incoherence.

Manifestly, the clique of ideologues surrounding Mao did not take kindly to Deng's reappearance, nor to the "restoration" policy it represented. The principal members of this clique were the four mentioned earlier: Wang Hongwen, Jiang Qing, Zhang Chunqiao, and Yao Wenyuan. These individuals launched their indirect attack on Zhou Enlai through the media, which was then under the control of Yao Wenyuan. It was in the environment of the power struggle just described that USLO came into existence and began to operate in Beijing. Outwardly, Beijing appeared calm, but behind the scenes, above all in the sacred confines of the Zhongnanhai Party Headquarters, tensions must have been running high.

The first open indication of retaliation by the pragmatists against the "Maoists" occurred in August 1973, with the convening of the Tenth Congress of the Chinese Communist Party. Martha and I were awakened one night in our nine-story apartment building by the loud sound of drums and shouting; looking out the window we saw a procession of college-age youths pass by beating a huge drum mounted on a wagon and shouting slogans acclaiming the "great victory" of the Tenth Party Congress. What this "victory" amounted to, at least in part, was the insertion of an additional target for criticism alongside Confucius: Lin Biao. The anti-Confucius campaign now had become "the campaign to criticize Lin and Confucius," or "*pi* (criticize) *Lin, pi Kong* (for *Kong Fuze*, or "Confucius"), which was carried on at great length throughout China for many months.

I myself was never very clear as to what might link Confucius and Lin Biao, and I believe that the average Chinese must have had the same sense of bewilderment. Lin's sin was plotting against Mao—hardly the equivalent of "restoration of names." I do remember seeing a small box on the front page of the *People's Daily* the day after the tenth plenum that observed that the writer, a student, "had never understood the significance of the campaign to criticize Confucius until he had read the communiqué of the Tenth Party Congress," and had now dedicated himself to joining in the criticism of Lin Biao. Not until Dr. Kissinger arrived for a visit that November did the pieces fall into place. During dinner at the Great Hall of the People, I heard Zhou Enlai laughingly tell Dr. Kissinger, through an interpreter, of course, that he himself had taken advantage of the Tenth Party Congress to initiate the *"pi Lin"* aspect of the campaign. What Zhou's move did was to so thoroughly confuse the issue of who was being criticized, and for what, that the impact of the entire campaign was lost.

Combating the "Poisonous Weeds" of Western Culture

The next move was also Zhou's, as I look back on the events of those times. It involved Americans and the U.S. Liaison Office to the extent that we unwittingly provided an opportunity for Zhou to strike a blow against Jiang Qing and her clique. In October 1973 the Philadelphia Orchestra, under the conductorship of Eugene Ormandy, visited China on a cultural exchange, and it made quite a hit. As was its custom, the orchestra opened its rehearsals to music students, and it also played to packed audiences. The final performance, though, was the great event. Held in the Hall of the Nationalities, it was graced with the presence of Jiang Qing herself, accompanied by Yao Wenyuan. Jiang Qing was seated next to Ambassador David Bruce, and Yao Wenyuan next to Evangeline Bruce. Other USLO personnel were present, including Al Jenkins and his wife Martha, my wife Martha, and me.

The program was noteworthy in that the orchestra had been informed that it would play Beethoven's Sixth Symphony as a special request. All of the music the orchestra was to perform had been agreed upon prior to its departure from the United States, and Beethoven's Sixth definitely had not been included. When Eugene Ormandy protested the Chinese inclusion of the Sixth in the program and said the orchestra didn't have the music with it, he was told that Beethoven was a "must," and that the music would be flown in from Shanghai. Beethoven's Sixth was then duly played in fine professional style by the Philadelphia Orchestra, in a program that also included Respighi's "Pines of Rome" and ended with a rousing rendition of Sousa's "The Stars and Stripes Forever." The audience was thoroughly happy, and especially happy was the conductor of the Beijing Philharmonic Ensemble, Li Delun, who felt that a real breakthrough in culture and the arts, away from the "revolutionary" themes fostered by Jiang Qing, had been achieved thanks to the Philadelphia Orchestra's visit.

To my mind, there was no doubt but that the playing of Beethoven's Sixth had been initiated by Jiang Qing herself, recalling the episode during Kissinger's October 1971 visit when this particular symphony had been featured prominently in the cultural program hosted by Jiang Qing in the Great Hall of the People. On that occasion there had been gasps of surprise from the cadres and their wives who were present when Beethoven's music was heard, perhaps for the first time publicly since the Cultural Revolution began.

Adding to the special nature of the orchestra's final performance in Beijing, after the program the senior people from the Philadelphia Orchestra and USLO, including Eugene Ormandy and his wife, David and Evangeline Bruce, Al and Martha Jenkins, and Martha and I, were directed into a narrow reception room at the side of the Hall of the Nationalities, where Jiang Qing, Yao Wenyuan, and Li Delun were waiting to congratulate the orchestra's conductor. Nancy Tang was along as interpreter. Jiang Qing set out to charm Eugene Ormandy, first giving him a personally autographed book on Chinese music (in Chinese, naturally), and then handing him a small plastic envelope of cassia flowers, which she said she had picked herself that afternoon in her garden.[2] These blossoms were intended to be given to the members of the Philadelphia Orchestra, she said, who could either smell them (here she sniffed the fragrance herself), or else "they could put them in their tea." On this note, the interview closed, and the orchestra went back to a triumphal late night dinner at its hotel. The next day, it departed from Beijing, seen off by most members of USLO, who had particularly enjoyed their playing of "The Stars and Stripes Forever" at the concert.

It might have been assumed that with the Philadelphia Orchestra's departure, the Sixth Symphony episode was over, but it didn't turn out that way. About two weeks later when I went to the office and opened my copy of *People's Daily*, I was confronted on the inside front page with a long article containing a great many Chinese characters new to me. Consulting my Chinese-English dictionary, I finally determined that the article represented an attack on Western "program" music, *especially* pieces such as Beethoven's Sixth Symphony and Respighi's *Pines of Rome*—the two major pieces on the Philadelphia Orchestra's program—because music such as this "watered down the revolutionary enthusiasm of the masses."

It seems clear to me that Zhou Enlai had succeeded in gaining enough access to the *People's Daily* to generate this attack, which was patently targeted against Jiang Qing, the originator of the attacks against him in the anti-Confucius campaign. She had left herself and her crony Yao Wenyuan exposed for "watering down the revolutionary enthusiasm of the masses" as a result of attending—and probably determining at least part of the content of—the Philadelphia Orchestra's final performance. Jiang

Qing's enjoyment of the lilting melodies in Beethoven's Sixth was surely well known in China's inner party circles (I had seen it myself in October 1971, see chapter 4); the less familiar *Pines of Rome* was an added bonus for those seeking an excuse to embarrass her on ideological grounds.

If one thought that this episode represented the last shot fired in the running battle between the ideologues, represented by Jiang Qing and her clique, and the more moderately inclined group led by Zhou Enlai, such was not the case. Some few weeks after reading the *People's Daily* blast against Western program music, I again found myself confronted in my early morning reading of the *People's Daily* with an article containing an unusual number of unfamiliar words on the subject of *"Ang Dong Ni Ang Ni Wu Ru Zhong Guo."* Once more obliged to consult my dictionary, I worked it out that *"Ang Dong Ni Ang Ni"* was the well-known Italian film director Antonioni and that he had made a film on China that allegedly insulted or debased that country and its people.

Antonioni's sin, according to the *People's Daily*, was that in making his film he had ignored the achievements of the New China and concentrated on the old. For example, while shooting a scene of the great railroad bridge at Nanjing, of which the Chinese are particularly proud because it was designed and built entirely by Chinese with no Soviet help, Antonioni's camera had panned from the bridge to a little boy standing on the river bank wearing the traditional Chinese infants' trousers with an open split in the seat. Chinese indignation against Antonioni for failing to play up the New China reportedly knew no bounds, and even the People's Police traffic director in front of the Tian An Men was quoted as expressing his rancor against Antonioni's alleged insults to China. Of course, Antonioni had been allowed into China to make the film by Zhou Enlai himself, and it was the information department of the Foreign Ministry, answerable to Zhou, that had issued the permit. Jiang Qing and her cohorts had caught out Zhou and his Foreign Ministry supporters.

A nationwide campaign against Western culture followed, which influenced Chinese throughout the nation. Both *People's Daily* articles described above were the origin of this campaign, which caused the cancellation of the visit of at least one European symphony orchestra and put all resident foreigners on edge. The daughter of the Lebanese ambassador on one occasion, while driving with the son of the Belgian ambassador, made the mistake in a tourist shopping area of putting her cigarette lighter up against her eye as if it were a miniature camera. She and her friend were immediately surrounded by a horde of angry Chinese and accused of being spies. They both spent hours in the local public security precinct station trying to convince the Public Security Bureau cadres that she had been joking and that the cigarette lighter was not a camera.

In another similar incident, an American couple, friends of ours visiting with a Canadian delegation, were detained at length for innocently taking a picture that didn't show China at its revolutionary best. We had advised them to ask their guide if there were any objections to taking pictures of scenes that caught their attention, and the wife had done so in Shanghai's Bund as a river boat was docking. After the guide had said "okay," though, a door in the boat's deckhouse opened, and a little boy emerged and proceeded to urinate in the river just as the picture was being taken. The two Americans were taken to the local precinct house, where the officials demanded that the wife give up the film, which she refused to do. The result was that they were "struggled," that is, questioned and shouted at, all night before the public security people finally gave up and let them go. Martha and I happened to be on our way to Hong Kong by air at this time, and we encountered them at the airport in Shanghai, both badly shaken.

The effects of this anti-Western campaign did not wear off for months, and for the Chinese, cultural malfeasance could become a major sin. Wu De, the mayor of Beijing when USLO was established, was one of the victims, having been guilty of some obscure cultural crime having to do with the play "Thrice up Peach Mountain," which was staged under his jurisdiction, and he lost his job as a result. (I never could determine just what was ideologically wrong with this play.) Wu De, I believe, was a member of the Zhou Enlai faction—or at least he was more conservative or pragmatic when compared with the "Gang of Four." Although I suspect that few Chinese knew what was behind the blast of anti-Westernism and its accompanying criticism of domestic cultural presentations, the *People's Daily* had set the line, which was followed everywhere. If it had served the purpose of deflecting criticism away from Zhou Enlai, it was also turned against him; inevitably, various Chinese officials were caught in the middle of the ongoing battle for ideological high ground raging between the Maoists and the moderates.

Among the Chinese officials who must have had difficulty steering safely between the two "lines" struggling for power in China was Qiao Guanhua, who by this time had become foreign minister, replacing Ji Pengfei. In the company of his peers, Qiao always appeared to me to be insecure and tense, although when he was in a more or less completely foreign environment, such as at a diplomatic affair, he was much more relaxed. I noted his tenseness once when he was guest of honor at a dinner given by George and Barbara Bush, who had by then replaced the Bruces at the top of USLO (see below). Seated on Qiao's right, I became aware that he was nervously bouncing his right knee the whole evening. Sitting across from him were his wife and several other members of the Foreign Ministry. This was at a time when the outcry against Western culture and what became known as "poisonous weeds" (Western-influenced and nonideological ways of doing things) was at its height, and Qiao—a long-time supporter of Zhou Enlai—certainly appeared ill at ease.

In contrast, I learned that at a party given in his honor by the chiefs of mission of all the Scandinavian countries to honor the twenty-fifth anniversary of their common exchange of diplomatic relations with China, Qiao, who was unaccompanied, enjoyed himself hugely and drank liberal draughts of aquavit, scotch whiskey, wine at dinner, and after-dinner brandy or liqueurs. Indeed, at a dinner party given by Qiao for all USLO personnel shortly after the office opened, with only one or two minor Foreign Ministry officials and interpreters present, Qiao had behaved in much the same way, opening his Mao jacket and enjoying the liquid refreshments to the utmost.

Mao Zedong in his more lucid moments was evidently aware of the forces at work around him. Not too long after USLO opened, he asked several members of its staff to attend a basketball game. David Bruce and Al Jenkins attended. (I missed it due to my first bout with Beijing's pervasive upper respiratory infections.) During the game, a few words were exchanged privately between Mao and David Bruce, during which Mao pointed to the inevitable duo with him as interpreters, Nancy Tang and Wang Hairong, and referred to them as "those spies."[3] Evidently Mao had drawn the conclusion, not a mistaken one in my judgment, that the two had attached themselves to the Jiang Qing faction. Indeed, the influence of these two must have become increasingly great as Mao's periods of lucidity diminished, and foreign visitors were obliged to rely upon what they heard from Nancy Tang and Wang Hairong as the true words of Mao.

An example of the potential influence of the two interpreters was provided to me by the ambassador of a NATO country with whom I was quite close and who had been present when his visiting prime minister had called on Mao. Upon entering Mao's study, two female nurses standing on each side of the chairman had heaved Mao erect from his chair while the elderly gentleman babbled something that to the visitors was entirely unintelligible. The interpreters without blinking an eye went through the formality of telling their distinguished visitor how pleased the chairman was to see him and how the visit would improve the good relations between their two peoples.[4]

It seemed plain to me that the factional confrontation in the CCP was bitter indeed, and that it was fueled in part by the failing health of not only Mao Zedong but also Zhou Enlai, although the issue of these leaders' health was not discussed publicly. The *People's Daily* often showed Mao (at times looking rather emaciated and senile) greeting foreign guests, one of whom early on in our stay was Imelda Marcos from the Philippines, or conferring with senior personalities in China, such as Wang Hongwen.

Zhou Enlai, also weakening during this period due to his prostate cancer, left Deng Xiaoping to carry the burden of state, but this was not made official. As of Henry Kissinger's November 1974 visit Deng presided over the bilateral discussions. (When Kissinger met with Deng and his colleagues in the Great Hall that November, Deng glanced to his left or right after every statement, as if to reassure himself that he had said the right things.) Rumors of Zhou's health problems were confirmed in the summer of 1974 by the visit of Senator Henry A. ("Scoop") Jackson, who succeeded in visiting Zhou in the hospital and reported that oxygen equipment was ready for use outside Zhou's room.

The Philadelphia Orchestra incident aside, USLO managed to escape much of the onus of the anti-Western campaign. Kissinger may well have determined the reason during his November 1973 visit, when he met with Chairman Mao. Accompanied only by U.S. Liaison Office Chief David Bruce, Kissinger had a long, philosophic chat with the chairman, who was then enjoying a lucid moment. (Photographs of the meeting were published by the Chinese media to indicate continuing friendship.) Mao made it clear that Soviet expansionism still operated upon his mind.[5] Mao did, however, mention that, "the U.S. was trying to stand on China's shoulders to get at the USSR."[6] The "marriage" between the United States and China, if that was what it might have been called, was obviously one of convenience and not the result of any great bond between our two governments. In fact, as the internal struggle within the CCP went through its various twists and turns, USLO would occasionally go for weeks without any contact with Chinese officialdom. Perhaps we were fortunate that the infighting diverted attention from USLO and U.S.-China relations.

There was, nevertheless, one sad episode in which USLO indirectly became entangled in internal Chinese politics. It was a case in which our senior political officer, Nick Platt, while driving to the Ming Tombs and the Great Wall with his family and visiting parents, struck a young Chinese girl on a bicycle who suddenly came out of a side road and crossed his path. She suffered serious head injuries as a result of the accident. Although Nick commandeered a truck to take her to the nearest hospital that could handle such injuries, the girl died. He was profoundly distressed by this tragic outcome of the accident.

In response to a telephone call from Nick, I accompanied him to the Public Security Bureau headquarters near the Beijing Hotel and sat with him during a preliminary hearing. Later, the PSB investigated the skid marks on the road and concluded he had been exceeding the speed limit. Whether or not this was true, we were not permitted to dispute it. The girl was an only child, the mother was distraught, and, as we were told by the PSB, "Feelings in the commune where the girl lived were very high": this was the crux of the matter. Eventually we settled the unfortunate affair (much to the relief of the PSB) by making an *ex gratia* payment of 20,000 *yuan*, but without acknowledging any fault on Nick's part. Ironically, the payment was made by the Chinese-owned People's Insurance Company, and not by the U.S. government. The aftermath was rather bitter, though, for the Foreign Ministry pointedly told us that in cases of this nature the country concerned customarily withdrew the officer "voluntarily." So the Platt family regretfully eventually had to leave Beijing. My reading of this situation was that while the PSB tried to act in a fair manner, the "feelings," that is, the political reaction of the commune members, conditioned as they were by anti-Western propaganda, certainly played an important part in this case. The U.S. government "voluntarily" withdrew Nick in order not to imperil U.S.-China relations. It is possible that failure to resolve this issue promptly could have benefited those elements in the CCP who opposed the rapprochement with the United States.

Throughout the early period following USLO's opening, Zhou Enlai was instrumental in keeping China on a more or less even course. His worsening illness, which meant absences from the political scene, surely must have deprived his adherents of much of his wisdom and protection. Zhou remained true to his principles, as was exemplified by his speech at the National People's Congress in January 1975, when his main theme was China's need for modernization (this was the first mention of the "four modernizations" of agriculture, industry, national defense, and science and technology). However, when the Party journals carried Zhou's speech, they also printed an article blasting "bourgeois liberalism" and strongly directing the Chinese people to oppose such thinking. Along with the incessant campaign against "poisonous weeds," this seemed to be evidence that the ideologues were able to muster considerable power. In fact, when President Gerald Ford visited China in the latter part of 1975, he found Deng Xiaoping strangely uncommunicative on matters that previously had been discussed regularly with the United States (see below). Deng was obviously under pressure and very much on the defensive.

Zhou Enlai's death on 8 January 1976 was followed later by large-scale pro-Zhou demonstrations in Tian An Men Square on "*qing ming*," the traditional day in China for mourning the dead, which fell on 5 April. These occurred spontaneously when many ordinary Chinese, especially students, attempted to place funeral wreaths in honor of Zhou at the Monument to Revolutionary Martyrs but were deterred by public security personnel. The demonstrations gave the ideologues the chance they needed to get rid of Deng Xiaoping on the grounds that he had failed to keep proper order. Deng then disappeared for the second time. With Zhou dead and Deng gone, the "Gang of Four" took over.

The growing accession to power of the Gang of Four, which lasted only until Mao Zedong's death in September 1976, did not mean a complete return to the ideological precepts of the past. An illustration of this was the Chinese response to a speech by Kim Il Sung of North Korea. In May 1975, Kim paid a state visit to China (by rail, since he never traveled by air). At the banquet in his honor at the Great Hall of the People,[7] to which representatives of all the diplomatic missions but USLO were invited, Kim proclaimed that in the event of widespread civil disturbances in South Korea, it would be the North's "proletarian international duty to come to the aid of its brethren in the South, and the only thing that would be lost was the military line of demarcation." This speech had obviously been intended to seek Chinese backing for a North Korean military attack on the South following the North Vietnamese victory in Vietnam. However, China's response, given by Li Xiannian, repeatedly stressed the theme of "peaceful reunification." When Kim Il Sung returned to Korea, he also was speaking in terms of "peaceful reunification." Chinese caution regarding another conflict in Korea must have prevailed.[8]

To the outside world, at least, pragmatism and national self-preservation predominated; nevertheless, the political atmosphere in China, especially in Beijing, was tense to the point sometimes of being explosive. Highly placed leaders were dropping out of sight, and from what we in USLO could observe, no Chinese, from our cook to Premier Zhou Enlai, felt himself safe from the ideological struggles to determine the direction for China's future. The "struggling" against the Belgian and Lebanese teenagers mentioned above is but a small example of the tension under which the Chinese lived.

Some of the bitterness that surrounded the protagonists in the struggle that persisted long after Mao's death surely was due to Mao's violation of a fundamental Confucian principle: the prince owed his loyalty to the lord, but the lord in turn had an obligation to return that loyalty to his supporters and protect them. Mao, in attacking the very people who had stood by him through the many years of civil war and struggle, was acting in a way that violated the very essence of Chinese political and cultural tradition. Many of Mao's one-time adherents felt that their loyalty had been betrayed; this contributed to their antipathy to Chairman Mao and his ideology.

New USLO Leadership

While China was in the throes of its leadership struggle, we in USLO had a sudden leadership change of our own. In August 1974 David Bruce called me to his office and showed me a telegram from the State Department informing him that he was to be replaced by George Bush, then chairman of the Republican National Committee. This abrupt change was a real shock to Bruce, as it was to me. The explanation that eventually emerged was simple enough: George Bush had been a serious contender for the office of vice president of the United States when Spiro Agnew resigned, and when Gerald Ford had received the job, Bush had been offered as a consolation prize virtually any U.S. government job he wanted; he had picked chief of the U.S. Liaison Office in Beijing. Another consolation prize was being offered to Bruce, the ambassadorship to the NATO Alliance, based in Brussels. I urged him to accept this appointment despite his reservations, for it would allow him to leave his Beijing post with dignity and, based on his European service, put him back on familiar ground where he could make a real contribution. On departing, though, he remarked to me as we walked to the airplane that he was "very sad." He had already told me that he had not necessarily intended to stay in China for a full tour, but he at least wanted to pick his own time for leaving.

The Chinese greatly respected David Bruce: on or near the eve of his departure they arranged in his honor a "palace-style" dinner in the Summer Palace area where the Empress Ci Xi had often dined and watched Chinese opera. It was an extraordinary occasion, in that the dinner was served after the Summer Palace officially closed, and we had the whole place to ourselves.[9] The moon was shining on the Kunming Lake, and from across its waters we could hear the sound of Chinese music ("revolutionary," of course, but still very evocative) from the radios of peasants who lived nearby. The effect of this hospitality was to recall China's past, and it made a profound impression on all of us.

David Bruce's departure left me as chargé d'affaires, since Al and

Martha Jenkins had already departed, and the Bushes were not due until October. It was under these circumstances that I represented the United States at the huge dinner in the Great Hall of the People held by the Chinese every year on 30 September for all "foreign guests" to celebrate the anniversary of the establishment of the People's Republic of China on 1 October 1949. With me were Evangeline Bruce, who had remained behind in Beijing to close out the Bruces' household, and Martha. Even though we were seated at the farthest table from the head table and the stage due to our anomalous diplomatic status (we ranked just below the PLO contingent), the slight was greatly mitigated in that the head of the Americas and Pacific Ocean Areas (or Oceanian) division of the Foreign Ministry, Lin Ping, and his seniormost associates, were our table hosts. This occasion was the last public appearance by Zhou Enlai, although, as I have mentioned above, Zhou did make a key speech at the National People's Congress the following January. Another guest at this function was Ajitorop, successor to Aidit as leader of the Indonesian Communist Party (PKI), indicating that—nominally, at least—the Chinese Communist Party still supported revolutionary movements elsewhere, including in Southeast Asia.[10]

When George and Barbara Bush arrived, they plunged vigorously into the USLO and Beijing scene, working hard to learn all they could as quickly as possible about China and its current problems, and touring the city and its environs. A typical sight in the fall of 1974 was seeing the Bushes, both wearing face masks, riding bicycles into the teeth of the grit-laden wind that seemed to be blowing constantly from the direction of the Gobi desert. USLO officials soon learned to admire George Bush, who listened carefully to the opinions of those who had been in Beijing longer than he had. He also began to study Chinese with USLO's Chinese teacher.

An early task Mr. Bush had was to pay a formal call on Deng Xiaoping, then acting in Zhou Enlai's place, in the Great Hall of the People. The conversation was most friendly, with Deng eloquently describing plans for "mechanizing" Chinese agriculture, which up to then, he said, was like "manicuring the land" (here he made a motion with his fingers similar to the opening and closing of scissors). I couldn't help but wonder how mechanization of Chinese agriculture could proceed very far without creating a vast unemployment problem. (This issue in part has been resolved more recently with the disbandment of the communes by allowing the "townships," the successors to the communes, to establish their own small-scale industries, many of which are thriving. But thousands of peasants continue to flock into the cities.)

In November 1974 Dr. Kissinger made another visit to China, hoping once again to see Chairman Mao. This hope was not realized. The chairman, it seemed, was not in Beijing, and it would be "inconvenient" to arrange a visit to wherever it was that he was residing. It was Mao's habit to leave Beijing when the weather started to turn cold, and we suspected at the time that he was not in good enough physical shape to meet with Kissinger. Neither was Zhou Enlai in shape to preside over the visit of a distinguished foreign visitor (or at least this was what we assumed), and the result was that the formal talks between Kissinger and his Chinese counterpart were with Deng Xiaoping, who filled in for Zhou. (Kissinger did have a rather brief thirty-minute hospital meeting with Zhou Enlai, however.)

The Kissinger party was unusually large, Dr. Kissinger having brought with him not only Assistant Secretary for East Asian and Pacific Affairs Philip Habib, but also Assistant Secretary for Public Affairs Robert Anderson, plus all their assorted staff assistants. It was at this meeting, mentioned earlier, that Deng Xiaoping seemed to be looking to his colleagues seated to his left and right for assurances that he was following the correct party line.

As a consolation prize to Kissinger for not seeing Chairman Mao, the Chinese arranged a trip by air to the beautiful and historic city of Suzhou for Dr. and Mrs. Kissinger and other senior people in his party, including those from USLO. George and Barbara Bush headed the USLO contingent. I somehow doubt that the chance to view Suzhou's scenery compensated Kissinger for not seeing Mao, but for the rest of us, including the Chinese who accompanied us, it was a grand excursion. Few, if any, of our Chinese hosts had ever visited Suzhou, a city world-famous for its gardens, which evidently had escaped the depredations of the Red Guards. There is a Chinese poem about Suzhou that declares "*Shang You Tian Tang, Xia You Su Hang*" (above, there is heaven, on earth there are Suzhou and Hangzhou). The gardens in the city—a favorite retirement spot for high-ranking officials in the Imperial era—were indeed lovely.

Following the Suzhou visit, the Kissingers returned to the United States from Shanghai, taking Barbara Bush with them for a Christmas visit to her home. Not long afterwards, George Bush departed on a trip to Washington, D.C., where he was to be inaugurated for a year as president of the prestigious Alfalfa Club. He traveled to Washington by way of Pakistan in response to a long-standing invitation from President Bhutto to visit his country. In Pakistan he did not see Bhutto, who at that moment was struggling for his political, and as events turned out, his physical life, but Bhutto sent him on a tour of the Khyber Pass area, where he had lunch at the officers' mess of the Khyber Rifles. Here he contracted a vicious strain of amoebic dysentery that nearly laid him low; in Washington he stayed on his feet long enough to deliver a brilliant acceptance speech at the Alfalfa Club, after which he collapsed. He was then admitted into Georgetown Hospital for a recovery that took several weeks. Not until after his recovery did he return to Beijing, and during his absence I again acted as chargé d'affaires.

While the USLO Chief was away, I had another opportunity to meet with Deng Xiaoping and to see him in action at close range. The occasion was the visit to China in early December of Mike Mansfield, then still a senior member of the U.S. Senate. Deng Xiaoping gave a luncheon in honor of the senator, to which I was also invited. Mike Mansfield's visit came at a period in U.S. politics when he was pushing hard for the withdrawal of all U.S. troops from Europe, and he was very anxious to have some support for this policy from senior leaders of other countries. Therefore, during the luncheon he asked Deng if he, Deng, didn't think that the United States was overextended militarily.

Deng's response was to stand up at the table, spread open his hands, and press down on the tabletop with his fingers extended, saying that the United States was like his fingers—its power was stretched out in a great many places (Deng was referring primarily to U.S. deployments in Asia), but each "finger" was vulnerable to being cut off by strong opposing forces. Deng's response to Mansfield reminded me of the briefing I had received the previous year while visiting the former Chinese Communist headquarters in Yan'an concerning Mao Zedong's strategy when Kuomintang troops were attacking the city and it was about to fall. Mao, I was told, had withdrawn Communist forces from Yan'an to induce the Kuomintang to overextend its armies and in this way make them more vulnerable to counterattack.[11] I'm sure that Deng's words pleased Senator Mansfield, even though I never had any indication afterwards that he used Deng's line in his campaign to get U.S. troops out of Europe.

A vignette of Deng Xiaoping's part in the CCP's revolutionary history emerged from this luncheon: at one point Mike Mansfield referred to Deng as "General," which caused Deng immediately and forcefully to contradict the senator. He had never been a military man, Deng said; his role in the military campaigns had been strictly political.

News reports covering both Kissinger's and Mansfield's visits to China dwelt on the fact that while Kissinger had met with Zhou Enlai for only thirty minutes, Mansfield had spent fifty-five minutes with Zhou. As a result, it was speculated in the Beijing diplomatic corps and the press that this discrepancy could be taken as a snub to Kissinger, allegedly because the United States was moving too slowly on normalizing diplomatic relations. Mike Mansfield was said to have confirmed Chinese impatience over the slow pace of normalization.[12] We in USLO discounted the possibility of a snub, recalling in this respect how Dr. Kissinger and Zhou Enlai enjoyed talking to each other—we attributed the time difference to the state of Zhou's health.

USLO and Cambodia

Over the course of about one year, from the spring of 1974 to 1975, USLO was intermittently involved in the political/military events in Cambodia, although, despite David Bruce's and my best efforts, the situation there intruded more into our consciousness than our activities. The tragic fighting in Cambodia between Cambodia's national forces and the Vietnamese-supported Khmer Rouge, with the resultant Communist takeover and accompanying slaughter of hundreds of thousands of Cambodian people, was one of the most agonizing experiences in U.S. military and diplomatic history. Responsibility for this situation unquestionably lies with the U.S. Congress, whose increasingly hostile attitude towards U.S. involvement in Cambodia eventually led to cessation of U.S. bombing of Khmer Rouge forces, and finally, to a cut-off date for all military assistance to the non-Communist Khmer.[13] The Khmer Rouge also did their part by refusing any hint of compromise.

Kissinger writes that in David Bruce's first formal meeting with Zhou Enlai on 18 May 1973, Zhou raised the question of Cambodia and said that "the only way to find a solution was for the parties concerned to implement fully all the subsidiary clauses of Article 20 [of the Vietnam Armistice Agreement]," which meant the withdrawal of all foreign troops (including, of course, the Vietnamese forces). During his November 1973 visit to China, Kissinger subsequently said, through Zhou Enlai, that the United States would not oppose Sihanouk's return to Phnom Penh under appropriate—but unstated—conditions.[14]

Apart from David Bruce's 18 May meeting with Zhou Enlai, however, we in Beijing were cut out of the information loop on the situation in Cambodia. Nevertheless, the problem of how best to resolve the fighting in Cambodia in a manner acceptable to all contestants did not leave our minds, and as the agony continued, as described fully by Kissinger in chapter 8 of his book *Years of Upheaval*,[15] David Bruce and I put our heads together and sent a telegram to Kissinger proposing that the United

States in fact should make an effort to reintroduce Sihanouk into the drama on the grounds that he possibly retained some influence among the Cambodian people and that his presence in Beijing might make him accessible to USLO. A peremptory rejection was our response; we concluded that whatever might then be going on, Kissinger wanted no one but himself to have a hand in it. Our telegram was sent in approximately May 1974, around a year after our arrival in Beijing.

Sometime not long afterwards a Khmer Rouge delegation headed by Ieng Sary and Khieu Samphan came to Beijing, and when, during a press conference given by the Khmer Rouge, Prince Sihanouk positioned himself on the stage in an effort to take part, he was ignored by the Khmer Rouge representatives and virtually shoved off the platform. This episode certainly indicated to us that his influence with the Khmer Rouge, if not with the Cambodian people, was minimal.

Following the arrival of George Bush as the new USLO chief, and actually only a few weeks before the fall of Phnom Penh, we in USLO, particularly George Bush and I, found ourselves drawn back into Cambodian political events. The cause was USLO's receipt of a letter from Prince Sihanouk in March 1975 requesting the help of the U.S. government to safeguard his collection of Cambodian music and musical instruments, left behind in his palace in Phnom Penh when he departed the country in 1970. He was worried about the safety of these items as the Khmer Rouge forces approached the city, and he asked if the U.S. government might be able to take charge of them and get them out of the country to Thailand before the city fell. We of course informed the State Department and our embassy in Phnom Penh. (To the best of my knowledge they did manage to evacuate Sihanouk's collection, although I've never heard of it since.) In addition, thinking that his letter might be a last-minute effort by Sihanouk to become involved in the outcome in Cambodia, we asked State's permission, which was granted, to see if he wished any further contacts with us to discuss "matters of common interest."

After a certain amount of sparring around, we did hear from Sihanouk, and I was asked by George Bush to meet with Sihanouk's chef de cabinet, Phung Peng Cheng, to discuss what steps might be taken. My discussions, naturally held under the close guidance of George Bush, took place mainly in the office of the French deputy chief of mission, Jean Malot (later French ambassador to China); they proceeded desultorily for several weeks, with Sihanouk apparently acting coy. The final act of this drama came in the early morning hours around the first of April, when a "NIACT" ("night action") cable from State instructed me to get in touch with Phung Peng Cheng "urgently" within the next few hours to establish whether or not Sihanouk was willing to take any action in the developing situation in Phnom Penh.

On this particular occasion, with much appreciation of Jean Malot's tolerance, at 6:30 A.M. I met with Phung Peng Cheng in the Malot apartment and conveyed, I hope, the anxieties under which Washington was laboring—the Khmer Rouge were only a few miles from Phnom Penh—and the fervent hope that Sihanouk might be able to play a part. Sadly, this whole effort came to naught: in the next day or so we received a letter from Sihanouk stating that he would "do nothing which would offend the Khmer Rouge." Sihanouk had read the handwriting on the wall—correctly, it seems. If we at USLO had been able to act earlier, though, perhaps things could have been different. In making our contacts with Sihanouk, we took pains to keep the Chinese informed, and their only reaction was to wish us well.

The *Mayaguez* Incident

Another USLO concern involving the Khmer Rouge in Cambodia took place while George Bush and I were both in Beijing: the *Mayaguez* incident. This involved a U.S. merchant ship belonging to the Sea-Land Corporation, which was engaged in transshipping containers to and from larger Sea-Land vessels in Hong Kong and assorted Southeast Asian ports. The ship, the *Mayaguez*, was seized off the Cambodian coast by the Khmer Rouge a few days after Phnom Penh fell. The captain had radioed a distress signal while sailing well outside the three-mile limit, he claimed, but the *Mayaguez* was nevertheless boarded, its crew taken prisoner, and the ship moved to an island off Sihanoukville, or Kampong Som, Cambodia's principal port. Official Washington was outraged and determined not to let what was regarded as piracy go unanswered; it wanted rather to make a show of force against the Khmer Rouge.

Again USLO received a NIACT, which directed us immediately to seek out the (North) Vietnamese embassy in Beijing and inform them that unless the ship and crew were released forthwith, military action would be taken to recover both. There was no other way known to Washington of contacting the Khmer Rouge. This telegram arrived in the afternoon of a day in mid-April; it happened that George Bush was on a trip to the Great Wall and Ming Tombs with some visiting VIPs, so the action was mine. What I did was to have USLO's chief political officer, Don Anderson, who spoke fluent French transcribe the ultimatum into French and carry the transcript to the Vietnamese embassy.

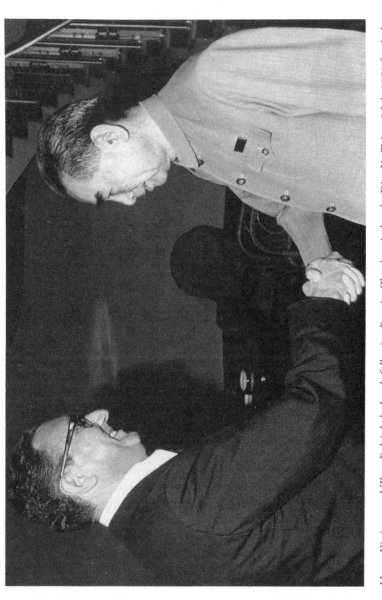

Henry Kissinger and Zhou Enlai shake hands following Premier Zhou's arrival at the Diao Yu Tai on 9 July 1971 for the beginning of Sino–U.S. talks. This historic handshake between China's premier and a senior U.S. official was the first such encounter since U.S. Secretary of State Dulles turned his back and refused to take Premier Zhou's hand at the 1954 Geneva talks. (Chinese government photo)

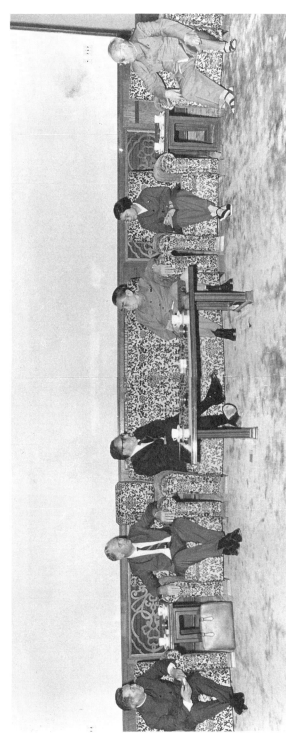

Preceding the formal discussions on 9 July 1971, between Zhou Enlai and Henry Kissinger, there was a less formal conversation over a cup of tea—a typical Chinese custom. The photo shows, (l to r): Huang Hua, the author, Dr. Kissinger, Premier Zhou, Nancy Tang (interpreter), and Marshal Ye Jianying. (Chinese government photo)

First talks with Premier Zhou Enlai, 9 July 1971 (l to r): Nancy Tang, Zhou Enlai, Yeh Jianying, Zhang Wenjin, Xiong Xianghui, Winston Lord, the author, Henry Kissinger. (Chinese government photo)

Lunch at the Diao Yu Tai, 11 July 1971, before departure for Pakistan. Around the circle (l to r): Winston Lord, the author, Henry Kissinger, Richard Smyser, Xiong Xianghui, Wang Hairong, Ye Jianying, Ji Chaozhu, Premier Zhou, Tang Wensheng, Huang Hua; others not identifiable, except that Han Xu is probably on Winston Lord's right. (Chinese government photo)

Richard Nixon is greeted by Zhou Enlai upon arrival in Beijing, 21 February 1971. (L to r): Mrs. Nixon, President Nixon, Premier Zhou, Wang Hairong, Ye Jianying, Han Xu, Li Xiannian. (Chinese government photo)

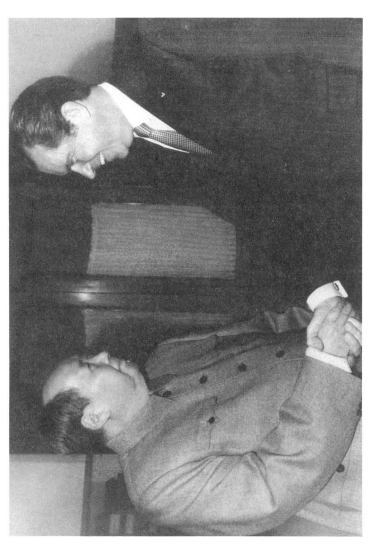

Chairman Mao Zedong and President Richard Nixon shake hands at beginning of their meeting in Beijing, 21 February 1972. (Chinese government photos)

Mao Zedong and Richard Nixon in Mao's study in the Zhong Nan Hai, 21 February 1972. (L to r): Zhou Enlai, Nancy Tang (interpreter), Chairman Mao, President Nixon, Henry Kissinger.

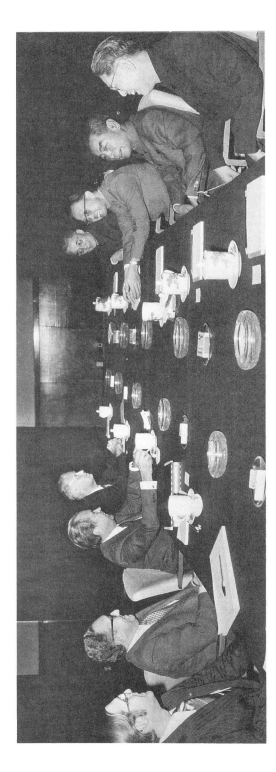

President Nixon's first substantive meeting with Premier Zhou Enlai at the Great Hall of the People on the afternoon of 22 February 1972. (L to r): Winston Lord, Henry Kissinger, President Nixon, the author, Zhang Wenjin (advisor to Premier Zhou), Ji Chaozhu (interpreter), Premier Zhou, Vice Foreign Minister Qiao Guanhua. (Chinese government photo)

Richard Nixon negotiating with Zhou Enlai at the Great Hall of the People, 23 February 1972. On the U.S. side (l to r): Henry Kissinger, President Nixon, the author; on the Chinese side (r to l): Zhang Wenjin, Premier Zhou, Vice Foreign Minister Qiao Guanhua. The painting on the wall is of Chairman Mao Zedong writing in his study (located in a cave) at Yan'an. (White House photo)

In his first official act as USLO chief, George Bush signs October 1974 agreement sending archaeological exhibition to the United States. (L to r, seated): Bush and the Chinese vice minister of foreign affairs in charge of cultural matters; (standing): Lynn Pascoe, Brunson McKinley, and Donald Anderson from USLO, the author, Wu Zhungzhao, curator of Beijing's Palace Museum, Nancy Tang, and unidentified staff of State Administrative Bureau of Museums. (Chinese government photo)

George Bush, U.S. Liaison Office chief, and author at Great Wall, October 1974. On left side of photo is Foreign Service inspector William N. Stokes. (photo by Martha Holdridge)

Author at Beijing University memorial to Edgar Snow, October 1974. Half of Snow's ashes were interred at this site, the other half in the United States. (Photo by Martha Holdridge)

USLO Chief George Bush and author with "responsible person" of Beijing subway during visit in January 1975. (Author's collection)

Author and wife, Martha Holdridge, with leaders of the Hua Shan Commune Revolutionary Committee near Wuhun, February 1975. (Author's collection)

Vice president's party en route to Beijing from New Zealand, May 1982, to discuss arms sales to Taiwan. (L to r): Barbara Bush, the author, Don Gregg (vice president's foreign affairs advisor), Nancy Bearg Dyke (deputy to Don Gregg), Peter Teeley (press secretary to the vice president), Chase Untermeyer (executive assistant to the vice president), Vice President Bush. (White House photo by Cynthia F. Johnson, personal photographer to the vice president)

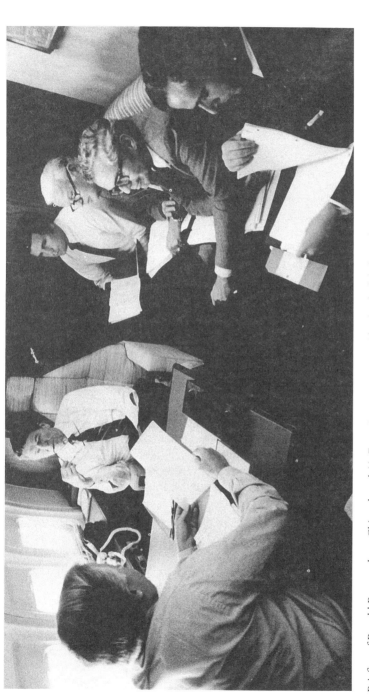

Briefing of Ronald Reagan about China aboard Air Force 1, en route to president's scheduled speech in Denver, Colorado, 1982. (L to r): Secretary of State Alexander Haig, President Reagan, unidentified man, author, Don Gregg, the vice president's foreign affairs advisor and later ambassador to the Republic of (South) Korea. (White House photo)

Don promptly complied, after first telephoning for an appointment.
He reported on his return that his presence had been greeted with a great
flurry of excitement, this being the first contact any American official in
Beijing had ever made with any members of the Vietnamese embassy.
The message itself had also caused great excitement, and the Vietnamese
originally refused to accept it but eventually did, saying they would inform Hanoi. We again told the Chinese of our contact, and received a
neutral response, which we took to mean that the Chinese would interpose no objections. This was all that we could do, other than to inform
Washington. By this time George Bush had returned from his Great Wall-
Ming Tombs trip, and he approved fully of what we had done.

As it happened, the deadline of the ultimatum expired before any
Khmer Rouge response took place, and a contingent of U.S. Marines came
in by helicopter to the island where the *Mayaguez* was held and took
over both ship and island, unfortunately with some American losses. The
Marines discovered that the crew of the *Mayaguez* was not aboard the
ship but had been taken to Kampong Som; within a few hours, however,
a launch appeared from Kampong Som with all the crew members, and
the ship was permitted to proceed.

The *Mayaguez* episode was virtually my last official concern in Beijing,
since I had received orders transferring me from USLO to Singapore as
ambassador—subject, of course, to confirmation by the Senate. Before
leaving, Martha and I went through the usual round of farewell parties,
one of which was a luncheon in my honor at the International Club, for
USLO officers only, hosted by Lin Ping. During the luncheon, Lin asked
me when I thought that diplomatic relations between China and Singapore might be established. I replied that my understanding was that Singapore would not act before Indonesia, given Indonesia's sensitivity about
China and Chinese. Lin Ping's response was, "Ah, then that will take
a long time." He was correct—Indonesia did not reestablish diplomatic
relations with China until 1990, fifteen years after my June 1975 departure
from Beijing, with Singapore following soon after. (Singapore had in the
interim permitted the exchange of trade missions and allowed a branch of
the [People's] Bank of China to operate.)

Martha and I left China with some regret but also a certain amount of
combat fatigue. We were simply tired of hearing too many "*bu fang
bien*"s ("It's not convenient") and "*bu qing chu*"s ("It's not clear"), the
standard responses from Chinese officials to requests (such as for permission to travel) and to difficult questions. We were tired of the circumscribed existence we had lived for two years. On the other hand, we had
traveled to quite a few parts of China, obtained first-hand a sense of what

was going on politically and economically, and enjoyed the opportunities to see for ourselves some of the great monuments and cultural centers of China's historical past. Everywhere we went we had made sure that the local museum was on our itinerary, and we had taken photographs of many exhibits not normally seen by outsiders. Our final going-away present was a trip to Datong, capital of the Northern Wei Dynasty, through which Buddhism had entered China around the fourth and fifth centuries C.E. There we were fortunate enough to visit both the Yongang Caves, a famous collection of Buddhist temples carved out of the solid rock of the hills of Northern Shanxi, and Datong itself, where a temple complex dating back to the Liao Dynasty, consisting of the *Shang Hua Yuan Si* and the *Xia Hua Yuan Si*, or Upper and Lower Hua Yuan Monasteries, still stands, from which Chinese Buddhist missionaries carried their faith to Japan. In Datong we also visited a factory manufacturing coal-burning, steam-driven locomotives, which was one of China's largest enterprises of this nature; a notable feature of this factory was the large number of workers, among whom only a few seemed to be working.

At the time of my family's visit to Datong, the only previous foreign visitors had been President Georges Pompidou of France and his party, since Datong was a closed city. Not only was it the site of many coal mines, the locomotive factory, and the Yongang Caves, but it had a heavy concentration of PLA troops, being on the main invasion route into China from the Mongolian People's Republic. Having the chance to travel to this closed city of strategic importance to both historical and modern China was to me a fitting close to my Chinese odyssey.

I believe that it's worth observing that on the political side, when the time came for my departure, I was able to leave behind a going concern—a diplomatic establishment that differed very little from an embassy and that was carrying on normal day-to-day relations with the Chinese Foreign Ministry and other ministries of the Chinese government. The Chinese, in their liaison office in Washington, were in a similar position. Ten years earlier, the attainment of such a status would have seemed unthinkable to both sides. The question of ultimate normalization of diplomatic relations was not one of "whether," but of "when," although none of us at USLO saw an early solution taking place. I take great satisfaction in having been a part of the process that not only brought the United States and China closer together, but also provided the basis for addressing joint problems in a continuing way at the highest levels of our respective governments.

Chapter 10

Buildup to Full Normalization

Some policy adjustments but no dramatic breakthroughs were achieved in U.S.-China relations during the three years that I was in Singapore, 1975–1978. Perhaps the most positive achievement was that during this period, both in the latter days of the Nixon administration and again in the Ford administration, the United States reiterated five major points to assure the Chinese of American sincerity in pursuing normalization: (1) the United States would acknowledge the Chinese position that there was but one China and that Taiwan was a part of it; (2) the United States would not support a Taiwan independence movement; (3) as the United States withdrew its military and diplomatic presence from Taiwan, it would assure that the Japanese did not come in as a replacement; (4) the United States would support any peaceful solution to the Taiwan situation and would not support Taiwan in any military action against China; and (5) the United States would seek to achieve normalization.[1]

President Gerald Ford paid a visit to Beijing in November 1975, after first visiting South Korea, in hopes of improving U.S.-China relations. Zhou Enlai must have been near death, and his chosen successor, Deng Xiaoping, was reportedly preoccupied—perhaps with the implications for him of Zhou's passing. Deng had little to contribute from the Chinese side to the U.S.-China relationship, other than to state again China's concerns about the Soviet Union. While in Beijing President and Mrs. Ford and their daughter Susan had the privilege of an audience with Chairman Mao. The chairman laboriously rose from his chair and "shuffled across the floor" to greet his visitors; according to President Ford, he spoke in a "low growl" that required each interpreter (presumably Nancy Tang and Wang Hairong) to write down what they thought Mao had said and check it with him. Otherwise, Mao impressed President Ford as being in full command of his senses.[2] He demonstrably was not in good physical condition.

Subsequent to the Ford family's meeting with Mao Zedong, the chairman had an additional meeting with President Ford, George Bush, Dr. Kissinger (who since August 1973 had served as secretary of state), and Presidential National Security Assistant Brent Scowcroft. In that meeting, according to Ford, Mao expressed his deep suspicions of the Soviet Union and his hope that the United States would stand up to the Soviets.

During the several meetings President Ford had afterward with Deng Xiaoping, the president declared that he tried without success to draw Deng out about further steps towards normalization of U.S.-China relations, only to find Deng "polite but firm" and seemingly "in no hurry to press for full diplomatic relations or the termination of our [the United States's] long-standing commitments to Taiwan."[3] Given Deng's situation vis-à-vis the "Gang of Four," his reticence was not surprising. President Ford departed for the Philippines with little to show for his visit to China, and Kissinger fails to mention this visit in either of his two books covering his tenure at the White House and the Department of State.

A View from Southeast Asia

I was not entirely cut off from China during my Singapore assignment. One Saturday afternoon in early 1976 Prime Minister Lee Kuan Yew telephoned to ask me to come to his official residence to discuss a visit to China that Prime Minister and Mrs. Lee were about to undertake in response to a Chinese invitation (despite the lack of diplomatic relations). What the prime minister wanted in particular from me, drawing on my experience in China, was advice on how to conduct himself in his conversations with senior Chinese leaders, which he expected would be tough, thanks to Singapore's past history of opposing the extension of Chinese influence into Southeast Asia. My advice to Lee was to stand firm on principle; the Chinese would certainly take advantage of any effort on the part of their guest to curry favor by agreeing with them on significant policy issues, but would not respect him for doing so. At the same time, I urged Lee to be absolutely courteous in his responses. This approach seemed to have worked, for after his return Lee telephoned me to thank me for my advice.

I also picked up one tidbit about life in Beijing during the "Gang of Four" era from Mrs. Lee, who during one of the prime minister's typically casual poolside parties after their return from China, referred to her experiences at the cultural event in the Great Hall of the People to which virtually all high-level visitors were subjected. Mrs. Lee mentioned that she had been seated between Jiang Qing and the wife of a senior Chinese government official, and that Jiang Qing and the official's wife had talked across her—a very impolite thing to do from her standpoint as a guest of the Chinese—and the two had spoken about "getting" so-and-so, and how someone else needed to be watched closely and might have to be removed. "They didn't think I spoke Chinese," said Mrs. Lee, who, like her husband, was English-educated, "but I did!" Her description of this scene gives a glimpse into the climate of intrigue and conspiracy in Beijing during the "Gang of Four" period.

Back in the United States, the Ford-versus-Carter presidential election campaign was underway. Carter hardly endeared himself to leaders of East Asian countries friendly to the United States when he made one of his platform planks the unilateral removal of U.S. forces from South Korea. Lee Kuan Yew, for one, was incensed, and on 8 August 1976, he took me aside at the reception following the Singapore National Day parade to explode, "What's that man thinking of?" What Lee and other East Asian leaders saw in this platform proposal was the beginning of a drawdown of U.S. military strength in the region that could not but affect the balance of power unfavorably for their countries. The Japanese, too, were deeply concerned, and I cannot believe that China, with its preoccupation with the Soviet threat, could have felt pleased by a U.S. withdrawal from South Korea, even if North Korea stood to benefit from any realization of Carter's plans.[4]

Fortunately, after Carter's election, the groundswell of public opinion against the unilateral withdrawal of U.S. troops from Korea, both in East Asia and within Carter's own administration, was strong enough to force a reversal of the decision. My old friend and colleague, William Gleysteen, who was ambassador to South Korea at this time, told me of the bitterness with which the newly elected president accepted the weight of opinion against him. Traveling to Korea personally to convey his change of mind, President Carter literally shook his finger at Ambassador Gleysteen in the limousine that was taking them to President Park Chung Hee, saying something like, "Look what you have forced me into!" Carter obviously took the reversal, which was surely the best course for the United States, as a personal affront.

It was at about this same time that U.S. ambassadors throughout East Asia were asked their opinion of what the consequences would be if the United States were to relinquish *all* its bases in the region. Only one of my colleagues responded with a reply supporting such a move.[5] I have no idea whether serious consideration was being given to relinquishing all the U.S. bases, but Carter's stand relative to the U.S. forces in South Korea suggests there was more to it than just idle curiosity.

Bearing in mind China's concerns about the growth of Soviet military strength in the Pacific, I can't help but believe that the Chinese at that time would also have tacitly agreed to the preservation of the U.S. military role in the Pacific. As I have frequently pointed out, the U.S. policy of counterbalancing the Soviet military buildup in the East Asian region was well understood and appreciated in Beijing.

The Changing of the Guard in China

As a consequence of the massive pro-Zhou Enlai demonstrations in Tian An Men Square on 5 April (see p. 154), the scale of which was unprecedented, rivaled only by the 3–4 June prodemocracy demonstrations in 1989, the Gang of Four had their pretext for "getting" Deng for failing to preserve order in Beijing. Deng again vanished from the scene, as before to be given refuge in Canton by Marshal Ye Jianying. His opponents then took command.

Speaking of command, it was about this time that Mao supposedly gave his blessings to a new successor by uttering the words, "With you in charge, I am at ease." This particular successor was Hua Guofeng, an experienced but colorless party leader from Shanxi. The Gang of Four must have known that Mao couldn't last much longer and had chosen Hua over Wang Hongwen on the grounds that the latter was simply too stupid to fill Mao's shoes. (Stories abounded in Beijing about Wang Hongwen's lack of the necessary leadership qualities and his perceived closeness to Jiang Qing.[6]) Perhaps they also reasoned that Hua would be a pliable member of their group. Judging by a film I viewed of an interview Hua granted a foreign visitor, he was hardly the hard-bitten old campaigner of Deng Xiaoping's caliber, but rather seemed weak and somewhat effeminate.

The biggest event in China in 1976 was Mao Zedong's death. By the time of his demise, Mao was confined entirely to his bed and unable to speak even the "growls" Gerald Ford had described; in fact, in his last hours he was placed in a respirator, according to Harrison Salisbury, who apparently had good access to eyewitnesses of the chairman's final hours.[7] Mao died in the early morning of 9 September 1976.

Mao's would-be successors, the Gang of Four, who watched his passing and were in a state of agitation as a result, were only able to agree on a single action: to bury Mao's preserved body in a special mausoleum to be constructed on the south side of Tian An Men Square, facing north, in contradiction of all Chinese tradition. But while they were still wrangling over this particular issue, Marshal Ye Jianying, at that time vice chairman of the Party's Military Affairs Commission, was active in his own channels. Ye succeeded in convincing senior military leaders that their own personal security would be at risk if Jiang Qing and other members of the Gang of Four took over control of the government and Party. One of these military leaders was Wang Dongxing, the commander of unit 8341 of the PLA, which was responsible for the security of the top leaders in Beijing. For Wang Dongxing, a former commander of Mao's personal bodyguard in the Yan'an era, his was a crucial personal decision, and a crucial decision for China's future as well.

On the night of 6 October, with the assistance of Wang Dongxing, a "palace coup" was successfully staged under Ye's direction in the Western Hills area favored by the top people for meetings and residences: in a matter of hours all of the Gang of Four were seized and placed under house arrest. (Later they would be brought to trial for treason.) Following their arrests, Ye telephoned old associates who were strongly critical of Mao and the Gang, with one especially important telephone call going to Deng Xiaoping in Canton telling him that he could come back to Beijing and, as Harrison Salisbury has put it, "return to center stage."[8] Deng was truly like the mythical phoenix, rising not once but twice from the ashes of a fire to assume a new life. He returned to Beijing in mid-1977.

Inevitably, a certain amount of confusion and infighting took place along with Deng's return, including an effort by Hua Guofeng to hang on to his position as Mao's successor. In the course of the next few years (1977–1980), however, Deng was able to bring about the removal of Hua Guofeng as chairman. In replacing Hua, Deng did not take over as Party chairman, the position Hua had occupied. Deng never assumed the top position in a formal sense but preferred to operate from his leading positions in the Party Politburo and the Military Affairs Commission. He became chairman of the latter body. Deng also brought in as his own possible successor and secretary-general of the Party a long-time adherent, Hu Yaobang.

The 11th CCP congress took place in August 1977. It confirmed Deng's rise to power and at least partially cleared the decks of the old leadership, although sufficient numbers of the "Old Guard" supporters of Mao Zedong remained in positions of power to cause trouble for Deng later on. The new leadership was thus in place, along with new domestic policies that differed drastically from those of Mao, and that in reality reversed them. Full implementation of these policies nevertheless had yet to be achieved.

The Carter Administration Moves Ahead

As Deng Xiaoping's star ascended, the Carter administration took over in the United States. In addition to focusing on relations with the Soviet Union, always the preeminent U.S. concern, the new administration began to consider the merits of working to improve relations with China. Leonard Woodcock, then the president of the United Auto Workers' Union, has mentioned to me that when he was called to the White House in February 1977 and offered the job of chief of the U.S. Liaison Office in Beijing, President Carter told him that he, Carter, attached highest priority to improving U.S.-China relations.[9]

According to Harry Harding in his book *A Fragile Relationship*, shortly after Carter took office the Carter administration began an internal assessment of U.S. policy towards China and of the prospects for establishing diplomatic relations with Beijing.[10] Leading this internal assessment was President Carter's assistant for national security affairs, Zbigniew Brzezinski, who initiated a review of the "voluminous" memoranda of conversation with the Chinese recorded by the Carter administration's predecessors. As outlined by Brzezinski,

> That review was initiated by my NSC staffer for Chinese affairs, Professor Michel Oksenberg. In the months to come, he was to play a central role in moving the American-Chinese relationship forward, in developing the conceptual framework for it, and in helping me overcome some of the key obstacles. Much of the progress achieved in U.S.-Chinese relations is due to him and to his effective collaboration with his very able State Department colleagues, notably, Richard Holbrooke and Roger Sullivan. When it became clear later in the year, and very much so after 1978, that I was inclined to push for more rapid movement in the U.S.-Chinese relationship than was Secretary Vance, this little cluster of senior officials would often meet in my office and coordinate the needed initiatives directly with me.[11]

From April to June 1977 a more formal review of the subject of normalization was commissioned under the rubric of Presidential Review Memorandum No. 24 (PRM-24).[12] Both protagonists and antagonists of normalization had their say: The pronormalization group argued that a failure to complete the process begun by the Shanghai Communiqué would lead to Beijing's imposing severe restrictions on U.S.-China economic and cultural ties and might even cause China to seek accommodation with the Soviet Union. In addition to forecasting a decline in these ties if normalization did not proceed, this faction also took the position that an improvement in U.S.-China relations would cause the Soviets to be more accommodating to U.S. interests. The antinormalization group maintained that any dissatisfaction in Beijing over relations with the United States arose because Beijing placed a lower priority on the establishment of diplomatic relations than it did on cooperation with Washington against Soviet expansionism, and that Washington's "naive" pursuit of détente with the Soviet Union was responsible for any Chinese dissatisfaction. The weight of the argumentation in PRM-24 lay with the pronormalization group, with whom the president clearly sided, judging by his comments to Leonard Woodcock. After considerable discussion, their views prevailed.[13]

In PRM-24 the Carter administration had another bridge to cross—to decide whether or not to accept the three principles that the Chinese had laid down for normalization in 1975: the United States had to (1) abrogate its Mutual Defense Treaty with Taiwan, (2) end official relations with Taiwan, and (3) withdraw all its remaining forces from Taiwan. Ultimately, PRM-24 accepted these three conditions, at least in broad outline, as necessary to achieve progress. As Harry Harding points out, the Carter administration accepted that the United States had already tacitly agreed to all three conditions. The Shanghai Communiqué had committed the United States to withdrawing its forces and installations from Taiwan, at least insofar as "conditions in the area improved"; President Ford had accepted the condition that the United States would maintain only unofficial relations with Taiwan after normalization; and Kissinger had concluded that the Mutual Defense Treaty could not be maintained in the absence of formal U.S.-Taiwan diplomatic ties.[14] (Frankly, I'm not certain just where or when it was that Kissinger had reached such a conclusion, but its logic is inescapable.)

Carter's secretary of state, Cyrus Vance, was convinced that the three Chinese principles would have to be accepted, but he retained reservations, the most important being that the United States should continue to sell arms to Taiwan. Vance, I suspect, was motivated by concern over the firestorm that would be ignited in U.S. domestic policy by the strong pro-Taiwan element in the Congress and among elements of the public if U.S. arms sales to Taiwan were cut off. Vance also believed that while the post-normalization U.S. relationship with Taiwan would be an unofficial one, it would still be necessary to maintain U.S. Government personnel on the island in some capacity to handle such details as consular business and protection of American citizens resident on Taiwan.

Setting the stage for moves towards normalization, President Carter made a speech at Notre Dame University in May 1977 stating, "We see the American-Chinese relationship as a central issue of our global policy, and China as a key force for global peace. We wish to cooperate closely with the creative Chinese people on the problems which confront all mankind, and we hope to find a formula which can bridge some of the difficulties which still separate us."[15]

In August 1977 the Carter administration made its first attempt to normalize U.S.-China relations. Secretary of State Vance, accompanied by Phil Habib and Dick Holbrooke, made a trip to Beijing, where they met first with Foreign Minister Huang Hua and then with the newly elevated Deng Xiaoping to discuss further steps in the normalization process. According to Cyrus Vance in his book *Hard Choices*, the best the Chinese were willing to offer on the normalization issue was along the lines of the formula used with the Japanese: Beijing would tolerate an unofficial U.S. relationship with Taiwan only via a nonofficial presence through an "ostensibly private organization."[16]

Given all the PRM-24 discussions in Washington, it came as a matter of considerable surprise that "for political reasons" (unstated, but possibly related to Vance's concern that pushing the China issue too strongly might have interfered with U.S. relations with the Soviet Union), Vance took what he termed the "maximum position" in his meeting with Huang Hua of insisting on U.S. government personnel remaining on Taiwan in an official capacity, even though he was willing to allow the Mutual Defense Treaty to "lapse" and even though he stipulated that the U.S. military withdrawal from Taiwan would be completed.[17] He went on to say that the American presence on Taiwan would not be diplomatic in character—despite the official status of U.S. personnel—but would be an informal one without a flag or the U.S. government seal. (In his book, Vance fails to mention the arms sales issue, but it can be assumed that someone on the U.S. side, perhaps Vance himself, did in fact bring it up with the Chinese.) Vance's position was embodied in a draft joint communiqué, which he was prepared to present if the Chinese response was favorable.

The formula Vance offered to Deng in August amounted to setting terms Deng was bound to reject: so long as official Americans remained on Taiwan as such, this would be tantamount to trading the liaison office in Beijing for the embassy in Taiwan, in other words, making a switch. Anyone who was familiar with the workings of our liaison office in Beijing and who knew that we enjoyed all-but-complete diplomatic relations with China would have known that such a course would fail. China simply could not accept a similar all-but-diplomatic U.S. relationship with Taiwan and would, as it had already done tacitly, draw a line against anything more than overtly unofficial U.S. links with Taiwan.

By this time Leonard Woodcock was firmly established in Beijing and was present at the talks Vance conducted with the Chinese leaders. In a conversation with me, he said that Deng Xiaoping's reaction to Vance's proposal was cold, although polite, but once the proposition of the switch was laid before him, all discussion of further steps towards normalization ceased. Also according to Woodcock, Deng said nothing derogatory at the time, but when another American delegation, this one private (including, among others, Kay Graham of the *Washington Post* and Arthur Sulzberger of the *New York Times*), came to Beijing several weeks later, Deng granted it an audience during which he characterized his meeting with Vance as a setback in Sino-American relations.[18] I personally find it difficult to understand how it was that Vance, either on his own initiative or under instruction, took such a sterile course.

In October 1977 I accompanied Prime Minister Lee Kuan Yew and his chosen successor, Goh Chok Tong, to Washington on official calls on various U.S. government officials, the president of the World Bank, and members of Congress. At that time I heard from various sources other feedback from Cyrus Vance's trip to Beijing. They all added up to the same conclusion: Vance's August trip to China was as Deng described—a setback to U.S.-China relations. There were some who went so far as to describe it as a "disaster."

Having burned its fingers over the August 1977 Vance visit to China, the reaction of the Carter administration and the State Department was to put the whole question of U.S.-China normalization on hold for several months while focusing on other issues, notably the relationship with the Soviet Union but also the conclusion with Panama of the treaty on the future of the Canal Zone. In November 1977 the outgoing Chinese liaison office chief in Washington, Huang Zhen, invited National Security Adviser Brzezinski to visit Beijing for further discussions on normalization, and Brzezinski entered into a prolonged struggle with State over the merits of taking such a trip.[19] He also continued to push for a more positive U.S. response to China's concerns on a whole range of issues—without much success.

President Carter, over State's objections, eventually authorized Brzezinski to make the visit. Also, in February 1978, Brzezinski began to hold regular meetings in Washington with Chinese Liaison Office Chargé Han Xu about normalization and other topics of mutual interest. Brzezinski journeyed to Beijing in May 1978. On that trip he was authorized to inform the Chinese that the Carter administration wanted to accelerate the normalization of relations and to this end was willing to accept all three of China's basic positions, namely repudiation of the U.S.-Republic of China Mutual Defense Treaty, downgrading of U.S.-Taiwan relations to a genuinely nonofficial nature, and withdrawal of U.S. military forces from Taiwan.[20] According to Brzezinski, once he had reached China and met with Deng Xiaoping, he told Deng that "the president has made up his mind to normalize relations with the PRC." Brzezinski was also directed to tell the Chinese that the United States was resolved to stand up against the Soviets.[21]

Accompanying Brzezinski on his visit to Beijing were four very capable men with diverse specializations: Morton Abramowitz from the Defense Department (he was actually a Foreign Service officer on detail), to help discuss overall military intelligence and also assist on a proposal for an exchange of military delegations; Richard Holbrooke of State, to consult on the expansion of cultural and economic cooperation; Ben Huberman, from the staff of Frank Press, the president's adviser for science and technology, to raise the possibility of an expansion in scientific cooperation, to include a possible visit to China by Dr. Press; and Michel Oksenberg, Brzezinski's "closest adviser on Chinese affairs," who was to work closely with Brzezinski on his presentations to the Chinese leaders.[22] Quite clearly, the scope of the Brzezinski mission was very broad and seemed designed to anticipate Chinese agreement on normalization.

While Carter and Brzezinski were prepared to go this far, Brzezinski's instructions retained a proviso that the U.S. Mutual Defense Treaty with Taiwan would remain in force for a year after normalization—the wording of the treaty stated that it could be invalidated by either party after a year's notice—and that U.S. arms sales to Taiwan would continue. Brzezinski was also told to inform the Chinese that despite the firm U.S. stance against the Soviets, the United States would seek to pursue START talks with the Soviet Union simultaneously with the U.S.-China normalization talks. The relationship with the Soviet Union was very much in the minds of all the foreign policy leaders in Washington.

Brzezinski's reception in China was much warmer than that accorded Vance, and he was photographed on top of the Great Wall pointing an AK-47 towards, according to newspaper quotes, what he termed the Soviet "Polar Bear." Brzezinski notes that he said something to the effect that the second person up the wall—after himself, of course—would be packed off to Ethiopia to confront the Cubans. This remark was also picked up by the American press.[23] Nevertheless, despite the welcome Brzezinski received, the normalization process still remained on hold, perhaps due in considerable part to the United States's continued arms sales to Taiwan. I have heard that Brzezinski tried to downplay the arms sales issue with the Chinese and referred to it only indirectly while in Beijing. The issue was not addressed directly until September 1978, when President Carter raised it with Chinese Liaison Office Chief Chai Zemin in Washington and said that the sales would proceed. President Carter also declared, "We expect a peaceful resolution on the issue of Taiwan."[24]

After returning from Beijing, Brzezinski met on 20 June 1978, with President Carter and Secretary Vance to discuss his trip and follow-up action. In this meeting, closely held and strictly limited in size, the president and his secretary of state and national security adviser laid down the final negotiating strategy and set the target date for normalization: 15 December 1978. On the arms sales issue, as the 15 December date approached, the Chinese showed signs of balking on normalization because of continued U.S. arms sales to Taiwan. To help placate the Chinese, Brzezinski noted on 15 December, "We made it clear that we will continue after a one-year pause during which the [Mutual Defense Treaty with Taiwan] is being abrogated."[25]

Normalization's Relationship to Chinese Domestic Concerns

It is conceivable, and in fact highly probable, that in 1977 and 1978, lack of resolution of China's domestic issues distracted Deng Xiaoping and deflected his attention from the normalization issue. It can be postulated that Deng was not in a position to address the normalization question fully until he had put his own domestic house in order, which among other things involved steering the deliberations of the Third Plenum of the 11th CCP Central Committee. This meeting took place in October–November 1978.

The Third Plenum of the 11th CCP Central Committee was one that, in the words of China's CCP General Secretary Jiang Zemin at the CCP's 14th Party Congress fourteen years later in October 1992, "brought order out of chaos. . . . Thanks to the victory in smashing the Gang of Four, we saved the country from calamity. . . . [Prior to the Third Plenum, however,] the political, ideological, organizational, and economic confusion left over from the Great Proletarian Revolution was still extremely serious."[26] In addition to the general confusion mentioned by Jiang Zemin, supporters of Mao Zedong's dogma, or at least leaders who opposed Deng Xiaoping's reform program, remained in positions of power.

During the Third Plenum, Deng was able to strengthen his hand considerably and to solidify his leadership role, as well as gain support for his definition of the future directions of the party and the country.

Following the Third Plenum, Deng could more readily address policies dealing with the growing exigencies in PRC relations with Vietnam, along with U.S.-China normalization, and also his domestic reforms. (An issue of some significance to China was its problems with Vietnam due to the growing relationship between Hanoi and Moscow, as will be discussed in chapter 11.) As Jiang put it in his 14th Party Congress speech, cited above, "The 1978 Third Plenary Session of the 11th CPC [CCP] Central Committee and the *central leading collective with Comrade Deng Xiaoping as the nucleus which was formed at the session, undertook an arduous mission to achieve a great turning point in history, thus opening up a new period in the development of China's socialist cause*" (emphasis added).[27]

With the exception of my Washington visit in 1977, I was obliged to watch all of the foregoing developments from a distance, but in June 1978 I returned to Washington, where I found myself detailed from the State Department to the Intelligence Community Staff. In theory, the Intelligence Community Staff coordinated the intelligence collection and analysis efforts of the diverse government agencies active in this field: I had access to the outputs of all of them. Further, within a few months I was reassigned to the National Intelligence Council, physically located in the CIA, as national intelligence officer for China. (Eventually, my area of responsibility included all of East Asia and the Pacific.) These positions gave me an excellent vantage point from which to look at developments in China.

As I assumed my new posts, the U.S.-China relationship was about to take a major turn. For Deng Xiaoping, the Third Plenum of the 11th CCP Central Committee was a crucial test, which when he successfully passed it, gave him a dominant role in determining both China's domestic policies (this meant above all economic reform, though some political reforms such as "democracy wall" were originally tolerated) and its foreign policies, which were described by Jiang as "opening up to the outside world." For two years Deng had, of necessity, been concerned primarily with bringing order out of chaos at home. With the closing of the Third Plenum, Deng was in position to look to the outside world.

For U.S. foreign policy and Zbigniew Brzezinski as well as for Deng Xiaoping, 1978 marked a crucial turning point. Because Brzezinski overrode the objections of Secretary of State Cyrus Vance on proceeding rapidly towards normalization of U.S. relations with China, it became evident that the initiative for foreign policy again rested with the White

House, with Brzezinski the person to whom the president turned first for advice and for operational management. (This development proved true not only with respect to China, but for other areas of the world as well.)

President Carter and National Security Advisor Brzezinski did not hesitate to pursue the course of normalizing relations with China. In September 1978, talks were resumed in Beijing between USLO Chief Leonard Woodcock and Foreign Minister Huang Hua, and occasionally with Deng Xiaoping himself, and also in Washington between Brzezinski and Chinese Ambassador Chai Zemin, or in his absence, Chargé Han Xu. In Beijing, Deng appeared as anxious as Brzezinski to normalize. During the talks between the Chinese and the U.S. representatives, though, one serious issue remained to be overcome: the U.S. resolve to continue arms sales to Taiwan. To the Chinese, the United States's maintenance of a program of arms sales to Taiwan was incompatible with the principle already accepted by the United States that Taiwan was a part of China. From the Chinese perspective, by selling arms to Taiwan the United States was involving itself in China's internal affairs, something that Jiang Zemin later, in his 14th CCP Congress speech, termed "impermissible." Reservations on normalizing relations in the face of continuing U.S. arms sales to Taiwan went right to the top of the Chinese leadership, including Deng Xiaoping.

Chapter 11

The Impact of Vietnam and Cambodia on Normalization of U.S.-China Relations

Given the strong Chinese feelings against American insistence on continuing arms sales to Taiwan, Deng Xiaoping needed some overriding factor to use to justify normalization of U.S.-China relations regardless of the arms sales issue. This factor could only have been the growing tension between China and Vietnam over Cambodia, with the Soviet Union standing behind Vietnam.

China and Vietnam

In September 1978, about the time I was assigned to be national intelligence officer for China, I became aware of the tremendous influence that Vietnam and Cambodia exercised on U.S.-China relations. It was at this time that the American intelligence community noted Vietnam's military buildup against Cambodia, which occurred contemporaneously with the growing Chinese support for the Khmer Rouge in Cambodia.

The complex interplay of interests in Indochina involved the Soviet Union as well as China, Cambodia, and Vietnam. In July 1978 Vietnam joined the Council for Economic Mutual Assistance (CEMA), the Soviet-dominated Eastern European equivalent of the European Community (EC); within months, on 4 November, North Vietnam signed a Treaty of Friendship and Cooperation with the Soviet Union, which contained some military overtones. It was after the signing of this treaty that the Soviets moved into the former U.S. base at Cam Ranh Bay to set up facilities for docking and refueling Soviet warships enroute from Vladi-vostok and Petropavlosk across the Indian Ocean to the Soviet-dominated island of Socotra in the Red Sea. Soviet "Bears," long-range reconnais-sance aircraft, were also based at Cam Ranh Bay, as were, eventually, a squadron of MIG-21s, plus other installations for keeping track of U.S. military movements in the Western Pacific. Neither Cam Ranh Bay nor Socotra rivaled Subic Bay and Clark Field in terms of facilities, but they were nevertheless important adjuncts to the long-range projection of So-viet naval and air power.

These developments demonstrated that Vietnam had aligned itself with the Soviet bloc. The Soviets, by signing the treaty with Vietnam and by their deployment of naval and air power at Cam Ranh Bay, appeared to be identifying themselves firmly with Vietnam as a military ally. The U.S. intelligence community certainly saw the Soviet-Vietnamese relationship in this light.

In the meantime, between July and December 1978, Vietnam began a military buildup along the Cambodian border that was highly suggestive of an intention to attack Cambodia. This was especially pronounced in the area known as the "Parrot's Beak," an area of Cambodian territory wedged into South Vietnam's Tay Ninh Province. There are those who argue that Vietnam's military buildup and subsequent attack on Cambo-dia were intended to rescue the Cambodians from the horrors that had been inflicted on that unfortunate country by the Khmer Rouge under the leadership of Pol Pot. The Khmer Rouge had taken the opportunity of the U.S. military withdrawal from Cambodia (see chapter 10) to take over and unleash a reign of terror in which hundreds of thousands, or even millions, of Cambodians died.

I don't for one minute accept the thesis that Vietnam attacked Cambo-dia to deliver the country from Pol Pot and the Khmer Rouge. Vietnam's own history of concern for human rights was, and remains, poor in the extreme. Rather, what motivated Vietnam was most likely the "legacy of Ho Chi Minh"—the thesis espoused by Ho and reportedly expressed on his deathbed that all of the lands in Indochina formerly controlled by the French rightfully should fall under Vietnam's control. Thus, Vietnam was not attempting to halt the killings in Cambodia; rather, it simply used the international opprobrium against the Khmer Rouge to justify before foreign public opinion an invasion that was basically motivated by a de-sire for territorial aggrandizement. Vietnam had long since established its hegemony over Laos.

Of crucial importance in Vietnam's apparent determination to attack Cambodia was that China, for its own reasons, had staked out Cambodia as falling within China's sphere of influence and not Vietnam's. This Chinese proprietary role in Cambodia had been affirmed by a number of important steps: there had been visits to Cambodia by leading Chinese personalities including Guo Moruo, a leading member of China's cultural establishment, and Deng Yingchao, Zhou Enlai's widow. In addition, the Chinese had established an economic aid program in Cambodia that included the construction of a textile mill, and it had set up a military assistance program in Cambodia that embraced the provision of MIG 15–17 aircraft to Cambodia and the stationing there of a Chinese military mission. These steps were but the public manifestations of a special relationship between China and Cambodia—I feel sure that China conveyed word to Vietnam via diplomatic or Party channels that Cambodia was off limits for Vietnam.

I suspect, too, that in the course of providing high-level attention to Cambodia and bolstering it economically and militarily, China was also trying to use its influence on Pol Pot to behave more humanely towards the Cambodian people. Word of the "killing fields" in Cambodia had already reached the outside world, and China itself stood to be tarred with the same brush as Pol Pot if the killings continued. Indeed, towards the end of the Pol Pot regime, there appeared to be a tapering off of the atrocities against the Cambodian people committed by the Khmer Rouge under his command, conceivably as a result of Chinese "advice."

What interests did China have in Cambodia? My surmise is that China resented the increasingly warm relations between Vietnam and the Soviet Union, which was regarded by China as a hostile entity. It will be recalled that China had for a time attempted to interfere with shipments of Soviet military supplies to Vietnam through Chinese territory (see chapter 1), and the Chinese were deeply concerned over the possibility that Vietnam could turn into a channel to extend Soviet power into areas adjoining China's southern borders. Vietnam and Laos were already lost to China, although Chinese troops had been quietly moved into areas of Laos contiguous with China, and China had assisted the Vietnamese in keeping communications lines open during the Vietnam War. The complete domination by Vietnam of all three former French Indochinese states would have been a serious strategic setback to the Chinese, who ever since the People's Republic of China was established in 1949 have consistently displayed a sensitivity towards being "surrounded" by hostile forces. Only Cambodia remained outside the Vietnamese orbit following the U.S. withdrawal in 1975, and the Chinese from their standpoint would have had little option but to help Cambodia, despite the odious nature of the Pol Pot regime.

Vietnam quite obviously remained undeterred by the Cambodian-Chinese relationship, bolstered perhaps by the impression created by its joining CEMA and its Treaty of Friendship and Cooperation with the USSR that the Soviet Union would back Vietnam in whatever it planned to do vis-à-vis Cambodia. In fact, to clear the decks of possible Chinese fifth columnists, some months before the Vietnamese actually attacked Cambodia, they expelled their entire Chinese minority from the region formerly known as North Vietnam. This step involved the movement into China of several hundred thousand Sino-Vietnamese, many of whose ancestors had been living in Vietnam, particularly in Hanoi and Haiphong, for generations. To the Washington intelligence community, it definitely seemed that Vietnam was girding itself for a war against Cambodia and was prepared to ignore whatever warning signals Beijing had sent.

The Chinese, for their part, were beginning to respond in kind. A foreign diplomat stationed in Beijing who visited Yunnan Province about the middle of December 1978 watched an enormous column of Chinese military vehicles loaded with troops, artillery, and tanks pass by going southward on the road between Kunming and the border town of Lang Son.[1] China was responding to Vietnam's moves by making its own military preparations, in the event that Vietnam failed to heed China's warnings.

In addition to military preparations, however, China needed to take political actions to offset the presumed backing that Vietnam enjoyed from the Soviet Union as a result of Hanoi's joining CEMA, signing the Treaty of Friendship and Cooperation, and permitting the Soviets to use Cam Ranh Bay as a base. And only one power was capable of balancing off the Soviets: the United States. Accordingly, the Chinese—most certainly under the guidance of Deng Xiaoping, who had consolidated his power in the Third Plenum of the 11th CCP Central Committee and so was in a position to set China's foreign policy course—took another look at the question of normalizing relations with the United States. Despite Zbigniew Brzezinski's promising visit in May 1978 and the talks that resumed in September, the issue of normalization of U.S.-China relations had still to be resolved, with U.S. arms sales to Taiwan remaining a major obstacle. With Deng free to focus on the issue and the events in Indochina in the background, in the short span of two weeks or so in the final two months of 1978, an agreement on U.S.-China normalization was worked out that both parties could accept.

"Normalization" Finally Achieved

The parameters of the U.S.-China rapprochement on normalization had already been set by the United States in a meeting between President Carter and Chinese ambassador Chai Zemin on 19 September 1978 (see chapter 10), during which Carter set forth the following conditions:

1. The U.S. presence on Taiwan after normalization would be unofficial.
2. American commercial, cultural, and other relations with Taiwan would continue.
3. Sale of selected defensive arms to Taiwan after normalization would also continue.
4. The United States would issue a public statement expressing hope for a peaceful resolution of the Taiwan problem (between China and Taiwan).
5. Termination of the U.S.-Taiwan Mutual Defense Treaty would be expected in accordance with the terms of the treaty, which provided for termination upon one year's notice by either party.[2]

I can't assume that Sino-Vietnamese and Sino-Soviet relations were the only elements that figured in the delay in negotiations on normalization that occurred between May 1978 and the final agreement reached in November. Deng clearly needed to establish his dominance over the Party leadership against some well-dug-in conservatives, which he succeeded in doing at the Third Plenum of the 11th CCP Central Committee in November 1978. Relations with the United States were but one of several elements Deng had to contend with at that time. It was only after Deng had won out over his critics that the question of U.S.-China relations could be addressed and negotiations pursued, but in an atmosphere made much more urgent by Vietnam's threatening military posture against Cambodia. One of the conditions set by President Carter in September that, if accepted by Deng, would have to be forced down the throats of Deng's detractors in the CCP, was the American insistence on maintaining arms sales to Taiwan. Otherwise, the course of events would have been smoother.

The negotiators of the final agreement were USLO Chief Leonard Woodcock on the U.S. side, and on the Chinese side, Deng Xiaoping, Foreign Minister Huang Hua, and Assistant Foreign Minister Zhang Wenjin. Secretary of State Vance and Assistant Secretary Richard Holbrooke also had important roles, but that the transcripts of the normalization talks were later stored in the White House situation room files speaks strongly as to where the center of gravity lay.

The issues involved on each side in the normalization process were fairly extensive. On the Chinese side was a desire for an unequivocal commitment to the concept that Taiwan was part of China; that, accordingly, all diplomatic relations between the United States and Taiwan should cease; and that the United States-Republic of China Mutual Defense Treaty should be voided. (Deng Xiaoping's concerns over continuing arms sales to Taiwan were stifled for the moment.) On the U.S. side was a desire for a Chinese commitment, tied to the Chinese position on ending the Mutual Defense Treaty with Taiwan and breaking diplomatic relations, that China would not use force to reunite Taiwan with the mainland. What was finally worked out was a joint statement along the lines of the Shanghai Communiqué, in which each side stated its position without challenging the position of the other side. (See appendix B.)

On 15 December 1978, the agreement on normalization of U.S.-China relations was announced to a startled world (at least I personally was startled, as were the authorities on Taiwan). The agreement itself was to take effect 1 January 1979. Actually, normalization required four separate documents to make the key points desired by each side: a government-to-government Joint Communiqué on the Establishment of Diplomatic Relations Between the United States of America and the People's Republic of China dated 1 January 1979, in which the United States acknowledged that Taiwan was part of China, and both sides agreed that normalization served the cause of peace; a statement by President Carter that the United States would "continue to have an interest in the peaceful resolution of the Taiwan question"; a further U.S. statement reiterating that the United States continued to have an interest in the peaceful resolution of the Taiwan question and "expects that the Taiwan issue will be settled peacefully by the Chinese people themselves" (see also chapter 3); and a Chinese statement declaring that, "As for the way of bringing Taiwan back to the embrace of the motherland and reunifying the country, it is entirely China's internal affair." (See appendixes B and C.)

In the announced agreement normalizing relations with China, the United States said it would terminate the Mutual Defense Treaty with Taiwan following a year's grace; it withdrew diplomatic recognition from the "Republic of China on Taiwan," and it declared that an unofficial relationship would be set up in its place that would be much more truly unofficial than that which Cyrus Vance had proposed in August 1977. The United States further declared that all of its military personnel were to be withdrawn from Taiwan within four months. Nothing was said in any of the normalization documents about terminating U.S. arms sales to Taiwan—in light of subsequent events, a very significant omission. In fact, going back to the Carter-Chai conversation of 19 September 1978, it had been made clear to the Chinese that arms sales would continue (however, there was nothing said that the issue could not be addressed again after normalization).

On the Chinese side, the Chinese did not challenge the U. S. premise that reunification of Taiwan with the mainland would be by peaceful means, although this issue was declared to be entirely China's internal affair; China challenged neither the continuation of a nonofficial relationship between the United States and Taiwan nor the validity of ongoing commercial and cultural relationships. Most importantly, the Chinese did not address the issue of continued sale of U.S. arms and military equipment to Taiwan. This last feature must have been a bitter pill for Deng Xiaoping and the Chinese leadership to swallow, but swallow it they did—for "strategic reasons," as one of their senior diplomats, Zhang Wenjin, told me two years later, when the issue had become a major irritant in U.S.-China relations. Zhang's words, that Deng Xiaoping tolerated these continued sales to Taiwan for "strategic reasons," fit precisely into my thesis that the Chinese wanted and needed the relationship with the United States to balance off the Soviets in their impending campaign against Vietnam.

Although the normalization agreement was speeded by the Cambodian situation, long-term implications were inherent in it. Both sides were able to set aside (at least for the moment) the Taiwan issue and to conduct relations in a conventional manner that provided for enhanced economic and political benefits for both. China became much less isolated and much more accepted as a member of the world community; the United States gained wider entry into China's economic market, and with a much-enhanced ability to address mutual U.S.-Chinese political and military concerns.

Deng Xiaoping's Visit to the United States

The normalization agreement also included an invitation extended by President Carter to Deng Xiaoping for Deng, or anyone else he might designate, to visit the United States the following January. Deng jumped at the chance, and his impending visit was contained in the normalization announcement of 15 December. Here was the crux of the matter, in my judgment: the Chinese established—at least as far as the outside world was concerned—a special relationship with the United States via Deng Xiaoping's visit, in addition to getting much of what they wanted with respect to the removal of the United States as an obstacle to the reunification of Taiwan with China. Deng's trip to the United States began on 29 January 1979, and it had the effect of placing the United States in China's corner in the same way that the Soviet Union appeared to be in Vietnam's corner in the showdown then building in Cambodia. On 24 December 1978, the Vietnamese had invaded Cambodia and in a relatively short period of time had not only reached the Mekong River and Phnom Penh, but had sent their forces all the way to Battambang, in Western Cambodia. A failure by China to respond would have represented an immense loss of face, as well as posing a strategic threat to China's southern borders. China's response was to build up its forces adjacent to Vietnam, and to prepare to attack across the border.

What Deng Xiaoping had in mind in introducing the United States into the Cambodian equation can be discerned from the public statements he made while in the United States. In addition to Washington, D.C., Deng visited other cities, including Atlanta and Houston, and a constant theme of his public remarks was, "It may be necessary for China to teach Vietnam a lesson." What he said in his private Oval Office meeting with President Carter and National Security Advisor Brzezinski remains closely guarded, but in his speech at the east wing of the National Gallery in Washington on the eve of his departure from Washington, he sounded a very bellicose note that was notably hard on Vietnam and the Soviet Union and could be taken as a harbinger of a Chinese attack on Vietnam. I was standing near Deng and clearly heard through the translator what he said. To my surprise, no startling news headlines appeared the next day. I believe news accounts of the speech did not pick up on Deng's theme at least in part because listeners did not clearly hear what Deng said, owing to the poor acoustics in the building.

In addition to sounding an alarm regarding China's intentions toward Vietnam, Deng in his speech significantly showed his understanding of U.S. concerns about Taiwan by saying, "We wish from the bottom of our hearts to resolve [the reunification] question in a peaceful way, for that will be advantageous to our country and to our nation. This wish was clearly expressed in the message of the Standing Committee of our National People's Congress [on 1 January 1979] to our compatriots on Taiwan. I should say that after the normalization of relations between China and the United States, the chances of a peaceful solution have become greater."[3] While not amounting to a renunciation of force, Deng's statement, along with the 1 January 1979 message, gave the United States and Taiwan sufficient grounds to assume that China would adopt a peaceful approach to the reunification issue.

In any event, if Deng had used his belligerent National Gallery theme in his meeting with President Carter, no subsequent statement came from the White House tending to discourage a Chinese attack on Vietnam. Hence, Deng got what he wanted: a tacit U.S. endorsement of a Chinese military action against the Vietnamese. To emphasize this, on the way back to China from the United States, Deng stopped in Japan and made his point clearly, "It *will* be necessary to teach Vietnam a lesson," implying that the United States had acquiesced in China's military plans. Thus, by expediting U.S.-China normalization, even at the cost of continued arms sales to Taiwan, and coming to the United States to speak about "teaching Vietnam a lesson," Deng figuratively put the United States behind China in the coming showdown with Vietnam, balancing off the Soviet identification with Vietnam.

Michel Oksenberg, who held the same NSC position during the Carter administration that I had occupied during the Nixon administration, has postulated in discussions with me that Deng's eagerness to complete normalization of relations with the United States was further impelled by the upcoming Carter-Brezhnev summit, which was scheduled for May 1979. According to this thesis, Deng wanted to ensure that China would not be overlooked by either the United States or the Soviet Union during their summit and also that U.S.-China relations would be firmly in place by this time. It makes sense to assume that Deng also had this factor in mind, although I place heavier weight on Deng's determination to "teach Vietnam a lesson."

China Attacks Vietnam

China's actual attack on Vietnam did not immediately follow Deng's U.S. visit, since the Chinese evidently needed more time to mobilize their forces from their central reserve and to position these units along the Vietnamese border. The shooting began on 19 February 1979, Chinese time, when Chinese forces crossed the Vietnamese border in the vicinity of Lang Son and in several other widely separated places. Vietnamese resistance was reportedly intense, and the Chinese forces discovered that neither their equipment nor their training were designed for the kind of fighting they encountered, in which they had to eliminate Vietnamese troops dug into caves in the range of hills separating China from Vietnam. Little if any air power was used by either side, and the battle turned into a slugging match between infantry units, in which the Vietnamese had the advantage of knowing the terrain and of fighting from prepared positions. Some reports place Chinese losses as heavy as 30,000 men.

Nevertheless, by early March the Chinese had taken the important Vietnamese border town of Lang Son, and their forces had advanced across the range of hills dividing Vietnam and Cambodia to reach the lowlands of the Red River Delta. At this point, the Chinese did what they had done against the Indians in Assam in 1962: they simply stopped fighting, turned around, and marched back into China. From their standpoint, Vietnam had been taught its "lesson," and the Chinese saw to it that the war was kept a limited one. The Chinese withdrawal occurred on 9 March 1979, only three weeks after the campaign had been launched. By keeping the fighting to this scale, China showed that it did not desire a larger conflict designed to drive the Vietnamese out of Cambodia, but rather was content to punish Vietnam for its invasion. The Vietnamese had taken the Chinese attack seriously enough, though, to move main force units from various places in North Vietnam and Cambodia to the border area adjacent to China.

As for the Soviet Union, apart from some propaganda blasts, it did nothing of any consequence to support Vietnam during the period that the Sino-Vietnamese fighting was under way. Perhaps to show that it did possess palpable military strength, in mid-March it undertook extensive military maneuvers in its far eastern military region, which had earlier been set up as a "front" under the command of a senior marshal, and which included the Mongolian People's Republic (MPR), territory that had long been an invasion route into China's vital areas. Five Soviet divisions were stationed in the MPR. Among other moves, these maneuvers involved a paratroop drop north of the MPR, which unfortunately for the Soviets was spoiled when the paratroops were dropped in a heavy wind and were scattered all over the landscape.

The Chinese did not undertake any special reinforcement of their troops along the Soviet and Mongolian borders, except to put them in a state of alert, and the Soviet maneuvers seemed to impress them as being nothing more than sheer bluff. There is no way of telling what influence the Chinese alignment with the United States played in preventing a Soviet attack on China to back up Vietnam, but Soviet military planners presumably could not rule out some form of U.S. reaction if the Soviet Union's forces became involved.

A curious development after the withdrawal of the Chinese forces from Vietnam was that the official CCP press remained silent about the fighting for two months. It printed no claims of a great victory, and the Chinese masses were left in the dark as to what had taken place. As I recollect, it was with reference to this same period that Chinese media later referred to a "cold wind" having blown through the party structure. I took this to mean that Deng Xiaoping's adventure against Vietnam had not been received with universal acclaim by his colleagues, and that he was under some criticism from other CCP leaders over the episode, particularly due to the high number of Chinese casualties. Other changes in Deng's policies from those of Mao may also have been under fire. It wasn't until late April or early May that the Chinese press suddenly blossomed with great accolades for the forces that had fought the Vietnamese, and awards for valor were handed out profusely.

Deng Xiaoping's Post-Vietnam Reform Program

Just about the same time that the Chinese press was hailing the victory over Vietnam, the media quoted Deng as proclaiming, "seek truth from facts," and "the sole criterion of truth is practice." This sounds very much in character for the man who had allegedly stated that he didn't care whether a cat was black or white so long as it caught mice, but the effect of these two new statements was to redefine Marxism-Leninism-Mao Zedong thought in such a way as to declare that if a measure worked, it was Marxist-Leninist, and if it didn't work, it was not. Deng appears to have won a double victory over his critics: the first, in declaring the campaign against Vietnam a victory in which the Vietnamese had indeed been taught a lesson, and the second in redefining China's version of Marxism in such a way as to replace ideology with practicality as the guiding principle for the development of the state. (I have noted that Jiang Zemin's speech at the 14th CCP Congress in 1992 underscored the importance of Deng Xiaoping's redefinition of Marxism-Leninism-Mao Zedong thought.)

It is perhaps worth reiterating as part of this sequence of events that Deng had won an important victory regarding both domestic and foreign policy at the Third Plenum of the 11th CCP Central Committee in October-November 1978. At this plenum, Deng succeeded in forcing a separation between the Party bureaucrats and what might be called the technocrats in the management of the economy, in that the Party was divorced from direct management of economic enterprises. These were to be run by technically qualified managers while the Party authorities were to concentrate on political rather than economic affairs. This change was obviously of enormous significance. It appears that Deng may well have gone into the normalization negotiations with the United States fresh from winning a victory over the long-established Party leadership, and hence was in a good position to "seize the moment, seize the hour" on normalization, as Mao Zedong might have put it. Nevertheless, internal struggles continued, as indicated by the hiatus in hailing China's strike against Vietnam as a "great victory."

The National People's Congress (NPC) in August 1979 confirmed Deng's policies as state policy, and Zhou's "four modernizations" were at last established as the "general line of the state." China's priorities among the "four modernizations" were also made very clear at this NPC: development of agriculture came first, followed by light and heavy industry, in that order, so as to produce more consumer goods, then national defense, followed by science and technology. The basis of China's reform program, which remains in effect to this day despite the setbacks following the Tian An Men bloodshed 3–4 June 1989, had been established. This program has focused on economics almost to the exclusion of politics. "Democracy wall," for example, survived only a few months in the fall of 1979, and China's intellectuals have undergone periods of relaxed controls followed by intensified restrictions. The reform program has now proceeded far enough and long enough, however, that it would be almost impossible for any Chinese leader to try to turn back the clock.

China's current economic system developed from the 1979 reforms: the "responsibility system" in agriculture, which in addition to replacing the communes with townships, allocated township land to peasant families to farm and permitted these farm families to pass this land on to their descendants; the establishment of small-scale industries in rural areas to soak up surplus manpower; the granting of rights to the peasants to retain for their own use all crops that exceeded quotas set by the state; the continuation of rural free markets; the payment of annual bonuses to city workers for exceeding quotas (a practice frequently abused by paying bonuses regardless of productivity); and the separation of the Party from the day-to-day management of farms and factories.

In addition, "special economic zones" were set up in various parts of coastal China, notably in Shenzhen across from Hong Kong, which were permitted substantial latitude in setting regulations to attract foreign capital and that granted employers the right to fire unsatisfactory workers, thus ending the so-called "iron rice bowl" (guaranteed jobs and income). The leadership was still reluctant to face up to the problems of China's price structure; significant differences between prices set by the government and the free market prices for the same goods led both to inflation and corruption, as those with access to government-supplied raw materials or supplies sold them to the free marketers or to small-scale enterprises at a raised price. State-owned enterprises remained the major area of Chinese investment (and are still a heavy drain on China's financial resources). But the contrast was marked between the Soviet Union's reforms, which left agriculture largely untouched, and those in China, where 80–85 percent of the people were still located on the farms; they responded enthusiastically to the changes in the new system.

Reaction in the United States and Taiwan to Normalization

While the joint announcements by Beijing and Washington of normalization came as a stunning surprise to some, overall public and press reaction in the United States was surprisingly mild and generally favorable. For example, *Newsweek* magazine of 8 January 1979 quoted leading U.S. figures as saying that the normalization agreement was simply a logical extension of the Shanghai Communiqué; there was no national uproar among the American people, who took the action calmly. The main focus of public attention during the weeks following the 15 December 1978 announcement of normalization was on the impending visit of Deng Xiaoping, rather than on Taiwan, and then on Deng's actual visit when it occurred.

On Taiwan, however, the situation was inevitably quite different. In the first instance, the United States did not provide Taiwan with advance word of the joint U.S.-China 15 December announcement on normalization. The news came as a bombshell. The only prior notification consisted of a few hours grace provided by our then-ambassador, Leonard Unger, to Chiang Ching-kuo, who had succeeded his father, Chiang Kai-shek, as president. The ambassador spent several hours tracking down Chiang on the night of 15 December, finally reaching him at 2:00 A.M. at his residence. The outrage on Taiwan was extreme and widespread, undoubtedly helped along by the attitudes of the government officials who felt betrayed. I have frequently wondered if it might have been possible for the United States to have found some way to cushion the blow, but I am forced to admit that I really can't think of anything that would have mitigated Taiwan's agitation.

Shortly after the formal date of U.S.-China normalization on 1 January 1979, President Carter sent Deputy Secretary of State Warren Christopher to Taiwan to "explain" the matter to the authorities there. After he was met at the Taipei airport by Ambassador Unger, and the two had boarded their limousine for the trip back to Taipei, the vehicle was surrounded by a crowd of as many as 20,000 screaming, abusive people, who cursed and spat at the two occupants in the rear seat. They stoned the car, breaking its windows and rocking it back and forth, thoroughly terrorizing the two passengers. Only by driving away through a narrow side street was it possible for the driver to escape the crowd. It was obvious that a demonstration of such a nature and on such a scale could not have taken place without official connivance. President Carter was outraged when informed of the episode and wanted to recall Christopher immediately, but in the end he let the mission proceed. Probably a major element in Christopher's visit was reassurance to Taipei that the arms sales would not be stopped.

Meanwhile, back in Washington, increasing criticism of the normalization agreement came from within the ranks of Taiwan's many supporters in the Congress. The administration had sent a carefully worked-out Taiwan Enabling Act to Congress that would provide for the establishment and maintenance of a nonofficial relationship between Taiwan and the United States (for example, U.S. government personnel assigned to the American Institute in Taiwan, or AIT—the name of the unofficial U.S. agency—would temporarily resign their commissions without loss of seniority). During the formulation of the original Taiwan Enabling Act document, I was privileged as NIO for the region to be at the White House to hear presentations by Roger Sullivan, deputy assistant secretary of state in the East Asia bureau, charged with overseeing Taiwan affairs and the Office of People's Republic of China and Mongolian Affairs. When this act reached Congress, though, Taiwan's supporters, principal among whom were Republican Senator Jesse Helms of North Carolina and Democratic Senator John Glenn of Ohio, the administration's version, drafted by State, was rewritten by the Congress into the Taiwan Relations Act, which was much firmer in expressing U.S. support for Taiwan than had been originally envisaged. President Carter signed this act into law.

Notably, while still incorporating the concept of unofficiality found in the original document, although perhaps in much stronger and more definitive terms than had been used initially, the Taiwan Relations Act, or TRA, had this to say about continued U.S. arms sales to Taiwan:

(a) . . . The United States will make available to Taiwan such defense articles and defense services in such quantity as may be necessary to enable Taiwan to maintain a sufficient self-defense capability.

(b) The President and the Congress shall determine the nature and quantity of such defense articles and services *based solely upon their judgment of the needs of Taiwan, in accordance with procedures established by law. Such determination of Taiwan's defense needs shall include review by United States military authorities in connection with recommendations to the President and Congress.* (Emphasis added.)

(c) The President is directed to inform the Congress promptly of any threat to the security or the social and economic system of the people of Taiwan or any danger to the interests of the United States arising therefrom. The President and the Congress shall determine, in accordance with constitutional processes, appropriate action by the United States in response to any such danger.[4]

Two important points emerge from this language: first, the determination of what "defense articles and services" were to be made available to Taiwan remained entirely a U.S. responsibility, a proviso that, as will be seen, would come to haunt the TRA drafters; and second, it was further suggested that the United States might intervene in the Taiwan Strait area if a threat against Taiwan were posed by some hostile force, which could only be China. Indeed, elsewhere in the TRA are the words that "peace and stability in the area are in the political, security, and economic interests of the United States and are matters of international concern," and "to make clear that the United States decision to establish diplomatic relations with the People's Republic of China rests upon the expectation that the future of Taiwan will be determined by peaceful means."[5]

Going one additional step, the TRA restated the validity of international treaties binding the United States and Taiwan (with the exception of the Mutual Defense Treaty, about which nothing is said and which was repudiated in the U.S. Statement on Normalization), and it specifically gave the Overseas Private Investment Corporation permission to function in Taiwan as it does in other parts of the world. The intent of the TRA drafters was obviously to leave the status quo between Taiwan and the United States as little disturbed as possible. China duly protested the TRA as interference in its affairs, but in the end let it stand without any action. "Strategic reasons" must have again played an important part in China's acquiescence. And with the TRA in effect, anti-U.S. activities on Taiwan died down. Within a period of weeks, the United States had appointed its first chief of the American Institute in Taiwan, Charles T. Cross, who had been born in China, served in Singapore as ambassador, and spoke excellent Chinese. Taiwan's counterpart entity in the United States, the "Coordination Council for North American Affairs," or CCNAA, was also set up and operating within a short period of time. An entirely new relationship had come into being involving China, Taiwan, and the United States in a way that could not have been envisaged at the time of the Shanghai Communiqué.

Chapter 12

Normalization's Status during the Carter and Reagan Years

The Carter Administration

During President Carter's last two years in the White House, two contradictory lines emerged in the normalization process. On the one hand, the Carter administration rapidly broadened U.S.-China contacts on diplomatic, military, economic, cultural, and other fronts; on the other, it continued and actually expanded arms sales to Taiwan, once the one-year moratorium informally agreed to by the United States in normalizing relations with China had passed.[1] Given the PRC's strong antipathy to the United States's maintaining a military relationship with Taiwan, this contradictory policy towards China was a growing source of tension in U.S.-China relations, although it was not directly addressed until well into President Reagan's first term. Then, for over three years our military relationship with Taiwan was a source of recurring problems in the budding new U.S. relationship with China.

To broaden U.S.-China ties, the Carter administration worked vigorously in 1979 and 1980 to expand the new relationship. In his book *Fires of the Dragon*, David Kaplan details the expansion of ties and notes that

In the year or so since recognition, progress between the U.S. and China had been remarkable. The United States opened its first consulates in China in thirty years, in Canton and Shanghai, while China reciprocated with offices in San Francisco and Houston. Congress overwhelmingly approved a major trade agreement, granting China most-favored-nation trade status [MFN] and boosting trade to record levels. After the long break in relations, U.S. and Chinese officials were feverishly at work on some three dozen other treaties, pacts, and protocols covering everything from aviation to education.

Tourism and scholarly exchanges had also grown rapidly. . . . In the strategic
area, too, the United States reached new levels of cooperation. . . . Unknown
at the time, PRC officials also were joining the CIA in a covert operation to
supply arms to Afghan rebels fighting the Soviets. . . . [2]

On economic matters, the Carter administration's activities included
setting up not one, but two joint commissions to address economic and
financial relations: the Joint Commission on Economics and the Joint
Commission on Finance, headed on the U.S. side by the secretary of commerce and the secretary of the treasury, respectively. There was no real
reason to have two joint commissions instead of one, except that the two
secretaries concerned were both jealous of their own prerogatives. The
two commissions did serve the purpose, however, of providing the United
States with a another cast of characters on the Chinese side with whom
to discuss matters of mutual concern.[3] One such concern was China's
interest in building what became known as the *San Men*, or "Three
Gorges" dam on the upper reaches of the Yangtze River, in which the
U.S. Army Corps of Engineers was regarded by both sides as a possible
participant, thanks to the corps's long experience building flood control
projects. (In fact, the engineers had once made a survey of China's Three
Gorges region in the Chiang Kai-shek era at Chiang's request with the
construction of a dam—or dams—in mind.)

The continuing U.S. arms sales to Taiwan reached an all-time high of
over $550 million in President Carter's last year in office. (Allowing for
inflation, this figure was $835 million in 1982 dollars, the year the United
States and China directly addressed the arms sales issue.) An additional
complication for the succeeding administration was a virtual promise by
the Carter administration to Northrop Aircraft that it would be permitted
to sell to Taiwan the upgraded version of the F-5E/F series of fighter
interceptor jets.[4] Presumably, Carter agreed to this because the upgrade,
the F-5G, was in the U.S. view strictly a defensive aircraft. (The PRC,
however, did not see it this way.)

The F-5E/F was already being coproduced on Taiwan and had become
the mainstay of Taiwan's defensive air strength. The F-5G, which later
became known as the F-20 "Tigershark," was designed to be a quantum
jump in terms of speed and all-around capabilities, containing a single
engine that was more powerful than the twin engines in the F-5E/F, and
having better avionics and weaponry than its predecessor. However, the
F-5G had one built-in design limitation: its "loiter time" was limited, so
that it could only remain over a target as far away from Taiwan as the
China mainland for approximately fifteen minutes, and therefore it was

not suitable for backing up a military attack by Taiwan against the mainland. The F5-G was strictly a fighter-interceptor, in other words, a defensive aircraft. Disagreements with China over this interpretation would come to plague the Reagan White House.

The presidential election campaign heated up in 1980, with George Bush opposing Ronald Reagan for the nomination as the Republican candidate and Jimmy Carter running for the Democratic candidacy. When Ronald Reagan's candidacy gained momentum, the China issue began to loom as a factor in the presidential campaign, for Reagan had been known as a particular friend of Taiwan since, following Nixon's visit to China, he had been sent to Taiwan by President Nixon in 1972 to reassure President Chiang Kai-shek that U.S. support for "the Republic of China on Taiwan" remained in effect. After Reagan had asked George Bush to be his running mate, and Bush had accepted, the new vice presidential candidate went to China in August 1980 to counter any fears by the top Chinese leadership that Ronald Reagan would be a "loose cannon" on the question of U.S. relations with China. George Bush, of course, was particularly well equipped to undertake this mission on the basis of his knowledge of China and his personal relationships with senior Chinese leaders gained during his tenure as chief of the U.S. Liaison Office in Beijing.

To my own surprise, I found myself caught up in the preparations for the Bush China visit. I was one of three national intelligence officers (NIOs) who flew from Washington to the Bush family residence in Kennebunkport, Maine, to brief the vice presidential candidate on the military situation affecting China and its neighbors in the region, namely, the Soviet Union and Vietnam. My particular contribution was to describe what we knew about the Chinese military organization and order of battle, including what little we could put together about the minor Sino-Vietnamese border skirmishes going on at that time. My two colleagues described Vietnam itself and the Soviet forces in the Soviet Far Eastern military region. We were instructed not to touch upon Chinese internal politics; others, it seems, would do that when we finished. These others, as we discovered when we were leaving the briefing room, were Ray Cline, a long-time partisan of Taiwan, Richard Allen, an equally firm friend of Taiwan, and James R. Lilley, who had been my predecessor as NIO for China in the National Intelligence Council.[5]

The Bush visit to China could hardly be called an unqualified success. Because of his own good standing with the Chinese, I believe Bush was able to provide some reassurance about the Reagan-Bush policy towards China if the two were elected, but the effect was spoiled by a press conference given by candidate Reagan on 23 August 1980, when Bush was on the point of leaving Beijing. In this press conference Reagan remarked that Taiwan was really a country and should be treated as such (he referred to it as the "Republic of China"), that the United States should restore diplomatic relations, that Taiwan should be provided with whatever arms it believed it needed to defend itself, and as a final completely contradictory afterthought, that the United States should work to improve relations with the People's Republic of China. *Newsweek* magazine covered this episode with the caption, "Bush Bombs in Peking."[6] To compound the complexity of the situation, the Chinese called U.S. Ambassador Leonard Woodcock to the Foreign Ministry to protest the Reagan press conference, after which Ambassador Woodcock was ambushed by Western reporters on the steps of the Foreign Ministry. He then gave an impromptu press conference in which he said that, in effect, he agreed with the Chinese, since U.S. policy toward China had been established in two joint communiqués and was well known.

Despite this seeming American vacillating on the subject of its China policy, some ongoing contact continued at the official level in the late months of the Carter administration; for example, People's Liberation Army Chief of Staff Geng Biao visited Washington in the fall of 1980 at the invitation of the secretary of defense and presented Pentagon officials with a list of some fifty-plus military items China wished to buy from the United States. Nothing came of Geng's initiative at this time, however.

I had my one and only contact with President Carter at about this same time. CIA Director Admiral Stansfield Turner asked me to accompany him to the White House to brief President Carter on China, on the economic, political, and military situations as perceived by the intelligence community. The president had no particular comment, other than to remark that the normalization of relations with China might well be the single most important event for which his administration would be remembered.

The Early Days of the Reagan Administration

With the election of Ronald Reagan as president and George Bush as vice president, I found myself rapidly drawn into the new administration. One of the President's early appointments was that of General Alexander M. Haig Jr. as secretary of state,[7] who shortly afterwards called me to his transition office in the State Department and offered me the position of assistant secretary of state for East Asia and the Pacific. Haig, it seems, had remembered me from the days when we both worked on the Kissinger NSC staff. I had not expected to be in line for the position but promptly accepted. Four years on the NSC staff plus my previous assignments in the region had given me ample experience.

Accordingly, as of the first workday in January 1981, I moved back to the State Department, where I remained as assistant secretary of state-designate until May, when conservatives in the Senate who had been sitting on my appointment finally gave up, and I was confirmed. I replaced Richard Holbrooke in this position.

From the moment I first sat at the assistant secretary's desk, I found myself caught up in serious issues affecting U.S.-China relations. The first of these concerned what had been reported in the Taiwan and American press as an invitation to several senior personalities from Taiwan to attend the Reagan-Bush inaugural ceremonies as an "official" delegation. In fact, there was no such thing as an "official" invitation, since the list of invitees had been drawn up by the Reagan-Bush inaugural committee, a nongovernmental body. Nevertheless, the publicity given to the invitees from Taiwan was enough to arouse the ire of the Chinese, and China's ambassador in Washington, Chai Zemin, let it be known that if the Taiwanese delegation showed up, he wouldn't.

Believing that the new Reagan administration emphatically did not need the headache of beginning its life with a crisis over China policy, I set out to try and put a stop to the presence at the inauguration of the representatives from Taiwan, who consisted of the secretary general of the Kuomintang (KMT) Party, the governor of Taiwan, and the mayor of Taipei. In this task I had the support of Jim Lilley, who had been working for the 1980 Reagan-Bush presidential campaign. Lilley immediately got in touch with some of his friends on Taiwan to point out the disadvantages to Taiwan of an early fight over China policy that the presence of their delegation would cause; meanwhile I worked through a member of the inaugural committee, Anna Chennault, to say the same things. Mrs. Chennault, the widow of General Claire Chennault, the famous head of the World War II "Flying Tigers" (she was also a niece of senior Chinese official Liao Chengzhi, the person in charge of overseas Chinese affairs for Beijing) immediately got in touch with her high-level contacts on Taiwan to explain the circumstances. As a further step, I telephoned Ambassador Charles Cross in his office in the American Institute on Taiwan (AIT) in Taipei, on an open line, to make my points, expecting that there was a good chance of the call being monitored.

The upshot was that none of the Taiwan representatives appeared at the inaugural ceremonies. The governor of Taiwan suddenly discovered that he had urgent business at home; the mayor of Taipei had not yet left for the United States and canceled his trip; and the secretary general of the KMT, who was already in the United States, came down with a case of "diplomatic flu," for which he was hospitalized in a facility outside Alexandria, Virginia. Jim Lilley and I paid a consolation call on him in his hospital room.

In this manner one crisis was averted. I have to admit that I personally felt like the villain in an old-fashioned melodrama over this situation, especially with respect to the secretary general of the KMT, but I believed we had followed the only possible course. Chinese ambassador Chai Zemin duly showed up at the inaugural ceremonies, and the U.S.-China relationship remained where it had been—more or less on track.

My own and Jim Lilley's activities served to point up the next issue that had to be faced: Taiwan's desire to acquire the F-5G fighter-interceptor (also known as the "F-X"). Unquestionably, Taiwan's willingness to be flexible on the inauguration issue was linked to a desire not to compromise its chances of obtaining this new, high-performance aircraft. To further complicate the scene, news items in both the American and Taiwan press quoted the chief of staff of Taiwan's Air Force as expressing confidence that the new Reagan administration would come through for Taiwan with the F-5G.

The China mainland press immediately launched a barrage of criticisms, not just over the aircraft, but over continued arms sales to Taiwan in general, thus reviving an issue that had been relatively quiescent for the last year or so. China's press also renewed criticisms of the Reagan press conference of the preceding year and allegations that the United States under Reagan would turn back the clock and attempt to reverse normalization. This spate of criticism, which to my mind reached unprecedented levels of vitriol, was to last almost until the time when, over eighteen months later, the United States and China finally concluded a joint communiqué on arms sales to Taiwan.

While we in State were still digging into our new duties, we were hit by yet another issue with great potential for setting back U.S.-China relations: the level at which U.S. and Taiwan officials could meet. This question came up in an unexpected setting. South Korean President Chun Doo Hwan had been invited to visit Washington as the second chief of state or head of government to make such a visit.[8] (Chun's visit was in fact a reward for his agreeing to switch the sentence against detained South Korean opposition leader Kim Dae Jung from execution to house arrest.) I was part of the entourage that met President Chun at the Reflecting Pool after his helicopter had flown him in from nearby Andrews Air Force

Base and that accompanied the South Korean group in the motorcade to the diplomatic waiting room in the White House. There we all waited for Chun's meeting with President Reagan. As the group of South Korean and American dignitaries was milling around waiting for the two presidents to get together, I was approached by Richard Allen, who had become President Reagan's national security advisor. Allen told me that he had talked to President Reagan a couple of nights earlier and had gotten Reagan to agree to office calls, that is, to permit Taiwan officials to call on U.S. officials in their offices in the various departments of the government, including State.

Office calls? I was deeply disturbed by this prospect. I knew how seriously the Chinese would be watching the level of contacts between Taiwan's "unofficial" representatives and their U.S. counterparts. If the head of the Coordination Council for North American Affairs (CCNAA) could call on the secretary of state or senior officials in the State Department building, China's fears about a reversal of U.S. policy towards recognizing Taiwan as a country rather than as a province of China, hence vitiating past assurances on maintaining a "one China" policy, would be realized. This would jeopardize the painstaking work of years to establish and build a relationship with this important member of the world community. The issue of the level of calls would certainly be closely monitored in Beijing, since high-level calls would also be tantamount to according diplomatic recognition to Taiwan. In light of the chill that ensued when Cyrus Vance in 1977 had suggested what amounted to a switch between an embassy in Taiwan and the liaison office in Beijing we could expect that "official" calls would be deeply resented in China, with unpredictable consequences. A problem already existed, for on his own Dick Allen had invited the head of the CCNAA to call on him in his office in the Old Executive Office Building adjacent to the White House.

I had no alternative but to apprise Secretary Haig about what had transpired and hope that he could walk the matter back from where Dick Allen and the president had left it. What Haig eventually arranged was a compromise: working-level officials from Taiwan could make "business" calls on their working-level counterparts in departments other than State, but senior officials could only meet with *their* counterparts at "unofficial" receptions, dinners, or other similar functions held outside U.S. government property. Business-level calls included those made in the Pentagon, where Taiwan officials were permitted to go, but not in uniform and not using their titles of military rank. I subsequently made a point of going to private receptions in honor of the KMT "Double Ten" National Day (10 October), which were separate from the public reception given by CCNAA in some Washington hotel. I also made a point of meeting personages like the governor of the Bank of Taiwan off government premises, as in a function room in a hotel.

The basic principles of this compromise on U.S.-Taiwan official interactions are still in effect. (There was a stretching of the arrangement in early 1992 when Carla Hills, President Bush's special trade representative, visited Taiwan—a step offset by the visit of the U.S. secretary of commerce to Beijing. Further, in September 1994 the Clinton administration decided to permit office calls, both ways, by senior U.S. and Taiwan officials of economic or technical departments, such as housing, agriculture, and transportation, but not involving the White House, State, or Defense. These shifts reflected strong pressures from pro-Taiwan political forces in the United States.)

In March 1981, tension in the U.S.-China relationship was alleviated somewhat when President Reagan met with Chinese ambassador Chai Zemin. In his characteristic outgoing style the president reassured Chai that while the United States would not forget "old friends," that is, Taiwan, it would also abide by the two joint communiqués covering U.S.-China relations. The president also assured Chai that the United States would remain sensitive to Chinese concerns about arms sales to Taiwan, although he made no promises about ceasing these sales, which in fact were called for by law under the Taiwan Relations Act. I believe that Chai left the meeting relatively happy, even though all the clouds in U.S.-China relations had not been dispelled. We met in the Cabinet Room of the White House, with Secretary Haig sitting next to the President. With Chai Zemin were several members of his staff, including my old acquaintance and friend, Ji Chaozhu, who served as interpreter.

About this time we in the State Department began to give some thought to establishing a more equitable relationship between the United States and Taiwan on the one hand and China on the other, when it came to arms sales. As matters then stood, there was a complete embargo on arms sales to China; we began to consider whether this might not be changed to permit the sale of weapons of a purely defensive nature on a case-by-case basis and to treat China as a "friendly, nonallied state." Discussions on this subject began within the U.S. government bureaucracy, in which State and the Commerce Department advocated change, and the Pentagon, backed by elements in the CIA, strongly resisted. Commerce's more forthcoming position, expressed by Undersecretary Lionel Olmer, who chaired the interdepartmental meetings, was that arms exports would help the U.S. economy.[9] Those on the opposing side believed that we would simply be arming a potential enemy of the United States. Ultimately, the matter went to the full National Security Council, and by June those who favored a change had won. The question then was simply when and how to announce the decision.

Several considerations drove this shift in policy on arms sales to China. For one, the Chinese had begun to show signs of restiveness because Taiwan was still receiving arms, and the Chinese press was continuing to spew out criticism over such sales, with the clear intention of deterring sale of the F-5G. For another, Deng Xiaoping and others had dropped broad hints to visiting Americans that China would like to improve its military power by buying U.S. arms. And finally, it was considered by some in Washington to be in the U.S. national interest to help China face the Soviet Union with more powerful weaponry. This was a logical outgrowth of policies already initiated in the Carter administration to strengthen the "strategic relationship" between the United States and China by extending it into military and other security realms.

The Haig Visit to Beijing

The question of arms sales to China was finally settled on the eve of a visit to the PRC by Secretary Haig. He had already begun to consider the merits of paying a visit to Beijing to meet the Chinese leaders personally when, fortuitously, Deng Xiaoping sent him a message in June expressing the hope that the secretary could visit China "soon."[10] Secretary Haig had already agreed to attend a meeting with the foreign ministers of the five ASEAN states (Association of Southeast Asian Nations, then consisting of Singapore, Malaysia, Thailand, Indonesia, and the Philippines; more recently, Brunei and Vietnam have been added), who customarily met with five "dialogue partners": the United States, Japan, Canada, Australia, and New Zealand, with observers from the European Community and Papua-New Guinea. The ASEAN meeting with the dialogue partners was scheduled to follow its annual foreign ministers' meeting, set for early July 1981 in Manila; therefore, it was worked out at the National Security Council level in the form of a NSDD (National Security Decision Directive),[11] that Haig would go first to China, then to the ASEAN postministerial meeting in Manila. Thus, he would need to leave for China around the end of June. Following his Manila visit, Haig would then go on to an ANZUS (Australia-New Zealand-U.S. Security Pact) Council meeting scheduled to take place in Wellington, New Zealand, on the heels of the ASEAN session.

It was planned that in China Secretary Haig would inform the Chinese of the policy change on selling arms to China and invite the chief of staff of the People's Liberation Army, or his representative, to visit Washington again in the fall with a list of defensive weaponry that China might wish to buy from the United States. At this point the willingness of the United States to sell arms to China would be made public. In fact, we had already agreed among ourselves on the commercial sale of some thirty or more of the items on the list that Geng Biao had brought the previous year. The president instructed Haig, in addition to addressing the arms sales question, to discuss the strategic relationship between China and the United States, including the shift in China's status to that of a "friendly, nonallied state," and to explore "the question of finding a modus vivendi on Taiwan, including the parameters of unofficial relations and arms sales."[12]

Secretary Haig duly departed on his long swing through East Asia and the Southwest Pacific towards the end of June 1981, and I went with him, along with several members of my staff with China backgrounds. Richard Burt, then assistant secretary for public affairs, was also a member of the party, as was General Vernon A. Walters, who came as a kind of roving adviser. A fairly sizable press contingent was included, sitting in the back of the airplane.

Once in Beijing and established at the now-familiar Diao Yu Tai (the State Guest House), we commenced our talks with the Chinese. One took place with the Chinese military, headed by Geng Biao, in the Great Hall of the People. It touched on the matter of arms sales, about which the Chinese agreed to forward a list of items they desired—which, in fact, they sent rather promptly—and also provided an opportunity for Haig to reiterate the strategic interests that Americans and Chinese shared. Deputy PLA Chief of Staff Liu Huaqing was designated to visit the United States to engage in further discussions of the arms sales issue. (Actually, other events intervened, and the Liu Huaqing visit did not take place until much later. A major factor in China's cancellation of the Liu Huaqing visit, I believe, was the growing tension in the fall of 1981 over continued U.S. arms sales to Taiwan.)

A second talk took place with a new member of the Chinese leadership, Premier Zhao Ziyang, whom we met in one of the lesser palaces of the Forbidden City (*Gu Gong*) on the other side of the Zhongnanhai lake from Chairman Mao's former residence. Zhao was accompanied by a number of senior Chinese, including Foreign Minister Huang Hua. Here again the advantages of the strategic relationship between the United States and China were reviewed, and the secretary pointed out that the United States wanted to remain a reliable friend of China. Zhao Ziyang took this opportunity to repeat China's stand that the Taiwan issue was strictly an internal matter that could be managed if we adhered to the two joint communiqués, and he expressed confidence in China's ability to cope with the Soviet threat. General Walters made what was to me an interesting observation after this session to the effect that Zhao had seemed rather uncertain and, after having made his points, had looked to his colleagues, as if for confirmation that he had followed the right line. Walters's evaluation of Zhao was reminiscent of the way that Deng Xiaoping had appeared to me at the meeting with Henry Kissinger in November 1974, when Deng had seemed to lack a certain degree of confidence. Both were very new in their positions when the meetings took place.

When we finally met with Deng Xiaoping, again in the Great Hall of the People, Deng this time displayed no signs of hesitation, but was quite firm in expressing irritation over continued U.S. arms sales to Taiwan and the failure of the United States to live up to several commitments made to China during the Carter administration. He was polite about it, though, and listened carefully, if with some difficulty hearing,[13] to Secretary Haig's discourse on the way that the U.S. government functioned and how Congress was an important factor affecting the speed and scope of activities. At the conclusion of this meeting, Deng asked Haig and me to join him in a brief private session in a back room of the conference hall, and taking only an interpreter with him, he proceeded to bring up the question of U.S. troops in South Korea. Couldn't we find a way to remove them, or if not, at least to move them down to the southern part of the Korean Peninsula away from the Demilitarized Zone? Here I must assume that Deng had been asked by his North Korean friends to bring up the subject of the troops, and he was dutifully complying. In any event the Chinese showed themselves to be as anxious as we were to see peace preserved on the Korean Peninsula.[14]

The final item on Secretary Haig's program was a press conference, delivered on the eve of our departure from Beijing on the top floor of the *Min Zu*, or Nationalities Hotel. On this occasion Haig delivered a straightforward if somewhat censored account of his conversations with the Chinese leaders, and then hit the press with what seemed to me a real "clanger" (to use the British expression) by stating for the first time that the United States was now prepared on a case-by-case basis to sell defensive arms to China.

According to the NSDD to which I have referred, the news of this crucial policy change was not to be made public until the visit later that year by Liu Huaqing, and I was hard-pressed to explain why the secretary made it public in China at that time. In his book *Caveat*, Haig refers to leaks in the *New York Times* and the *Washington Post* occurring shortly after the NSC had reached its decision, thus in effect making the question of security theoretically moot. Haig has since told me that Bernard Gwertzman of the *New York Times* had indeed learned of the decision. Regardless of leaks, though, to bring up the subject while in China in front of both our own press party the Chinese and foreign press stationed in Beijing was to give enormous publicity to this subject. Indeed, it became a headline issue all over East Asia, and it deeply colored Haig's discussions with the ASEAN foreign ministers in Manila. I must admit that at the time my colleagues and I were more than a little taken aback by this particular revelation and bewildered as to its motivation, but I can't rule out the possibility that the president authorized Haig to say what he did. In any event, it caught Washington by surprise as well and caused resentment in some conservative quarters.

The following morning when we departed Beijing for Manila, we were seen off at the airport by various Chinese dignitaries, headed by former foreign minister Ji Pengfei, at this point, I believe, a vice chairman of the Standing Committee of the National People's Congress. But before we boarded our aircraft, one more act remained in this particular drama. Zhang Wenjin, who at that time was an assistant foreign minister ("*Fu Li Bu Zhang*") came up to me with an English-language press ticker item reporting that on the preceding day President Reagan had given a press conference in which he had repeated much of the pro-Taiwan rhetoric that had caused George Bush so much trouble in Beijing the year before. Although I can't be sure, I speculate that the president's remarks, reassuring as they were to Taiwan, were in response to Haig's words in his press conference the previous evening about arms sales to China. What were the Chinese to make of these remarks, Zhang wanted to know, and how did they square with the assurances of good faith that Secretary Haig had been making over the last several days? I showed the ticker item to the secretary and told him that I would use as a response a line that the Chinese had frequently used with us: "Pay attention to what we do, not to what we say." This I did, taking a certain amount of perverse pleasure in doing so, given the history of past Chinese propaganda attacks against the United States, after which the Chinese had used the same line with us. We then boarded the aircraft and flew off to Manila.

Haig's Manila stop was dominated by the news from Beijing about U.S. arms sales to China. The press hounded the secretary to elaborate on the subject, and in the ASEAN postministerial dialogue sessions, this was the element every foreign minister wanted to address, whether in one-on-one sessions or in the full five-on-five meetings. In fact, the final five-on-five meeting, which was televised, might just as well have been called a five-on-one affair, since all the questions from the ASEAN foreign ministers seemed to be directed at Secretary Haig, to the extent that it appeared the ministers were ganging up on him—they had virtually no questions for the other invited guests. Although Secretary Haig handled himself very well and managed to get across the line that the United States was definitely not abandoning its ASEAN friends, I'm sure that he was glad when the proceedings were over.

One issue did make its way through both the foreign ministers' meeting and the postministerial dialogue: the question of addressing Vietnam's occupation of Cambodia, which we were then calling "Kampuchea" in keeping with that country's traditional name. The ASEAN foreign ministers, supported by all the dialogue partners, agreed to propose in the UN that an international conference on Kampuchea be convened by the United Nations in the latter part of July. This was duly proposed in the UN by ASEAN and passed by a vote in the General Assembly.

With the ASEAN postministerial dialogue behind us, the ANZUS Council meeting in Wellington seemed almost anticlimactic. Our Australian and New Zealand friends—this was some years before New Zealand took itself out of ANZUS by rejecting the U.S. "no confirm, no deny" formula about the possible presence of nuclear weapons aboard its visiting warships—offered understanding, and in the case of both countries, superb hospitality. No cracks in the ANZUS alliance were visible, and it was possible for the secretary to reassure members about U.S. constancy, although the antinuclear sentiment in New Zealand was already present and growing, particularly within the Labour Party.

Scarcely had we returned to Washington than Secretary Haig traveled to New York for the UN International Conference on Kampuchea, taking me along as part of his party. Around one hundred countries were present on this occasion, with only the Soviet bloc and some of the more pro-Soviet or anti-U.S. nonaligned countries absent. The Chinese were also present on this occasion. My general mandate was to keep track of all the East Asian countries present and to act as liaison with the anticommunist Kampuchean factions headed by former prime minister Son Sann and former chief of state Prince Sihanouk, on both of whom I paid personal calls; my particular task was dealing with the Chinese delegation, headed by Vice Foreign Minister Han Nianlong.

The ASEAN nations and the majority of the other countries taking part in the conference favored wording in the final resolution that would demand the withdrawal of "foreign forces" from Kampuchea and the subsequent creation through free elections of a neutral, sovereign,

independent country, carefully not mentioning Vietnam by name as having committed aggression, to avoid hardening the Vietnamese position.
The Chinese, on the other hand, demanded that the aggressor be identified and condemned. U.S. policy was to support those parties most directly involved, namely, the ASEAN countries and the noncommunist
Kampuchean factions, since the former were the ones who had called for
the conference, and the latter had borne the brunt of the guerrilla warfare
then raging in Kampuchea, particularly in the areas adjacent to the Thai
border.

It fell to my lot to try to talk the Chinese out of their hard-line position
and into going along with the majority. To this end, I made a special trip
to the Chinese UN Mission, where the Chinese delegation was housed,
to call on Han Nianlong to urge acceptance of the wording preferred by
the majority and to point out the advantages of identifying China with
the ASEAN countries. I found him rigidly opposed. We must have gone
around the track on the merits of the respective positions at least three
times, with the Chinese delegation showing no signs of give. Later that
day in the delegates' lounge Secretary Haig tried himself to induce Han
Nianlong to yield, but with no outward sign of success. China's insistence
on going against the majority might well have made the International
Conference on Kampuchea, or "ICK," as we called it, a failure, but ultimately the Chinese came to see this point and did change their stance.
Fortunately for questions of world peace, the Chinese were beginning to
draw away from previously immutable ideological positions and to perceive the merits of adjusting to the points of view of other countries.

The result was a virtually unanimous condemnation of Vietnam's aggression against Cambodia/Kampuchea, since everyone knew that the
only "foreign forces" in that country were Vietnamese, but leaving the
Vietnamese a way out if they chose to take it. The ICK recommended
that a representative be picked to tour the countries present to discuss
how they might cooperate to induce the Vietnamese to withdraw, and it
was the Danish foreign minister who was chosen by the ICK for this task.
The job was a thankless one, but he tried admirably. I believe that the
ICK did add weight to the successful resolution that the ASEAN countries placed before the UN General Assembly that year, and in every
subsequent year, with a growing margin of support, until a Vietnamese
troop withdrawal actually occurred, for the withdrawal of "foreign
forces" and the creation of a neutral, sovereign, independent Cambodia/
Kampuchea.

There was one minor spot of embarrassment for Secretary Haig. At a
reception given by the ASEAN delegates following the adoption of the

ICK resolution, Khieu Samphan, who represented the odious Khmer Rouge, forced his way through the throng of diplomats and managed to have himself photographed shaking hands with the secretary, who of course had never met him before and who had no idea who he was. I did not recognize Khieu Samphan either, and so could not warn Haig. The press took great delight in printing this photo. At this same reception I took the opportunity to congratulate the Chinese delegation for changing its stand.

At any rate, despite the background static from Beijing over U.S. arms sales to Taiwan, the United States and China had managed to cooperate on an issue of considerable international importance and to keep their relationship functioning.

Chapter 13

Working towards a U.S.–China Joint Communiqué on Arms Sales to Taiwan

Studies and Ultimatums

About the same time that Alexander Haig set off on his June 1981 visit to Beijing, the NSC decided that the U.S. government should study the question of whether Taiwan really needed the F-5G to defend itself against a Chinese attack. This question derived from the wording of the Taiwan Relations Act (TRA) (see chapter 11), in which it was stipulated that "the President and the Congress shall determine the nature and quantity of . . . defense articles and services [made available to Taiwan through the Military Assistance Program (MAP)] based solely on their judgment of the needs of Taiwan, in accordance with procedures established by law."[1] The study was assigned to the Department of Defense (DoD) on the grounds that it was in the best position to gauge Taiwan's needs in relation to China's military capabilities for launching an attack against Taiwan. Another study undertaken at about the same time by the Defense Intelligence Agency (DIA) addressed the effects on Deng Xiaoping's position of an F-5G sale to Taiwan.

While these studies were under way, the Mexican government in October 1981 was host to a North-South conference of chiefs of state or heads of government at the resort city of Cancún, which President Reagan and Secretary Haig attended. There they met with Chinese Premier Zhao Ziyang and Foreign Minister Huang Hua. Upon the president's and Haig's return from Cancún, Haig informed me that Huang Hua had demanded a "date certain" for the cessation of U.S. arms sales to Taiwan.

According to Haig in his book *Caveat*, the president had listened to Zhao outline a nine-point plan, devised by Deng Xiaoping and publicly

211

announced by the PRC in January 1979, for reuniting Taiwan with Mainland China. This plan, already rejected by Taiwan, would have permitted Taiwan to retain its own armed forces, its own social and economic systems, and its own foreign economic and cultural relations, in exchange for accepting China's five-star flag. Both Zhao and President Reagan ran out of time and departed from the meeting to attend to other commitments, leaving Foreign Minister Huang Hua with the task of conveying to Haig the Chinese demand for a fixed date for U.S. cessation of arms sales to Taiwan, plus assurances that such arms sales would in any one year not exceed the highest level of the Carter years and would decline year by year until they ceased.[2] Huang Hua subsequently repeated this position at the end of October in Washington, where he had come for discussions with Secretary Haig following an appearance at the United Nations General Assembly (UNGA). At that time Huang explicitly threatened that if the United States did not respond with a "date certain," China would downgrade diplomatic relations with the United States. (It had already downgraded relations with the Netherlands from the ambassadorial to the chargé level over the Dutch sale of two submarines to Taiwan.)

From Haig I had heard of Huang Hua's demand at Cancún for a date certain for the cessation of arms sales to Taiwan, but I was not familiar with the other aspects of Huang Hua's remarks to the secretary. But both in New York, where I had accompanied Haig to the UNGA session, and later back in Washington, China's assistant minister for foreign affairs, Zhang Wenjin, informed me in no uncertain terms of China's firm position against the sale of the F-5G to Taiwan. What had apparently stiffened the Chinese attitude was a series of leaks from the White House that the United States intended to sell enough arms to China (again, through MAP channels) to stifle predictable Chinese complaints over significant arms sales to Taiwan, perhaps including the F-5G. I called on Zhang in New York at the Chinese delegation offices, where he gave me a stiff lecture about arms sales to Taiwan, particularly the F-5G, although he appeared more relaxed about the F-5E/F coproduction, leaving the impression that China did not challenge this particular arrangement. Later, Zhang called on Deputy Secretary William P. Clark in Washington and was more diplomatic but made it very clear that China could live with the existing coproduction in Taiwan of F-5E/F aircraft, but it would be compelled to react strongly, as by downgrading U.S.-China relations, if the United States sold the F-5G to Taiwan. Zhang's wording and tone left no room for doubt on this particular issue.

In conducting talks during Huang Hua's post-UNGA visit to Washington, the U.S. and Chinese sides first met on 29 October in one of the secretary of state's seventh floor conference rooms at the department. Here, as Haig makes clear in *Caveat*, he took a strong line against the cessation of arms sales (or a "date certain") and also firmly rejected other aspects of Huang's position, including the Chinese allegation that the United States was attempting to create "two Chinas," as well as the Chinese threat to downgrade relations.[3] Perhaps to cut the sting of his words, though, and to try to meet Huang at least part way, Haig announced— much to my surprise, since he hadn't discussed any particular position with me or my associates—that there would be no increase in quantity or quality of U.S. arms sales to Taiwan, nor would the value of such sales exceed the highest level reached during the Carter administration. In this way, Haig went some distance towards meeting Huang's demands. Immediately after this meeting, the director of China mainland affairs, William Rope, and I put Haig's position down in writing in the form of "talking points" for the secretary to use in further talks with Huang Hua. Haig also took those points to the president, who in turn accepted them as a basis for ongoing discussions. Despite the concessions on quality and quantity of arms sales, our position was quite tough; we did not accept "ultimatums" such as that made by Huang.

In this way, although with no full meeting of the minds, movement on the arms sales issue had in fact occurred. Thanks to Secretary Haig's statement—which, as of the time of his first meeting with Huang Hua, had not to the best of my knowledge been cleared with the White House—the U.S. stand had been modified to some extent to meet China's objections to our continued arms sales to Taiwan, although we were certainly locked in as far as no increases in quantity or quality were concerned. In putting forward his position, Haig may well have been responding to what Zhang Wenjin had told us about the F-5E/F coproduction line in Taiwan being bearable, even if the quantum jump to the F-5G was not. In any event, after some further inconclusive discussions between Haig and Huang Hua, Huang and his party returned to China without any further exchanges on the arms sales issue. Haig and Huang Hua agreed, though, that the arms sales question was to be further addressed in Beijing between Zhang Wenjin and the U.S. ambassador to China, Arthur Hummel, starting in December 1981.

Another development had occurred a month or so earlier in Washington when the DoD study of Taiwan's military requirements was completed. The study found that Taiwan did *not* need the F-5G to defend itself against the air power that China was then capable of mustering against it. The study determined that Taiwan's F-104s, which by then had been in service on the island for some years but were still potent fighter-interceptors, plus its F-5E/Fs (the F-5F was simply a two-seated training version of the F-5E but otherwise had the same capabilities) were more than sufficient to cope with Chinese air strength. China's air power consisted of a mix of Korean War–style MIG-15/17s; additional squadrons of MIG-19s, a follow-on to the MIG-15/17 roughly equivalent to the U.S. F-100; and a supply of MIG-21s, which remained its most potent air threat. The Chinese had been working on an indigenous successor to the MIG-21, known as the F-8, but progress on this aircraft was slow. They had also developed a variation of the MIG-19, known as the F-9, for use as an attack-bomber, but this was not in the same league as the MIG-21 or the F-5E. By way of comparison, the U.S. Air Force and Navy used the F-5E as the equivalent of the MIG-21 in the "aggressor" squadrons employed by the U.S. Air Force and Navy to simulate aerial combat with the aircraft then in use by communist forces worldwide.

Also, the second (DIA) study indicated that sale of the F-5G would result in a downturn in U.S.-China relations and a major set-back for Deng Xiaoping and his modernization program. Of course, the basic DoD study's findings leaked to the press and to interested members of Congress almost as soon as it was completed, and in December 1981 I had the task of lunching with the press and a few congressional staffers to confirm what had already been leaked. In addition, to reduce Taiwan's sensitivities over the loss of the F-5G, I confirmed what had also been leaked at approximately the same time: the United States would release the approximately $100 million already paid by Taiwan for spare parts to be used in Taiwan's aircraft inventory. The supply of these spares had been hung up for months pending the decision on the F-5G, and Taiwan badly needed them to keep its aircraft flying. The Chinese learned about the spare parts sale by means of the leaks, and they vehemently protested, in particular on the grounds that this decision had been made while talks on the whole arms sales issue were being conducted in Beijing. (Here again China showed its sensitivity to the United States making unilateral decisions involving its interests without its participation—in this case they were especially vehement because China's position against arms sales had already been clearly presented by Huang Hua in Washington). Secretary Haig reminded the Chinese that Huang Hua's position as expressed on 29 October had been an ultimatum, which the United States did not accept.[4]

Besides continuing the Hummel-Zhang talks in Beijing, the State Department's next effort to break the deadlock was to draft a letter to Premier Zhao Ziyang inviting him to visit the United States to observe the tenth anniversary of the signing of the Shanghai Communiqué. No reply to this letter was ever received. As outlined by Haig, "Ambassador Hummel in Beijing reminded the Chinese of the significance of this date and told them that the United States was not prepared to let such a historic decade end with a retrogression in Sino-American relations." Hummel also reminded the Chinese of the numerous decisions the United States had made to show good faith, such as expressing willingness to provide them with certain items of the military equipment they had requested. He added that measures to liberalize economic assistance, agricultural commodity assistance, import restrictions on furs and skins, and Export-Import Bank funding availability, would be submitted to Congress and that the administration would also ask Congress to repeal some of the trade and other legislation that impeded trade with China.[5]

My January 1982 Trip to China

In the absence of any tangible response from the Chinese, though, and in light of the evident fact that Hummel's talks with the Chinese were going nowhere, Secretary Haig decided that a more dramatic U.S. initiative was required to continue the discourse with the Chinese, with the hope of cutting off further disputes on the arms sales issue before they became too pronounced. At the heart of these disputes was the F-5G issue.

Haig directed me to head a small special mission to Beijing to meet with Zhang Wenjin and whatever other senior Chinese officials we could reach. Our mission eventually comprised, besides two State Department non–China area specialists and myself, Richard L. Armitage, at that time deputy assistant secretary for East Asian Affairs in the Bureau of International Security Affairs at the Pentagon; William Rope, director of China and Mongolia affairs in the State Department; plus my staff assistant David E. Brown. Ambassador Hummel would join us in Beijing, along with Vivian Chang, a Chinese-American member of the embassy staff, who would serve as interpreter.

Also on this mission were Robert Blackwill, deputy assistant secretary of state in the Political/Military Bureau, and John Davies, country director for Eastern Europe in the Bureau of European Affairs. The latter's task was to explain to the Chinese how the then-current Soviet pressures on Poland might connect with the U.S. arms sales to Taiwan. A possible point here was what seemed to be a Soviet buildup for an attack on Poland, which may have helped the president to withhold the F-5G from Taiwan in order to ease tensions with China, while continuing the

F-5E/F coproduction line (something we assumed the Chinese were pre-pared to accept); otherwise, the United States might have faced military and political crises both from the Soviets in Poland and from the Chinese in the Taiwan Strait.

My own task had several elements: first, informing the Chinese offi-cially, and certainly more formally than through the press leaks, that the United States would not sell Taiwan the F-5G; more important, I was to tell the Chinese that we wished to begin discussion of a joint communiqué that would place ongoing sales of U.S. aircraft and other defense items to Taiwan into a context acceptable to both the United States and China, and thus put aside this issue as a major item of dispute in our relations. To facilitate this approach, I carried a set of principles we were prepared to embody in a very tentative draft joint communiqué. These principles had been approved personally by the president.[6] I was further instructed to convey the information to the Chinese that the United States would con-tinue the F-5E/F coproduction line with Taiwan and would provide re-placements (via the MAP program) for aging or inoperable aircraft in Taiwan's air force.

Finding a context within which to manage the arms sales issue was becoming a necessity. During the latter part of 1981 the Pentagon had told State that according to law, the Defense Department would be obliged to inform the Congress no later than 20 August 1982, that the coproduction line of the F-5E/F would be extended. The dollar value of this extension would have been about $800 million in credits. Fortunately, this sum did not exceed the $835 million upper limit on arms sales to Taiwan set under the Carter administration, taking into account inflation since then (see chapter 12). Nevertheless, as we looked at the stage we had reached in our relationship with China over arms sales to Taiwan, we concluded that a failure to reach an agreement with the Chinese on this issue by the time of the announcement of the F-5E/F coproduction extension would cause an explosion in Beijing and in all probability would set back U.S.-China relations considerably. We could not predict the consequences, given the harsh anti-U.S. propaganda that was appearing constantly in the Chinese press over the arms sales issue, but we could not rule out a deterioration of U.S.-China relations, including the threatened downgrading of our mission in Beijing, for China, as noted, had already downgraded relations with the Dutch. We had worked too hard and too long to establish the foundation for meaningful, ongoing communications with this important nation of over a billion citizens to see such a regression in our relations.

It was with these principles and concerns in mind that, in accordance with Haig's instructions, our State Department delegation journeyed to

China. On 5 January 1982, Beijing time, our small group from Washington arrived long after dark at Beijing's airport, where we were met by Zhang Zai, chief of the Americas section of the Chinese Ministry of Foreign Affairs. To avoid a possible Chinese refusal of our visit, which would have left us in the position of carrying on a sterile dialogue on the arms sales issue by cable, we had not let them know in advance the purpose of our visit, so it was a very puzzled Zhang Zai who was there to greet us. All I could tell him at the time was that we had some important matters to discuss with the Foreign Ministry and that we hoped he could arrange a meeting with Zhang Wenjin or someone of similar rank the following day. While seeing us off, Zhang Zai said that he would see what he could do. I was to stay at the residence of Ambassador Hummel, along with Rich Armitage, Bill Rope, and David Brown; the other members of the party were housed at the Beijing Hotel. Zhang Zai telephoned the residence later in the evening to say that a meeting had, in fact, been arranged with Zhang Wenjin for the following afternoon.

In my briefcase I carried with me the texts of a laboriously drafted document that we planned to give to Zhang Wenjin at our meeting. The first section contained a statement to the effect that Taiwan's military needs were such that it did not require the acquisition of the F-5G, and we therefore had no plans to proceed with any such sale. In addition, the statement indicated that we would replace aging or worn-out items in Taiwan's air inventory to maintain its defenses at current levels. We hoped that this formulation would prove noncontroversial to the Chinese, who had lived with the level of Taiwan's military capabilities then current without challenge since the issuance of the Shanghai Communiqué in February 1972.

Also, as noted, I had the first of many drafts of a joint communiqué (or perhaps more properly, a "statement of principles") that would, we hoped, eventually bring agreement between our two sides on a *modus vivendi* covering ongoing U.S. arms sales to Taiwan. This second document noted that Secretary Haig had expressed to Foreign Minister Huang Hua in Washington the previous October that there would be no increase either in the quantity or quality of arms sales to Taiwan. It explicitly linked any possible future reductions in those levels to China's continuing the policy of not using force to reunite Taiwan with the China mainland. There was no reference to a "date certain" for cutting off arms sales, as Huang Hua had demanded, since this would contravene the TRA.

Evolving a formulation on arms sales to Taiwan to present to the Chinese had been a very time-consuming task, since the language had to be acceptable (or at least tolerable) not only to the Chinese, but importantly, to the powerful pro-Taiwan supporters group in the Congress who often reflected the views of Taiwan's top leaders. The crucial element was finding some way of relating our arms sales to Taiwan to China's nonuse of force, thus not disrupting the current DoD appraisal of Taiwan's "needs," and thereby assuring compatibility with the TRA. We realized at the outset that this would be the most difficult part of negotiating any agreement with the Chinese, since their firm position all along was, and in fact still is, that the "liberation" of Taiwan, or more politely, "reunification" with the mainland, was entirely an internal matter for the Chinese to decide.

Before departing for Beijing, I had already resolved that I would keep the Congress, or at least the appropriate East Asia subcommittees of the Senate and the House, fully informed of where our negotiations with the Chinese stood. On this question I had very much in mind the failure of the "Taiwan Enabling Act" to gain congressional support, partly because the Congress had not known in advance what the Carter administration was attempting to achieve. The result was that the TRA was substituted and passed overwhelmingly by both houses of Congress, leaving the president no alternative but to sign. We actually had no hope that the Chinese would accept our first initiative on the arms sales issue, but operated on the assumption that at least we could begin a process of give-and-take that would eventually lead to a statement acceptable to both sides. This initial draft was prepared partly by me and partly by Bill Rope.

Our talks with the Chinese leadership duly began the day following our arrival, on 6 January 1982, in one of the former foreign mission buildings that the Chinese had taken over as guest houses in the old Beijing Legation Quarter. It was a typically cold, gray winter's day in Beijing, and we found an equally cold atmosphere in the room where we met. Sitting across from us at the usual green baize table was Zhang Wenjin, who headed the Chinese delegation. On my right was Ambassador Hummel and on my left Rich Armitage, with the other members of the team farther down the table. To open, after thanking Zhang for seeing us on such short notice, I informed him that the United States had determined *not* to sell the F-5G to Taiwan and then handed him the text of the statement to this effect, which we proposed to issue in Washington at the State Department's regular noon briefing the following day. The statement made clear that Taiwan's needs could be met through aircraft of the type already in its inventory, namely, the F-5E/F and the F-104.

Zhang countered with a rather bitter diatribe against the whole policy of continued U.S. arms sales to Taiwan, referring among other matters to the release of spare parts, which had been become publicly known the preceding month. I responded by reminding him that Deng Xiaoping had in 1978 accepted normalization of relations with the United States without demanding a cessation of U.S. arms sales to Taiwan. It was at this point that Zhang remarked, "Ah, yes, but that was for strategic reasons" (see chapter 11). If Zhang was tough in his remarks, I was equally tough in my response, which rather startled my Pentagon colleague Rich Armitage, but I knew that our position had no give. Zhang nevertheless accepted the draft containing the principles for a joint communiqué that I passed to him and said he would study it. I informed him about the presidential approval of the principles in the draft, even though, as I added the next day, "the details have not yet been worked out."

That evening Zhang gave the traditional banquet for the group, during which I found him, contrary to his usual diplomatic style, rather acid and biting in his comments about our arms sales to Taiwan and about U.S.-China relations in general. Zhang's behavior, which I considered uncharacteristic of his normal, even-tempered and urbane self, suggested to me that the arms sales issue had become a very sensitive one indeed in the upper levels of the Chinese Communist Party. Nevertheless, in his remarks about the F-5G he indicated that the Chinese were prepared to accept the U.S. statement. We mutually expressed the hope that the next day we could go on from there to address the whole arms sales issue and ultimately arrive at a solution via a joint communiqué. After the banquet I returned with Ambassador Hummel to his residence, where we first advised Washington to go ahead and issue the statement on the F-5G and then began to prepare for bed.

Just then the telephone rang in the ambassador's study, and I understood that Zhang Wenjin was on the other end with a complaint about our draft statement on the F-5G. Since the only other extension on that line was in the master bedroom, I ran there to use the telephone on the bedside table and, with apologies, perched on the edge of the bed occupied by his wife, Betty Lou, who was lying there reading.

The gist of Zhang's complaint was that the section of the statement where we said we would replace aging or inoperable aircraft in Taiwan's inventory could be construed as leaving us free to upgrade Taiwan's capabilities, and it was therefore unacceptable. Thinking hard, I suggested that we amend the section to conclude: "with comparable aircraft."[7] (In putting this forward I had in mind that the Air Force of the Federal Republic of Germany had been operating F-104s acquired through the United States's FMS [Foreign Military Sales] program for some years but was anxious to release them because of a high rate of attrition, even though they had been very well maintained.) I also added, ". . . and by extension of the F-5E coproduction line in Taiwan." This language would convey both to our own people and to Taiwan that Taiwan's needs could be met by its existing inventory of aircraft, including continuation of our coproduction line. In fact, the statement made this point directly. Zhang told us he would get back to us on this, which he did about fifteen minutes later, saying that the Chinese side had agreed.

The problem then remained of getting the revised wording to Washington before the statement was issued at noon Washington time on 8 January. I immediately called back to my Washington office and gave the new language to my principal deputy, Thomas Shoesmith, and left it up to him to touch the appropriate bases in State and the White House. Fortunately, the time difference between Washington and Beijing gave us a little leeway—it was about 10:30 or 11:00 P.M. in Beijing, which was 11:00 or 11:30 A.M. in Washington. (This time discrepancy between Beijing and Washington came in very handy later.) To my infinite relief, in about half an hour Shoesmith called back to say that the amended wording was acceptable, and we immediately conveyed this message to Zhang Wenjin. Though Shoesmith had run into initial resistance, he had been assisted in his efforts by Alan Romberg, formerly in the State Department's East Asia Bureau but then in Public Affairs, who had carried the revised wording to the daily noon briefing. Then, after what had been a very eventful day, I went back to my own bedroom and retired for the night.

The next afternoon I again met with Zhang Wenjin in the same location to discuss our draft joint communiqué. As expected, Zhang had little use for the initial draft. The problem, again as I had expected, was the question of linkage, that is, relating our approach on arms sales, which we indicated would taper off over a period of time, to China's nonuse of force in reuniting the mainland and Taiwan. Zhang insisted on the standard Chinese position, which was that the "liberation" of Taiwan was an internal matter for the People's Republic of China, in which nobody else had the right to interfere. He did, however, agree to furnish us with a counterdraft, and I concluded from this exchange that we had achieved what we had sought: the beginning of a dialogue on a joint communiqué covering U.S. arms sales to Taiwan.

That same afternoon Zhang Wenjin put forward three conditions for continuing our talks: we would make public the fact that no weapons had been involved in the spare parts release of December 1981; that the process of releasing the spare parts had already been underway before President Reagan met with Premier Zhao Ziyang at Cancún; and that we contemplated no new transfers of arms to Taiwan in the next few months while talks on the subject were continuing. Zhao told me that it would be very helpful to China if we could make these points in an open context.

Thinking them over, I foresaw no particular difficulties, but while I let Zhang know that we would respond positively, I asked him to let us do it in our own time and in our own way. He agreed.[8] On the morning of the next day, John Davies met with a senior Foreign Ministry official (Han Xu, I believe). While Davies was busy with his talks, Zhang Zai escorted Bill Rope, David Brown, and me to visit the Lama Temple in Beijing's northwest quarter, which had been closed to foreigners during my assignment to USLO. I was intrigued on this visit to see that not only had the Lama Temple been completely refurbished (it reportedly had been badly torn up by Red Guards during the Cultural Revolution), but that it contained a contingent of yellow-robed Buddhist monks—signs of a political thaw in Beijing, even if the weather that morning was bitter cold.

There remained but one item of a ceremonial nature: I was able to pay a call on Deputy Prime Minister Ji Pengfei, which had the effect of putting an official high-level Chinese imprimatur on the work we had done with Zhang Wenjin over the preceding days. I then left for Washington via Tokyo, where I briefed my Japanese Foreign Ministry counterparts on the trip.

My meeting with Ji was covered by the press. *Newsweek* entitled its article on this event, "No FX for Taiwan, no joy in Peking." Of course, *Newsweek* was unaware of the previous contacts we had engaged in with the Chinese on the subject of the F-5G (or "FX"). According to the *Newsweek* item, Ji Pengfei had said to me with an alleged hint of disapproval, "You arrived on short notice and are leaving in a hurry," to which I was said to have replied, "Despite the short notice I was received very well." Ji was then quoted as concluding with the observation, "You are always welcome."[9]

To be frank, the Chinese were indeed disturbed about the issue, but in my judgment not because of the U.S. decision not to sell Taiwan the F-5G. That decision was in line with what they were prepared to accept based on what we had been told in New York and Washington by Zhang Wenjin. Rather, they were upset because China had not been a major player in the sequence of events leading up to my visit. On the preceding 13 December they had sent a protest note to us on the spare parts release, declaring in effect that China "will never accept any unilateral decision from the United States" concerning arms sales to Taiwan. Still, the deed was done; both sides could now proceed to the next item on the agenda, namely, formulating a joint communiqué on U.S. arms sales that would be acceptable to both sides and that would stand up to scrutiny by the U.S. Congress.

Vice President Bush's May 1982 Trip to China

During the following weeks and months, the drafting of a joint communiqué on the issue of arms sales to Taiwan turned out to be a tortuous
process. As I noted, we needed some form of linkage to China's nonuse
of force in reuniting Taiwan with the mainland, which China adamantly
resisted on the grounds that the whole subject was purely an internal
matter for the Chinese to decide. Meetings in Beijing between Ambassador Hummel and Zhang Wenjin or Zhang Zai initially took place once or
twice a week, and only later accelerated to daily sessions as 20 August
came closer. We discovered early on that we could not realize our hope of
completing the process by 28 February, the tenth anniversary of the
Shanghai Communiqué.

One of the particular problems we faced was that while our drafting
efforts were proceeding, we were being subjected to a level of invective in
the Chinese press that became so extreme that by March I was beginning
to wonder whether any further attempts were worthwhile. To read the
Chinese press, which was incessantly charging that the United States was
colluding with Taiwan and interfering in China's internal affairs, was to
wonder if we could ever succeed. In an effort to get a reading on the
Chinese attitude toward finally realizing a joint communiqué, I made arrangements to meet privately with Ji Chaozhu, who at this time was political counselor to the Chinese embassy in Washington. On the strength of
our long-standing acquaintance, I asked him outright if it was worthwhile
for us to continue our efforts. Ji seemed taken aback by my question and
urged me by all means to continue to seek agreement.

While our discussions with the Chinese were going on, I also continued
to keep the Congress constantly informed about what we were doing. I
was resolved that if an agreement could be reached with the Chinese on
arms sales to Taiwan, it would not be canceled out or redrafted through
any failure on my part to assure the appropriate briefing of the Senate
Foreign Relations Committee and the House Foreign Affairs Committee.
As a result, I met frequently with both committees, particularly their East
Asian subcommittees, to bring the members up to date on where we stood
at any given moment. This effort most often put me in touch with Senator
Charles Percy of Illinois, then chairman of the Senate Foreign Relations
Committee; Senator S. I. Hayakawa, chairman of the Foreign Rela-
tions Committee's East Asian subcommittee; Representative Clement
Zablocki, chairman of the House Foreign Affairs Committee; and Repre-
sentative Stephen Solarz, chairman of the House Foreign Affairs Committee's East Asian subcommittee. I would visit these leaders almost weekly,

sometimes in their committee rooms and sometimes in their offices on the Hill. I found all four quite sympathetic with what we at State were trying to do, but others were less so, particularly on the Senate Foreign Relations Committee, the home of several of the authors of the Taiwan Relations Act.

Our process of exchanging drafts and counterdrafts with the Chinese continued from March into April with little progress, despite Ji Chaozhu's encouraging words. Towards the end of April, the president decided to try to cut the knot by writing to Deng Xiaoping and Chinese Premier Zhao Ziyang to suggest that Vice President Bush, who was planning a visit to Japan and several other East Asian countries in May 1982, might visit China as part of his tour to discuss the arms sales issue. The vice president's previous service in China was considered a plus by the White House, since he had in all probability been regarded by the Chinese as a friend.

There was no immediate Chinese response, which suggested all the more strongly to us that relations with the United States were being debated at the highest levels of the CCP. The vice president ultimately departed on his East Asian tour with no word from Beijing about a stop in China. (All we received from Beijing at this time was editorializing in the press that continued U.S. arms sales to Taiwan would bring about a deterioration in U.S.-China relations, along with the admonition that "those who created the knot should be responsible for untying it."[10]) I accompanied Vice President Bush on this trip, as did Martha, since Barbara Bush was also along to accompany her husband. All of us aboard the vice-presidential aircraft hoped that at some point along the way we would hear from the Chinese and could add Beijing to the Bush itinerary.

I should add that Secretary Haig originally had reservations concerning a vice-presidential visit to China, perhaps on the grounds that the U.S.-China relationship could best be handled through State Department, rather than White House, channels, but he acceded to the White House decision that the trip be made if at all possible. We in State's Bureau of East Asian and Pacific Affairs, which in this case meant the China mainland affairs staff and myself, drafted two letters, to be signed by the president and carried by the vice president, expressing U.S. sincerity about reaching an agreement. One letter was addressed to Deng Xiaoping and one to Premier Zhao Ziyang. Along the way, in New Zealand on 3 May, after we had learned of China's agreement to a Bush visit, a third letter was drafted, addressed to CCP Chairman Hu Yaobang, in the chance, even though remote, that Mr. Bush might meet with him. The first two letters we sent by telegram to Beijing ahead of time, and we carried the actual texts along with us. The third letter was sent to Beijing by diplomatic courier.

We had three letters, each containing much the same wording, because we lacked advance knowledge of whom the vice president would meet in Beijing if the Chinese ultimately agreed to his visit. I was later asked by the Chinese, who were baffled by the existence of three letters, why we had acted in this way, and I gave them this explanation. Part of the problem was that Deng Xiaoping, clearly the top leader in China, had resigned from most of his governmental and party positions, even though all other Chinese leaders continued to defer to him. We considered it just possible that Hu Yaobang might substitute for Deng, and therefore we had to be prepared.

The vice president's route was first to Japan, where in addition to meeting with Prime Minister Nakasone he was invited to lunch by Emperor Hirohito in the Imperial Palace; then to Seoul for meetings with South Korean President Chun Doo Hwan; next to Singapore for a brief meeting with Prime Minister Lee Kuan Yew; next to Australia for a meeting with Prime Minister Malcolm Fraser, and finally to New Zealand for a session with Prime Minister Sir Robert Muldoon. During this entire time there was no word from the Chinese until shortly before the scheduled departure from New Zealand, when news of Chinese approval of a Bush visit finally arrived by means of a cable from our embassy in Beijing. This late Chinese response, even if favorable, came at the farthest point away from Beijing that was possible during the vice president's tour and necessitated a very long jump—from Wellington to Beijing with a refueling stop at Darwin, Australia—that took over twelve hours. Still, the importance of visiting Beijing transcended the inconvenience, and as if to make up for their delay in responding, the Chinese offered a day's rest in the scenic spot of Hangzhou (the same city where the Shanghai Communiqué was finalized) so we could recover from jet lag.

We could perhaps have been shot down on our landing in Hangzhou. For the first time in my experience with the Air Force's Special Air Mission squadron, the vice president's pilots made a mistake, confusing a Chinese military airfield for the civil airfield. Just as we were about to land, with wheels and flaps down and the jet engines reduced in power, the throttles of the engines were suddenly pushed forward, the wheels and flaps came up, and we circled some more until the correct airfield was finally sighted. I have subsequently wondered just what would have happened had our pilots not recognized their mistake.

At Hangzhou we were met by the Hummels. In addition to my getting together with the vice president and Hummel to go over the arms sales issue and to work out his presentation to the Chinese, we had a chance to enjoy walking around Hangzhou's famous lake. Our wives were able to visit the city and some of its well-known tourist sites. When they visited an old Buddhist temple, they were surprised to find it packed with worshippers, young people as well as old. What we all discovered in Hangzhou was that the city had become China's honeymoon capital, with hundreds of brightly clothed newlywed couples strolling hand in hand and enjoying both the amenities and each other's company. The bright clothing of the honeymooners (who, we were told, saved up their vacation time to go to Hangzhou to get married), combined with their obvious carefree behavior, was a portent of the many other changes that we were to see in China as a result of the reform program Deng Xiaoping had begun in 1979. Hangzhou was a delightful interlude.

Upon reaching Beijing, Vice President Bush presented the letters to Vice Premier Wan Li to be passed on to the addressees. The letters were of some considerable significance, for we had tried to draft them in such a way as to suggest U.S. flexibility on arms sales to Taiwan. All the letters contained the words, "We fully recognize the significance of the nine-point proposal of 30 September 1981, and the policy set forth by your Government as early as 1 January 1979."[11] This last reference was to the statement (I believe the same one mentioned by Deng Xiaoping when he visited Washington) that after normal diplomatic relations were established with the United States, China would take "current realities" into consideration in its relationship with Taiwan—perhaps a backhanded way of saying that China would seek peaceful reunification with Taiwan rather than military liberation. This same reference also amounted to a linkage of sorts between arms sales and peaceful reunification. In addition, a sentence was added in the president's letter to Zhao Ziyang saying, "We would expect that in the context of progress toward a peaceful solution, there would be a decrease in the need for arms by Taiwan." (Note again the reference to Taiwan's "needs.")

In the event, Vice President Bush did meet with Premier Zhao Ziyang and also with Foreign Minister Huang Hua. Most importantly, though, he was able to meet with Deng Xiaoping. Several of my Chinese friends who were present at the meeting or who had a hand in the evolution of U.S.-China relations have confirmed that this was *the* turning point in our difficult road towards agreement. We met with Deng Xiaoping and several associates from the Chinese Foreign Ministry in the Great Hall of the People in a U-shaped configuration, with Deng seated approximately in the bend of the U, the vice president on his right, Ambassador Hummel (the president's personal representative in China) on Bush's right, then myself and the other members of our party. On Deng's left were Zhu Qizhen, deputy director of the American and Oceanian Division, and other senior Foreign Ministry officials, including Zhang Zai.

Some minutes into the conversation with Deng, after the exchange of the usual welcoming statements, Deng suddenly suggested that he and the vice president go off to a separate room for a private conversation of about fifteen minutes. Deng and the vice president then rose, and together with Art Hummel and a Chinese interpreter they went to a small adjacent room. The fifteen minutes stretched out to half an hour and then an hour, leaving me to carry on a desultory conversation with Zhu Qizhen. Finally, after an hour had passed, Deng and the others reappeared, and the larger meeting ended. Thanks to this meeting, the vice president was successful in convincing Deng that the United States was unquestionably sincere in wanting an agreement on the Taiwan arms sales question, and Deng was won over, if any doubts on this matter remained in his mind. The Chinese customarily place great store in their assessment of the real intentions of those with whom they are negotiating. Following the meeting, I received no new negotiating instructions, but work did resume on a joint communiqué in both Washington and Beijing.

The vice president had a press conference after the meeting with Deng, and when asked about arms sales, he declared, "I'm not going to elaborate on the details of any negotiation," but went on to say that discussions of the arms sales issue would continue at the level on which they had been conducted since my trip in January, that is, by the State Department in Washington through Hummel in Beijing to the Chinese. Bush also added that he would carry back to Washington a much clearer perception of the Chinese position than had previously been held in Washington, although he did reiterate that the Taiwan Relations Act was the law of the land and would be observed.[12] For the record, two days later the Chinese did present a counterdraft to our most recent proposal, and the talks proceeded in a much improved atmosphere.

Before departing for home, the vice presidential party had the opportunity to watch a new play being staged in the southern part of Beijing. In keeping with the political climate of the times, the play was entirely nonpolitical. It had a plot reminiscent of the Arabian Nights: a young prince in what must have been Turkestan was being victimized by a plotter intent on seizing the throne; the villain (who wore black and was adorned with a flourishing black mustache, as were his followers) used a seductress to try to suborn the prince, and part of her act was to do a shimmy dance in a dress with a bare midriff. I heard gasps of surprise at this point from the surrounding Chinese and thought to myself that China had certainly come a long way from Jiang Qing's revolutionary opera. We all noticed that the young women on the streets were wearing dresses, silk stockings, and high heels instead of the shapeless coats and trousers of the Mao Zedong era. While "Democracy Wall" may have perished in 1979, many other aspects of reform in China had persisted, as witnessed in the newly-wed scene in Hangzhou.

Chapter 14

Agreement: The Joint Communiqué on Arms Sales to Taiwan

On returning to Washington we in State's East Asian and Pacific Affairs Bureau (EA/P) kept up our drafting efforts towards a joint communiqué on continued U.S. arms sales to Taiwan. Shortly after my return, I also was called on to testify before the Senate Foreign Relations Committee concerning what the administration was attempting to accomplish in our negotiations with China. There I ran into a real buzz-saw in the person of Senator John Glenn of Ohio, one of the original authors of the Taiwan Relations Act. Senator Glenn was outspoken in his criticism of our refusal to give Taiwan what it wanted in the way of military sales, especially high-performance aircraft, to which I could only reply that our sales were based upon Taiwan's needs, as had been specified in the Taiwan Relations Act that he himself had helped to frame.

Then, to my surprise, Senator Glenn began to berate me for not doing more to improve the United States's relations with China. At this point I felt I had to respond frankly and asked if I might do so. Senator Glenn did not object, whereupon I reminded him that China had protested the Taiwan Relations Act and regarded it as incompatible with the 1972 Shanghai Communiqué and the 1979 Joint Communiqué on the Establishment of Diplomatic Relations; hence, what Senator Glenn wanted us to do in increasing arms sales to Taiwan in keeping with his interpretation of the TRA was absolutely contradictory to improving relations with China. Senator Glenn turned red and made no further comments.

My schedule called for me to accompany the secretary of state to the annual ASEAN Foreign Ministers' meeting in late June in Singapore. But Secretary Haig, who was having his troubles with the White House staff at this time, chose not to go. Walter Stoessel, who had taken over as deputy secretary of state from Judge William Clark when the latter went to the White House as the president's national security adviser, went to Singapore in Haig's stead, and I accompanied him.[1] After the ASEAN meetings, I decided to visit some of the other countries in the region for which I was responsible, including Malaysia, Burma, and Thailand. My sense was that the handling of the joint communiqué was in good hands, Bill Rope's in Washington and Art Hummel's in Beijing, and I could safely spare a few extra days. It was in early July in Thailand, at the ambassador's guest house, that I heard the news over the Voice of America that Secretary Haig had resigned. I was stunned at the news and immediately sent a telegram to Haig expressing my regrets. I cut short any further travel plans and hurried back to Washington, where Walt Stoessel was functioning as acting secretary of state.

Upon returning to Washington from Southeast Asia, I found that despite the State Department's loss of an able and distinguished head, Haig's resignation was a blessing in disguise. His relations with the White House staff, that "hydra-headed monster," as he once termed it in my hearing—consisting of Michael Deaver, Edwin Meese, and James Baker—had become so poisonous as to bring the secretary's work to a virtual standstill.[2] Any proposed drafts of the joint communiqué on arms sales to China that he might have sent over to the White House would probably have been scrutinized with a magnifying glass, with any small point of contention requiring return of the document for redrafting. I cannot but give Al Haig credit for recognizing that his departure was a significant factor in our ability to reach an ultimate agreement with the Chinese on arms sales to Taiwan. In his book *Caveat*, he writes, "On reflection, it seems to me that my precipitous, albeit inevitable, departure from the Reagan Administration was the single act that made possible the solution of this critical question."[3] This is but one of many instances when, in my own experience, Al Haig's impeccable honesty—and refusal to be pushed around— contributed to the solution of a difficult problem. His resignation unquestionably speeded up the process of reaching agreement on the arms sales communiqué as the critical 20 August deadline approached.

Intense Last-Minute Negotiations

By this time the 20 August deadline for notifying Congress of the extension of the F-5E/F coproduction line in Taiwan was staring us in the face, so the pace of our activities in both Washington and Beijing had to quicken considerably. We had early on in our negotiations informed the

Chinese about this deadline, which surely must have had some bearing on the speed of their own drafting process. Both sides realized, in my opinion, that if the Congress renewed the U.S.-Taiwan F-5E/F coproduction agreement before release of a U.S.-China joint communiqué on the subject of continuing U.S. arms sales to Taiwan, U.S.-China relations would inevitably suffer.

Our daily routine came to be this: Bill Rope and I prepared and put in final form the instructions for Art Hummel in the evening, usually with me sitting behind Bill at the word processor and looking over his shoulder; these went to Acting Secretary Stoessel for clearance. To my recollection, Stoessel never changed a word. He was not a China hand and deferred to our judgment. After he had initialed the instructions document, he sent it to the White House for clearance and final transmittal. Again, I'm not aware that any changes were made in our draft at the White House. Judge Clark, like Walt Stoessel, was not a China hand, nor were the other members of the senior White House staff. With Haig gone, no lingering rancor between State and the White House came to my attention. At any rate, there seemed to be nothing in our drafts that conflicted with White House policy.

Here again the time difference between Beijing and Washington became our ally: in the evening, Washington time, we transmitted our instructions to Hummel in Beijing, where it was morning Beijing time, so they were on his desk ready for perusal early in his day, giving him ample opportunity to work out his presentation to the Chinese. Then, following his meeting in the afternoon with his opposite number in the PRC's Foreign Ministry, he sent us his report, along with comments and recommendations, which would reach us in the morning Washington time, and give us the rest of the day to work out our next draft. As the days of July and early August passed, the pace of our activities picked up, and tensions inevitably increased. Where meetings in Beijing between Hummel and his Chinese opposite numbers had occurred perhaps twice a week, they now took place daily, following the pattern I have described.

During this period, another factor introduced itself: the reaction of the Taiwan government, which, thanks to leaks from its supporters in Congress, was well aware of what we were doing to achieve a U.S.-China joint communiqué on arms sales to Taiwan. As we might have expected, a steady stream of editorial invective from Taiwan was directed against the U.S.-China negotiations on arms sales. In addition, while we were in the midst of our drafting process, I was contacted, indirectly of course, by the head of Taiwan's Coordination Council for North American Affairs and asked if I would accept and pass on to the Congress six points that

Taiwan wanted to ask the United States to use as guidelines in conducting its relations with Taiwan. These, I was told, would also serve as reassurance of a continued close relationship between the United States and Taiwan. The points were:

1. The United States would not set a date for termination of arms sales to Taiwan.
2. The United States would not alter the terms of the Taiwan Relations Act.
3. The United States would not engage in advance consultations with Beijing before deciding on U.S. weapons transfers to Taiwan.
4. The United States would not serve as a mediator between Taiwan and the mainland.
5. The United States would not alter its position regarding sovereignty of Taiwan (that is, while we would continue to regard Taiwan as part of China, the question of reunification would be left to the Chinese themselves, with our only stipulation being that reunification be by peaceful means). Nor would we exert any pressure on Taiwan to engage in negotiations with the mainland.
6. The United States would not formally recognize China's sovereignty over Taiwan.[4]

In looking these points over, I decided that none would cause the United States any trouble. In fact, we were already in agreement on all points: One of the basic issues in seeking a joint communiqué with Beijing on arms sales to Taiwan was to avoid a "date certain" for U.S. termination of such arms sales; there was no chance that the Congress would amend the TRA, even if we had wanted to do so; we regarded the nature and content of our arms sales as solely the concern of the United States within the parameters (no increases in quantity and quality) already agreed to with the Chinese; we had no intention of acting as a mediator between the PRC and Taiwan. From the time of the Shanghai Communiqué we had left their future relationship to be resolved by the Chinese people themselves, our only concern being that the solution be peaceful; the same philosophy covered the remaining two of the six points. Accordingly, I recommended in a memo to Walt Stoessel that the six points be agreed to by the United States. The White House, which continued to look after the interests of its "old friend," Taiwan, agreed. Word of U.S. acceptance of the six points was conveyed to Taiwan, and I also agreed to inform the Congress of our response. This I did on or about 27 July 1982.

I have referred to increased tensions as our deadline approached. These tensions came from the pressures to which we were subjected from five different directions: Taiwan, Beijing, the ever-shortening time, friends of Taiwan in Congress, and the White House itself, which, while wanting to see an agreement, also was resolved not to let down its old friends on Taiwan.

The pressures from Beijing can be perceived from an article by Christopher Wren, writing from Beijing in the *New York Times* of 14 July 1982, headlined ''China's Irritation with U.S. Growing,'' in which Wren listed a whole series of anti-U.S. editorials appearing in the mainland press that past week. The articles he referred to, published in the *People's Daily*, the *Beijing Review*, the magazine *Fortnightly Talk*, and the *Journal of International Studies*, all blamed the United States for the strains in U.S.-China relations over alleged U.S. deference to Taiwan. The most authoritative of these was the piece printed in the *Journal of International Studies* and reprinted in the *People's Daily*. Ten thousand words long, complete with forty-three footnotes, the article reviewed the whole history of the U.S. attitude towards Taiwan over the preceding four decades. Wren's article in the *Times* speculated, on the basis of his talks with foreign diplomats in Beijing, that Deng Xiaoping was under pressure from his own conservative critics to explain why his overtures to the United States had not halted its military sales to Taiwan. Al Haig's resignation was regarded by the Chinese as a possible indication that administration policy towards China could shift away from Haig's alleged pro-China stance.[5] On 11 July the *People's Daily* accused American conservative ''diehards'' of trying to undermine the U.S.-China talks and ''resurrect the old 'two-Chinas' policy.''[6]

The pressures from Taiwan's friends in the Congress came from frequent critics of China policy such as Senator Barry Goldwater of Arizona, who charged that people in the administration wanted to cave in to Red China and dump Taiwan.[7] They also came in the form of charges from Senator Glenn, which he delivered to me and repeated to the press, that the administration was failing to live up to both the letter and spirit of the Taiwan Relations Act. To counter these criticisms, on 28 July President Reagan gave a classified briefing (which promptly leaked) to pro-Taiwan senators and congressmen, in which he let it be known that while the State Department had informed China that there would be no increase in the quantity or quality of arms sales to Taiwan, the administration would notify Congress ''within two weeks'' (he inadvertently shortened the deadline by a week) of a new deal on F-5E fighters. Among the congressional participants in this briefing were Senators Goldwater, Steve Symms of Idaho, and William Armstrong of Colorado, and Representatives Jack

Kemp from New York, Edwin Derwinski of Illinois, and John Rousselot of California. Also present were Vice President Bush, Secretary of Defense Caspar Weinberger, and newly appointed Secretary of State George Shultz.[8] Secretary Shultz had been confirmed by the Senate on 16 July, and I believe that this was his first formal appearance in his new position. In his Senate hearing, Shultz had pledged to Senators Goldwater and Helms, perhaps the two most fervent supporters of Taiwan, that there would be no halt in American weapons to Taiwan and no slackening in implementation of the Taiwan Relations Act.

Nothing the president said at his briefing, however, contradicted the approach that we in State were taking with his approval on the arms sales issue. Congressional conservatives were said to have taken comfort from the president's commitment "not to abandon our longtime friends on Taiwan."[9] The president also reasserted, as he had in a press conference 27 July, a commitment to carry out the Taiwan Relations Act but said also that he wanted to continue the U.S. relationship with Beijing begun under President Nixon and continued under President Carter.[10]

Agreement Finally Reached

While all of this politicking was going on in Washington, those of us involved in the drafting process kept working away, with the result that by the first half of August we had all but bridged the gap between ourselves and the Chinese on the final wording. We followed the pattern set in the Shanghai Communiqué by having both sides set forth their own positions on the basic issues of the status of Taiwan and their respective relationships with the island before getting down to the crux of the matter in dispute, namely, the arms sales. The Chinese reiterated that "the question of Taiwan is China's internal affair," but added, "The message to compatriots on Taiwan issued by China on January 1, 1979 [see chapter 11], promulgated a *fundamental* policy [emphasis added] of striving for the peaceful reunification of Taiwan with the Motherland. The nine-point proposal put forward by China on September 30, 1981, represented a further effort under this fundamental policy to strive for a peaceful solution to the Taiwan question." Both the United States and China, in addition, endorsed a statement that "respect for each other's sovereignty and territorial integrity and noninterference in each other's internal affairs constitute the fundamental principles guiding United States-China relations."

For our part, we took due note of what the Chinese had said about the peaceful resolution of the Taiwan question in the two statements just quoted, as well as the line laid down in the 1979 Joint Communiqué on the Establishment of Diplomatic Relations, and declared that these created favorable conditions for the settlement of U.S.-China differences over arms sales to Taiwan. We went on to say that, *"Having in mind the foregoing statements of both sides* [emphasis added], the United States Government states that it does not seek to carry out a long-term policy of arms sales to Taiwan, that its arms sales to Taiwan will not exceed, either in qualitative or quantitative terms the levels of those supplied in recent years since the establishment of diplomatic relations between the United States and China, and that it intends to reduce gradually its arms sales to Taiwan, *leading over a period of time to a final resolution* [emphasis added]." The language I have just cited is embodied in the Joint Communiqué of 17 August 1982 (see appendix C). Our original draft at this juncture had concluded the sentence just quoted with the words, ". . . (resolution) of this difficult problem," but the Chinese had objected and so we removed them. This phraseology was, as I recollect, the last obstacle to reaching an agreement.

Thus, each side had moved very close to the position desired by the other. China had retained its insistence that resolution of the Taiwan question was its internal affair but had also declared that its nine-point proposal represented further efforts in its "fundamental policy" of seeking to reunite Taiwan with the mainland by peaceful means. On our side, we interpreted China's use of the expression *"fundamental* policy" (*da zheng* in Chinese) to mean "unchanging and long-term," an interpretation that I explained in some detail before the Senate Foreign Relations Committee. (Another interpretation was that the Chinese wording meant "great" and "formal.") China's wording gave us the latitude to state in general terms that "having in mind," that is, "on the basis of" the "foregoing statements of both sides," we did not seek to carry out a long-term policy of arms sales to Taiwan, that our arms sales would diminish "over a period of time," and that the arms sales would not exceed either in quality or quantity what had been previously provided to Taiwan, essentially by the Carter administration.

What we did not provide China, though, was a "date certain" for ceasing our arms sales, and in fact, the issue of a termination was left open-ended ("leading over a period to a final resolution"). Beijing's commentary to the contrary notwithstanding, we did achieve a form of linkage between Chinese adherence to a peaceful reunification policy and U.S. actions.

A precise interpretation of the joint communiqué will indicate that any change in China's "fundamental policy" would inevitably have its effects on U.S. arms sales to Taiwan, and, if carried to its logical conclusion, on the U.S. role in the Taiwan Strait as defined in the Taiwan Relations Act. In effect, arms sales to Taiwan could continue, even at a gradually reduced rate, so long as we observed the quality and quantity limitations and did not exceed in any one year the high point in sales of the Carter administration, as expressed, of course, in current dollars (in 1982 that was approximately $835 million). Cessation of arms sales would be achieved at some undefined point down the road. Nor was there any reference to an annual percentage of reductions. (After I left the bureau to take up an assignment as ambassador to Indonesia, I heard that such an allegation had been made in the press; however, that was not the case: we rejected the Chinese attempt to insert the words "progressive reduction" into the communiqué text.)

One factor was omitted in our discussions, nor was it ever alluded to by either side: Taiwan's latitude to purchase arms from commercial sources outside the framework of U.S. government arms sales to Taiwan, which involved U.S. government credits under the "MAP" (Military Assistance Program) voted on annually by Congress. The TRA also covered only U.S. government responsibilities for the supply of arms and military services to Taiwan. Privately, we assumed that Taiwan would probably look to the commercial arms market, as in fact it did in ordering two submarines from the Dutch, since its foreign-exchange reserves were more than adequate. We did not, however, actively encourage Taiwan to turn to the commercial arms market.

The finale of our long negotiating process was a cliff-hanger. On the assumption that we had gone as far as we could go, we sent out our last and what we considered our final draft to Beijing on Saturday, 15 August, Washington time, and I went to bed that night not knowing what the outcome would be. Then, early the next morning the telephone rang in my bedroom, and my wife informed me that State's Operations Center was on the line. I immediately answered, and learned that a flash message had just arrived from Beijing saying that the Chinese had accepted. At last we had reached accord on this critical and, up to then, divisive issue.

A great deal, of course, remained to be done before we could issue the agreed-upon version of the Joint Communiqué on Arms Sales to Taiwan. Prior to official issuance on the following workday, Monday, 17 August, I needed to take the final version of the joint communiqué to the Hill to justify it before the appropriate Congressional committees or leaders. That Sunday afternoon I was called to Secretary Shultz's private office, a small room off his more formal, official office, to go over the draft. He read the wording, grunted, and said, "Well, I guess it's about the best we could get," or words to that effect, leaving me with the clear impression that he was not entirely satisfied with what we had accomplished. He then told me and Bill Rope, who was also present, "You're going to take a lot of heat on this, but it's the right thing to do."

(I hasten to add that in February 1987 I was invited to a reception in the main diplomatic reception room in the State Department to honor the fifteenth anniversary of the Shanghai Communiqué, during which Secretary Shultz referred in his speech to the "three significant milestones in Sino-U.S. relations": the Shanghai Communiqué of 28 February 1972; the Communiqué of 1 January 1979, on Normalization of Relations; and the 17 August 1982, Communiqué on Arms Sales to Taiwan. Following his speech, he came up to me, shook my hand, and said, "Well, John, it's worked out pretty well, hasn't it?")

But before the Joint Communiqué on Arms Sales could reach the stage of public and press acceptance, I had to run the gauntlet: inform the Congress, especially those senators and representatives most interested in U.S.-Taiwan relations, and bear the brunt of their criticisms. I could also expect some echoes of those criticisms from the press and public. At the request of the White House, I asked for a meeting with the Senate Foreign Relations Committee so that the president could hear the members' views; the committee granted me a closed-session appointment on short notice on the morning of 17 August. The public release of the communiqué was to take place simultaneously in Beijing and Washington later that day.

When I outlined to the Senate Foreign Relations Committee the proposed terms of the Joint Communiqué on U.S. Arms Sales to Taiwan, pointing out the significance of the Chinese wording on their "fundamental policy" of "striving for the peaceful reunification of Taiwan with the Motherland," and of the lack of a "date certain" for termination of U.S. arms sales, I ran into a tirade of complaints from the pro-Taiwan senators that left me limp. I was also asked to return for an open session meeting, which I agreed to do. Returning to State in my car, I said to my legislative assistant, who had accompanied me, that it had been a rough session and that we might expect trouble in the future from that quarter—but it never came. Even at that time I had reached the conclusion that while some of the senatorial ire was genuine, a significant part of what was said was said for the record, allowing the senators to get off the hook with respect to their constituents and Taiwan by blaming State for what had happened, and not themselves.

On the afternoon of that same day, I also briefed Chairman Zablocki of the House Foreign Affairs Committee in his office in the Capitol, where he was accompanied only by his senior staff assistant. Zablocki was quite philosophical about the joint communiqué; he simply remarked that he hoped things would work out as we had anticipated. We assumed, correctly, as it turned out, that with his consent, or acquiescence, no further briefings of the House Foreign Affairs Committee were necessary.

The long-negotiated Joint Communiqué on Arms Sales to Taiwan was formally announced on the same day, 17 August 1982. No legislative action by the House or Senate was contemplated in response to that Joint Communiqué. It appeared that my efforts to keep Congress informed all along had paid off in general acceptance of this agreement.

Reactions to the Joint Communiqué

Despite a lack of organized opposition, the U.S.-China Joint Communiqué on Arms Sales to Taiwan was a controversial topic in concerned circles for some time. The White House was of great help in damping down congressional criticism, especially President Reagan's personal intervention on the afternoon of 17 August in inviting thirty senators and representatives for a briefing in which he explained how the United States had not undercut Taiwan.[11] When CBS commentator Dan Rather, in his 6:30 P.M. evening newscast remarked that Taiwan *had* been undercut, President Reagan actually telephoned Rather to deny that any such thing had occurred, and on 18 August, Rather carried this presidential intervention on his 7:00 P.M. program.[12] The president also issued a statement that declared that the joint communiqué was "fully consistent with the Taiwan Relations Act," adding also our intention to stand by an old friend and accord it the respect and dignity befitting such a relationship.[13] Bill Rope drafted this statement, and I approved it.

There were other official U.S. supporters of the joint communiqué as well, such as Senator Hayakawa, chairman of the East Asia subcommittee of the Senate Foreign Relations Committee, who was quoted as saying (with considerable accuracy, I might add), "There are enough ambiguities in the agreement so that no one should be seriously offended, no one should feel sold out." Senate Majority Leader Howard Baker said he was pleased with the document, in contrast to Senator Goldwater, who remained in character and termed it "a bad agreement."[14]

It might well be asked how it came to be that President Reagan, who as a candidate had taken such a strong pro-Taiwan stand in August 1980 had by August 1982 come to render such firm support to the joint communiqué. My own conclusion is that his support was based on his own convictions of what was good for the national interest. In addition, the lack of criticism from his associates in the White House (Baker, Deaver, Meese, and Judge Clark) indicates that all had come to perceive that the political damage to the Republican Party's cause would be far greater if the Reagan administration were to be blamed for a major setback in U.S.-China relations than if Taiwan received the degree of support about which Reagan, as a candidate, had spoken in August 1980. That year, 1982, was an election year, and the Republican leadership must have concluded that the last thing their party needed was a controversy over relations with China. (As it happened, the Republicans lost both houses of Congress, but China never became an issue in the campaign.) Moreover there was also the question of alternatives: how long could the United States follow a policy that would alienate China and create tensions in the Asia-Pacific region?

Those of us who had been deeply involved in the negotiations leading up to the issuance of the Joint Communiqué of 17 August 1982 were pleased with the high level of backing from the White House and not surprised by the negative tone of statements from Taiwan and even from China (see below). Our assumption was that if each was unhappy or had reservations, we must have done something right.

As far as American public opinion itself is concerned, it may be of some historical interest that not one of the major U.S. news magazines—neither *Time*, nor *Newsweek*, nor *U.S. News and World Report*—carried anything about the 17 August Joint Communiqué in their respective 23 August editions, the earliest date on which they could have reported the news, since all three had a 16 August deadline. Developments in Lebanon, it seems, had come to dominate major news coverage. The *New York Times*, however, did carry a favorable editorial concerning the joint communiqué on 19 August, which, in referring to Taiwan's future, concluded with the words, perhaps prescient in the light of contemporary developments: "The best real guarantee of the island's future is Peking's continued stake in American friendship and good will. To jeopardize this merely for better hardware would serve neither Taiwan's interests nor America's."[15]

Taiwan, as might have been expected, expressed great unhappiness over the joint communiqué, noting via a statement by a spokesman of its Foreign Ministry, "Now [that] the United States Government has mistaken the fallacious 'peaceful intention' of the Chinese Communists as sincere and meaningful and consequently acceded to the latter's demands to put a ceiling on both the quality and quantity of the arms to be sold to the Republic of China, it is in contravention of the letter and spirit of the Taiwan Relations Act, for which we must express our profound regret."[16]

Taiwan also took this opportunity to publicize in its media the six points I had earlier provided to the Congress (see above).

The Chinese also maintained reservations about the joint communiqué, saying in both a Foreign Ministry statement and a *People's Daily* editorial that the accord was "only the first step" towards solving the issue of arms sales to Taiwan and that continuation of the unofficial U.S. relations with Taiwan provided for in the TRA could lead to "another grave crisis."[17]

Actually, the reaction in China, at least in private, was much better than we could have anticipated. Shortly after the joint communiqué's issuance, Ambassador Hummel was summoned to a meeting with Deng Xiaoping in which Deng expressed his congratulations over the completion of the joint communiqué. For Deng, who beyond a doubt had been enduring criticisms from some of his more orthodox colleagues over continued U.S. arms sales to Taiwan (amply revealed by the anti-U.S. attacks on this issue in the Chinese press, as mentioned), the consummation of the joint communiqué on arms sales must have come as a great relief. Art Hummel has mentioned to me that the atmosphere of this meeting, as manifested by Deng and the other Chinese who were present, was one of considerable affability. Even the injection by the Chinese during the meeting of a demand for the return of Hu Na, China's foremost woman tennis player, who had defected and turned professional after a tennis tour of the United States that took her to several states, did not detract from this atmosphere. (I might add that as far as U.S.-China relations were concerned, the Hu Na episode was the only ripple I can remember disturbing the otherwise placid relationship we maintained during the rest of 1982. Things could have been worse if the Chinese had pressed the Hu Na case more vigorously, since there were several representations to State by congressmen to assure that we did not give into Chinese demands. But China allowed the event to pass into history.)

With the joint communiqué on arms sales out of the way and no further significant crises in U.S.-China relations darkening the horizon, the Pentagon went ahead with notifying Congress of its intention to continue the F-5E/F coproduction line with Taiwan, which amounted to credits of approximately $800 million in 1982 dollars. Purists might argue that this sum came close to exceeding the highest level of sales during the Carter administration, although the total possibly might have been spread over several years, but taking into account inflation since the Carter period, there was no violation of either the letter or the spirit of the joint communiqué. I cannot recall any particular reaction from Beijing, which as noted had been informed in advance about our intentions.

My last brush with the Congress over arms sales to Taiwan came around November 1982, when I was beginning to disengage as assistant secretary in preparation for assuming my post as ambassador to Indonesia. On this particular occasion I briefed the East Asia subcommittee of the Senate, joined by members of the House, on what we could do, and in fact were doing, to maintain arms sales to Taiwan within the parameters of the joint communiqué. Jesse Helms, one of the most vociferous critics in the Senate, arrived some time after my briefing had begun, missing all the positive things I had said, and remarked that he didn't really believe that the president of the United States was aware of what we "people in the State Department" had gotten him into through the joint communiqué. The senator was taken aback when I informed him that the White House had been with us every step of the way, and, in a really telling blow, informed him that the decision to send the vice president to China in May 1982 was made in the White House and not in State.

And so, finally, after fourteen years of negotiations, if 1968 is taken as our starting point in trying to improve relations with China, or more than a quarter century, if the 1955 ambassadorial-level talks are used as a beginning, the United States finally achieved a *modus vivendi* with China on the most contentious item dividing us. Our two countries could then proceed to other matters of mutual concern without the Taiwan issue poisoning the atmosphere. I would be the first to agree that the arms sales issue was left up in the air, with no conclusive end in sight, but with "enough ambiguities" (to quote Senator Hayakawa) to live with the situation indefinitely if neither side made any major changes in policy.

As I pointed out earlier, American investment in China has been considerable following U.S.-China rapprochement. China has achieved access to the United States as an important market for its exports, and tens of thousands of Chinese students have come to the United States to study. At the same time, American scholars and teachers have worked in China, U.S. businessmen have found China a land of opportunity (despite many unforeseen problems), U.S.-China diplomatic relations have been maintained at a level sufficiently high to address major bilateral and international concerns, U.S. newsmen have reported in depth on political and economic developments in China, and thousands of Americans have visited China as scholars and tourists. All this has contributed to the increased understanding between our two countries. Meanwhile, Taiwan has not sunk beneath the East China Sea but has developed its economy to unprecedentedly high levels and has implemented significant democratic reforms. U.S.-Taiwan relations of an unofficial nature continue, while a peaceful environment (but with two "glitches" in May 1995 and March 1996, as noted below) has generally been maintained in the Taiwan Strait.

Chapter 15

In Retrospect—and Looking Ahead

The effort to cross the divide between the United States and the People's Republic of China was at best tedious, time-consuming, frustrating, and fraught with difficulties. The discussion in chapter 8 of "two different social systems coexisting together" doesn't begin to tell all there is to know about the profound differences in the values under which each country operates or the complexities Americans encounter in working with the Chinese—and presumably the Chinese have in working with us. Before turning to the future of U.S.-China relations, it may be useful to briefly recap some of each country's fundamental values.

China's Cultural Heritage

China's basic ethical values date back over 2,500 years to the "Spring and Autumn" period of the Zhou Dynasty, when the authority of the Zhou kingdom had broken down and petty kings set their states against one another. At this point the towering figure of Confucius appeared on the stage of Chinese history. While he sought in vain among the warring states for a government post commensurate with his talents, Confucius nonetheless became revered in his own and future generations for his teachings, later collected in the so-called *Analects*. Confucius deplored the anarchy of his times and described in ideal terms the earliest days of the Zhou Dynasty, when its founders were supposed to have established a golden era of peace. To Confucius, the "Way" (or *Dao)* for men (and women as well) to return to this golden era was for them to play their assigned roles in a fixed society of authority. He summed it up in this statement: "Let the ruler be a ruler and the subject a subject; let the father be a father and the son a son."[1] Already the classic Chinese aversion to disorder (*luan*), or anarchy, was clearly evident. The so-called "five relationships" between ruler and subjects, father and son, husband and wife, elder brother and younger brother (applying also to elder sister and younger sister), and friend and friend, are also attributed to Confucius. Even before Confucius, the family became the core of Chinese society, but its role was codified under Confucius. The father was a patriarch, respected for wisdom, and the center of authority in the family. The ruler of the state was in turn the patriarch of all his people.

For the ruler, the measure of his success lay in his virtue and the contentment of the people, rather than his exercise of power. An important aspect of the ruler's duties was to perform ceremonial rites that placed the realm and Heaven in balance. If the realm was calm, and the needs of the people were being met, the ruler enjoyed the "Mandate of Heaven," which assured his continued rule and that of his successors—provided, of course, that his successors followed his example. If not, the Mandate of Heaven was withdrawn, and the nation was subjected to natural disasters, civil chaos, and foreign invasions, or all three, leading to the fall of the dynasty.

As for the individual, he or she was subordinated to all of those who in the social hierarchy were superior in rank. The status of women was definitely below that of men, but in Chinese classics such as *The Dream of the Red Chamber* the matriarch in a family—or even in a state, such as the empress dowager in the Qing Dynasty—exercised great influence even though nominally "behind the screen" (*zai mu hou).*

Confucius outlined a whole set of virtues both inner and outer that a ruler or a "gentleman" should possess, and observance of the outer virtues and associated rituals became extremely important as China's history progressed. The importance of rituals in China can be judged by the fact that during the imperial era, one of the emperor's principal duties was to perform rites such as (during the Qing Dynasty) praying at Beijing's Altar of Heaven on the first day of the new year and ceremoniously plowing at the Temple of Agriculture to assure a good harvest. The ultimate purpose of such rituals was to assure the stability and prosperity of the empire for the coming year.

Although Confucius accepted the stratification and authoritarianism of society and did not challenge the institution of a hereditary monarchy, he did leave room for reality. Inherent in the concept attributed to him of "rectification of names" (see chapter 9) was the implication that theory should conform to reality, or as was evidently meant by the Confucianists, reality should be made to conform to theory.[2] Here again are evident the seeds of the internal ideological dispute encountered by the staff of USLO when it opened in 1973, as different Chinese factions tried to interpret or distort the classic Chinese teachings in their own ways. Deng Xiaoping's "seek truth from facts" (see chapter 11) could be identified with the teachings of Confucius, if not of Marx and Lenin, while Mao and his ideological allies, certainly those who were attacking Zhou Enlai, tried to turn away from Confucius for his advocacy of what they called a return to feudalism.

Confucius was not the only proponent of an ethical philosophy in Chinese history. Others came along, some following in his footsteps, such as Mencius (Meng Zi), who elaborated on Confucian doctrine, and some critical of his "Way," such as Mo Zi, who opposed it and advocated instead an early form of totalitarianism. Taoism, which was epitomized by Lao Zi ("Old Master") and that defined man's rather insignificant role in relation to the universe, even predated Confucianism. By the fourth and fifth centuries C.E., Buddhism began to appear and to leave a permanent impression. But in China's typical syncretic way, all except Mo Zi's teachings were merged with Confucianism, as indicated in the Chinese classic book *Travels to the West* (*Xi You Ji*), which concludes with the admonition: "Remember, the three religions [Confucianism, Taoism, and Buddhism] are one," though its originator never intended Confucianism to be a religion. In spite of this, Confucius's teachings have certainly been the dominant feature in Chinese ethical and philosophical thought right up until the present time, carrying with them the set of values that most Chinese strive to attain, or to which they at least grant lip service.

It certainly can be argued that China's set of values has served the country well. Of all the nations in the world, China is the only one that can trace its history back in an unbroken line from the present to the first days of recorded history, the Shang Dynasty of (at a guess, since historical records are scanty) 1766 B.C.E., or at least to around the eleventh century B.C.E. I have even seen bronzes in the Shanghai Municipal Museum that are attributed to the period of the "Yellow Emperor," a mythical or semi-mythical figure who predated the Shang and who is credited with having done much to create the foundation of Chinese civilization and culture. To be sure, some foreign invaders were able to conquer China, but inevitably they adopted the values, systems, and culture of the more sophisticated Chinese and became indistinguishable from the Chinese. Ancient Egypt's civilization dates back further than China's, but its continuity was broken up by Greek and Islamic invaders (especially the latter), so that it has taken generations of archaeologists to recover the past and provide a picture of life under the pharaohs. China's "Middle Kingdom complex" to which I referred earlier (see chapter 7) can be attributed in large part to the country's historical continuity and long span of civilization, about which the Chinese are justifiably proud.

Cultural Heritage of the United States

The United States presents a marked contrast. Americans are the inheritors of the Judeo-Christian ethic, which tends to put more emphasis on the rights of the individual than on the well-being of society as a whole. A basic element in the evolution of American political thought, epitomized in Thomas Paine's pamphlet "Common Sense," was the rejection of a hereditary monarchy. This pamphlet, which was widely circulated in pre-Revolutionary America and could almost be regarded as the Bible of the American Revolution, has also been described as "the cry of a crusader out to destroy a selfish society dominated by a few gluttons of power, privilege, and possession."[3] "Common Sense" observed that, "*For all men being originally equals* [emphasis added], no one by birth should have a right to set up his own family in perpetual preference to all others forever."[4]

Paine's influence can be seen in the opening words of the American Declaration of Independence, as penned by Thomas Jefferson: "We hold these truths to be self-evident, that all men are created equal, that they are endowed by their Creator with certain inalienable rights, that among these are life, liberty, and the pursuit of happiness." There is nothing here about an orderly, structured, hierarchical society of the type glorified by Confucius, or about an absence of anarchy. The Declaration of Independence was the trumpet sounding the real beginning of the American Revolution and the underpinnings of America's subsequent political and social philosophy.[5] It is not surprising, therefore, that with the success of the American Revolution, Americans became imbued with the concept of extending the benefits of a democratic society to other parts of the world.

Accompanying this political idealism, a strong religious missionary strain has also long been present in the United States, which over the years developed a strong focus on China. American missionaries of various Christian sects were active throughout China. (My wife's grandfather was a Protestant missionary in Canton in the late nineteenth century.) The missionaries' affinity for China led to many contributions by the United States to China's modernization, such as the establishment of a significant number of the best middle schools and universities; among the latter were Yenching University in Beijing, Nanjing University in Jiangsu Province's capital at Nanjing, St. John's University in Shanghai (all Protestant), and Fu Ren University, a Catholic-sponsored institution in Beijing.

For many years, individual Americans contributed very substantial sums of money through their churches to support missionary activities in China, although in many cases these contributions involved significant personal or family financial sacrifices. Such contributions continued for well over a century, and even into the period of the Great Depression of 1929–1937. With this history of pro-Chinese sentiment in the United States, a nationwide outpouring of pro-Chinese support among Americans occurred after the Sino-Japanese clashes, beginning with the *Lugou-qiao* incident in 1937 and continuing throughout World War II. When during that period Madame Chiang Kai-shek (Soong Mei-ling) visited the United States and addressed both houses of Congress to ask for more U.S. support, she was widely acclaimed. The average American initially made little distinction between the Kuomintang or the Chinese Communists, and Edgar Snow's *Red Star over China* became a best-seller.

American's pro-China feelings were displayed even earlier after the so-called "Mukden (Shenyang) Incident" of 1931, which the Japanese used to seize control of Manchuria. The United States, under the leadership of Secretary of State Henry M. Stimson, stood alone among all of the nations of the world in calling for economic sanctions against Japan to halt its aggression against China. In point of fact, the United States did consider that it had a special relationship with China, dating at least as far back as its use of the Boxer Indemnity (the sum paid by China for losses by foreign interests caused by the Boxer Rebellion of 1900) to finance Chinese students coming to the United States to pursue higher education.

Returning to the present, I believe that the United States's strong anti-communist zeal in the post–World War II era, plus the missionary-inspired compulsion to spread the religious "word" that dominated American ecumenical thought for over a century, prompted Americans on moral grounds to reject Chinese Communist political principles and with them the government of the People's Republic of China. Secretary of State John Foster Dulles was not alone in regarding Chinese Communism as being intrinsically evil. This rejection undoubtedly added to the complexities surrounding normalization of U.S.-China relations (see chapters 10 and 11). It was fortunate for both sides that in the late 1960s or early 1970s a strain of pragmatism, or realism, was present in the minds of both sides' leaders. Therefore, in the face of the need to confront a common adversary, the Soviet Union, we were able to work out compromises in our respective ideological and cultural principles that enabled normalization to proceed. In the long run, however, serious differences persist, not only because of the specifics of unfolding current events, but also due to the inherent difficulty of bringing the nearly antithetical U.S. and Chinese social and political values into a reasonable balance.

Post-Normalization Problems

China maintains that a viable U.S.-China relationship is contingent upon the United States continuing to live up to both the letter and spirit of the three joint communiqués (see appendices A, B, and C). The United States has maintained firmly that the key element in U.S.-China relations, as epitomized in the joint communiqués or in accompanying statements, is China's adherence to a policy of nonuse of force in reuniting Taiwan with the mainland. As of the conclusion of the Joint Communiqué on Arms Sales to Taiwan in 1982, the U.S. relationship with China appeared to be on track, the Soviet Union still posed a serious military threat to both the United States and China, and it seemed that if differences appeared, they could be dealt with in a normal, diplomatic way.

What no one on either side anticipated was the furor that arose in the United States during the Bush administration over the human rights situation in China. This situation, of course, was China's brutal official repression on 3–4 June 1989 of the Tian An Men demonstrations. The scars of the bloody episode in Tian An Men Square, when China's leaders turned the People's Liberation Army against the demonstrators, still deeply trouble U.S. relations with China and will not be easily overcome. Television coverage of the events before, during, and after those days was watched worldwide and left indelible impressions on much of the U.S. public. Helping to keep the issue alive for some time was the press coverage of the U.S. decision to grant asylum (in Beijing) to Fang Lizhi, a leading proponent of more democracy in China and perhaps China's best-known dissident (critic of the Chinese leadership), who after the shooting started in Tian An Men Square fled with his wife to the U.S. embassy and then lived there for a full year. The riots, the bloodshed, and subsequent treatment of dissidents sensitized the American media and public to the broad issue of human rights in China.

Prior to the Tian An Men episode, U.S.-China relations had relaxed to the point that the United States had removed some of its strategic controls on sales to China of weapons-related technology. Toward the end of the Bush administration, the United States even allowed a satellite manufactured by the Hughes Aircraft Company in the United States to be launched in China by a Chinese "Long March" rocket. (After being suspended as a consequence of the Tian An Men clashes, this strategic relationship has since been partially renewed.) The effect of the "Tian An Men Massacres," as the American press called the tragic episode, on the U.S.-China relationship was that the American people and some government officials publicly began to call into question every aspect of that relationship, and in turn, China adamantly adhered to a hard-line response that left very little room for negotiation.

The efforts made by the Bush administration following the Tian An Men bloodshed to induce China to accept an interpretation of human rights more in keeping with U.S. and Western traditions, were failures. The visit to Beijing by National Security Adviser Brent Scowcroft and Deputy Secretary of State Lawrence Eagleburger to Beijing in July 1989, when the gunsmoke over Tian An Men had scarcely cleared, must have occurred at a time when the Chinese leaders themselves were still assessing the implications of the situation, in terms of both foreign and domestic policy; they were in no position to focus on human rights in any positive way. The second visit by Scowcroft and Eagleburger the following December may have been more productive, but the Chinese certainly did no more than give lip service to improving human rights, and a televised toast by Scowcroft to the existence of a warm U.S.-China friendship left an unfortunate impression that the United States was in some way acquiescing in Chinese policy. Moreover, the first Scowcroft-Eagleburger visit to Beijing was supposed to have been kept secret, but it inevitably leaked from Washington and cast further shadows over the whole episode.

In the meantime, through the economic reforms initiated by Deng Xiaoping, China has made giant strides in modernizing its economy, above all by freeing up the productive zeal of its millions of farmers (80–85 percent of the population) by eliminating the communes and returning to what amounts to family farming. The establishment of small-scale industrial enterprises in the "townships," which have succeeded the communes, has also left the rural sector of the economy demonstrably much better off than at any time in recent decades, despite widespread corruption and inefficiency. In the urban areas, living standards have also improved markedly because of the modification of China's larger-scale industrial economy to permit a large and increasingly significant component of private, or joint public-private enterprise. This latter modification requires a heavy component of foreign investment, a recourse to market capitalism, and rejection of Mao Zedong's basic concept that it is wrong to get rich. China is manifestly moving forward rapidly in its economic growth.

In a visit to Beijing in 1992, I was amazed at the extent to which entire streets in the city were lined with small kiosks selling a whole host of consumer goods produced, I assumed, by the small-scale industries in the townships, which have soaked up some of the excess manpower in the rural areas. (I recall here my reservations over Deng Xiaoping's remarks to George Bush in 1973 about mechanizing Chinese agriculture, on the grounds that a great surplus of manpower would be created thereby—see chapter 9.) The remarkable change I observed was in the space of just one year, since my 1991 visit. A 1994 visit to Jing De Zhen in Jiangxi Province also showed impressive economic activity taking place there.

Having been granted Most Favored Nation (MFN) treatment by the Carter administration, China turned to the United States as a major market for its exports, leading to a Chinese trade surplus of over $30 billion in 1994, with the total still growing. But China's MFN status has been threatened by those in the Congress, the press, and the American populace as a whole who would attach conditions, that is, require distinct improvements in China's human rights performance, to MFN's renewal. In 1992 a bill before the House of Representatives calling for conditionality passed overwhelmingly and was passed by the Senate as well, but not by enough votes to override a presidential veto.

In 1993 President Clinton supported extension of MFN using executive action without major congressional resistance, while at the same time calling on the Chinese to improve human rights practices; in 1994 he defied the critics in Congress and the press, not to mention a number of dedicated and highly vocal human rights organizations, to de-link China's MFN status from human rights considerations. Similar extensions of MFN for China were made in 1995 and 1996. American businesses with large commitments to China may have had much to do with the president's switch on Chinese human rights from his position during the 1992 presidential campaign. The only condition he imposed was to halt the import of Chinese-made firearms, both military and sporting, into the United States. However, elements in Congress, the press, and elsewhere continue to press for sanctions against China based on the human rights situation. This question may well arise again.

Other economic issues (with political implications) have also arisen to plague U.S.-China relations: China's growing trade surplus with the United States, coupled with a stubborn resistance to opening its own markets fully to U.S. goods; its alleged use of prison labor to produce items for export to the United States; and its lack of "transparency" in commercial dealings with U.S. interests, by which is meant the practice of lower-level Chinese authorities seeming to conclude commercial contracts, only to add later that full approval had yet to be obtained from higher-level authorities, and so on up the line. Protection in China of U.S. intellectual property rights also remains a serious problem: the United States has threatened high tariffs on Chinese goods in the amounts said to be lost by Chinese pirating of CDs, computer software, and tapes—between $2 and $3 billion annually—and the Chinese have warned of retaliation. Following agreement in early 1995 on the issue of protection of intellectual property, China began to crack down on pirating of copyrighted materials, but in the United States, neither businessmen nor the government were satisfied.

On China's side, there has been resentment at its exclusion from the World Trade Organization (WTO) as a developing country, for which it blames the United States, although in fact a prime factor has been China's resistance to providing certain data required for WTO membership, such as budgetary figures. Nevertheless, China has been inclined to regard its exclusion as a U.S.-engineered act designed to "contain" it, despite the support of other WTO members of China's exclusion pending its submission of the required data.

Military Buildup and Arms Sales Issues

Also troublesome is the question of China's modernization of its military technology and its sale of some of this technology to potential trouble spots in the Middle East. Most notable is China's alleged sale to Pakistan of the M-11 missile, a short- to medium-range vehicle capable of being modified to carry a nuclear warhead—a sale that China does not admit has taken place. There has also been a flurry of commotion within the U.S. intelligence community and in the press over China's alleged sale to Iran of chemicals for manufacturing mustard and nerve gas—a sale that seems to have been disproved by the U.S. search in Saudi Arabia of a Chinese ship en route to Iran that allegedly carried such chemicals; the search revealed no cargo of this nature. However, China had already sold Iran its Silkworm missile, a surface-to-surface type derived from the "Scud" of the former Soviet Union. These missile sales may have been in disregard of China's pledge in 1992 to abide by the Missile Technology Control Regime (MTCR) guidelines, even though China did not sign the MTCR.

China has defended all of its missile-related sales as being within the parameters of the MTCR; when Lynn Davis, under secretary of state for international security affairs, went to China in July 1993 to seek clarification of Chinese missile sales and missile-related sales to Pakistan, one source familiar with the visit declared that "the Chinese were completely contemptuous. . . . They just stiffed her, saying that [they] have abided by the MTCR guidelines."[6] In 1995, a new complication was injected over the Chinese decision to sell nuclear reactors to Iran, despite evidence that Iran is going all out to develop atomic weapons. China has since informed the United States that this sale has been "postponed."

As a consequence of the M-11 transaction, the United States on 25 August 1993 announced sanctions on the sale of military-related technology to ten Chinese companies, a decision taken, as one U.S. observer put it, "more in sorrow than in anger." Another U.S. official added, "We felt we had no choice."[7] Chinese reaction was prompt and harsh. Its official Xinhua News Agency called the move a "naked hegemonous act," while the Chinese vice foreign minister said to U.S. Ambassador J. Stapleton Roy, "Now that the U.S. has resumed these sanctions, the Chinese government has been left with no alternative but to reconsider its commitment to the MTCR." He went on to say, "The U.S. government shall be held responsible for all consequences arising therefrom."[8] (Once the Clinton administration backed away from restrictions on MFN, some U.S. military sanctions were eased, as already noted, and some high-level military contacts were undertaken.) In 1996, Secretary of State Warren Christopher said that the United States would not impose further sanctions on China because of its sale of nuclear technology to Pakistan, in this case 500 ring magnets suitable for use in plutonium-producing centrifuges.

American actions in the military sphere have also figured in the strains on the U.S.-China relationship. During the 1992 presidential campaign, George Bush patently violated the 17 August 1982 Joint Communiqué on Arms Sales to Taiwan by authorizing General Dynamics Corporation (now Lockheed-Martin) to sell 150 F-16 jets to Taiwan. This sale was clearly a political move to garner votes in Texas by saving jobs at the General Dynamics plant there. According to the U.S.-based Taiwan publication *Free China Journal,* the F-16 sale would amount to $6 billion[9]—a sum far exceeding anything that had been on the books previously. I consider it a striking piece of irony that George Bush, who did so much to make the 17 August 1982 joint communiqué a reality, was the individual who first broke its terms. The United States has subsequently sold Taiwan four E2-C surveillance aircraft, 70 percent of the cost being borne by Taiwan, and the remainder, for the radars, paid for through U.S. Military Assistance Program (MAP) channels. In addition, the United States has leased three *Knox*-class frigates to Taiwan (with six more to come),[10] pre-

sumably through MAP channels, and along with the three ships will provide through MAP between thirty-eight and forty-one Harpoon antiship
missiles worth $68 million.[11] A Taiwan application to purchase Mark-48
torpedoes to go with these ships is still awaiting approval. A further U.S.
arms transaction began in July 1993 when the Pentagon commenced selling Taiwan twenty-six new "Kiowa Warriors" (improved UH-53 helicop-
ters) of the same type as those intended for the U.S. Army.[12] And once
President Bush made the F-16 sale decision, the French followed with a
sale to Taiwan of sixty Mirage jet fighters. France has also sold Taiwan six
LaFayette-class frigates, similar to French navy ships, which have a
"stealth" configuration.[13]

Additional modernization of Taiwan's defenses has taken place with the
roll-out of Taiwan's Indigenous Defense Aircraft (IDA),[14] which, to my
knowledge, uses American Garrett engines and has enjoyed technical assistance from Grumman in its development. Besides the IDA, Taiwan has
launched five ships of a new class of locally built frigates, which bear a
striking resemblance to the *Oliver Hazard Perry* class of frigates currently
in service with the U.S. Navy, which were built by Bath Iron Works of
Maine.[15]

For its part, China has moved to improve its own military capabilities.
It has bought twenty-six SU-27 aircraft from Russia and may also have
purchased an unknown number of Russian MIG-29s. Reports also alleged
that the Chinese have been exploring the purchase of the still-uncom-
pleted aircraft carrier now at Sevastopol, either from Russia or Ukraine,
whichever claims ownership. Latest reports indicate that this vessel,
which is about 85 percent completed, is quietly rusting away at its berth,
but according to the March 1995 *U.S. Naval Institute Proceedings*, China
has announced plans to have two 45,000-ton carriers in operation by the
next decade. Moreover, it is either building or buying from Russia a substantial submarine fleet, including at least four Russian *Kilo*-class subs.[16]
It already has a small number of nuclear-powered guided-missile submarines.

China is also putting into service an indigenously designed class of frigates, probably with weapons and electronics acquired from European
sources, and it has continued to modernize its *Luda*-class destroyers
based on designs obtained from the former USSR.[17] Demonstrating its
growing "blue-water" naval capabilities, several years ago China sent a
small task force consisting of a destroyer, a frigate, and an oiler into the
Indian Ocean in the vicinity of India's Andaman Islands.

These military developments accompany Chinese claims to the presumably oil-rich Spratly Islands in the South China Sea near Borneo and

the southern Philippines, plus much of the South China Sea itself. While China professes an interest in the peaceful resolution of the conflicting claims to the Spratlys (in addition to China, Malaysia, the Philippines, Vietnam, Brunei, and Taiwan all lay some claim to the islands), China's capability to use force cannot be discounted, certainly not by those nations that abut the South China Sea and also regard the Spratlys as theirs. In fact, China has laid claim to almost the entire South China Sea, even though it has said that it will not interfere with peaceful navigation in this zone.

To their credit, the Chinese have not begun a buildup of military forces along the mainland areas adjacent to Taiwan—at least not of a major nature such as to suggest any intention of attacking the island, although Chinese naval patrol boats have been trying to stop the extensive smuggling between Taiwan and the mainland. However, in a more threatening stance, following the "private" visit to the United States by Taiwan President Lee Teng-hui in May 1995, China conducted two land-based missile test firings into East China Sea waters adjacent to Taiwan. In another gesture, in March 1996 China released a newsreel and still photographs showing amphibious landing maneuvers on its East China Sea coast. In the United States and elsewhere in the world, the press took these maneuvers as an attempt to influence Taiwan's presidential elections later that same month. The Taiwan stock exchange dropped sharply in response to these episodes. The United States reacted by positioning two aircraft carrier task groups built around the *Nimitz* and the *Independence* near the northern and southern entrances to the Taiwan Strait, but *not* inside it. Nor was there any statement by the United States that it was prepared to defend Taiwan against an attack from the China mainland, although there was considerable U.S. editorial criticism of China's missile tests and maneuvers in 1995 and 1996.

Taking all these military developments together, despite the lack of an active Chinese military threat along the Taiwan Strait, groups critical of China could argue that the military balance in the Strait had been or was in the process of being upset. Proponents of sales of F-16s to Taiwan could thus maintain that the 150 F-16s were "needed" to modernize Taiwan's forces in response to China's acquisition of the twenty-six SU-27 aircraft from Russia, in accordance with the provisions of the Taiwan Relations Act. Furthermore, the annual cost after adjustment for inflation of the United States's sale of the F-16s was possibly (albeit remotely) within the sales parameters established by the 17 August 1982 joint communiqué, despite the total cost of some $6 billion.

Nevertheless, once the U.S. sale of the F-16s was announced, the

Chinese began to threaten again that they would not adhere to the MTCR provisions. A senior Chinese diplomat told me that U.S. military sales of ships and aircraft to Taiwan, plus the sanctions, "put great pressure" on the Chinese leaders, for not having retaliated, especially with respect to the high-technology Harpoon missiles. A news item in the *Washington Times* of 10 September 1993 explicitly reported a Chinese threat of retaliation, once more in the form of not observing the principles of the MTCR. U.S. officials commenting on China's reaction were at pains to describe the sanctions (see above) stemming from the M-11 sale as the lightest action that could be taken under U.S. law. However, a "well-placed" East Asian diplomat was quoted as saying that Chinese retaliation for the perceived insult and loss of face was "virtually certain" and cited "a widespread reaction in the [East Asian] region that the Clinton administration failed to grasp what the ramifications of its action would be."[18]

In response to reports of a Chinese military buildup, I was told by a number of senior Chinese officials that China was not interested in initiating a military conflict in the region, since its main energies were directed toward trying to manage the economic problems of a population exceeding 1.2 billion people. For such a colossal task, they said, a peaceful environment, both domestic and regional, would be essential for at least fifty years.

Politics

On the political side, the policy the United States had carefully followed for years of not allowing senior administration officials to visit Taiwan was first breached in 1992 (see chapter 12), when Carla Hills, then the U.S. trade representative, was permitted a visit to discuss the United States's unfavorable balance of trade with Taiwan. (Members of the U.S. Congress have been frequent visitors to Taiwan, but their presence does not carry the same cachet as that of a senior administration official.) Also, the Clinton administration made some additional modifications of this policy (see chapter 12). Although still just a cloud on the horizon, there was a feeling in some U.S. quarters that, as Stephen Green of the Copley News Services' Washington Bureau put it, Taiwan deserved U.S. diplomatic recognition due to its economic strength and democratic reforms.[19] Green argued that the United States ought to "stop the charade of denying the reality of Taiwan and fully recognize it as a vital, independent and democratic nation." Some elements in the U.S. Congress picked up on this theme: Democratic Senator Paul Simon, a member of the Senate

Foreign Relations Committee, was quoted in the *New York Times* of 8 September 1994 as saying, "Taiwan has a multiparty system, free elections, and a free press—the things we profess to champion—while we continue to cuddle up to the mainland government, whose dictatorship provides none of these things." The same sentiments were reportedly expressed by the chairman of the Republican-dominated Foreign Affairs Committee, who before Taiwan's March 1996 presidential elections also said that he intended to extend a formal invitation to the expected victor, Lee Teng-hui, to pay an official visit to the United States.

At the same time, the breakup of the Soviet Union and perhaps the demise of communism in Russia as well, caused many Americans to question the strategic need for the United States to maintain close relations with China. Strategic issues manifestly were a significant catalyst in bringing the United States and China closer together, but many have asked whether such a close relationship was still necessary.

During this same period, the Clinton administration announced— surely intended to assuage congressional supporters of Taiwan—that it would expand official ties with Taiwan, while continuing not to recognize it as a country separate from China. This decision was promptly attacked by lawmakers of both parties as falling short of treating Taiwan with respect. Other administration concessions included supporting Taiwan for membership in the WTO and allowing certain senior officials (not in State!) to have contacts with Taiwan officials and to visit Taiwan. Under the new policy, Taiwan's office in the United States was permitted to change its name from Coordinating Council for North American Affairs to the Taipei Economic and Cultural Office in the United States. Also, senior Taiwan officials transiting the United States en route to other countries were now permitted to remain in the United States for twenty-four hours—the upshot of an incident in May 1994 when Taiwan's president, Lee Teng-hui, while traveling to Central America, was not allowed to debark from his aircraft while it refueled in Hawaii.[20]

This latter incident caused so much resentment among supporters of Taiwan in the U.S. Congress that in May 1995 the U.S. government yielded to congressional pressure and decided to issue a visa to Lee to visit his alma mater, Cornell University, in an allegedly private capacity, to receive an honorary degree. This move created enormous rancor in China. Adding to China's bitterness was that Secretary of State Christopher had assured the Chinese a week earlier that this visa would not be issued. Had Lee's visit been really "private," the problem would not have been so great, but it received massive publicity, both in the United States and Taiwan, and on his return to Taiwan, Lee compounded the strains by expressing the hope that he could make similar visits to major European countries.[21]

Recalling the United States's traditional policy of supporting neither two Chinas, nor one China, one Taiwan, nor an independent Taiwan—the established basis for the U.S.-China relationship—the course advocated by Stephen Green, Paul Simon, and other like-thinkers would surely be devastating to this relationship.

Following Lee Teng-hui's highly public "private" U.S. visit, China recalled its ambassador in Washington, Li Daoyu, for "consultations." Ambassador Roy's departure from Beijing at the expiration of his term left neither country with an ambassador in the other's capital. Li Daoyu returned a few months later, and Ambassador Roy was replaced by James Sasser, a former, now defeated, Democratic senator from Tennessee close to the White House but with no previous China experience. Sasser's nomination was held up in the Senate for weeks by Jesse Helms, chairman of the Senate Foreign Relations Committee, who was holding this and more than a dozen other nominations hostage to domestic political considerations. But China's decision to return Li Daoyu to the United States was followed by reiterations from several high-ranking U.S. officials, including Secretary of State Christopher, that our policy of supporting but one China remained unchanged.

Glancing at the Future

Following the Tian An Men incident, my personal belief had been that the toughest issue to handle in U.S.-China relations was human rights, but the questions of trade, intellectual property rights, and military sales now seem inextricably bound up in the situation. Even more critical at the close of 1996 was the question of U.S. policy regarding Taiwan.

With 3,500 years of history behind them, 2,500 of them dominated by the Confucian ethic, it is extremely hard for Chinese leaders to accept the thought that the United States, with a history of only a little more than 200 years, could have evolved a set of moral values that transcend their own and that should be used to determine China's relations with the United States, or indeed, of China's domestic interpersonal and government-to-people relationships. (By extension, the Chinese reject pretensions by any other nation, based on cultural, economic, or military superiority, to dictate to China the moral terms of its international or domestic relations.) The "Middle Kingdom complex" is alive and well in Beijing in the late 1990s. At the minimum, China will demand that it be

treated as an equal, in keeping with its rubric of "equality and equal benefit" ("*hu li ping deng*").

The present Chinese leaders hope to manage China's economic reforms
in such a way that their political system, above all the maintenance of
national stability and the leadership of the Communist Party, will not be
disturbed as economic strides continue. Perhaps this is possible, but in all
likelihood, economic reforms will in due course lead to political reforms.
However, any such changes must come from within if they are to last, not
be imposed from without; otherwise, there may be a backlash at the top
leadership level that will hurt, not help, the cause of political reform.

The clash of values remains unresolved internally. While I was ambassador in Singapore, I was privileged to be present to hear then–prime minister (now senior minister) Lee Kuan Yew argue with Patricia Derian, then
the State Department's assistant secretary for human rights and humanitarian affairs, over the sociopolitical viewpoints each represented. Lee
Kuan Yew, whom I heard on several occasions describe himself as "the
last Victorian," certainly was and is a staunch Confucianist as well. He
and his followers have attempted to inculcate Singapore's younger generation with Confucian virtues. Derian, on the other hand, is a veteran of the
civil rights movement in the American South, with its frequent clashes
between civil rights demonstrators and local authorities, a struggle that
epitomized the "rights of man" beliefs inherent in the U.S. Constitution.
She completely dismissed Lee's view that the well-being of society takes
precedence over individual rights and that detainees in Singapore only
needed to forswear violence to be released. The two talked past each other
for the better part of two hours and never came to a meeting of the minds.

So where do we go from here in our relationship with China? Some
people in the Congress, the press, and even the administration would still
attach improvement in China's human rights performance and observance
of democratic principles as a prerequisite to Chinese access to MFN treatment. Questions of the trade imbalance, China's handling of intellectual
property rights, and Chinese military sales must also be taken into account. China, however, while declaring itself determined to preserve its
opening to the outside world, absolutely rejects what it construes as foreign interference in its internal affairs. As Jiang Zemin declared before the
fourteenth Party Congress of 13 October 1992, "When it comes to issues
involving national interests and state sovereignty, China will never con-
cede to outside pressure."[22]

Beyond a doubt, the question of U.S. policy toward Taiwan is an important—if not the most important element—in Jiang's definition of "national interests and state sovereignty," and consequently the Chinese will

adamantly oppose any move we might make away from the "one China" concept. Indeed, the Taiwan issue has become a vital element in the U.S.-China relationship, which in the period to come could approach critical mass after years of quiescence, attributable to adherence of both China and Taiwan to the status quo established as a consequence of the three joint communiqués governing U.S.-China relations.

The United States should handle all these issues carefully, without slipping back into a prenormalization state of mind, and should take China's threats of retaliation seriously. We've begun to cut things very close. If MFN is again tampered with, if no solution is found for the dispute over China's monitoring of U.S. intellectual property rights, or if Taiwan's status is enhanced to near-diplomatic levels, the United States would lose whatever leverage it possesses in its attempts to improve U.S.-China relations. In the economic sphere, China is over time capable of shifting its focus on exports to Europe, Japan, Southeast Asia, Russia, and the Third World, and to turn to Europe and Japan for high-technology imports and to countries such as Canada, Australia, and Brazil for food grains. The bitterness generated by job losses in China until its export economy becomes readjusted would simply add to the poison in U.S.-China relations. As a footnote to this troubled situation, the economy of Hong Kong, which serves both as an entrepôt and export center for goods entering or leaving China, could suffer deeply.

One almost-certain result of Chinese retaliation would be the drying up of the flow of Chinese students to the United States—some 40,000 to 60,000 in 1996, and between 120,000 and 130,000 students since 1979—thus denying to China the store of knowledge that these students may provide to advance the modernization of China's economy, and also depriving China of the window on democracy that has been opened by the students. Furthermore, the nations of East Asia would all be deeply dismayed if a significant deterioration in U.S.-China relations were to occur, since they have relied upon the United States for years to help maintain regional stability.

Always lingering, too, is the question of what China's attitude would be towards reunification of Taiwan with the mainland should U.S.-China relations deteriorate—would China again threaten to use force? China's growing military power and renewed budgetary attention to the modernization of its armed forces will in any event make it a power in its own right in the Asia-Pacific region, one that certainly must be reckoned with. A point to bear in mind is that the only formal reference by China to following a "fundamental policy" of reuniting Taiwan with the mainland by peaceful means occurs in the 17 August 1982 Joint Communiqué on

Arms Sales to Taiwan. If this communiqué is vitiated, either by U.S. actions, moves by Taiwan toward independence, or both, the Chinese could again threaten to use force against Taiwan, with incalculable consequences for the United States. Given the American people's widespread objection to sending troops to such trouble spots as Bosnia, what would be their attitude to the reintroduction of U.S. military forces into the Taiwan Strait area to protect the island against a Chinese attack?

In taking a look at the future of U.S.-China relations, I am well aware that this task has been ably performed by others, notably Harry Harding in his book *A Fragile Relationship*²³ and the Atlantic Council and the National Committee on United States-China Relations (NCUSCR) in their policy paper entitled *United States and China Relations at a Crossroads*.²⁴ Both reach essentially the same conclusion: the United States should encourage a less confrontational mode of dealing with China, and China should reciprocate. Harding writes that the United States should strive for a normal rather than a special relationship with China, one that would be more "nuanced and less moralistic" than it has been since China's suppression of the Tian An Men demonstrations.²⁵ In the Atlantic Council-NCUSCR publication, a strong argument is made for a "vigorous, intelligent engagement" with China in which differences such as human rights could be discussed quietly through diplomatic channels and not made a public centerpiece of our relationship.²⁶ All of us who contributed to the Atlantic Council-NCUSCR publication agreed that the United States should avoid toying with the basic principles upon which U.S.-Chinese relations were normalized, so as to let the parties most directly concerned, Taiwan and the PRC, work out their own solution. In fact, they appeared to be doing just that until after Lee Teng-hui's U.S. visit, when China broke off talks between its Association for Relations Across the Taiwan Straits and Taiwan's Straits Exchange Foundation—both ostensibly nongovernmental bodies.

The Clinton administration has either heeded the Atlantic Council–NCUSCR argument or reached the same conclusion on its own: it has begun speaking of maintaining a "positive" or "constructive" engagement with China and denied that it was trying to "contain" that country.

As for human rights, in my own experience I have always found the Chinese willing to listen to another point of view on a variety of subjects, so long as the viewpoint is expressed in a way that does not turn it into a formal issue in mutual relations. When that does occur, the Chinese tend to fall back on their definition of principle, which leaves little margin for flexibility. Conversely, private conversations can bring results, and a resumption of high-level talks on political, economic, and military issues appears to be in order as a necessary first step. I attribute the fact that Fang Lizhi and his wife were eventually permitted to leave China, first for England and then for the United States, in part to advice that American sinologists gave the Chinese behind the scenes. I anticipate similar receptivity to other human rights issues as well, as perhaps foreshadowed by China's release of some of the leaders of the Tian An Men demonstrations. Subsequent heavy-handed Chinese treatment of other dissidents, however, including the re-arrest of Wei Jingsheng, the originator of the 1979–1980s "Democracy Wall," and of Wang Dan, a leader of the 1983 student demonstrations, may have offset any public relations gains achieved through other releases. The Harry Wu case, in which China arrested and convicted an American citizen of Chinese origin for espionage, set off a storm of indignation among U.S. human rights groups. In an apparent gesture toward the United States, Wu was expelled from China without serving a sentence. This cleared the way for First Lady Hillary Clinton to ignore U.S. human rights critics and attend the September 1995 UN Conference on Women in Beijing, and also improved the atmospherics for President Clinton's meeting with Chinese President Jiang Zemin during the UN General Assembly session in October 1995 and again at the Philippine APEC meeting in 1996. These developments, along with resumption of military contacts, may indicate an upturn in U.S.-China relations.

China's movement on the human rights issue may seem slow, but as Jiang Zemin made plain in his fourteenth Party Congress speech, the Chinese are extremely wary of appearing to act as a result of "outside pressure" that could be construed as interference in their internal affairs. Still, the Chinese should take to heart America's concerns and try to do their part in sustaining a working relationship with the United States by finding ways within their own system to extend lenient treatment to more of those accused of political "crimes" such as the Tian An Men demonstrations. Such steps would not only help to put this vexing problem behind both nations but ease tensions between China's leadership and its educated people, who are badly needed for modernization. Chinese restraint toward Taiwan would also be helpful, provided that Taiwan itself does not take actions that would be construed on the China mainland as trending toward an independent Taiwan.

Moreover, China should exercise greater sensitivity to the United States's concerns on issues such as arms sales to rogue regimes, access to Chinese markets, and protection of intellectual property rights. American businessmen have also encountered serious problems with corruption in China, a problem that is of widespread and growing concern to multitudes of Chinese at all levels. The United States should also make a greater effort to understand China's cultural and political sensitivities, and downplay its chosen role as the arbiter of morality for China, as well as for other countries.

While working on this book, my primary intention has been to look at the enormous obstacles that had to be overcome by both the United States and China to achieve a reasonably balanced, give-and-take way of dealing with one another. From the beginning, the central issue has been the question of Taiwan and how to find a way for both China and the United States to set this question aside so as to be able to maintain "normal" political, economic, and military relationships of benefit to both, while—for the United States—not cutting off friendly (but unofficial) links with Taiwan. I have also outlined the human rights, economic, and military problems that must also be addressed. My hope has been that by looking at the past as well as the present, a retrogression in relations can be avoided.

But, as a parting word, I want to leave the thought that even in the absence of a mutual threat from the former Soviet Union, it is still very much in the best interests of both China and the United States to maintain a relationship based on reality. To cite only a few reasons: the United States remains the world's strongest military power and the world's largest market, while China is becoming an economic giant, an important market, and a regional power and remains a strong voice in the Third World and possessor of the veto power in the UN Security Council. I am one with the late President Nixon in his remark that "it's far better to talk to the Chinese than to fight them." Having lived through the entire period of the ups and downs in the relations of the United States with the People's Republic of China, I would hate to see another generation of diplomats and sinologists compelled to go through the same sort of trying experiences that many of us in the foreign policy community endured over twenty-five years or more to put U.S.-China relations back on course. Neither does China need another long period of strained relations with the United States. In political, social, economic, and military terms, the stakes are too high.

Appendix A

The Shanghai Communiqué, 28 February 1972

President Richard Nixon of the United States of America visited the People's Republic of China at the invitation of Premier Chou Enlai of the People's Republic of China from February 21 to February 28, 1972. Accompanying the President were Mrs. Nixon, U.S. Secretary of State William Rogers, Assistant to the President Dr. Henry Kissinger, and other American officials.

President Nixon met with Chairman Mao Tse-tung of the Communist Party of China on February 21. The two leaders had a serious and frank exchange of views on Sino-U.S. relations and world affairs.

During the visit, extensive, earnest and frank discussions were held between President Nixon and Premier Chou En-lai on the normalization of relations between the United States of America and the People's Republic of China, as well as on other matters of interest to both sides. In addition, Secretary of State William Rogers and Foreign Minister Chi P'eng-fei held talks in the same spirit.

President Nixon and his party visited Peking and viewed cultural, industrial and agricultural sites, and they also toured Hangchow and Shanghai where, continuing discussions with Chinese leaders, they viewed similar places of interest.

The leaders of the People's Republic of China and the United States of America found it beneficial to have this opportunity, after so many years without contact, to present candidly to one another their views on a variety of issues. They reviewed the international situation in which important changes and great upheavals are taking place and expounded their respective positions and atittudes.

The U.S. side stated: Peace in Asia and peace in the world requires efforts both to reduce immediate tensions and to eliminate the basic causes of conflict. The United States will work for a just and secure peace: just, because it fulfills the aspirations of peoples and nations for freedom and progress; secure, because it removes the danger of foreign aggression. The United States supports individual freedom and social progress for all the peoples of the world, free of outside pressure or intervention. The United States believes that the effort to reduce tensions is served by improving communication between countries that have different ideologies so as to lessen the risks of confrontation through accident, miscalculation or misunderstanding. Countries should treat each other with mutual respect and be willing to compete peacefully, letting performance be the ultimate judge. No country should claim infallibility and each country should be prepared to re-examine its own attitudes for the common good. The United States stressed that the peoples of Indochina should be allowed to determine their destiny without outside intervention; its constant primary objective has been a negotiated solution; the eight-point proposal put forward by the Republic of Vietnam and the United States on January 27, 1972 represents a basis for the attainment of that objective; in the absence of a negotiated settlement the United States envisages the ultimate withdrawal of all U.S. forces from the region consistent with the aim of self-determination for each country of Indochina. The United States will maintain its close ties with and support for the Republic of Korea; the United States will support efforts of the Republic of Korea to seek a relaxation of tension and increased communication in the Korean peninsula. The United States places the highest value on its friendly relations with Japan; it will continue to develop the existing close bonds. Consistent with the United Nations Security Council Resolution of December 21, 1971, the United States favors the continuation of the ceasefire between India and Pakistan and the withdrawal of all military forces to within their own territories and to their own sides of the ceasefire line in Jammu and Kashmire; the United States supports the right of the peoples of South Asia to shape their own future in peace, free of military threat, and without having the area become the subject of great power rivalry.

The Chinese side stated: Wherever there is oppression, there is resistance. Countries want independence, nations want liberation and the people want revolution—this has become the irresistible trend of history. All nations, big or small, should be equal; big nations should not bully the small and strong nations should not bully the weak. China will never be a superpower and it opposes hegemony and power politics of any kind. The Chinese side stated that it firmly supports the struggles of all the oppressed people and nations for freedom and liberation and that the people of all countries have the right to choose their social systems according to their own wishes and the right to safeguard the independence, sovereignty and territorial integrity of their own countries and oppose foreign aggression, interference, control and subversion. All foreign troops should be withdrawn to their own countries.

The Chinese side expressed its firm support to the peoples of Vietnam, Laos and Cambodia in their efforts for the attainment of their goal and its firm support to the seven-point proposal of the Provisional Revolutionary Government of the Republic of South Vietnam and the elaboration of February this year on the two key problems in the proposal, and to the Joint Declaration of the Summit Conference of the Indochinese Peoples. It firmly supports the eight-point program for the peaceful unification of Korea put forward by the Government of the Democratic People's Republic of Korea on April 12, 1971, and the stand for the abolition of the "U.N. Commission for the Unification and Rehabilitation of Korea." It firmly opposes the revival and outward expansion of Japanese militarism and firmly supports the Japanese people's desire to build an independent, democratic, peaceful and neutral Japan. It firmly maintains that India and Pakistan should, in accordance with the United Nations resolutions on the India-Pakistan question, immediately withdraw all their forces to their respective territories and to their own sides of the ceasefire line in Jammu and Kashmire and firmly supports the Pakistan Government and people in their struggle to preserve their independence and sovereignty and the people of Jammu and Kashmir in their struggle for the right of self-determination.

There are essential differences between China and the United States in their social systems and foreign policies. However, the two sides agreed that countries, regardless of their social systems, should conduct their relations on the principles of respect for the sovereignty and territorial integrity of all states, non-aggression against other states, non-interference in the internal affairs of other states, equality and mutual benefit, and peaceful coexistence. International disputes should be settled on this basis, without resorting to the use or threat of force. The United States and the People's Republic of China are prepared to apply these principles to their mutual relations.

With these principles of international relations in mind the two sides stated that:

—progress toward the normalization of relations between China and the United Staes is in the interests of all countries;

—both wish to reduce the danger of international military conflict;

—neither should seek hegemony in the Asia-Pacific region and each is opposed to efforts by any other country or group of countries to establish such hegemony; and

—neither is prepared to negotiate on behalf of any third party or to enter into agreements or understandings with the other directed at other states.

Both sides are of the view that it would be against the interests of the peoples of the world for any major country to collude with another against other countries, or for major countries to divide up the world into spheres of interest.

The two sides reviewed the long-standing serious disputes between China and the United States. The Chinese side reaffirmed its position: The Taiwan question is the crucial question obstructing the normalization of relations between China and the United States; the Government of the People's Republic of China is the sole legal government of China; Taiwan is a province of China which has long been returned to the motherland; the liberation of Taiwan is China's internal affair in which no other country has the right to interfere; and all U.S. forces and military installations must be withdrawn from Taiwan. The Chinese Government firmly opposes any activities which aim at the creation of "one China, one Taiwan," "one China, two governments," "two Chinas," and "independent Taiwan" or advocate that "the status of Taiwan remains to be determined."

The U.S. side declared: The United States acknowledges that all Chinese on either side of the Taiwan Strait maintain there is but one China and that Taiwan is a part of China. The United States Government does not challenge that position. It reaffirms its interest in a peaceful settlement of the Taiwan question by the Chinese themselves. With this prospect in mind, it affirms the ultimate objective of the withdrawal of all U.S. forces and military installations from Taiwan. In the meantime, it will progressively reduce its forces and military installations on Taiwan as the tension in the area diminishes.

The two sides agreed that it is desirable to broaden the understanding between the two peoples. To this end, they discussed specific areas in such fields as science, technology, culture, sports and journalism, in which people-to-people contacts and exchanges would be mutually beneficial. Each side undertakes to facilitate the further development of such contacts and exchanges.

Both sides view bilateral trade as another area from which mutual benefit can be derived, and agreed that economic relations based on equality and mutual benefit are in the interest of the people of the two countries.

They agree to facilitate the progressive development of trade between their two countries.

The two sides agreed that they will stay in contact through various channels, including the sending of a senior U.S. representative to Peking from time to time for concrete consultations to further the normalization of relations between the two countries and continue to exchange views on issues of common interest.

The two sides expressed the hope that the gains achieved during this visit would open up new prospects for the relations between the two countries. They believe that the normalization of relations between the two countries is not only in the interest of the Chinese and American peoples but also contributes to the relaxation of tension in Asia and the world.

President Nixon, Mrs. Nixon and the American party expressed their appreciation for the gracious hospitality shown them by the government and people of the People's Republic of China.

(Department of State Bulletin, Vol. LXVI, No. 1708
[March 20, 1972], pp. 435–438.)

Appendix B

Joint Communiqué on the Establishment of Diplomatic Relations between the United States of America and the People's Republic of China, 1 January 1979

The United States of America and the People's Republic of China have agreed to recognize each other and to establish diplomatic relations as of January 1, 1979.

The United States of America recognizes the Government of the People's Republic of China as the sole legal Government of China. Within this context, the people of the United States will maintain cultural, commercial, and other unofficial relations with the people of Taiwan.

The United States of America and the People's Republic of China reaffirm the principles agreed on by the two sides in the Shanghai Communique and emphasize once again that:

—Both wish to reduce the danger of international military conflict.

—Neither should seek hegemony in the Asia-Pacific region or in any other region of the world and each is opposed to efforts by any other country or group of countries to establish such hegemony.

—Neither is prepared to negotiate on behalf of any third party or to enter into agreements or understandings with the other directed at other states.

—The Government of the United States of America acknowledges the Chinese position that there is but one China and Taiwan is part of China.

—Both believe that normalization of Sino-American relations is not only in the interest of the Chinese and American peoples but also contributes to the cause of peace in Asia and the world.

The United States of America and the People's Republic of China will exchange Ambassadors and establish Embassies on March 1, 1979.

(American Foreign Policy Basic Documents,
1977–1980, 962–981)—document 507

China

Following is the transcript of President Carter's statement in Washington on normalizing relations with China, as recorded by the *New York Times* through the facilities of ABC News:

Good evening. I would like to read a joint communique which is being simultaneously issued in Peking at this very moment by the leaders of the People's Republic of China:

"Joint Communique on the Establishment of Diplomatic Relations Between the United States of America and the People's Republic of China, Jan. 1, 1979.

"The United States of America and the People's Republic of China have agreed to recognize each other and to establish diplomatic relations as of January 1, 1979.

"The United States recognizes the Government of the People's Republic of China as the sole legal Government of China. Within this context the people of the United States will maintain cultural, commercial and other unofficial relations with the people of Taiwan.

"The United States of America and the People's Republic of China reaffirm the principles agreed on by the two sides in the Shanghai Communique of 1972 and emphasize once again that: both sides wish to reduce the danger of international military conflict. Neither should seek hegemony—that is the dominance of one nation over others—in the Asia-Pacific region or in any other region of the world and each is opposed to efforts by any other country or group of countries to establish such hegemony.

"Neither is prepared to negotiate on behalf of any other third party or to enter into agreements or understandings with the other directed at other states.

"The Government of the United States of America acknowledges the Chinese position that there is but one China and Taiwan is part of China.

"Both believe that normalization of Sino-American relations is not only in the interest of the Chinese and American people but also contributes to the cause of peace in Asia and the world.

"The United States of America and the People's Republic of China will exchange Ambassadors and establish Embassies on March 1, 1979."

Yesterday, our country and the People's Republic of China reached this final historic agreement. On January 1, 1979, a little more than two weeks from now, our two Governments will implement full normalization of diplomatic relations.

As a nation of gifted people who comprise about one-fourth of the total population of the Earth, China plays, already, an important role in world affairs—a role that can only grow more important in the years ahead.

We do not undertake this important step for transient tactical or expedient reasons. In recognizing the People's Republic of China, that is a single Government of China, we're recognizing simple reality. But far more is involved in this decision than just the recognition of a fact.

'Long History of Friendship'

Before the estrangement of recent decades, the American and the Chinese people had a long history of friendship. We've already begun to rebuild some of the previous ties. Now our rapidly expanding relationship requires a kind of structure that only full diplomatic relations will make possible.

The change that I'm announcing tonight will be of great long-term benefit to the peoples of both our country and China—and I believe for all the peoples of the world. Normalization and expanded commercial and cultural relations that it will bring—will contribute to the well-being of our nation to our own national interest. And it will also enhance the stability of Asia. These more positive relations with China can beneficially affect the world in which we live and the world in which our children will live.

Special Message to Taiwan

We have already begun to inform our allies and other nations and the members of the Congress of the details of our intended action, but I wish also tonight to convey a special message to the people of Taiwan.

I have already communicated with the leaders in Taiwan, with whom the American people have had, and will have, extensive, close and friendly relations. This is important between our two peoples. As the United States asserted in the Shanghai Communique of 1972, issued on President

Nixon's historic visit, we will continue to have an interest in the peaceful resolution of the Taiwan issue.

I have paid special attention to insuring that normalization of relations between our country and the People's Republic will not jeopardize the well-being of the people of Taiwan.

Broad Ties with Taiwan Pledged

The people of our country will maintain our current commercial, cultural, trade and other relations with Taiwan through nongovernmental means. Many other countries of the world are already successfully doing this.

These decisions and these actions open a new and important chapter in our country's history and also in world affairs. To strengthen and to expedite the benefits of this new relationship between China and the United States, I am pleased to announce that Vice Premier Teng has accepted my invitation and will visit Washington at the end of January. His visit will give our Governments the opportunity to consult with each other on global issues and to begin working together to enhance the cause of world peace.

Negotiations Begun by Nixon

These events are the final result of long and serious negotiations begun by President Nixon in 1972 and continued under the leadership of President Ford. The results bear witness to the steady, determined, bipartisan effort of our own country to build a world in which peace will be the goal and the responsibility of all nations.

The normalization of relations between the United States and China has no other purpose than this: the advancement of peace. It is in this spirit, at this season of peace, that I take special pride in sharing this good news with you tonight.

Thank you very much.

—document 509

Texts of Statements from U.S., China and Taiwan

Following are the texts of the United States statement on Taiwan, provided by the White House; the official English text of the Chinese statement on Taiwan read by Chairman Hua Kuo-feng, provided by Reuters from Peking, and an unofficial English translation of the statement by President Chiang Ching-kuo of Nationalist China.

United States' Statement

As of January 1, 1979, the United States of America recognizes the People's Republic of China as the sole legal Government of China. On the same date, the People's Republic of China accords similar recognition to the United States of America. The United States thereby establishes diplomatic relations with the People's Republic of China.

On that same date, January 1, 1979, the United States of America will notify Taiwan that it is terminating diplomatic relations and that the Mutual Defense Treaty between the United States and the Republic of China is being terminated in accordance with the provisions of the Treaty. The United States also states that it will be withdrawing its remaining military personnel from Taiwan within four months.

In the future, the American people and the people of Taiwan will maintain commercial, cultural, and other relations without official government representation and without diplomatic relations.

The Administration will seek adjustments to our laws and regulations to permit the maintenance of commercial, cultural, and other non-governmental relationships in the new circumstances that will exist after normalization.

The United States is confident that the people of Taiwan face a peaceful and prosperous future. The United States continues to have an interest in the peaceful resolution of the Taiwan issue and expects that the Taiwan issue will be settled peacefully by the Chinese themselves.

The United States believes that the establishment of diplomatic relations with the People's Republic will contribute to the welfare of the American people, to the stability of Asia where the United States has major security and economic interests and to the peace of the entire world.

—document 508

China's Statement

As of January 1, 1979, the People's Republic of China and the United States of America recognize each other and establish diplomatic relations, thereby ending the prolonged abnormal relationship between them. This is a historic event in Sino-United States relations.

As is known to all, the Government of the People's Republic of China is the sole legal Government of China and Taiwan is a part of China. The question of Taiwan was the crucial issue obstructing the normalization of relations between China and the United States. It has now been resolved between the two countries in the spirit of the Shanghai Communique and through their joint efforts, thus enabling the normalization of relations so ardently desired by the people of the two countries. As for the way of bringing Taiwan back to the embrace of the motherland and reunifying the country, it is entirely China's internal affair.

At the invitation of the U.S. Government, Teng Hsiao-ping, Vice-Premier of the State Council of the People's Republic of China, will pay an official visit to the United States in January 1979, with a view to further promoting the friendship between the two peoples and good relations between the two countries.

—document 510

Taiwan's Statement

The decision by the United States to establish diplomatic relations with the Chinese Communist regime has not only seriously damaged the rights and interests of the Government and the people of the Republic of China, but has also had a tremendously adverse impact upon the entire free world. For all the consequences that might arise as a result of this move, the United States Government alone should bear full responsibility.

In the past few years, the United States Government has repeatedly reaffirmed its intention to maintain diplomatic relations with the Republic of China and to honor its treaty commitments. Now that it has broken the assurances and abrogated the treaty, the United States Government cannot be expected to have the confidence of any free nation in the future.

The United States, by extending diplomatic recognition to the Chinese Communist regime, which owes its very existence to terror and suppression, is not in conformity with its professed position of safeguarding human rights and strengthening the capability of democratic nations to resist the totalitarian dictatorship.

The move is tantamount to denying the hundreds of millions of enslaved peoples on the Chinese mainland their hope for an early restoration of freedom. Viewed from whatever aspect, the move by the United States constitutes a great setback to human freedom and democratic institutions.

It will be condemned by all freedomloving and peaceloving peoples all over the world.

Recent international events have proven that the United States' persuance of the "normalization" process with the Chinese Communist regime did not protect the security of free Asian nations, has further encouraged Communist subversion and aggressive activities and hastened the fall of Indochina into Communist hands. The Government and the people of the Republic of China firmly believe lasting international peace and security can never be established on an unstable foundation of expediency.

Regardless of how the international situation may develop, the Republic of China, as a sovereign nation will, with her glorious tradition, unite all her people, civilian and military, at home and abroad, to continue her endeavors toward progress in the social, economic and political fields. The Chinese Government and the people, faithful to the national objectives and their international responsibilities, have full confidence in the future of the Republic of China.

Late President Chiang Kai-shek repeatedly instructed the Chinese people to be firm with dignity and to complete the task of national recovery and national reconstruction. The government and people of the Republic of China have the determination and the faith, which they will exert to their utmost, to work together with other free peoples in democratic countries to conquer Communist tyrannical rule and its aggressive policy. Henceforth, we shall be calm and firm, positive and hardworking. It is urged that all citizens cooperate fully with the Government with one heart and one soul, united and determined to fight at this difficult moment. Under whatever circumstances, the Republic of China shall neither negotiate with the Communist Chinese regime, nor compromise with Communism, and it shall never give up her sacred task of recovering the mainland and delivering the compatriots there. This firm position shall remain unchanged.

—document 511

Appendix C

United States-China Joint Communique
(on Arms Sales), 17 August 1982

(1) In the Joint Communique on the Establishment of Diplomatic Relations on January 1, 1979, issued by the Government of the United States of America and the Government of the People's Republic of China, the United States of America recognized the Government of the People's Republic of China as the sole legal government of China, and it acknowledged the Chinese position that there is but one China and Taiwan is part of China. Within that context, the two sides agreed that the people of the United States would continue to maintain cultural, commercial, and other unofficial relations with the people of Taiwan. On this basis, relations between the United States and China were normalized.

(2) The question of United States arms sales to Taiwan was not settled in the course of negotiations between the two countries on establishing diplomatic relations. The two sides held differing positions, and the Chinese side stated that it would raise the issue again following normalization. Recognizing that this issue would seriously hamper the development of United States-China relations, they have held further discussions on it, during and since the meetings between President Ronald Reagan and Premier Zhao Ziyang and between Secretary of State Alexander M. Haig, Jr., and Vice Premier and Foreign Minister Huang Hua in October, 1981.

(3) Respect for each other's sovereignty and territorial integrity and non-interference in each other's internal affairs constitute the fundamental principles guiding United States-China relations. These principles were confirmed in the Shanghai Communique of February 28, 1972 and reaffirmed in the Joint Communique on the Establishment of Diplomatic Relations which came into effect on January 1, 1979. Both sides emphatically state that these principles continue to govern all aspects of their relations.

(4) The Chinese government reiterates that the question of Taiwan is

China's internal affair. The Message to Compatriots in Taiwan issued by China on January 1, 1979 promulgated a fundamental policy of striving for peaceful reunification of the Motherland. The Nine Point Proposal put forward by China on September 30, 1981 represented a further major effort under this fundamental policy to strive for a peaceful solution to the Taiwan question.

(5) The United States Government attaches great importance to its relations with China, and reiterates that it has no intention of infringing on Chinese sovereignty and territorial integrity, or interfering in China's internal affairs, or pursuing a policy of "two Chinas" or "one China, one Taiwan." The United States Government understands and appreciates the Chinese policy of striving for a peaceful resolution of the Taiwan question as indicated in China's Message to Compatriots in Taiwan issued on January 1, 1979 and the Nine-Point Proposal put forward by China on September 30, 1981. The new situation which has emerged with regard to the Taiwan question also provides favorable conditions for the settlement of United States-China differences over the question of United States arms sales to Taiwan.

(6) Having in mind the foregoing statements of both sides, the United States Government states that it does not seek to carry out a long-term policy of arms sales to Taiwan, that its arms sales to Taiwan will not exceed, either in qualitative or in quantitative terms, the level of those supplied in recent years since the establishment of diplomatic relations between the United States and China, and that it intends to reduce gradually its sales of arms to Taiwan, leading over a period of time to a final resolution. In so stating, the United States acknowledges China's consistent position regarding the thorough settlement of this issue.

(7) In order to bring about, over a period of time, a final settlement of the question of United States arms sales to Taiwan, which is an issue rooted in history, the two governments will make every effort to adopt measures and create conditions conducive to the thorough settlement of this issue.

(8) The development of United States-China relations is not only in the interests of the two peoples but also conducive to peace and stability in the world. The two sides are determined, on the principle of equality and mutual benefit, to strengthen their ties in the economic, cultural, educational, scientific, technological and other fields and make strong, joint efforts for the continued development of relations between the governments and peoples of the United States and China.

(9) In order to bring about the healthy development of United States-China relations, maintain world peace and oppose aggression and expan-

sion, the two governments reaffirm the principles agreed on by the two sides in the Shanghai Communique and the Joint Communique on the Establishment of Diplomatic Relations. The two sides will maintain contact and hold appropriate consultations on bilateral and international issues of common interest.

(American Foreign Policy Current Documents, Document 495, Chapter B, East Asia, 1982, Joint Communique Issued by the Governments of the United States and the People's Republic of China, Washington and Beijing, 17 August 1982, 1038–1039.)

Notes

Chapter 1—Root Causes of United States–China Differences

1. Mao Tse-tung, "On the People's Democratic Dictatorship," in *Selected Works of Mao Tse-tung,* vol. 4, English translation (Peking: Foreign Languages Press, 1969), 415.

2. The complexities of the 1944–1949 period from the U.S. government perspective are outlined in the so-called *"White Paper": United States Relations with China 1944–49,* Department of State Publication 3573, Far Eastern Series 30. (Washington, D.C.: Department of State Office of Public Affairs, 1949). Barbara Tuchman (*Stilwell and the American Experience in China 1911–1945.* [New York: Macmillan, 1971]) goes into the tangled United States-Kuomintang-Communist relationships during World War II. Another insightful account is by John Leighton Stuart (*Fifty Years in China.* [New York: Random House, 1954]), the U.S. ambassador to China at the time of the Kuomintang defeat. These are but a few of the many sources by American authors covering the period.

3. This information comes from U.S. Foreign Service colleagues present in Beijing at that time.

4. Department of State, *Foreign Relations of the United States 1950,* vol. 6, *East Asia and the Pacific* (Washington, D.C.: U.S. GPO, 1950), 6:270–78.

5. While Ambassador Hurley's efforts to reconcile KMT-CCP differences were genuine, in his 1945 resignation letter (see *"White Paper,"* note 2, 581–84), he complained bitterly about what he saw as the procommunist bias of his State Department subordinates, who, when he relieved them of duties in China, returned to State in position to supervise *him.*

6. Editorial, "Veterans of 'Forgotten War' Get Their Reward," *Washington Post,* 29 July 1995, A–20.

7. "United States Policy toward Formosa" (Acheson press conference), *Department of State Bulletin* 22 (23 January 1950): 79.

8. "Military Security in the Pacific" (Truman press conference), *Department of State Bulletin* 22 (16 January 1950): 113–14.

9. Now that the breakup of the Soviet Union has made many hitherto highly classified Soviet documents available, evidence has emerged as to the Soviet culpability in the North Korean attack on South Korea. According to an Associated Press report from Moscow carried in the *Washington Times* of 14 January 1993:

Two American historians said yesterday they have found proof in newly opened Soviet archives that Stalin approved the North Korean attack that began the Korean War in 1950. Western historians have long suspected that the Soviet dictator authorized the invasion. Kathryn Weathersby of Florida State University and David Holloway of Stanford University said the proof came in a newly declassified report that was prepared by the Soviet Foreign Ministry for Soviet leader Leonid Brezhnev in 1966. According to the report, Stalin gave North Korean leader Kim Il-sung permission for the invasion during meetings in Moscow in March and April of 1950. "Soviet military advisers helped draft the battle plans, and Stalin gave orders that all of Kim's desires for weapons and equipment should be met quickly," Mr. Holloway said. After visiting Moscow, Mr. Kim went to China, where he obtained approval for the attack from leader Mao Tse-tung, according to the report to Brezhnev. More than 60,000 North Korean troops streamed across the 38th parallel into South Korea on June 25, 1950, in an attempt to bring the entire country under communist rule.

I find it significant that the Chinese as well as the Soviets were asked in advance by Kim Il Sung to approve the North Korean attack. The timing of Kim's visits and then the attack itself, coming within months of the statements by Dean Acheson and President Truman, could be taken to indicate that both Stalin and Mao believed that the North Koreans could attack without fear of U.S. intervention.

10. It might be recalled that during the Korean War, President Truman removed General MacArthur from command of U.S. forces in Japan and Korea for proposing to introduce ROC troops into the Korean War as a means of diverting Chinese attention away from Korea and toward the area of the Taiwan Strait opposite Taiwan. MacArthur's proposal would have widened the war and was in contradiction of Truman's orders to MacArthur.

11. A PRC artillery bombardment of the offshore island of Quemoy, to which the ROC responded in kind, had occurred earlier in 1954; this event helped to focus U.S. attention on the Taiwan Strait. Chiang Kai-shek told Secretary of State Dulles on 9 September 1954 that he had waited four days for U.S. approval before responding (the United States never did give that approval). See *Foreign Relations of the United States, 1952–1954*, vol. 12 (Washington, D.C.: U.S. GPO, 1984), 905.

12. Interestingly, in 1954 and early 1955 the United States conducted high-level internal discussions on the desirability of requesting the ROC to withdraw its forces from the Offshore Islands, including Quemoy and Matsu. To the United States, committing its power and prestige to the defense of Taiwan and the Pescadores was something quite different from including the Offshore Islands in its

defensive perimeter, since the chances of a U.S. confrontation with the PRC were greatly enhanced thereby. The question of a total withdrawal of ROC troops from the Offshore Islands was discussed with President Chiang Kai-shek and other senior ROC leaders, who opposed the plan on the grounds that it would deeply affect the morale of the people of the ROC. Consequently, the status quo remained, although the United States never accepted the ROC concept of using Quemoy and Matsu as stepping-stones from which to recover the China mainland. See *Foreign Relations of the United States 1952–54,* vol. 12, Department of State Publication 9390 (1984), 1058, and *Foreign Relations of the United States 1955–57,* vol. 2, *China* (1986), 238–40 (both Washington, D.C.: U.S. GPO).

13. Nicholas D. Kristof, "Chinese Premier to Make a Rare Visit to Vietnam," *New York Times,* 30 November 1992 (datelined Beijing, 29 November). Citing unnamed Chinese sources, Kristof states that 300,000 Chinese "volunteers" took part in the Vietnam War on Hanoi's side, with 1,100 killed.

14. *Khrushchev Remembers,* with introduction, commentary, and notes by Edward Crankshaw, tr. and ed. by Strobe Talbott (Boston: Little, Brown, 1970), 472.

15. According to then-Soviet Foreign Minister Gromyko in his memoirs, as reported by Philip Taubman ("Gromyko Says Mao Wanted A-Bomb Used on GIs," *New York Times,* 22 February 1988, 1), Gromyko made a secret follow-up visit to Beijing later in August 1958, during which Mao Zedong asked him for Soviet cooperation in a plan to lure U.S. troops deep into China, presumably as an outgrowth of the Taiwan Strait situation, and then attack them with Soviet nuclear weapons. The PRC's willingness at that time to resort to nuclear weapons, even with a resulting loss of half of China's population, must have shaken the Soviets and contributed directly to their repudiation of the Agreement on New Technology for National Defense. It can be postulated that when the Soviets also withheld support for the PRC's attack on the Offshore Islands as a consequence of Mao's willingness to risk a nuclear war with the United States, the PRC then concluded that it had no alternative but to back away from the developing confrontation with the United States in the Taiwan Strait—hence Zhou Enlai's call on 6 September 1958 for a resumption of the U.S.-PRC ambassadorial-level talks in Geneva. On the other hand, China's attacks on the Offshore Islands may themselves have been precipitated by the belligerent stance taken by Khrushchev vis-à-vis the landing of U.S. troops in Lebanon in July 1958, when he threatened to turn supporting U.S. warships in the Mediterranean into "flaming coffins."

16. Lenin was born in Simbursk, Russia, on 22 April 1870, according to the Western calendar, but on 10 April according to the old-style Russian calendar.

17. Lin Biao, "Long Live the Victory of People's War!" *Peking Review,* 3 September 1965.

18. Stanley Karnow, *Mao and China: Inside China's Cultural Revolution* (New York: Viking Penguin, 1984), 480.

19. Conversation of the author with former ambassador U. Alexis Johnson, 1994, who was present on this famous occasion in 1954 and saw Mr. Dulles turn his back on Premier Zhou when the latter approached him with hand out-

stretched. Chinese ambassador Wang Bingnan, also present, has since denied that this snub actually happened. Ambassador Johnson found Wang Bingnan's denial inexplicable.

20. Edwin W. Martin, conversations with the author on several occasions.

21. U. Alexis Johnson commented to me in a letter written in 1994 concerning Dulles's willingness to accept Zhou Enlai's offer, as follows:

It was very clear to me that Dulles was using the necessity of the talks to placate both the American extremists on the right and the left as well as foreign sniping by pointing to the fact of a channel of communications between the two governments for anything either side wanted to raise. By keeping the agenda to prisoners, other issues could be avoided and Peiping [Beijing] could be tested. Having in mind Arthur Dean's walk-out from Panmunjom, he made it clear to me that he wanted to call all of the shots, and from the beginning he read every word of what he insisted be virtually verbatim reports. During the single day I was given for preparation [for the whole series of talks] my most guidance was when, riding back from the White House with him, I asked him how long the talks might go on. He replied, "Alex, if you are there six months from now you will have been a success." Incidentally, he made it plain that he, not Eisenhower, was calling the shots.

In subsequent years I confirmed my suspicion that Zhou En-lai's [Zhou Enlai's] approach was very much the same as Dulles's. When I once asked Wang Bingnan after reaching agreement to release all American prisoners, why they did not put us on the spot to proceed to the next item on the agenda [author's note: the last prisoner was released only after the Nixon visit], he said that they were worried that if they did so we would stop the talks.

22. U. Alexis Johnson with Jeff Olivarius McAllister, *The Right Hand of Power* (Englewood Cliffs, N.J.: Prentice-Hall, 1984), 254. Johnson gives a full account of the Geneva talks.

23. Johnson, *Right Hand of Power*, 258.

24. Johnson, conversations with the author in the fall of 1956, when I was briefly detailed as rapporteur to the talks.

25. Johnson, *Right Hand of Power*, 260.

26. Johnson, *Right Hand of Power*, 260.

27. O. Edmund Clubb, *Twentieth Century China*, 2nd ed. (New York: Columbia University Press, 1976), 371.

28. Clubb, *Twentieth Century China*, 372. It should be noted in connection with the Dulles-Chiang joint communiqué that the formulation restraining the ROC from using force to restore its position on the China mainland was the inspiration of former ambassador Marshall Green, who was then policy adviser to Assistant Secretary of State for Far Eastern Affairs Walter S. Robertson.

29. Assistant Secretary Bundy, conversations with the author, spring/summer 1994.

Chapter 2—The United States and China
Turn towards Normalization

1. Quoted in Mikhail Heller and Aleksander M. Nekrich, *Utopia in Power; The History of the Soviet Union from 1917 to the Present* (New York: Summit Books, 1986), 625–626.

2. Chinese acquaintances have corrected my initial recollection that the Chinese response time was three days.

3. Mao Tse-tung, *Selected Military Writings of Mao Tse-tung: Conclusions on the Repulse of the Second Anti-communist Onslaught*. Essay dated 8 May 1941 (Peking: Foreign Languages Press, 1967).

4. Stanley Karnow, *Mao and China* (New York: Viking Press, 1972). Karnow cites examples of public Sino-Soviet accusations and counteraccusations of border transgressions dating back to 1964.

5. The Zhou Enlai-Kosygin discussions at Beijing airport were mentioned by Zhou to Henry A. Kissinger and members of his delegation (of which I was a part) in October 1971 just prior to Kissinger's return to the United States. Zhou's references to his discussions with Kosygin, repeated subsequently by other senior PRC officials, took place in the same VIP room in which Zhou had spoken to Kosygin some two years earlier.

6. Richard M. Nixon, "Asia after Vietnam," *Foreign Affairs* vol. 46, no. 1 (September–October 1967), 111–125.

7. Marvin and Bernard Kalb, *Kissinger* (Boston: Little, Brown and Co., 1974), 228–229.

8. The instructions to the Warsaw embassy may be found in recently declassified State Department cables 20061 and 008061 of 14 January 1970.

9. Henry Kissinger, *White House Years* (Boston: Little, Brown and Co., 1979), 687. Note here the reference to the "five principles," which recalls the Chinese reply to State's letter of 17 September 1968.

10. Kissinger, *White House Years*, 686–87.

11. Joint interview of Marshall Green and author, 1988, in *A China Reader*, vol. 2, Foreign Affairs Oral History Program, Association for Diplomatic Studies and Training (ADST), Arlington Va., January 1995.

12. Paul Kreisberg in an ADST oral history interview by Nancy Tucker, quoted in "Memoirs of an Insider—Evolution of U.S.-China Policy 1956–1973," *A China Reader*, vol. 3, 7.

13. Seymour M. Hersh, *The Price of Power* (New York: Summit Books, 1983), 361.

14. *People's Daily*, 18 May 1970.

15. Kissinger, *White House Years*, 688.

16. Vernon C. Walters, *Silent Missions* (Garden City, N.Y.: Doubleday & Co., 1978), 526.

17. Walters, *Silent Missions*, 527.

18. Walters, *Silent Missions*, chapter 25, and Kissinger, *White House Years*, 696–697.

19. Kissinger, *White House Years*, chapter 18.
20. Kissinger, *White House Years*, 699.
21. Kissinger, *White House Years*, 701.
22. Walters, *Silent Missions*, 527–532.

Chapter 3—Secret Flight to Beijing, 1971

1. Henry Kissinger, "The Pakistani Channel," *White House Years*, 698 ff.
2. Edgar Snow, *The Long Revolution* (New York: Random House, 1971, 1972), 222.
3. At this point I can't be sure of the original means by which this discourse between Snow and Mao became public—Snow refers to it in his book (note 2), and it may have been picked up from Chinese sources by our press monitoring unit in Hong Kong.
4. Kissinger, *White House Years*, 736.
5. Many outside observers have referred to Wang Hairong as Mao Zedong's "niece." While I was stationed in China, though, I was told by Chinese who knew her that she was (and is) Mao's mother's *grandniece,* granddaughter of Mao's mother's sister. Mao's personal physician Li Zhixui, in the Chinese version of his book *The Private Life of Chairman Mao*, 622, identifies her as Mao's grandniece.
6. Kissinger, *White House Years*, 749.
7. Kissinger, *White House Years*, 749.
8. Kissinger, *White House Years*, 752.
9. Kissinger, *White House Years*, 753.

Chapter 4—Preparations for the Nixon China Trip

1. Henry Kissinger, *White House Years*, 777.
2. Kissinger, *White House Years*, 783.
3. Alexander M. Haig Jr., *Caveat* (New York: Macmillan, 1984), 202.
4. Kissinger, *White House Years*, 1051.
5. I had a personal soft spot in my heart for Harned Hoose and for the College of Chinese Studies, since my parents and I had met Dean Pettis when we lived there from early March into May 1937. I hadn't met Harned in 1937, but it's entirely possible that we were in Old Peking at the same time. Sadly, Harned (who was among the most enthusiastic of the American businessmen hoping to open trade ties with China) died in Guangzhou some years after the historic Nixon China trip from injuries sustained in a car crash.

Chapter 5—The Nixon China Trip and the Shanghai Communiqué

1. Richard Nixon, *The Memoirs of Richard Nixon* (New York: Grosset & Dunlap, 1978), 560–564; Kissinger, *White House Years*, 1058–1066.

2. Kissinger, *White House Years*, 1059.

3. This remark was prescient, for Qiao's death some years later was due to lung cancer.

4. Marshall Green, in joint interview with the author, ADST Foreign Affairs Oral History Program, 1988, in *A China Reader*, vol. 2, January 1995.

5. Kissinger, *White House Years*, 1083.

6. Kissinger, *White House Years*, 1084.

Chapter 6—Following Up the Nixon Visit

1. Marshall Green, "Evolution of U.S. China Policy 1956–1973: Memoirs of an Insider," manuscript, 41.

2. Green, "*Evolution of U.S. China Policy*," 43.

3. Green, "*Evolution of U.S. China Policy*," 45.

4. Seymour Hersh, *The Price of Power*, 523.

5. Hersh, *Price of Power*, 523.

6. Kissinger, *White House Years*, 1114.

7. See Li Zhixui, Mao Zedong's private doctor, in his book (in Chinese), *Chairman Mao Zedong*, 611.

8. Fortunately, neither Winston Lord nor I was on the Hanoi leg of the trip, having traveled commercially across the Pacific to meet Kissinger in Hong Kong, since everyone who had been on the Hanoi visit suffered a bout of dysentery thanks to the cuisine at the government guest house.

Chapter 8—Two Different Social Systems Coexisting Together

1. In winter, when we looked out our apartment window on what otherwise would be a clear day, the sun at 7:00 A.M. would be barely visible through Beijing's choking atmosphere. The incidence of upper respiratory infection among USLO personnel was quite high.

2. Simon Leys, *Chinese Shadows* (New York: Viking Press, 1977).

Chapter 9—USLO and Internal Chinese Political Developments

1. I personally have viewed a Chinese film made in July 1965 covering the meeting between Mao Zedong and Aidit, chairman of the Indonesian Communist Party (PKI), in which the two swung around so that Mao directly faced the camera. To my surprise, Mao's face was utterly bland, and his eyes were glazed, as if

his mind was wandering. If his health and mental problems had already begun, the influence of the ideologues around him on the inspiration and organization of the "Great Proletarian Cultural Revolution" could have been much greater than previously supposed.

2. I suspect that the usually infallible Nancy Tang may have mistranslated what Jiang Qing said concerning "cassia" flowers, since U.S. experts tell me that the cassia bloom is found only in tropical climates and has no aroma. The flowers may have been jasmine, which does bloom in the Beijing area and has a pleasant fragrance.

3. David Bruce informed me about Mao's evaluation of the two interpreters the following day.

4. Another similar tale made the rounds of Beijing and concerned the visit of Emperor of Ethiopia Haile Selassie. Mao had somehow mistaken Haile Selassie for Kwame Nkrumah of Ghana, who had just been overthrown by a coup d'état, and proceeded to extend his sympathies to the presumed Nkrumah, to express confidence that the people of Ghana would soon restore him to his rightful place, and to wish him well. The two interpreters, without missing a beat, had translated Mao's words into something like, "The chairman expresses his welcome to your Imperial Majesty and is confident that your visit will strengthen the friendship between the Chinese and Ethiopian peoples." It seems that one of the members of the Ethiopian embassy staff who had accompanied Haile Selassie on the call on Mao spoke enough Chinese to understand what had really been said. (He would have had to cut through Mao's heavy Hunan dialect to understand the chairman, though.)

5. Henry A. Kissinger, *Years of Upheaval* (Boston: Little, Brown and Co., 1982), 351.

6. Conversation of the author with David Bruce, who attended the meeting.

7. The Chinese, in their anxiousness to please their Korean guest, had served dog meat—a Korean delicacy—at the banquet. In doing so, they had alienated every Muslim in the diplomatic corps, to whom the dog is an unclean animal. The dish was listed on the menu as *"ragout du chien."* My friends from among the Islamic nations represented in Beijing were unanimous in criticizing this little touch designed to please Kim Il Sung.

8. *Hung Chi* ("Red Flag," the CCP journal), May 1975.

9. I had a special bonus from attending this farewell dinner, in that while escorting Evangeline Bruce I had come upon a copy of the party publication *Can Kao Xiao Xi*, or "Reference News," a summary of important foreign news and internal developments, which was restricted to senior party personnel and withheld from diplomats—a *"gao ji gan bu"* must have dropped it.

10. Aidit's death following the abortive Indonesian coup in 1965 left Ajitorop the head of the PKI, but he remained in exile in China. I have not heard anything about him for years, and in the light of the restoration of Sino-Indonesian diplomatic relations, his presence in Beijing, if it still continues, is not likely to be publicized.

11. See the two documents issued by the Central Committee of the CCP, "On the Temporary Abandonment of Yenan and the Defense of the Shensi-Kansu-Ningsia Border Region," Directive of November 18, 1946, and Circular of April 9, 1947, in *Selected Works of Mao Zedong*, vol. 4 (Peking: Foreign Languages Press, 1969), 129–132.

12. Joseph Lelyveld, "China's Attitude on U.S. Assayed," *New York Times*, 19 December 1974, 8.

13. *Khmer* is the ancient term used by the Cambodians to describe themselves.

14. Kissinger, *Years of Upheaval*, 686.

15. Kissinger, *Years of Upheaval*, 302–372.

Chapter 10—Buildup to Full Normalization

1. Zbigniew Brzezinski, *Power and Principle* (New York: Farrar Straus, Giroux, 1985), 198.

2. Gerald Ford, *A Time to Heal* (New York: Harper & Row/The Readers' Digest Association, 1970), 386.

3. Ford, *A Time to Heal,* 387.

4. I don't know who on Carter's staff had come up with this particular less-than-ingenious proposal. Richard Holbrooke, who was an active adviser to Carter during the campaign and who later became assistant secretary of state for East Asia and the Pacific, has denied that he had any role in the decision, but someone in Washington had certainly buried his head in the sand. Perhaps Carter himself had come up with the idea, which is not improbable if Carter's lack of knowledge of East Asia is taken into account.

5. Another of my colleagues put it this way, "We should hang on to what we have for as long as we can," a position with which I heartily agreed. In fact, I devoted a considerable amount of my time in Singapore to assuring the use of Singapore military facilities for ships of the U.S. Seventh Fleet in need of repair and obtaining permission to use Singapore's main military airport, at that time Tengah, for refueling and taking fresh foods aboard U.S. military aircraft bound for the U.S. base at Diego Garcia in the Indian Ocean. Singapore also became a place for rest and rehabilitation, or R & R, for personnel assigned to Diego Garcia. In this way, the basis was established for Singapore's later offer of base rights to the United States as a partial replacement for Clark Field and Subic Bay in the Philippines, even on a limited basis. Thanks for this remarkable offer must go to Prime Minister Lee Kuan Yew, who despite his being a long-time member of the Non-Aligned Movement, was a realist when it came to understanding the power balances of the East Asian region and of the world.

6. For a glimpse of the relationship between Jiang Qing and Wang Hongwen, see Roxane Witke, *Comrade Chiang Ch'ing* (Boston: Little, Brown, and Co., 1st

ed., 1977), 472; also, Harrison Salisbury, *The New Emperors* (Boston: Little, Brown, and Co., 1992), 223.

7. Salisbury, *New Emperors*, 369.

8. Salisbury, *New Emperors*, 373–374.

9. Leonard Woodcock, conversations with the author, 1992.

10. Harry Harding, *A Fragile Relationship* (Washington, D.C.: Brookings Institution, 1992), 78–79.

11. Brzezinski, *Power and Principle*, 198.

12. The Presidential Review Memorandum (PRM) format was a successor to the National Security Study Memorandum (NSSM) format initiated by Kissinger during his tenure as presidential national security adviser.

13. Harding, *A Fragile Relationship*, 77.

14. Harding, *A Fragile Relationship*, 78.

15. Brzezinski, *Power and Principle*, 198.

16. Cyrus Vance, *Hard Choices* (N.Y.: Simon and Schuster, 1983), 81.

17. Vance, *Hard Choices*, 82.

18. Brzezinski, *Power and Principle*, 202.

19. Brzezinski, *Power and Principle*, 203.

20. Brzezinski, *Power and Principle*, 208.

21. Brzezinski, *Power and Principle*, 207.

22. Brzezinski, *Power and Principle*, 208.

23. Brzezinski, *Power and Principle*, 223.

24. Brzezinski, *Power and Principle*, 229.

25. Brzezinski, *Power and Principle*, 231.

26. FBIS (Foreign Broadcast Information Service)—CHI-92-198-S, 13 October 1992.

27. FBIS—CHI-92-198-S, 13 October 1992.

Chapter 11—The Impact of Vietnam and Cambodia on Normalization of U.S.-China Relations

1. As a member of the intelligence community staff, I read his report.

2. Jaw-ling Joanne Chang, *United States-China Normalization: An Evaluation of Foreign Policy Decision Making.* (Denver: University of Denver Press [Colorado Seminary], 1986), 196–198.

3. The "Message to Compatriots in Taiwan" cited by Deng fails to say in so many words what Deng stated in his National Gallery speech about "resolving [the reunification question] in a peaceful way." The closest it comes is to say, "Our state leaders have firmly declared that they will take present realities into account in accomplishing the great cause of reunifying the motherland and respect the status quo on Taiwan and the opinions of people in all walks of life there and adopt reasonable policies and measures in settling the question of reunification so as not to cause the people of Taiwan any losses." (See *China Review*, 5 January

1979.) Of course, these words, along with announcing the cessation of the bombardment of Jinmen (Quemoy) and other Taiwan Strait islands and a series of proposals for future relations between Taiwan and the mainland, can certainly be construed as an appeal for "peaceful reunification."

4. *Taiwan Relations Act*, Public Law 96-8 96th Cong., 1st sess. [H.R. 2479]; April 10, 1979. 93, Stat. 15, Sec. 3, 93 Stat. 14.

5. *Taiwan Relations Act*, 93 Stat. 14, Section 2 (b), 93 Stat. 15, Sections 3 (a) and (b), 21, *U.S. Code Annotated*, 3301–3316.

Chapter 12—Normalization's Status during the Carter and Reagan Years

1. Other items already in the so-called "pipeline" continued to be sent in the interim.

2. David E. Kaplan, *Fires of the Dragon* (N.Y.: Atheneum, 1992), 300.

3. Michael Blumenthal, then secretary of the treasury, gave the NSC staff and other interested parties a briefing on a meeting in China that he had attended with YaoYilin, head of the State Council's Office of Economic Planning. According to Blumenthal, Yao had recited a litany of China's woes in implementing economic reforms, after which he had asked rather plaintively, "Do you have any suggestions, Mr. Secretary?" Blumenthal's answer had been brief and to the point: "Yes, try capitalism." While both Yao and Blumenthal treated this exchange as a joke, it is an ironic fact that in the China of today, market-based capitalism has greatly overtaken state-owned enterprises in producing desirable goods for export and for domestic consumption, and in generating foreign exchange earnings.

4. Tom Jones, then Northrup's CEO, in conversations with the author, 1981.

5. In 1981 Lilley succeeded Charles T. Cross as head of AIT in Taiwan and was later appointed ambassador to South Korea, then to China.

6. *Newsweek*, 1 September 1971.

7. To offset Alexander Haig's less-than-right-wing-conservative views on China, as well as on other subjects, the president appointed an old friend from his California days, Judge William P. Clark, as deputy secretary of state. I assume that the intention of the White House was to have Judge Clark keep Al Haig in line or at least from straying too far off the path of Republican conservative righteousness, but Judge Clark turned out to be a helpful and positive asset in his position, perceiving the political liabilities of too rigid a policy on U.S. relations with Taiwan.

8. The first had been Prime Minister Edward Seaga of Jamaica, who had just replaced a personage considered not so friendly to the United States, Sir Michael Manley.

9. There had already been a considerable dispute within the Washington bureaucracy over the sale of a high-speed computer to China, which it claimed it needed for its upcoming census; State and Commerce agreed on the sale, but the

Pentagon and the CIA opposed it on the grounds that the computer would have definite military applications. Ultimately, the sale went through.

10. Alexander M. Haig Jr., *Caveat* (New York: Macmillan, 1984), 205.

11. This was the new form of the old NSDM, or "National Security Decision Memorandum".

12. Haig, *Caveat*, 206.

13. Deng was already beginning to show signs that he was hard of hearing, and the task of interpreting was complicated as a result.

14. The subject of the Deng Xioaping-Haig talks, with the exception of the Korean element, is covered fully in Haig, *Caveat*, 207.

Chapter 13—Working towards a U.S.-China Joint Communiqué on Arms Sales

1. *Taiwan Relations Act* (see note 4, chap. 11).

2. Haig, *Caveat*, 210.

3. Haig, *Caveat*, 210.

4. Haig, *Caveat*, 211.

5. Haig, *Caveat*, 211–212.

6. In fact, my final instructions, which were cabled to Beijing after my departure from Washington, contained a number of revisions to these principles that had been personally directed by the president, thus strengthening my hand as we dealt with the Chinese.

7. *American Foreign Policy Current Documents, 1982* (Washington, D.C.: Department of State publication no. 9415, 1985), Document no. 483, 1025–26.

8. The sequence of events covering my visit to Beijing is covered in *American Foreign Policy Current Documents, 1982*. (See note 7.)

9. *Newsweek*, 25 January 1982.

10. *New York Times*, 10 May 1982.

11. Ibid.

12. Ibid.

Chapter 14—Agreement: The Joint Communiqué on Arms Sales to Taiwan

1. The U.S. delegation began the trip on a U.S. Air Force aircraft, which carried us only as far as Manila, where it burned out a small part for which there was no ready replacement, even at Clark Field. After we had all tried—and failed—to find last-minute commercial flights to take us on the last leg of our journey, we were obliged to accept the hospitality of President and Mrs. Marcos of the Philippines, who offered us the use of the aircraft aboard which Mrs. Marcos had just

returned from Libya and Saudi Arabia. In this way we finally reached Singapore. Later, State found that it had been charged $17,000 by the Philippine government for the use of the aircraft.

2. The problem dated back to the day Haig was named secretary of state by President Reagan; when entering State's building immediately afterwards, he said to an assemblage of State employees (including me), "I am the vicar." By this he meant that he would be the supreme foreign policy figure in the new administration. This immediately offended the members of President Reagan's White House staff, who felt that they, too, had a foreign policy responsibility. Haig's relations with this staff progressed steadily from bad to worse.

3. Haig, *Caveat*, 210.

4. These points were included in the Statement by the Republic of China [Taiwan] following the issuance of the 17 August 1982 joint communiqué, but were made public in the United States by me on 24 July 1982.

5. *New York Times*, 14 July 1982, A-2.

6. *New York Times*, 12 July 1982, A-5.

7. *New York Times*, 16 July 1982, A–6.

8. *New York Times*, 29 July 1982, A-1.

9. Ibid.

10. Ibid.

11. *New York Times*, 18 August 1982, A-1.

12. *New York Times*, 19 August 1982, A-12

13. *New York Times*, 18 August 1982, A-1.

14. *New York Times*, 19 August 1982, A-12.

15. Editorial, *New York Times*, 19 August 1982.

16. *New York Times*, 19 August A-26.

17. *New York Times*, 18 August A-12.

Chapter 15—In Retrospect—And Looking Ahead

1. Edwin O. Reischauer and John K. Fairbank, *East Asia, the Great Tradition* (Boston: Houghton Mifflin, 1958 and 1960), 28–29, 70–73.

2. Reischauer and Fairbank, *East Asia, the Great Tradition*, 703.

3. Robert Leckie, *George Washington's War* (New York: HarperCollins, 1992), 248–249.

4. Leckie, *George Washington's War*, 249.

5. Leckie, *George Washington's War*, 254.

6. *Far Eastern Economic Review*, 9 September 1993, 117.

7. Ibid.

8. *Washington Times*, 9 September 1993, 2.

9. *Free China Journal*, 4 September 1992, 1.

10. *Free China Journal*, 8 October 1993, 1.

11. *Aviation Week and Space Technology*, 30 August 1993, 57.

12. *Aviation Week and Space Technology*, 23 August 1993.

13. *Asia-Pacific Defense Reporter* (Australia), November/December 1995, 8.

14. *Free China Journal*, 30 December 1994, 1.

15. *Free China Journal*, 21 July 1995, 1.

16. *U.S. Naval Institute Proceedings*, March 1995, 112.

17. See note 8.

18. *Washington Times*, 17 August 1994, A–15.

19. *New York Times*, 8 September 1994, A-5.

20. *Washington Times*, 11 September 1994, A-7; also reported in *New York Times*, 11 September 1994, 14.

21. *Free China Journal*, 2 June 1995, 1.

22. Foreign Broadcast Information Service, CHI-92-198-S.

23. Harry Harding, *A Fragile Relationship: The United States and China since 1972* (Washington D.C.: The Brookings Institution, 1992).

24. Atlantic Council, *The United States and China: Relations at a Crossroads*, Policy Paper, (Washington, D.C.: The Atlantic Council Publications Office, February 1993).

25. Harding, *A Fragile Relationship*, 330–331.

26. Atlantic Council, *The United States and China*, executive summary, xxii.

Index

communiqué, 234–35; effect on normalization, 171–73, 177, 183–84; as internal matter, 204–5, 218, 220, 222, 234; reunification plans, 211–12, 234, 259; use of force, 91–92, 98, 184, 185, 260

Taiwan, U.S. arms sales to, 10, 99, 171, 174–75, 177, 182, 184, 192–93; aircraft, 196, 200, 211–14, 216, 240–41; amount of, 196, 213, 216, 217, 235; cessation date, 211–12, 217, 232, 235; Chinese criticism of, 200, 211–12, 216, 221, 233; effect on U.S.-China relations, 195, 212, 214, 220, 229, 233; effect on normalization, 177, 179, 182; linkage to peaceful reunification, 217, 218, 220, 222, 225, 235, 290–91n3; need for, 213, 225, 229, 254; recent, 252–55; spare parts, 214, 217, 218, 220, 221; unilateral decisions on, 214, 221. *See also* Joint Communiqué on Arms Sales to Taiwan; Taiwan Relations Act

Taiwan, U.S. position on, 7, 19–20, 46, 60, 165, 231–32, 238, 257; in briefings, 95, 99; CCNAA suggestions, 231–32; in joint communiqué, 75, 89, 90–92, *see also* Taiwan arms sale communiqué; normalization and, 171–75, 177, 184; official statement, 183, 184, 273; Reagan administration, 197–98, 234; in Taiwan Relations Act, 192–93

Taiwan Relations Act, 10, 192–93, 202; arms sales under, 211, 223, 254; changes, impossibility of, 232; effect on U.S.-China relations, 229; U.S. observance of, 233–34, 238

Taiwan Strait crisis, 9, 22

Taiwan-U.S. mutual defense treaty, 8, 9, 21–22, 93, 94, 99; abrogation, 171, 174, 183, 184, 193. *See also* U.S.-ROC Mutual Defense Treaty

Tanaka, Kakuei, 99, 106, 108

Tang Longbin, 54

Tang Wensheng (Nancy), 54, 56, 57, 62; as interpreter, 148, 165; Nixon's China trip, 85; as "spy," 151

Taoism, 245

Thailand, 52, 100, 101, 230; communism in, 16

Thanat Khoman, 52, 101

Thanom (Thai prime minister), 51, 52, 101

Thieu (Vietnamese president), 51, 52

Tian An Men Square demonstrations, 16, 248, 249, 260, 261

Tibet, 11–12

totalitarianism, early advocates in China, 245

trade mission option, 111

trade, 96, 195; corruption in, 261–62; embargoes, 7, 30, 31; Japan, 106; in joint communiqué, 90, 267; Most Favored Nation (MFN) status, 250, 258, 259; restrictions, 40–41, 48, 215; U.S.-China, 250–51, 257, 258

train travel, 128–29

travel restrictions by U.S., 40–41, 48; by China, 140

Truman, Harry, 5, 7, 94

Turner, Stansfield, 198

Unger, Leonard, 191

United Nations, Nixon anniversary dinner, 42; Chinese representation in, 50, 68, 75

United States: anticommunism in, 8–9, 247; arms sales to Taiwan, 10, 230–31, 252–55; Asian military deployments, 167–68, 180, 289n5; Asian strategic interests, 5, 7; China, 34; statements on normalization, 3, 270–72; contacts with China, *see* diplomatic contacts; cultural heritage and values, 246–48; defense of allies under "Nixon Doctrine," 31; foreign policy, 40–41, 78, 176–77,

About the Author

John H. Holdridge, a career Foreign Service officer, was senior staff member for East Asia at the National Security Council under Henry Kissinger in the Nixon administration (1969–1973), deputy chief of the U.S. Liaison Office in Beijing (1973–1975), U.S. ambassador to Singapore (1975–1978), national intelligence officer for East Asia and the Pacific (1979–1981), assistant secretary of state for East Asia and the Pacific (1981–1983), and ambassador to Indonesia (1983–1986). Since retiring in 1986, he has been a writer and consultant.

DATE DUE

HIGHSMITH #45115